Bizenghast Vol. 5
Created by M. Alice LeGrow

Development Editors - Jodi Bryson & Aaron Suhr
Lettering - Michael Paolilli
Cover Designer - Chelsea Windlinger
Miss Dinah's Wardrobe by - La Cucacaracha

Editor - Lillian Diaz-Przybyl
Digital Imaging Manager - Chris Buford
Pre-Production Supervisor - Lucas Rivera
Art Director - Al-Insan Lashley
Managing Editor - Vy Nguyen
Creative Director - Anne Marie Horne
Editor-in-Chief - Rob Tokar
Publisher - Mike Kiley
President and C.O.O. - John Parker
C.E.O. and Chief Creative Officer - Stu Levy

A  Manga

TOKYOPOP and  are trademarks or registered trademarks of TOKYOPOP Inc.

TOKYOPOP Inc.
5900 Wilshire Blvd. Suite 2000
Los Angeles, CA 90036

E-mail: info@TOKYOPOP.com
Come visit us online at www.TOKYOPOP.com

ISBN: 978-1-4278-0485-3

First TOKYOPOP printing: July 2008
10 9 8 7 6 5 4 3 2 1
Printed in the USA

Bizenghast

Volume 5

By M. Alice LeGrow

HAMBURG // LONDON // LOS ANGELES // TOKYO

Bizenghast

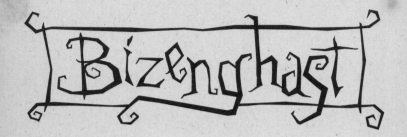

Contents

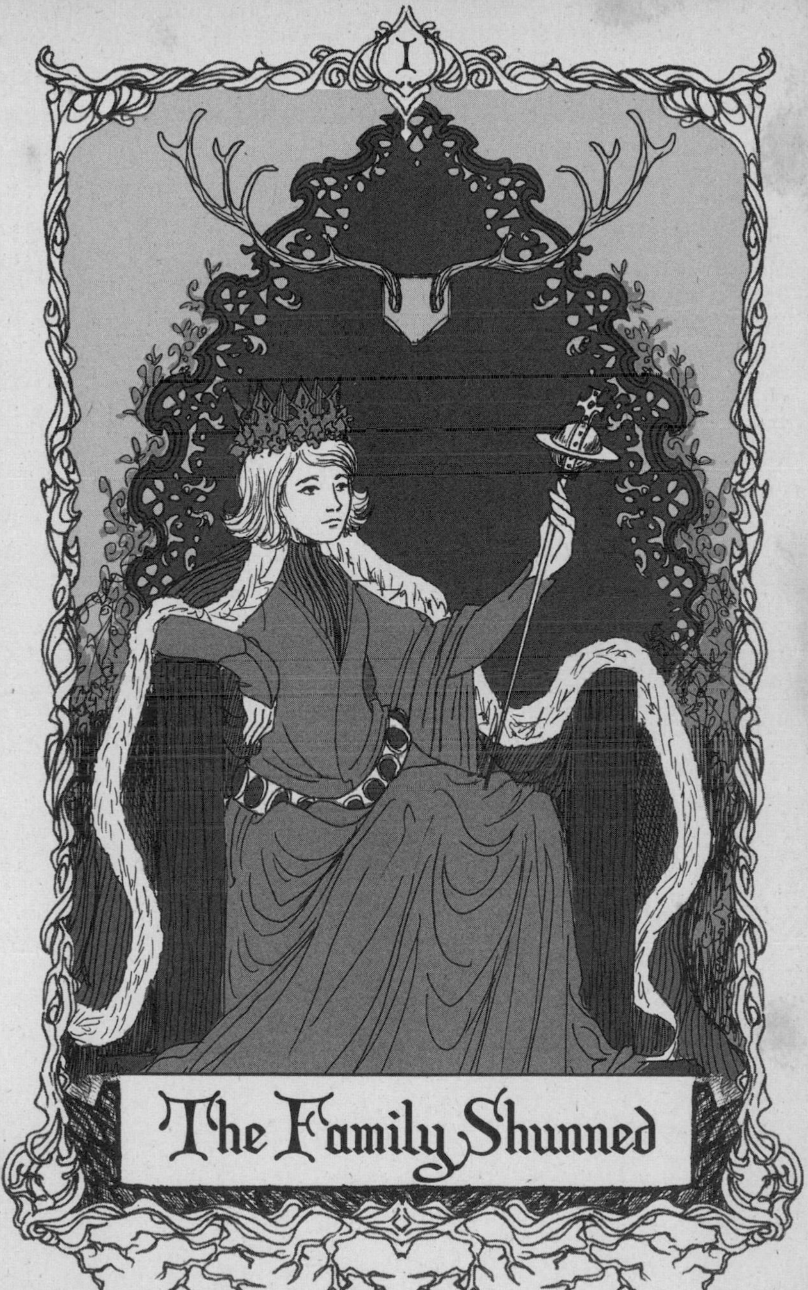
I
The Family Shunned

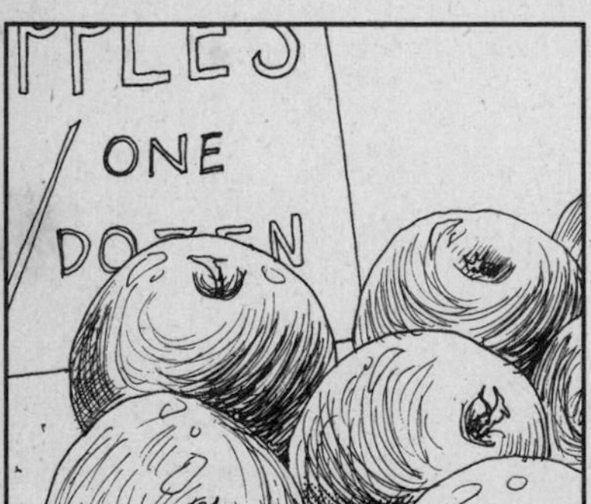
PPLES
ONE

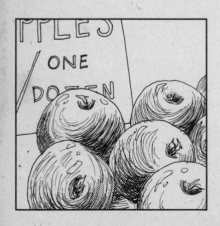

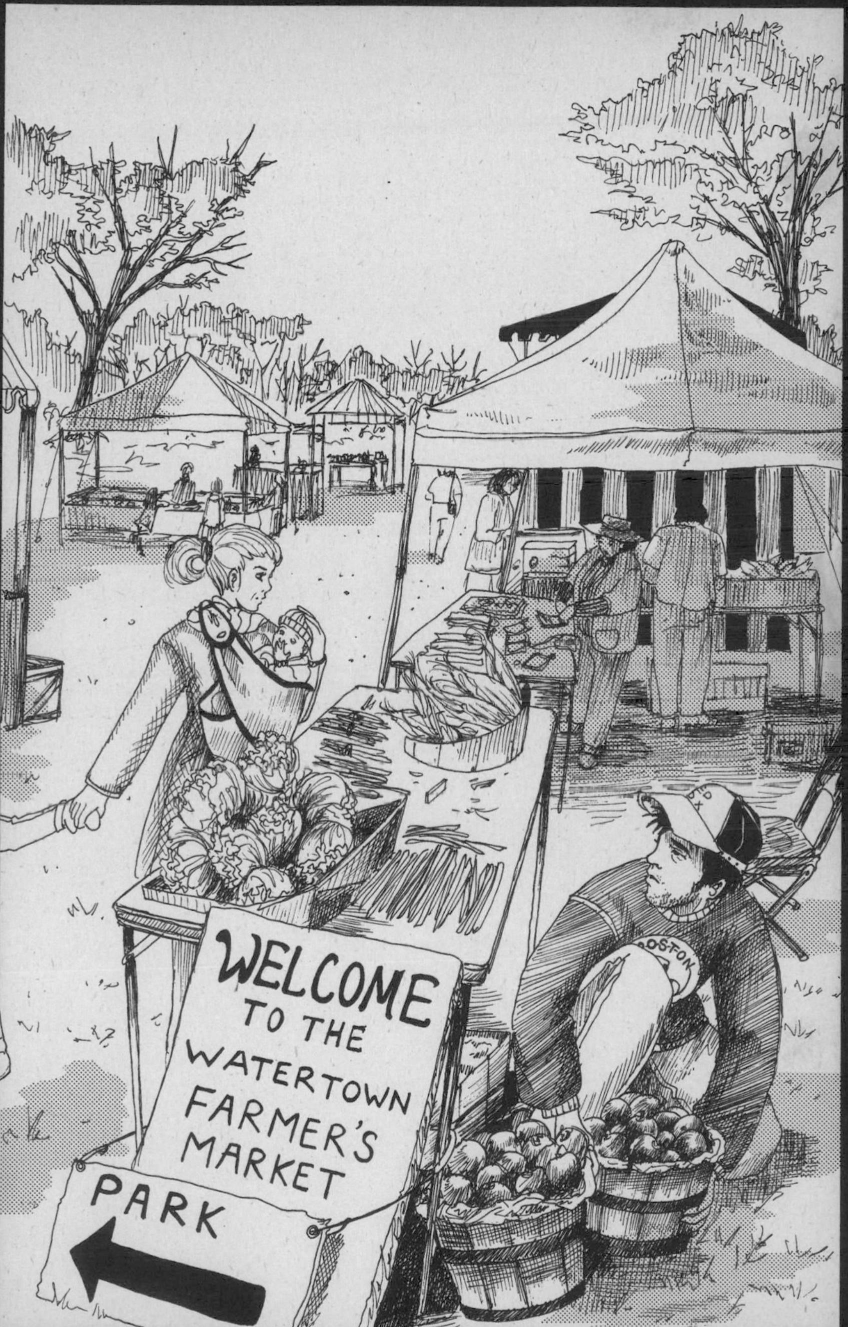
WELCOME
TO THE
WATERTOWN
FARMER'S
MARKET
PARK
BOSTON

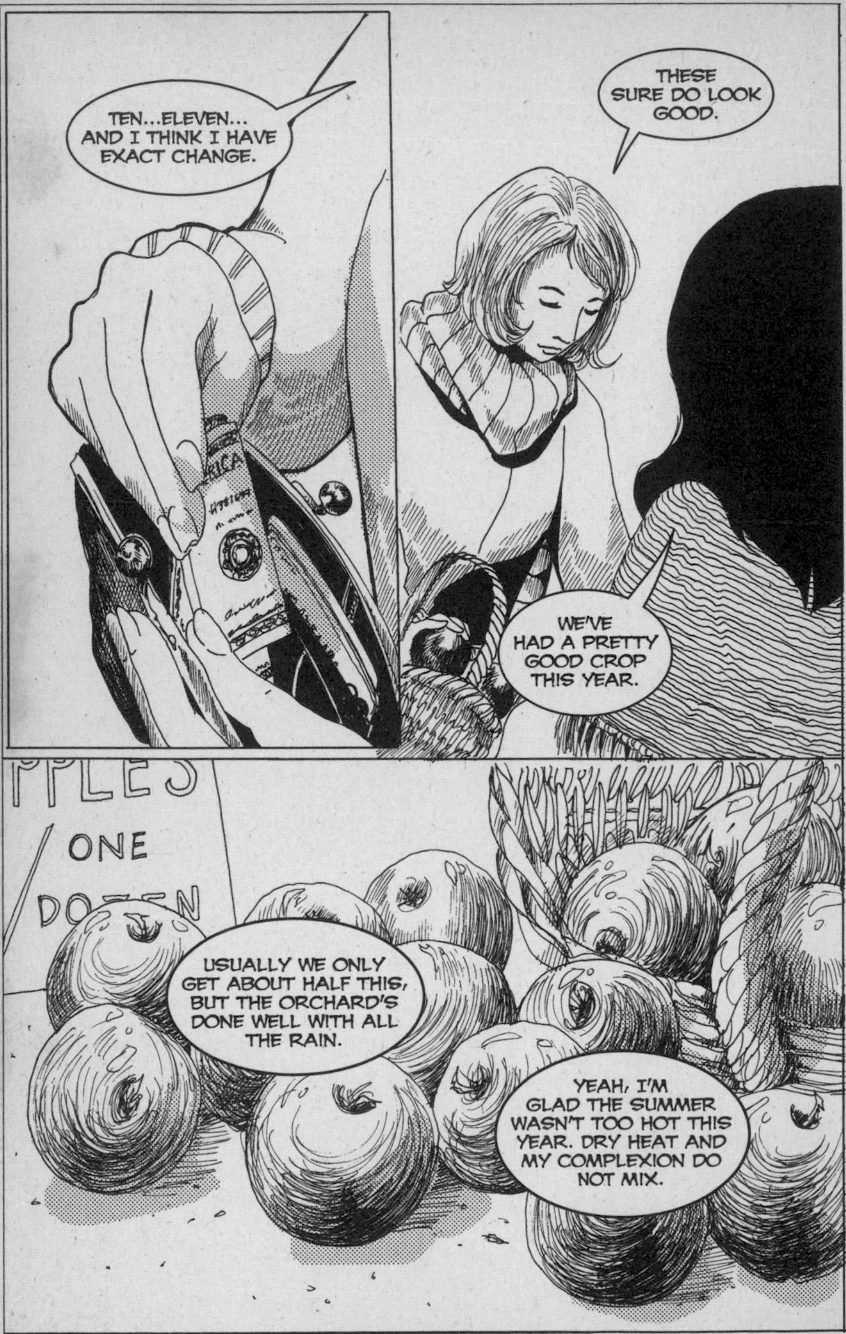
TEN...ELEVEN... AND I THINK I HAVE EXACT CHANGE.
THESE SURE DO LOOK GOOD.
WE'VE HAD A PRETTY GOOD CROP THIS YEAR.
PPLES
ONE
DOZEN
USUALLY WE ONLY GET ABOUT HALF THIS, BUT THE ORCHARD'S DONE WELL WITH ALL THE RAIN.
YEAH, I'M GLAD THE SUMMER WASN'T TOO HOT THIS YEAR. DRY HEAT AND MY COMPLEXION DO NOT MIX.

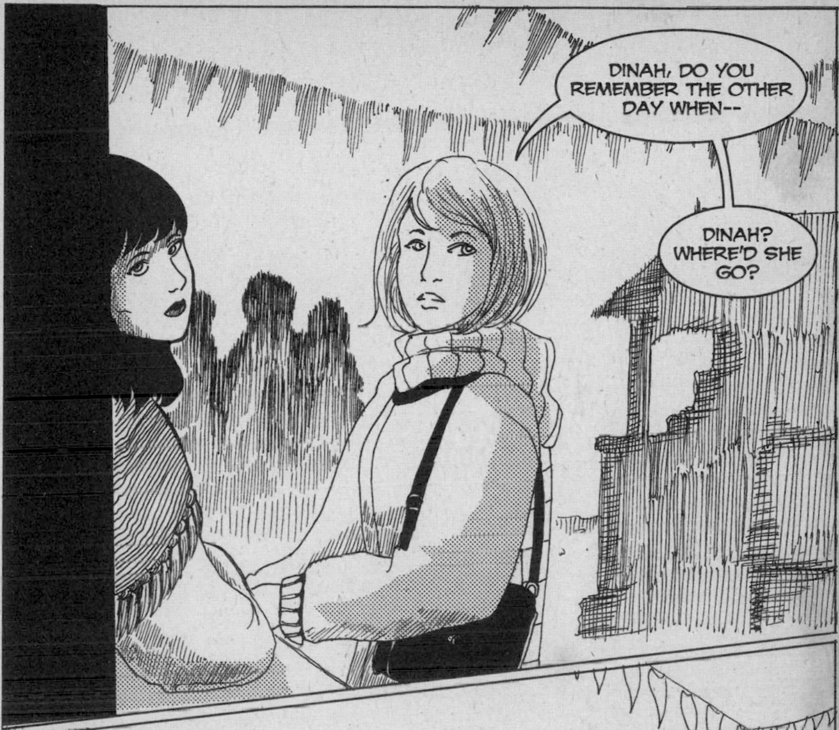
DINAH, DO YOU REMEMBER THE OTHER DAY WHEN--
DINAH? WHERE'D SHE GO?
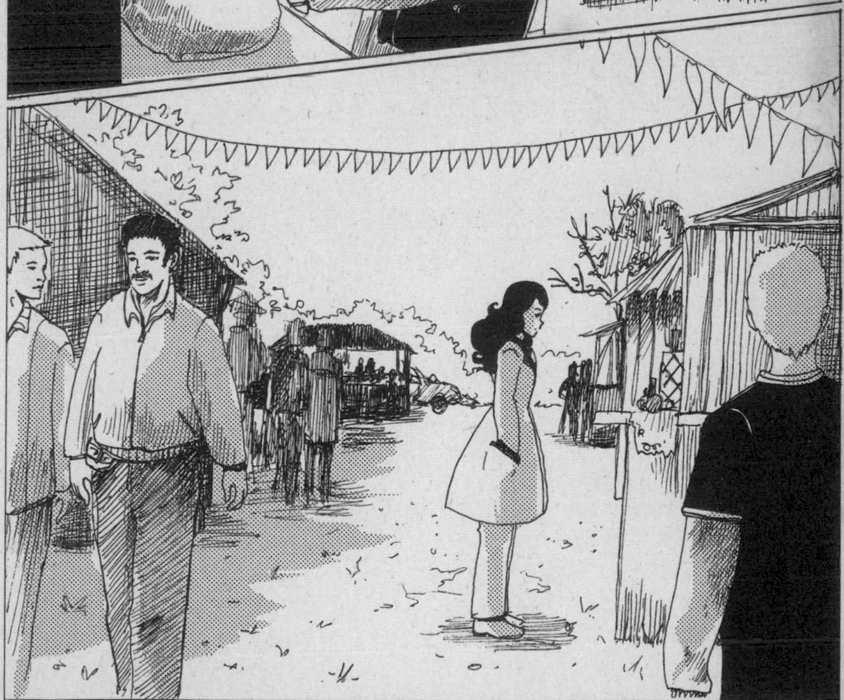

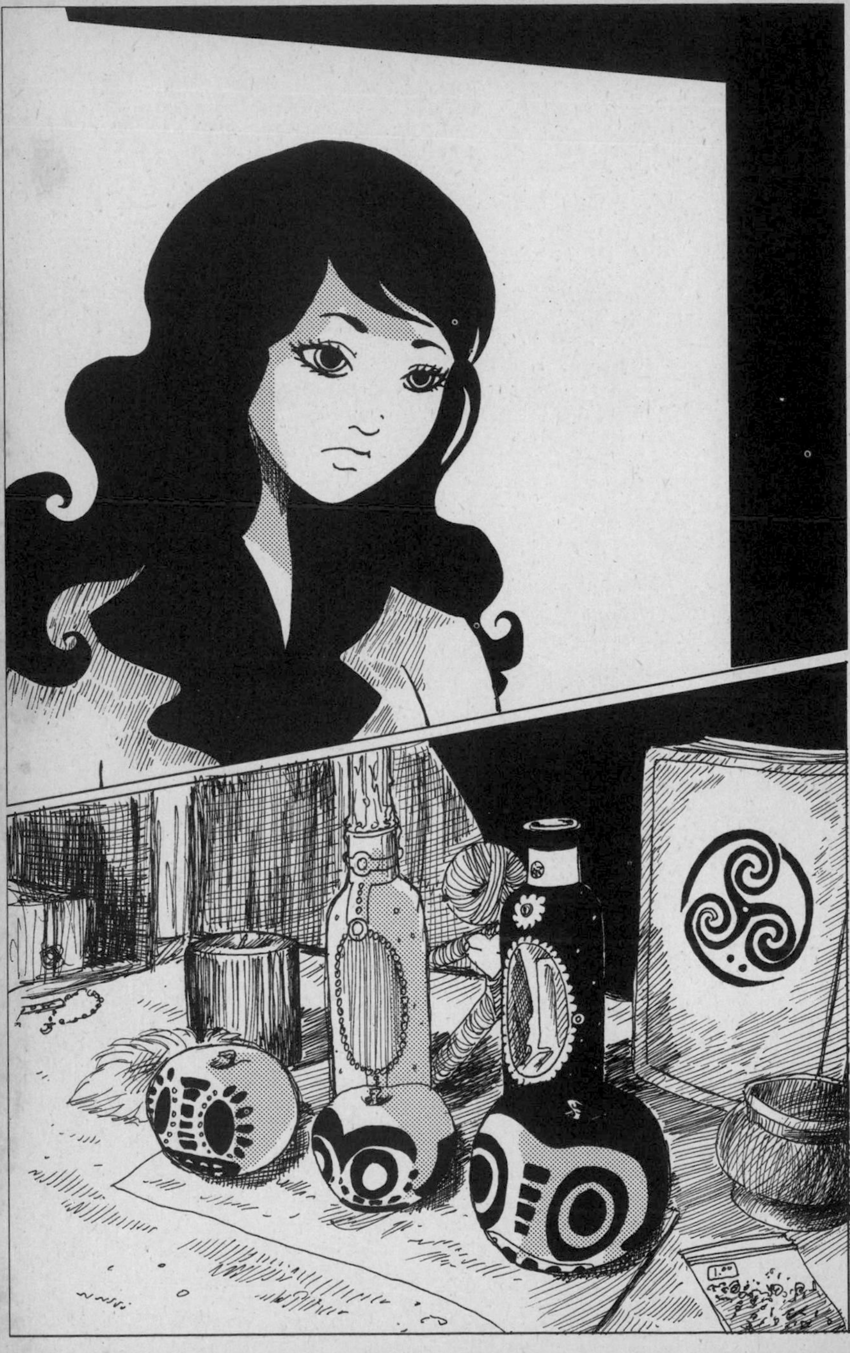
1.00

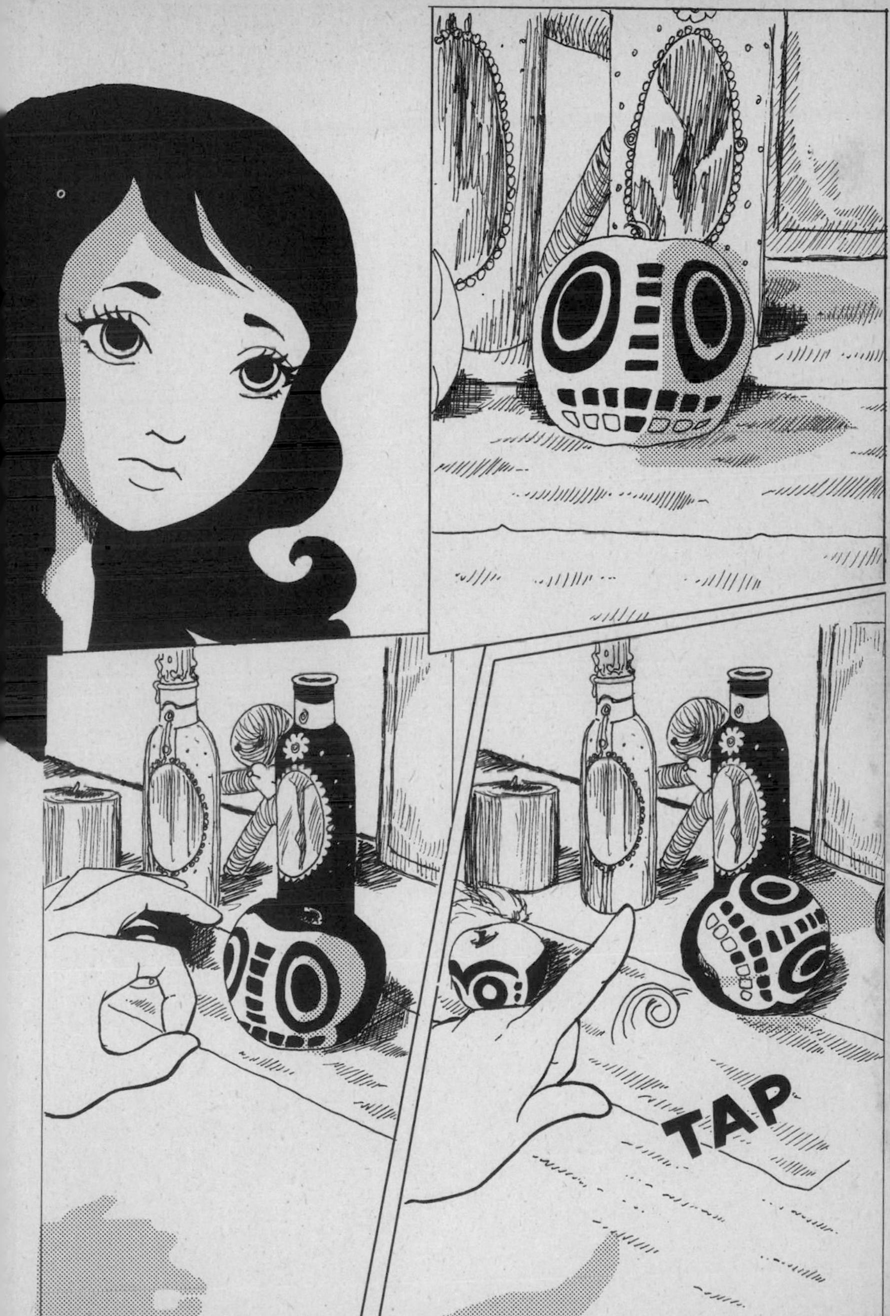
TAP

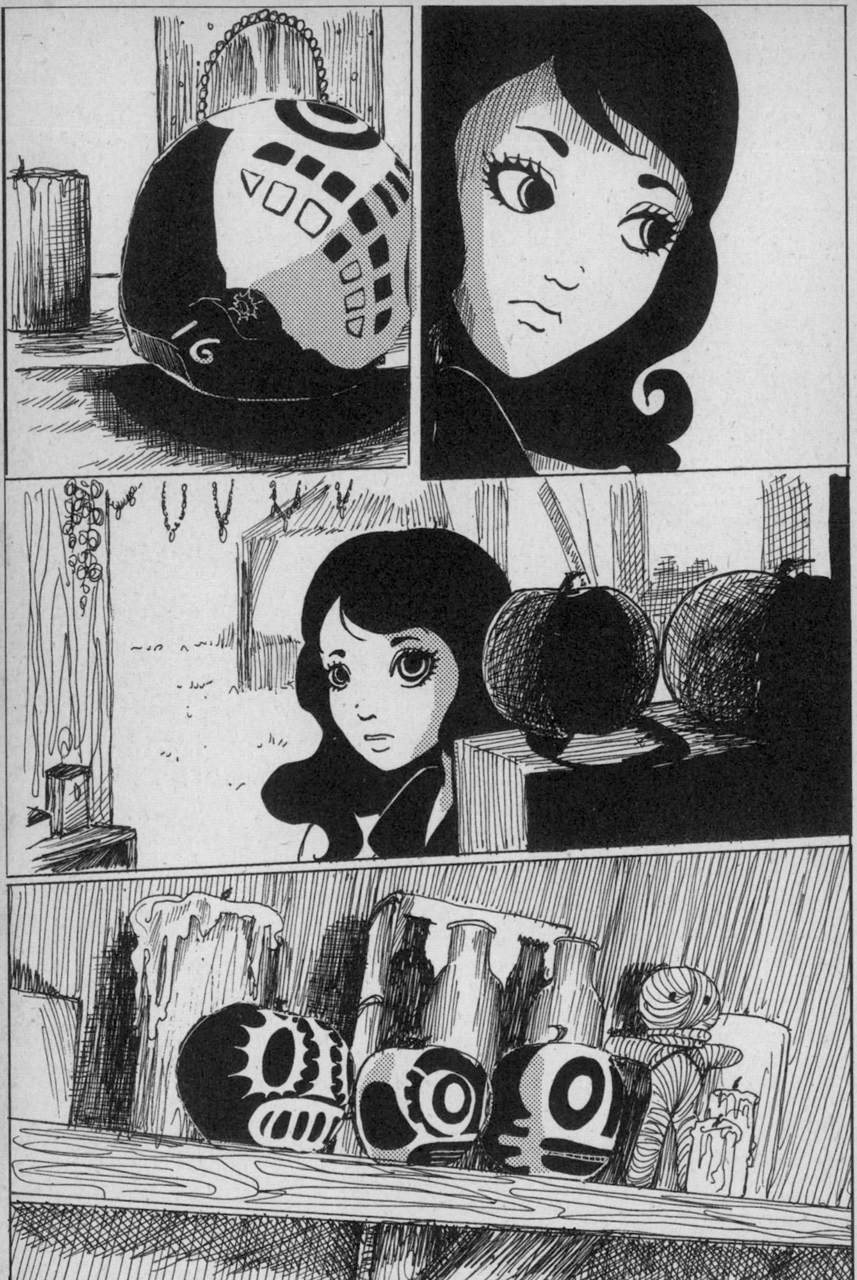

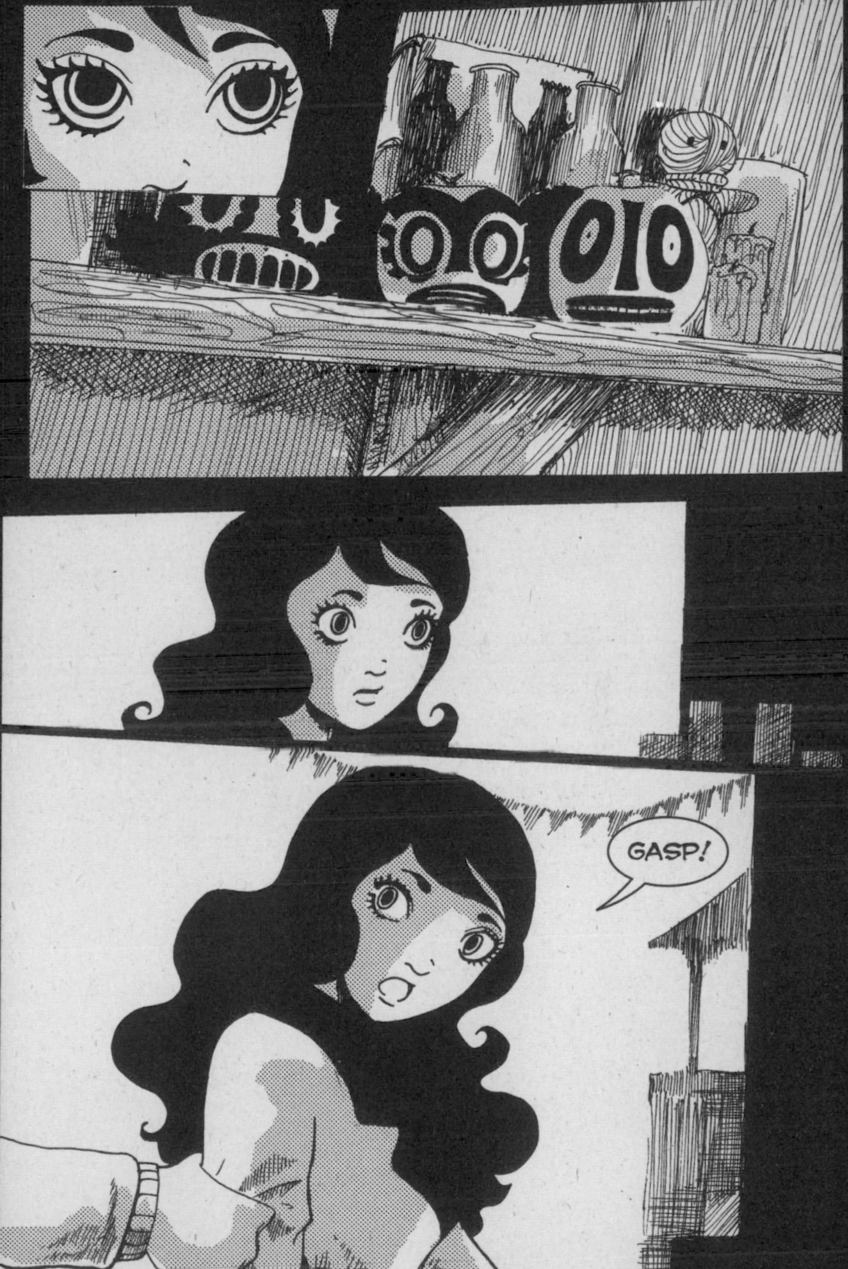
GASP!

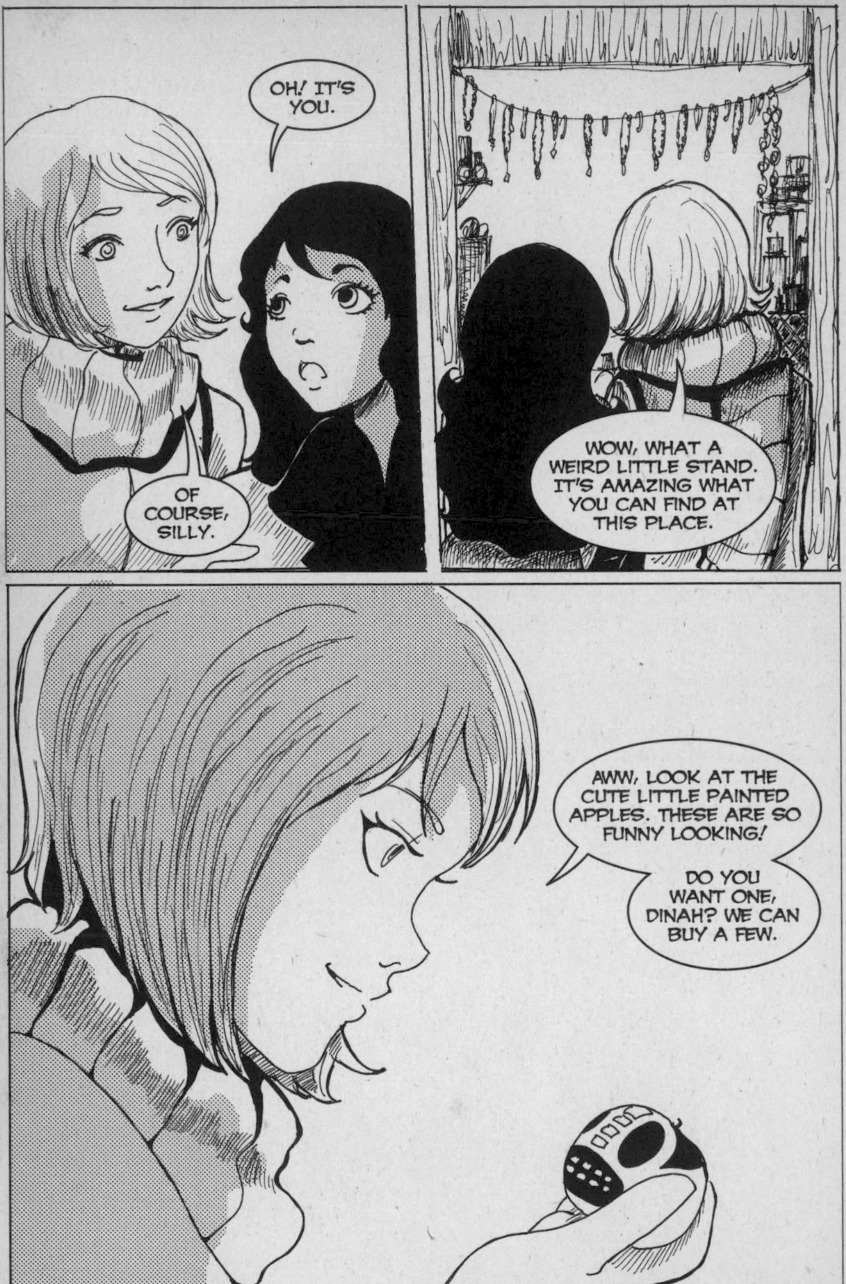
OH! IT'S YOU.
OF COURSE, SILLY.
WOW, WHAT A WEIRD LITTLE STAND. IT'S AMAZING WHAT YOU CAN FIND AT THIS PLACE.
AWW, LOOK AT THE CUTE LITTLE PAINTED APPLES. THESE ARE SO FUNNY LOOKING!
DO YOU WANT ONE, DINAH? WE CAN BUY A FEW.

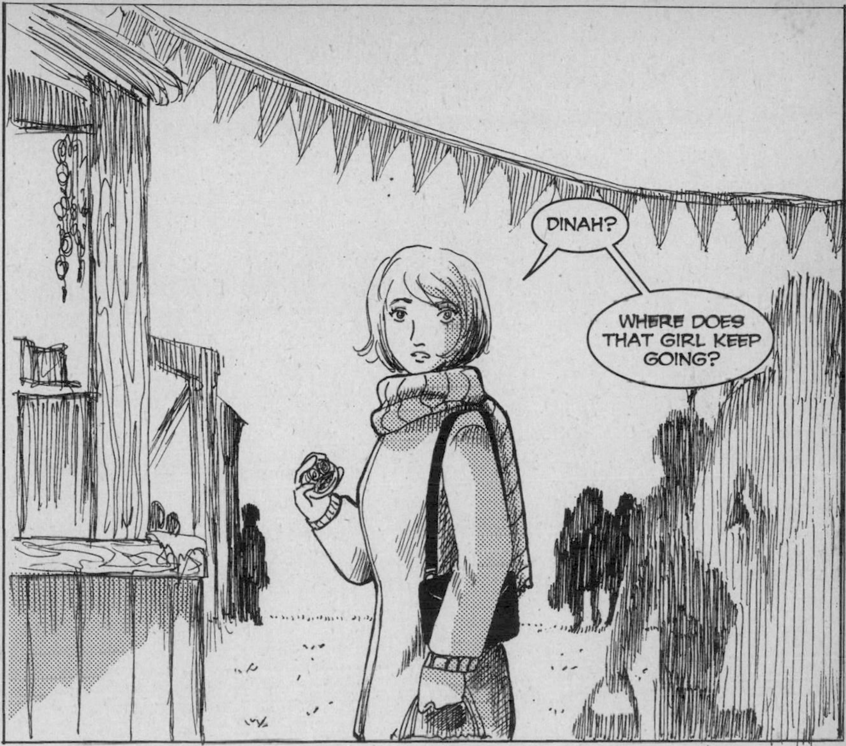
DINAH?
WHERE DOES THAT GIRL KEEP GOING?
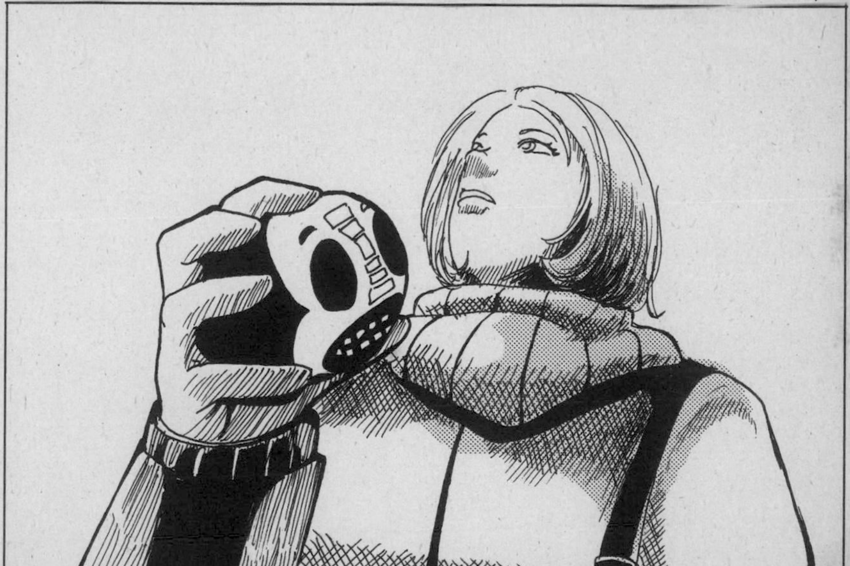

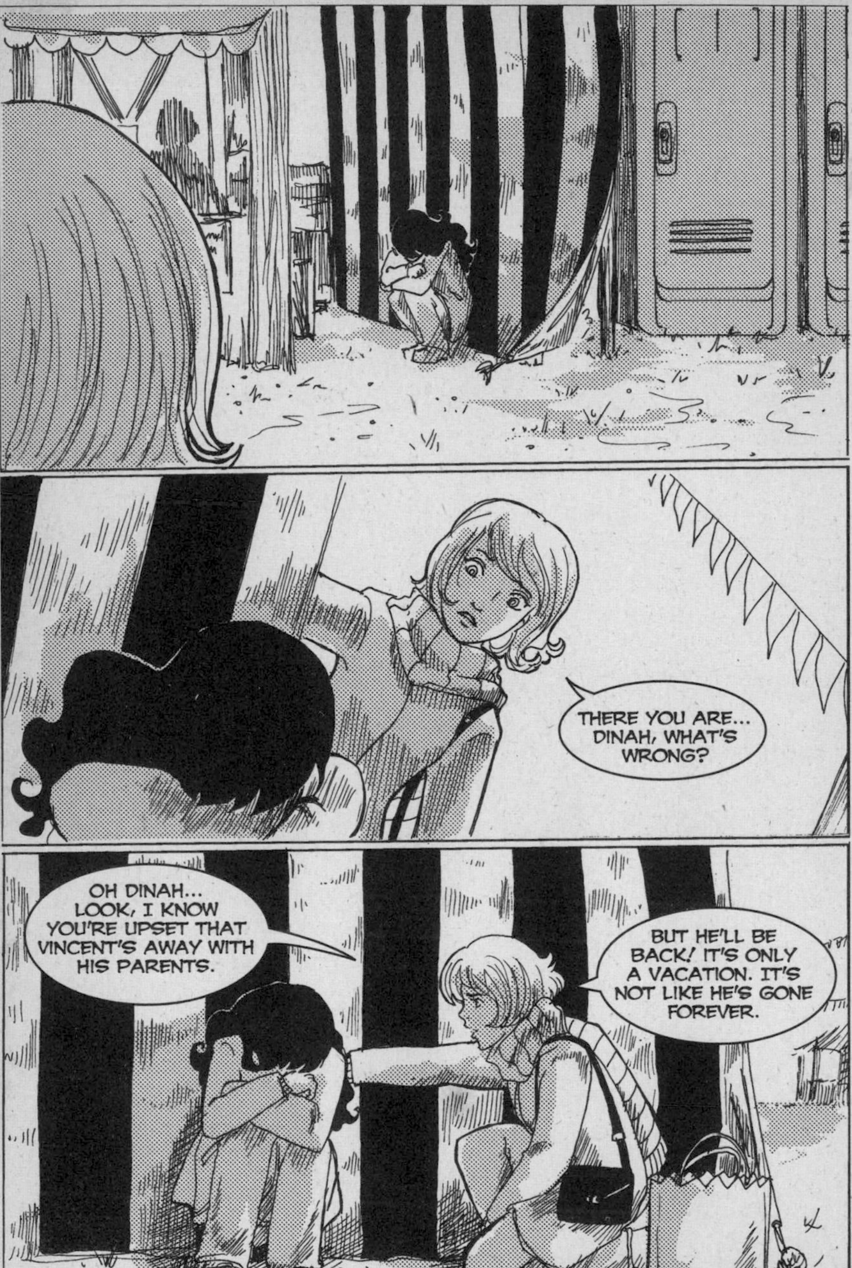
THERE YOU ARE... DINAH, WHAT'S WRONG?
OH DINAH... LOOK, I KNOW YOU'RE UPSET THAT VINCENT'S AWAY WITH HIS PARENTS.
BUT HE'LL BE BACK! IT'S ONLY A VACATION. IT'S NOT LIKE HE'S GONE FOREVER.

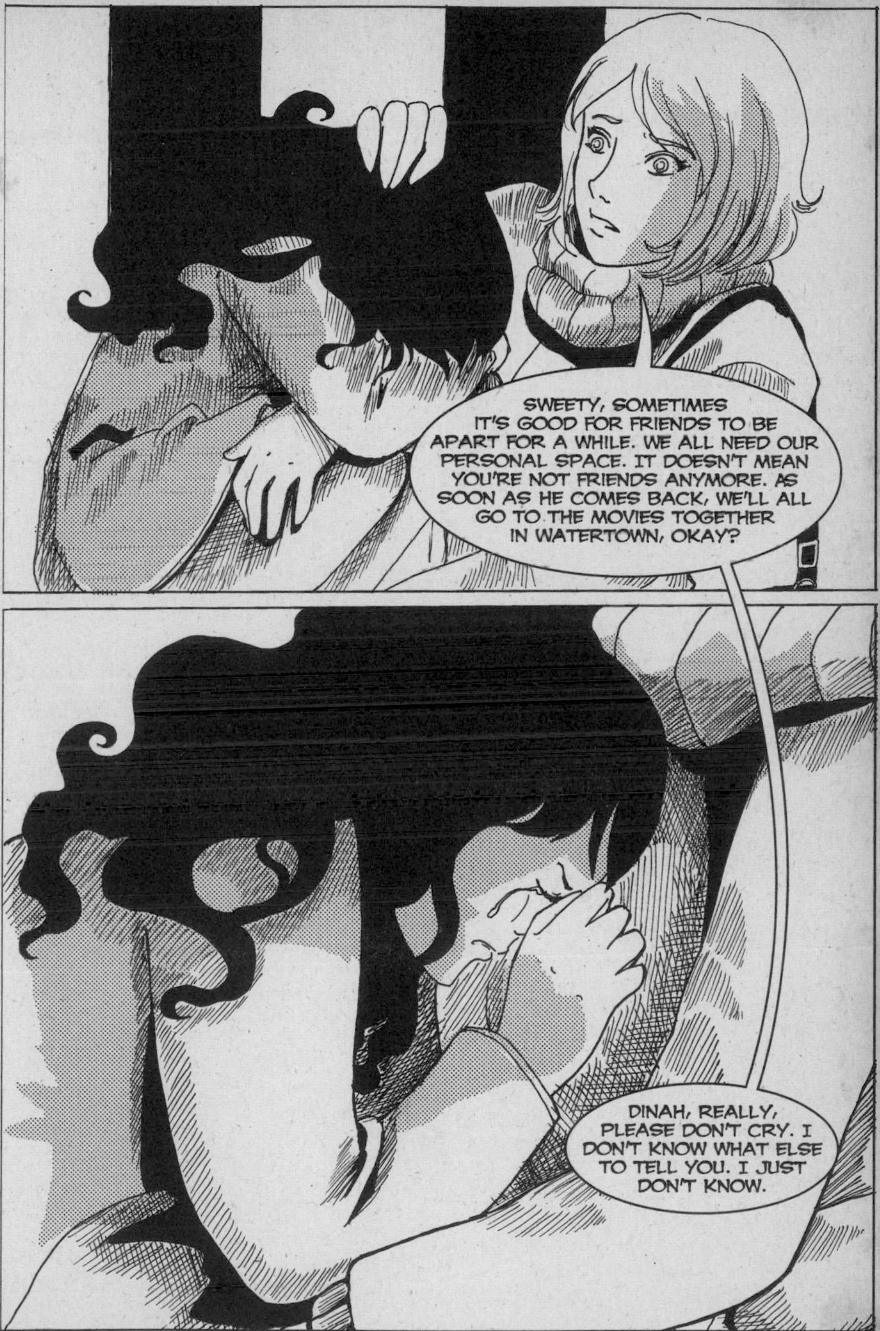
SWEETY, SOMETIMES IT'S GOOD FOR FRIENDS TO BE APART FOR A WHILE. WE ALL NEED OUR PERSONAL SPACE. IT DOESN'T MEAN YOU'RE NOT FRIENDS ANYMORE. AS SOON AS HE COMES BACK, WE'LL ALL GO TO THE MOVIES TOGETHER IN WATERTOWN, OKAY?
DINAH, REALLY, PLEASE DON'T CRY. I DON'T KNOW WHAT ELSE TO TELL YOU. I JUST DON'T KNOW.

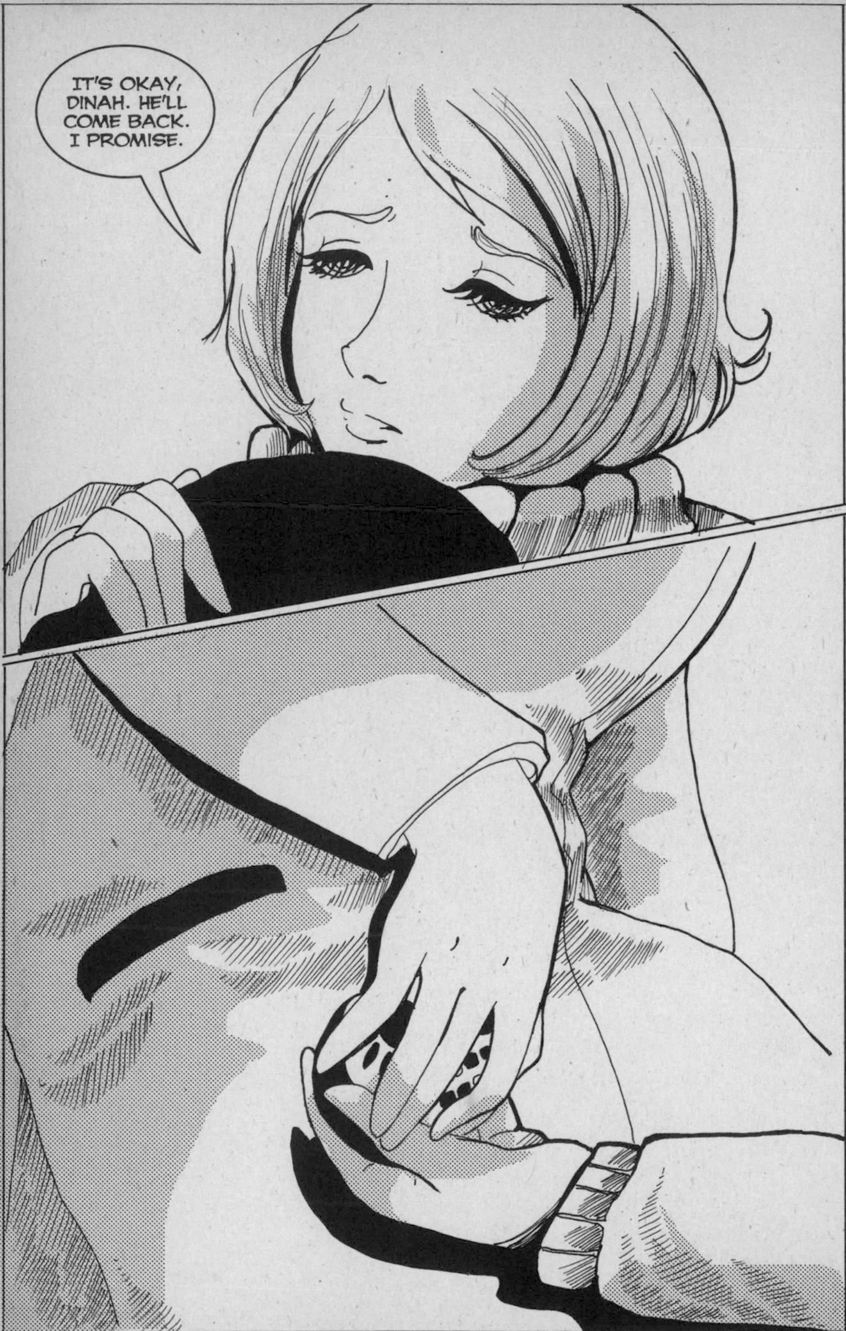
IT'S OKAY, DINAH. HE'LL COME BACK. I PROMISE.

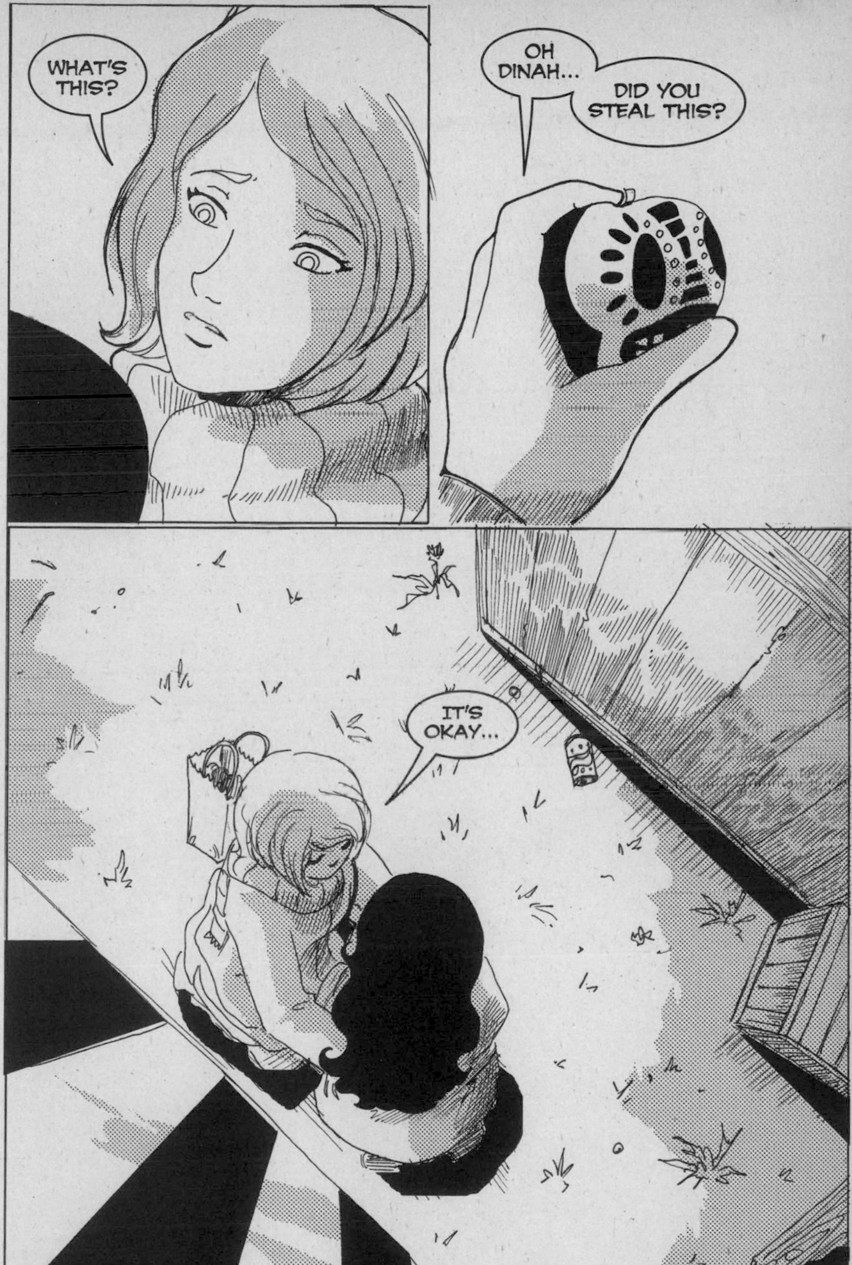
WHAT'S THIS?
OH DINAH...
DID YOU STEAL THIS?
IT'S OKAY...

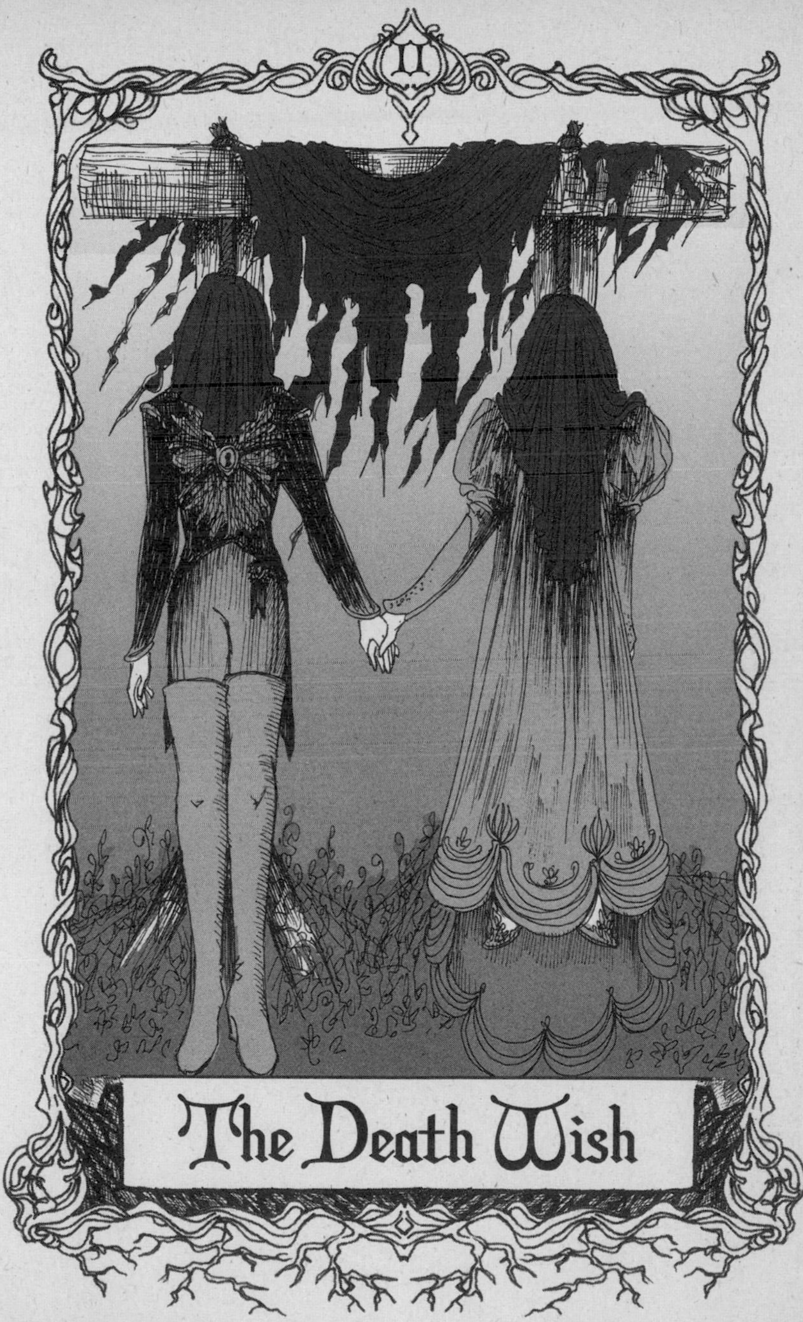
II
The Death Wish

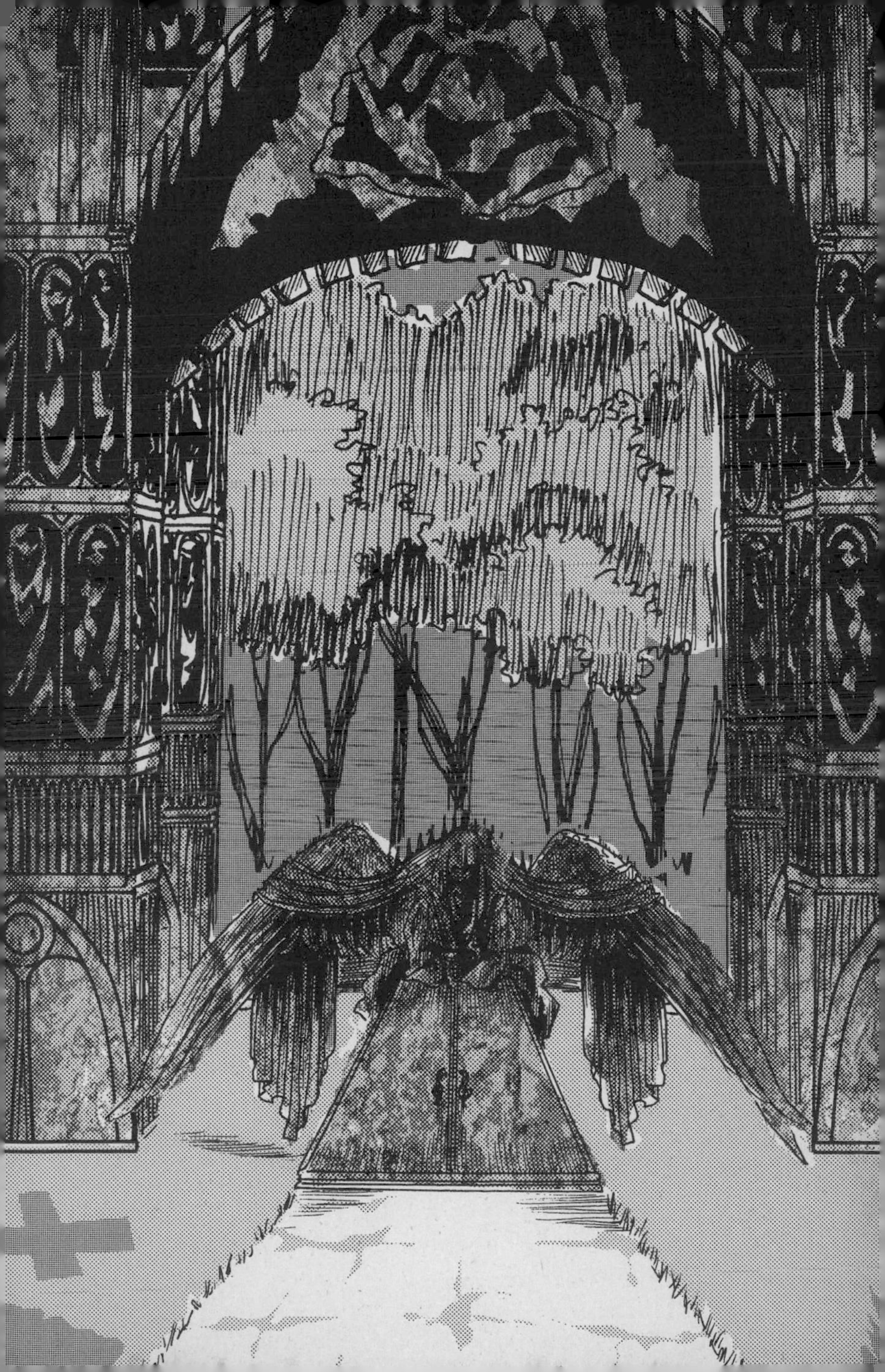

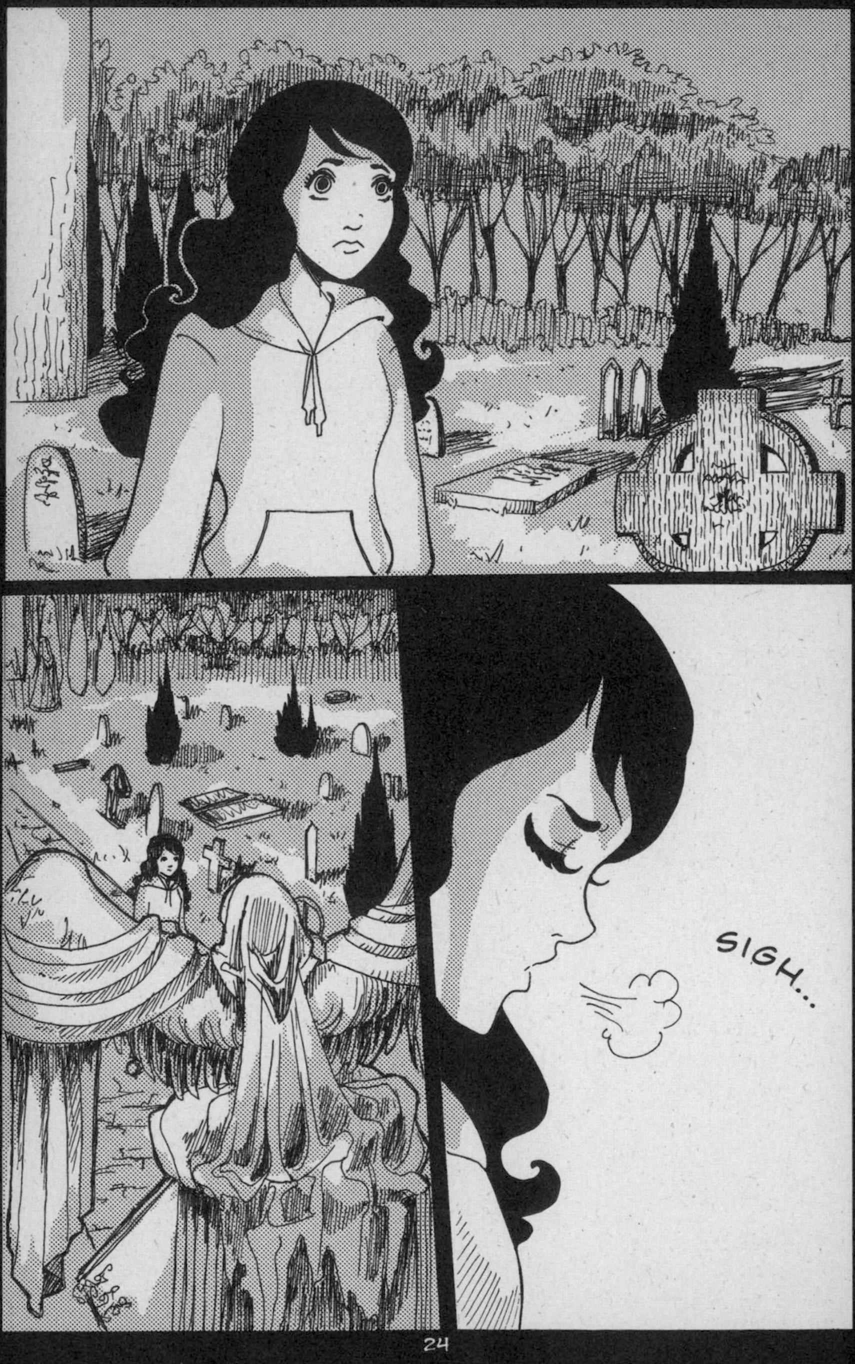
SIGH...

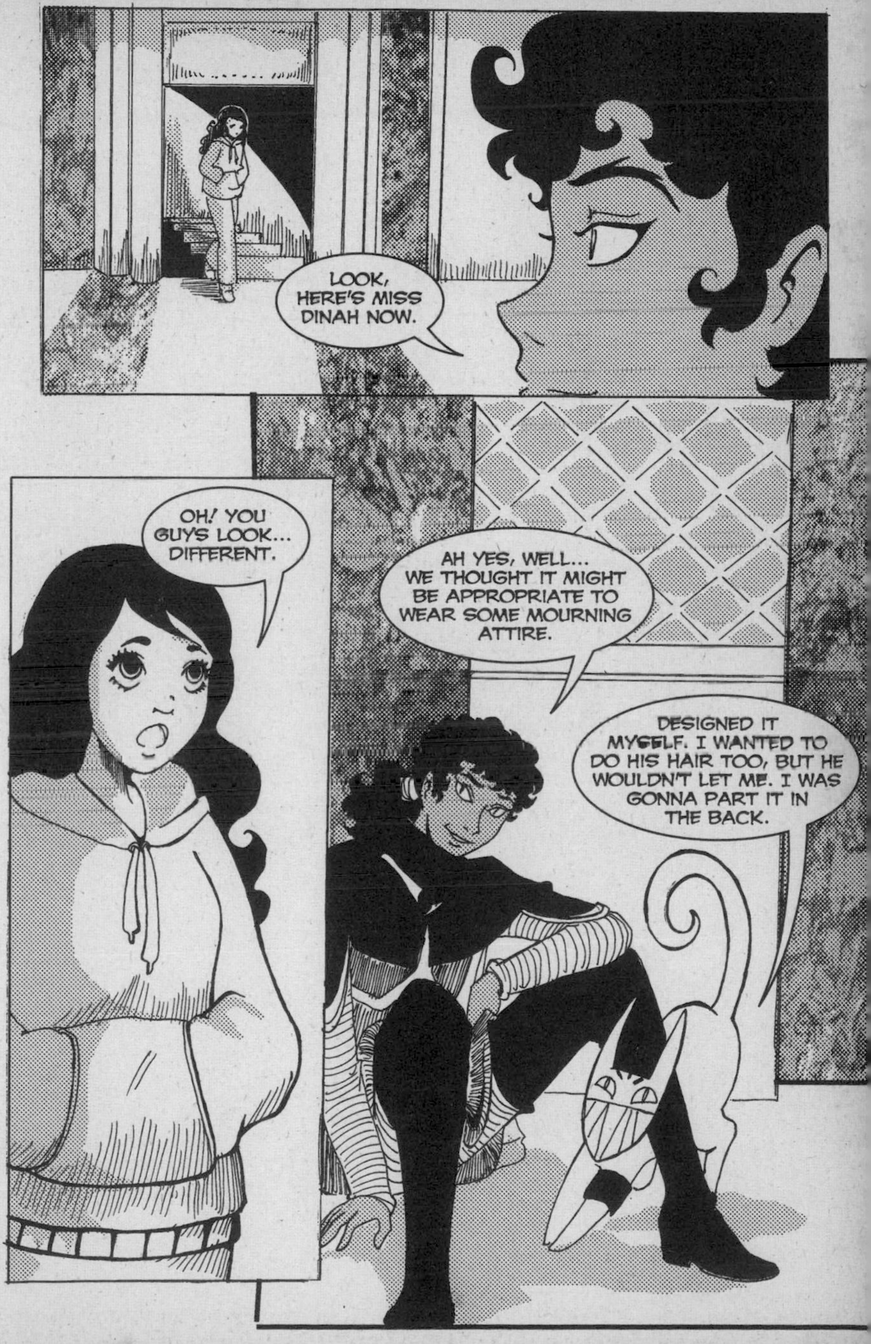
LOOK, HERE'S MISS DINAH NOW.
OH! YOU GUYS LOOK... DIFFERENT.
AH YES, WELL... WE THOUGHT IT MIGHT BE APPROPRIATE TO WEAR SOME MOURNING ATTIRE.
DESIGNED IT MYSELF. I WANTED TO DO HIS HAIR TOO, BUT HE WOULDN'T LET ME. I WAS GONNA PART IT IN THE BACK.

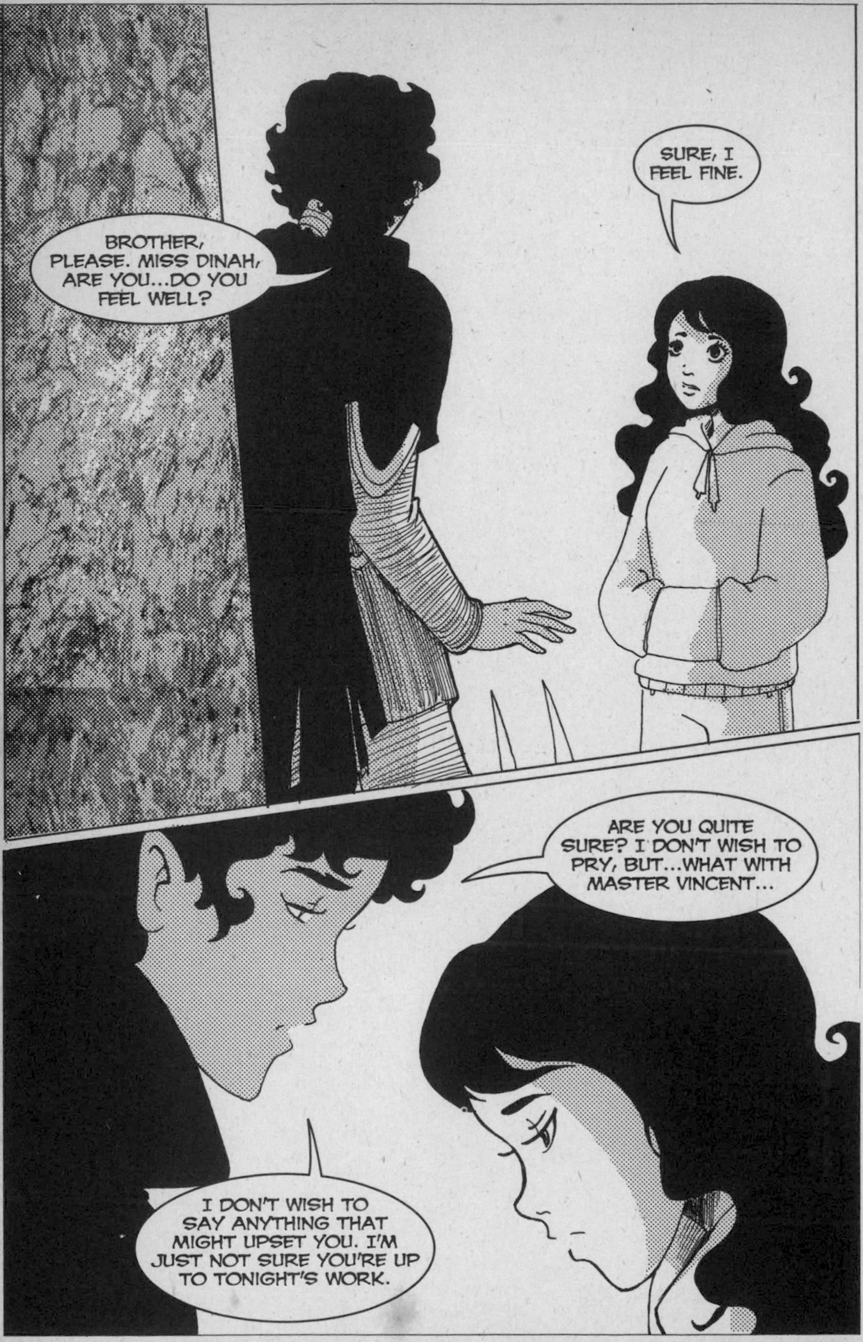
BROTHER, PLEASE. MISS DINAH, ARE YOU...DO YOU FEEL WELL?
SURE, I FEEL FINE.
ARE YOU QUITE SURE? I DON'T WISH TO PRY, BUT...WHAT WITH MASTER VINCENT...
I DON'T WISH TO SAY ANYTHING THAT MIGHT UPSET YOU. I'M JUST NOT SURE YOU'RE UP TO TONIGHT'S WORK.

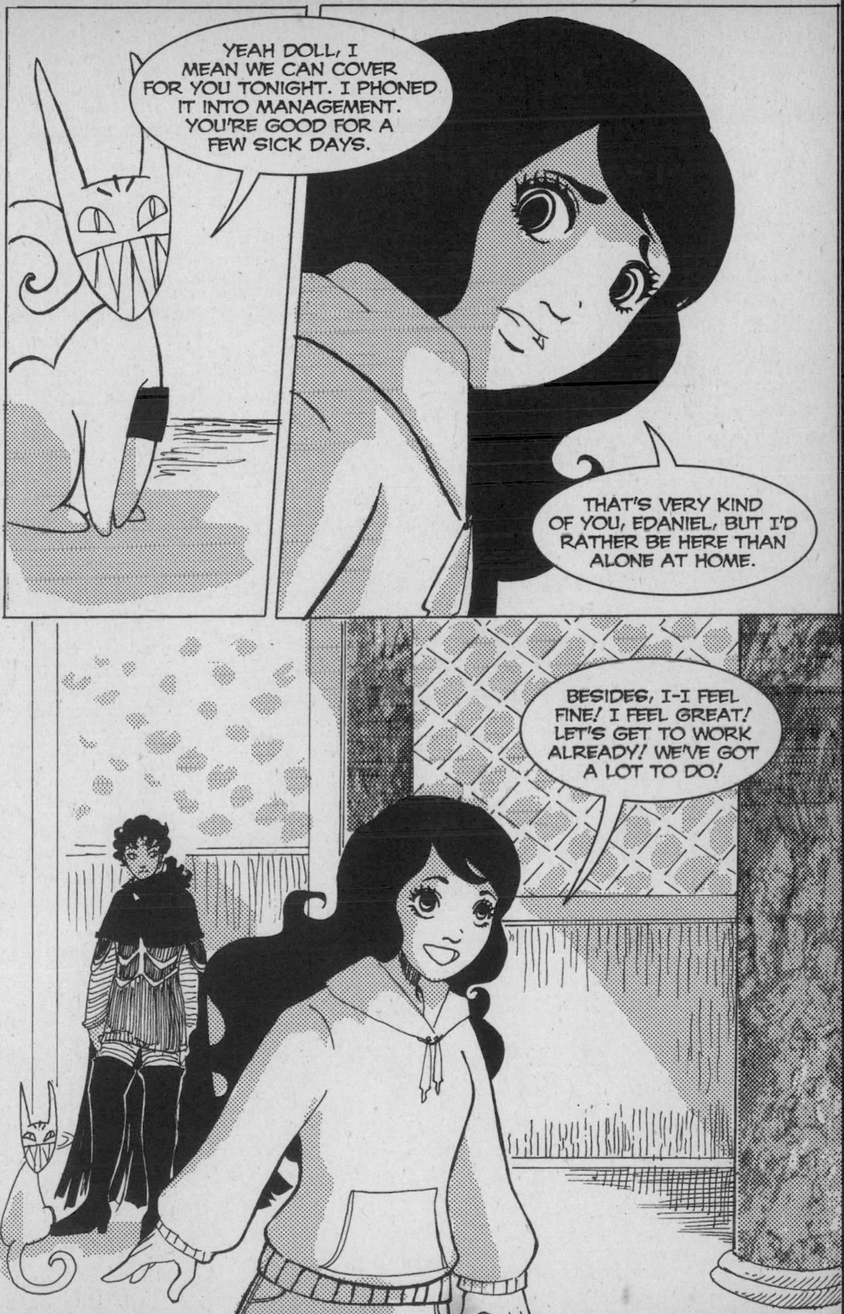
YEAH DOLL, I MEAN WE CAN COVER FOR YOU TONIGHT. I PHONED IT INTO MANAGEMENT. YOU'RE GOOD FOR A FEW SICK DAYS.
THAT'S VERY KIND OF YOU, EDANIEL, BUT I'D RATHER BE HERE THAN ALONE AT HOME.
BESIDES, I-I FEEL FINE! I FEEL GREAT! LET'S GET TO WORK ALREADY! WE'VE GOT A LOT TO DO!

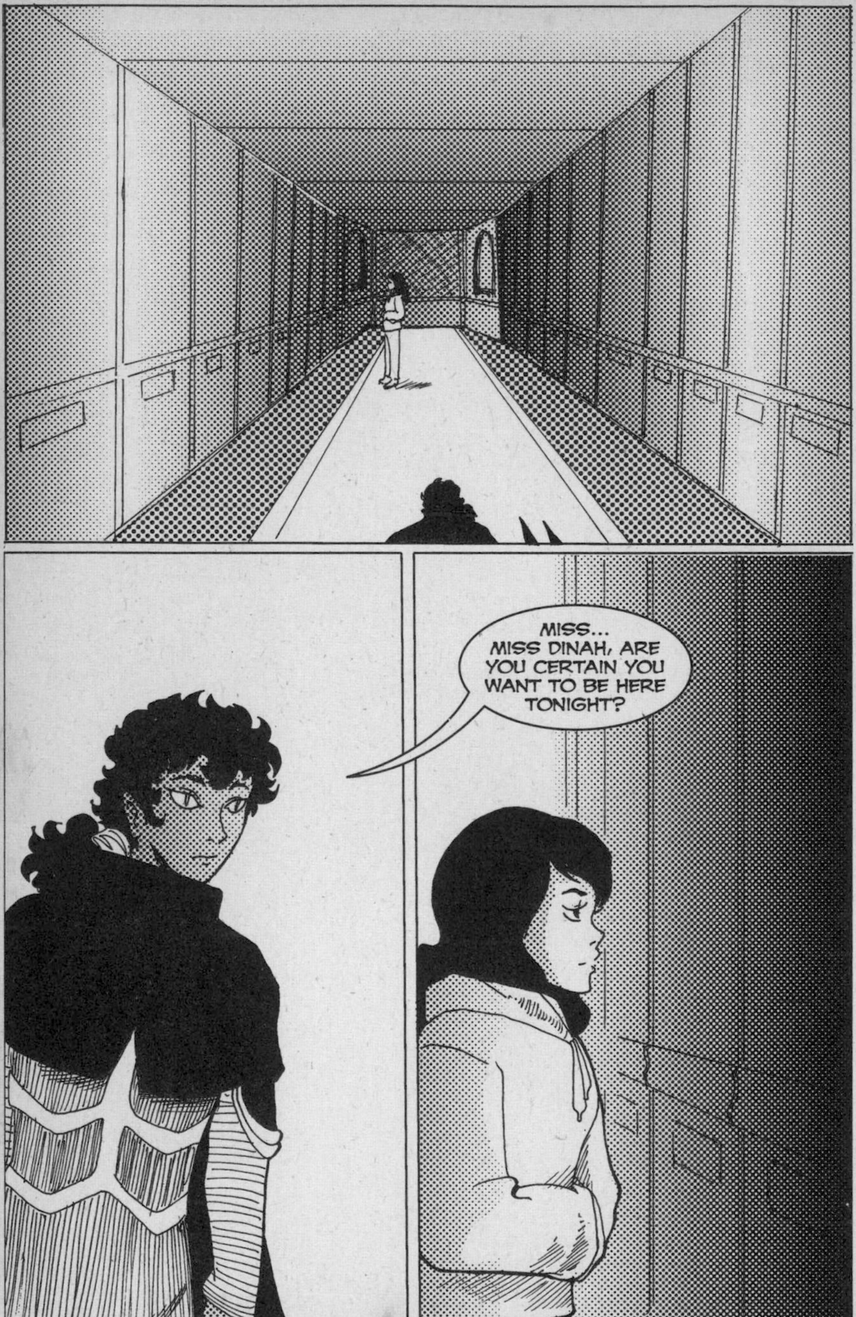
MISS... MISS DINAH, ARE YOU CERTAIN YOU WANT TO BE HERE TONIGHT?

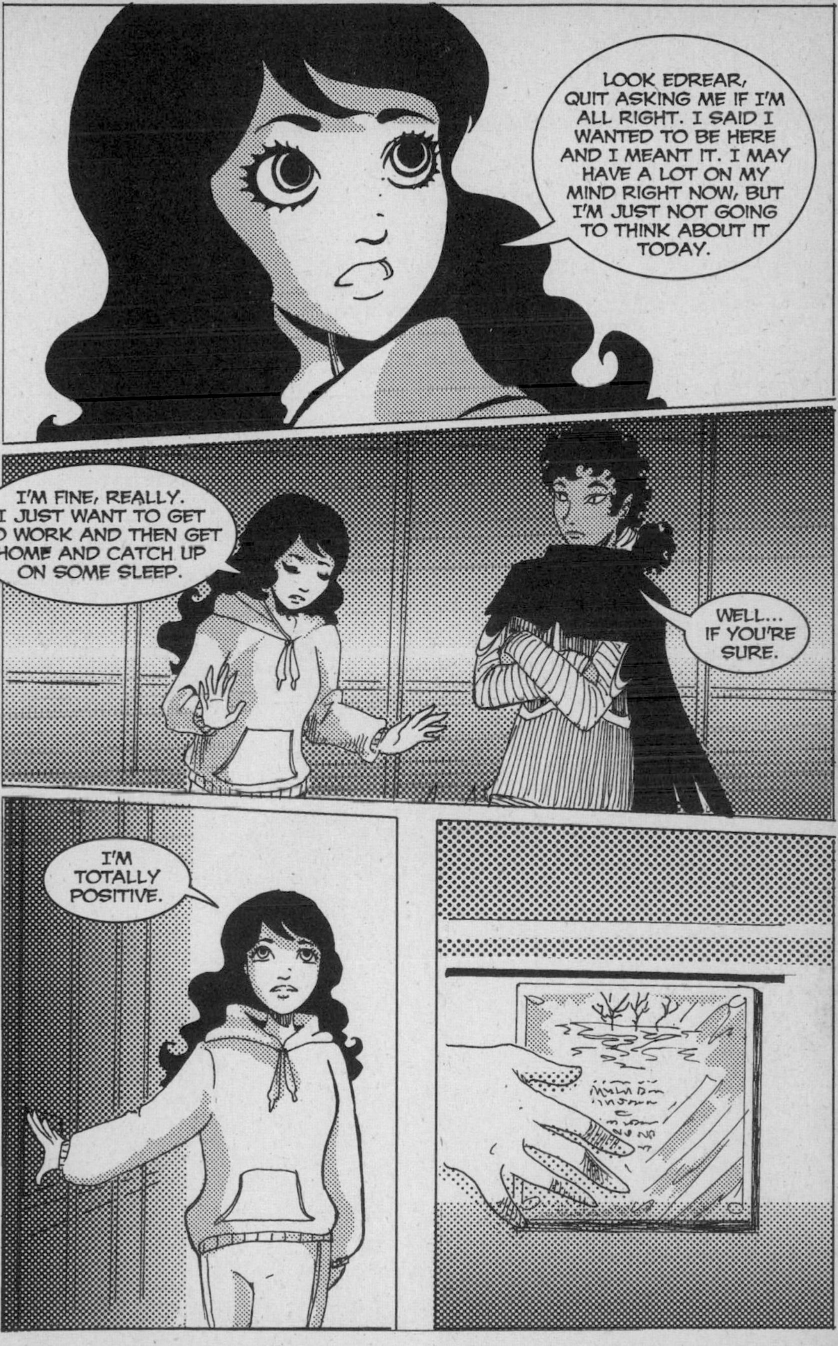

LOOK EDREAR, QUIT ASKING ME IF I'M ALL RIGHT. I SAID I WANTED TO BE HERE AND I MEANT IT. I MAY HAVE A LOT ON MY MIND RIGHT NOW, BUT I'M JUST NOT GOING TO THINK ABOUT IT TODAY.
I'M FINE, REALLY. I JUST WANT TO GET TO WORK AND THEN GET HOME AND CATCH UP ON SOME SLEEP.
WELL... IF YOU'RE SURE.
I'M TOTALLY POSITIVE.

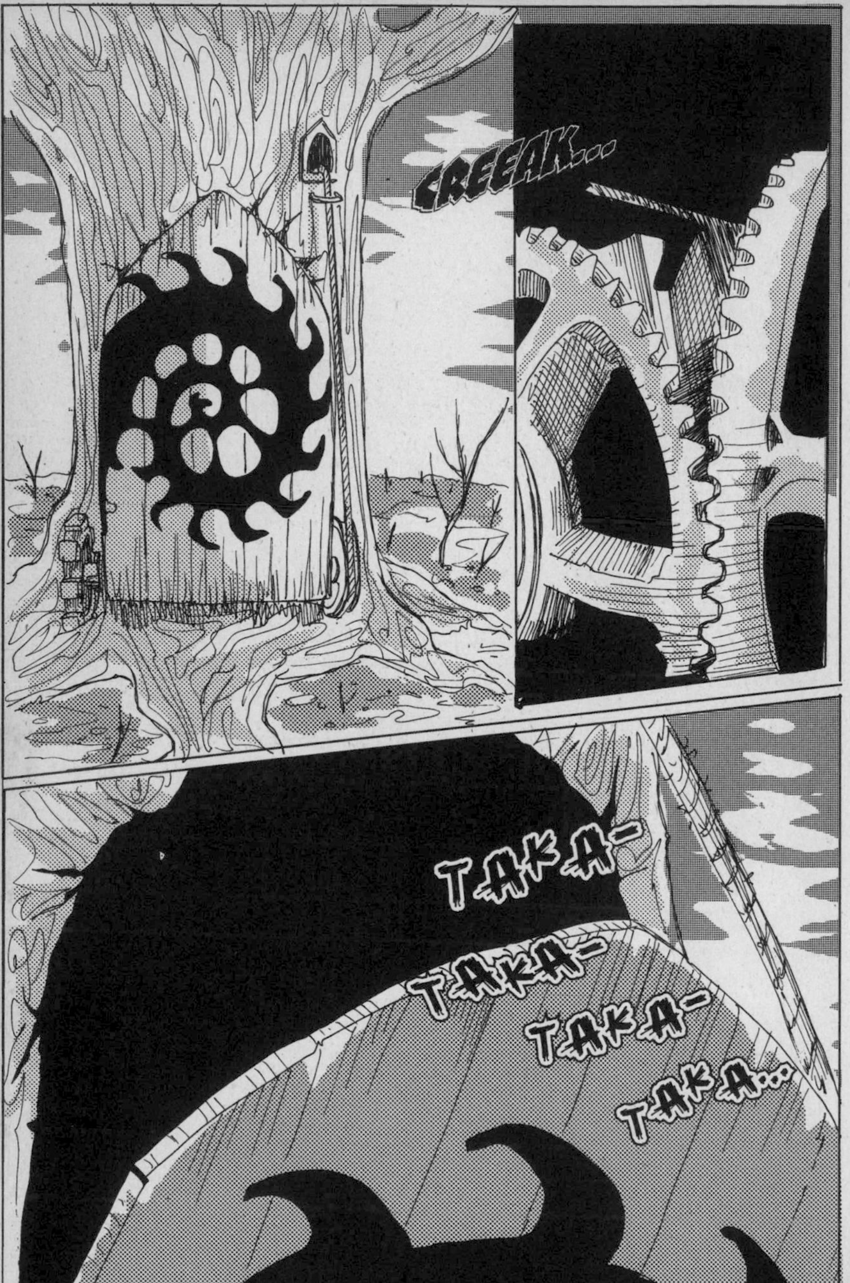
CREEAK...
TAKA-
TAKA-
TAKA-
TAKA...

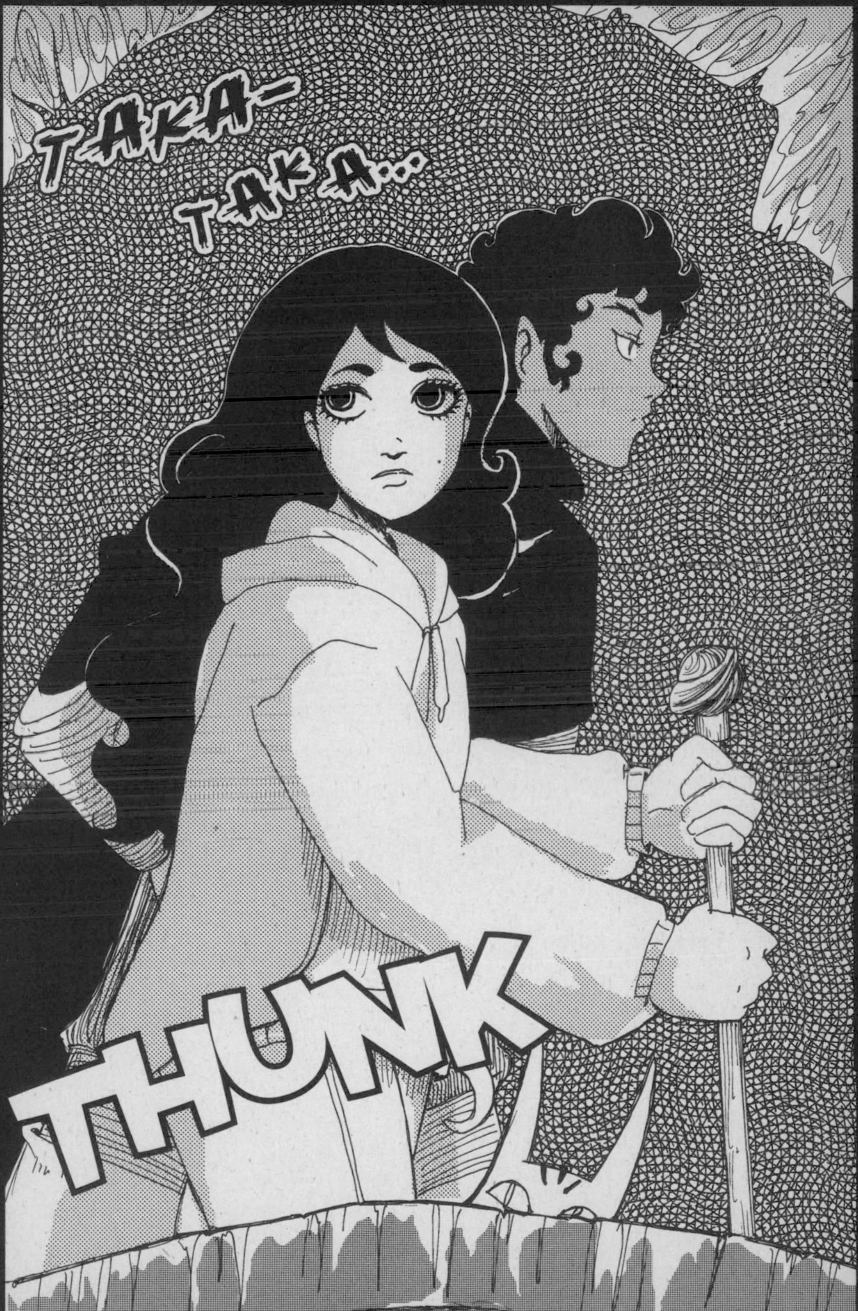
TAKA-
TAKA...
THUNK

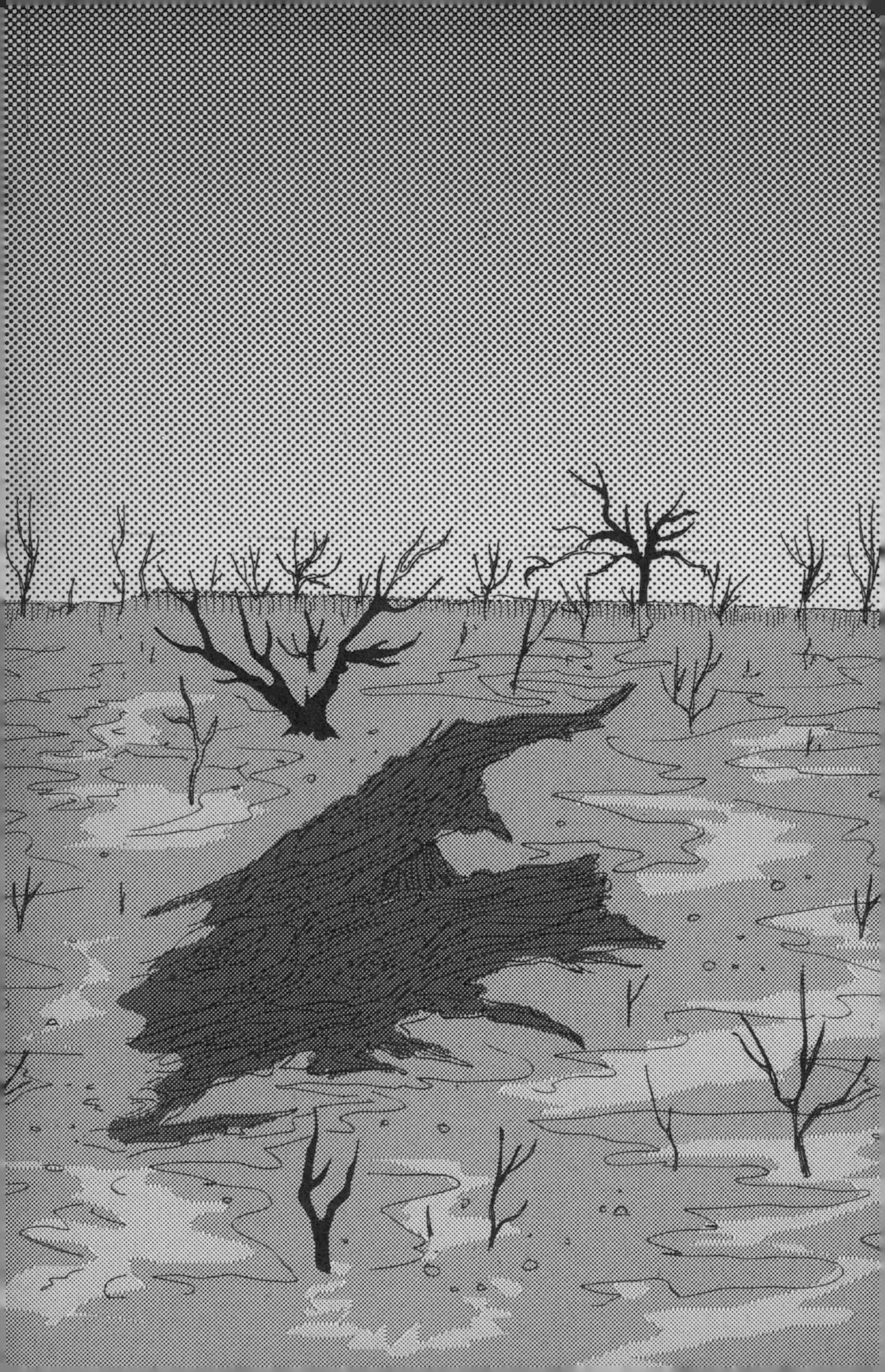

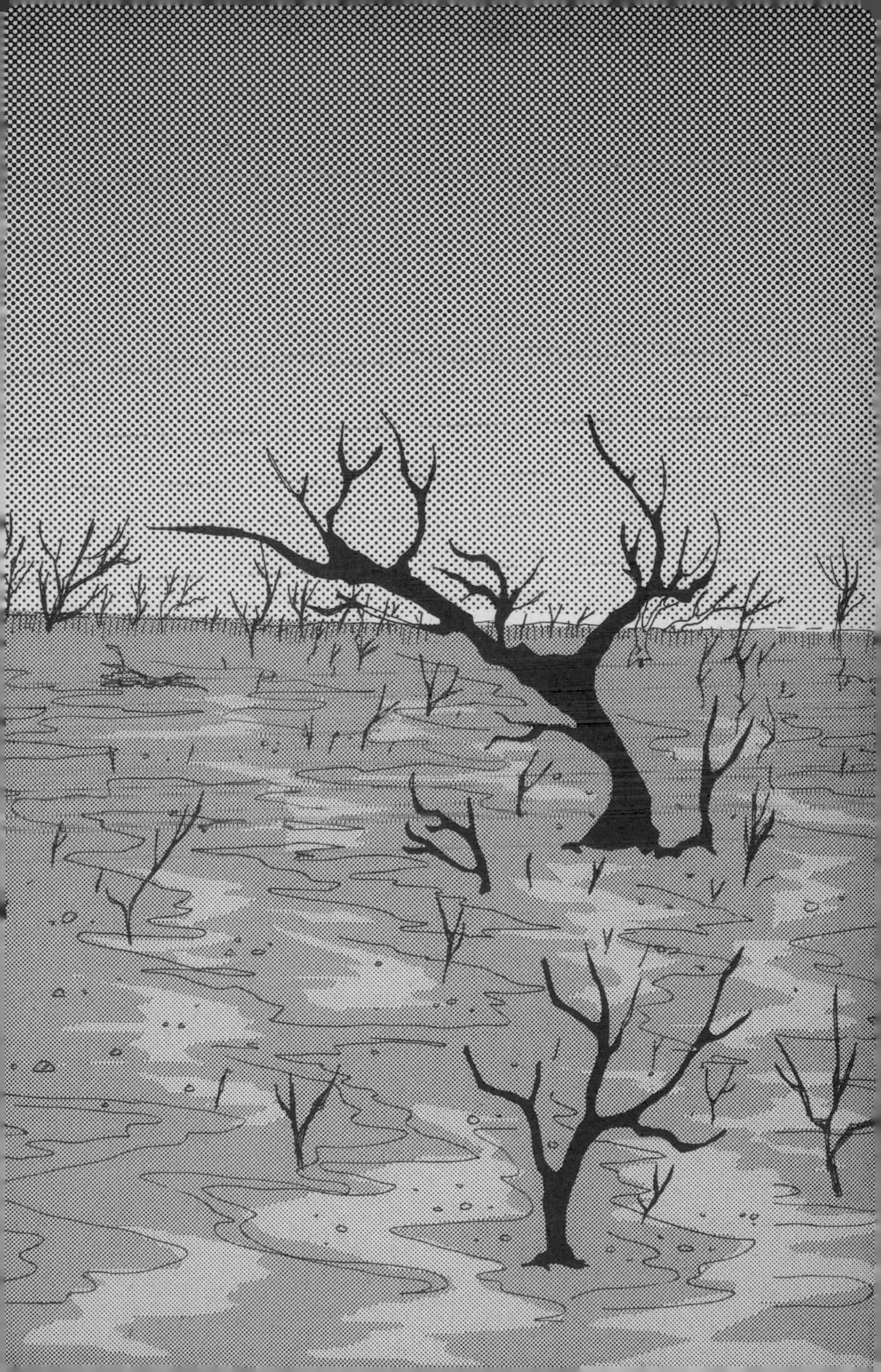

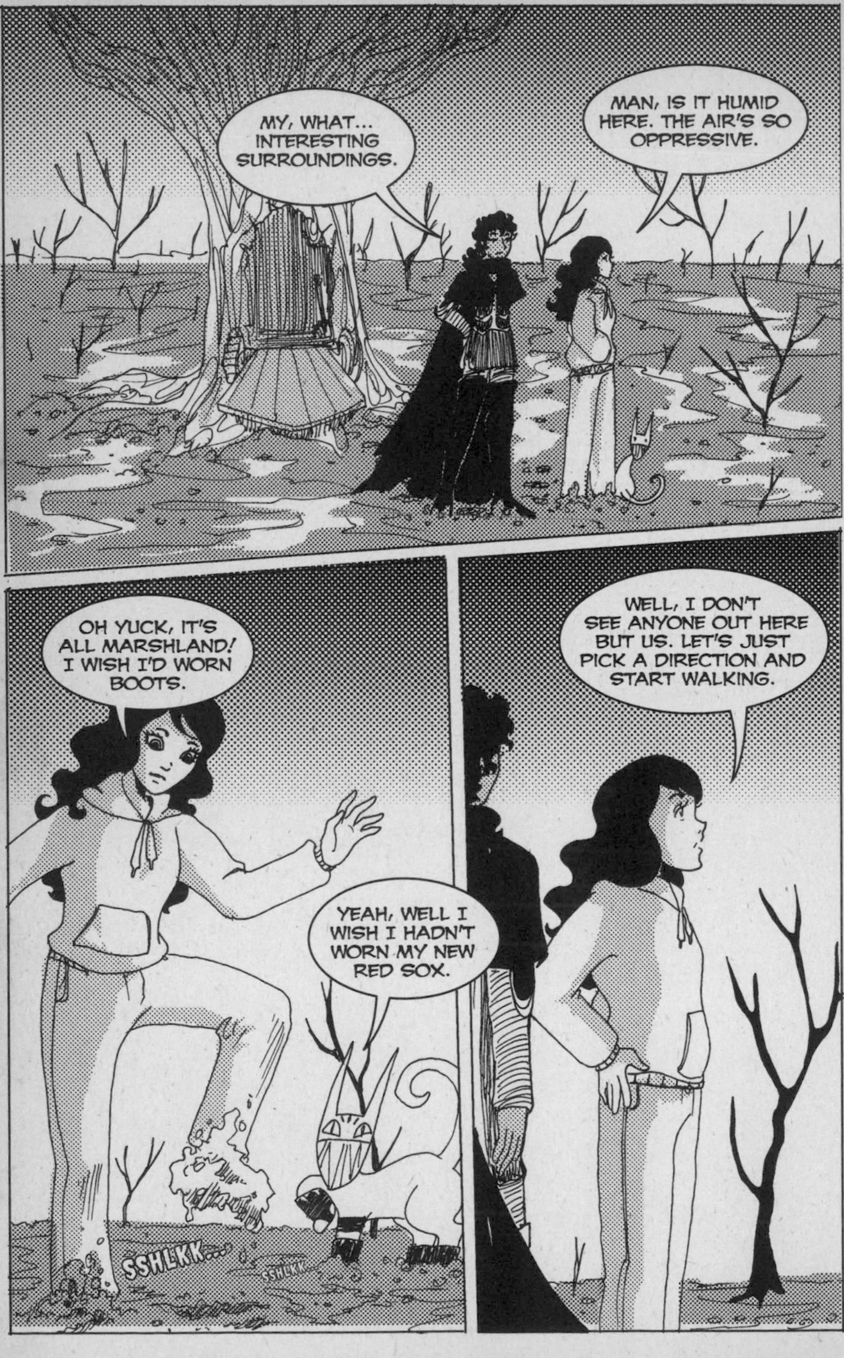
MY, WHAT... INTERESTING SURROUNDINGS.
MAN, IS IT HUMID HERE. THE AIR'S SO OPPRESSIVE.
OH YUCK, IT'S ALL MARSHLAND! I WISH I'D WORN BOOTS.
YEAH, WELL I WISH I HADN'T WORN MY NEW RED SOX.
SSHLKK...
SSHLKK...
WELL, I DON'T SEE ANYONE OUT HERE BUT US. LET'S JUST PICK A DIRECTION AND START WALKING.

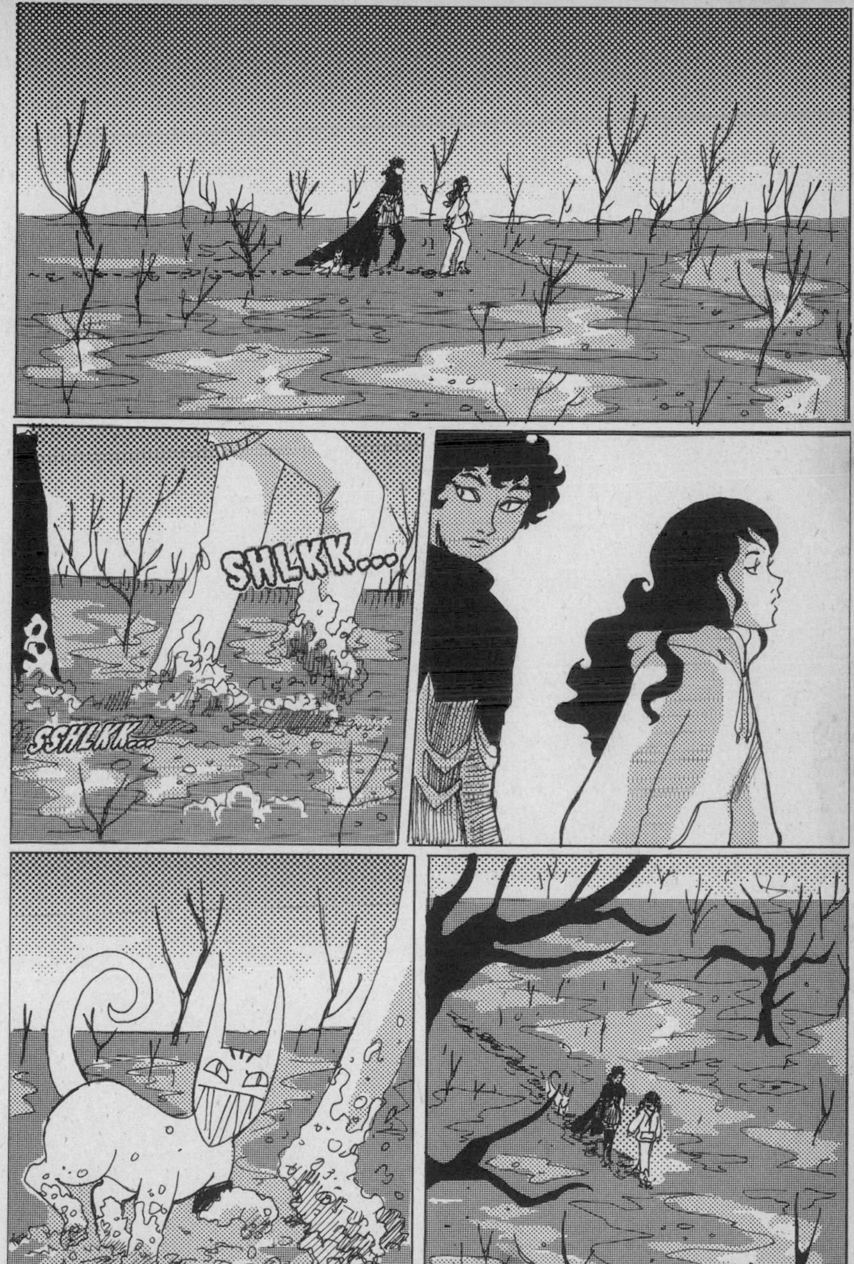
SHLKK...
SSHLKK...
SSHLKK...

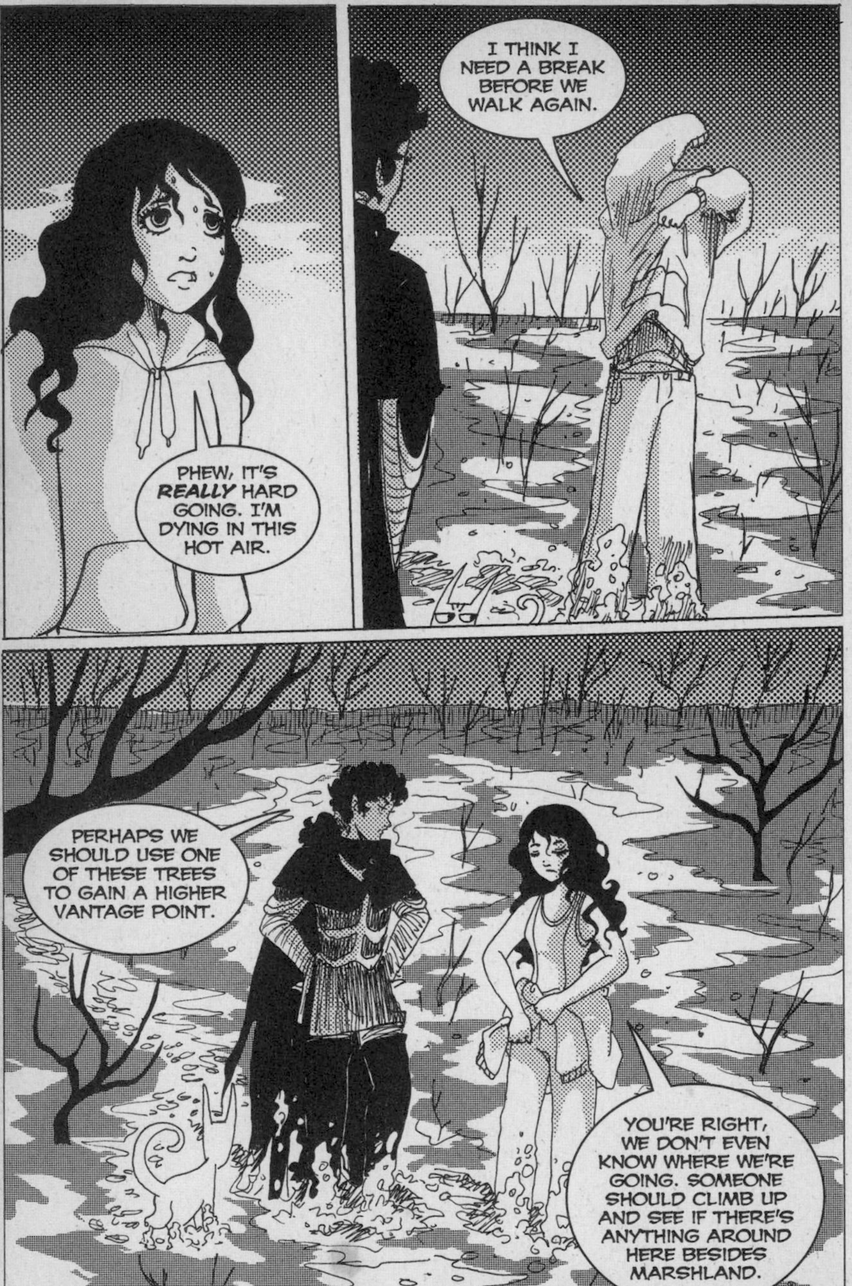
PHEW, IT'S *REALLY* HARD GOING. I'M DYING IN THIS HOT AIR.
I THINK I NEED A BREAK BEFORE WE WALK AGAIN.
PERHAPS WE SHOULD USE ONE OF THESE TREES TO GAIN A HIGHER VANTAGE POINT.
YOU'RE RIGHT, WE DON'T EVEN KNOW WHERE WE'RE GOING. SOMEONE SHOULD CLIMB UP AND SEE IF THERE'S ANYTHING AROUND HERE BESIDES MARSHLAND.

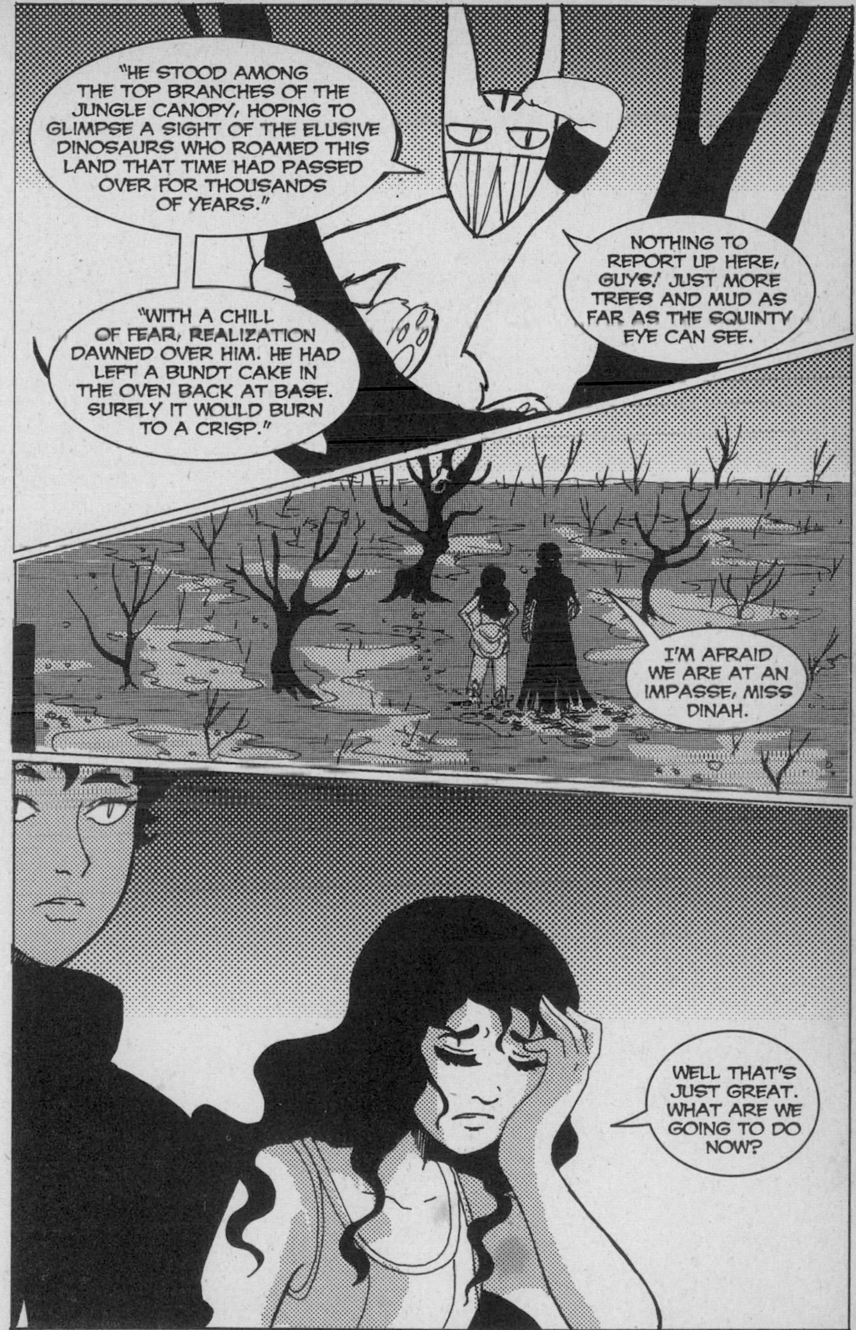
"HE STOOD AMONG THE TOP BRANCHES OF THE JUNGLE CANOPY, HOPING TO GLIMPSE A SIGHT OF THE ELUSIVE DINOSAURS WHO ROAMED THIS LAND THAT TIME HAD PASSED OVER FOR THOUSANDS OF YEARS."
"WITH A CHILL OF FEAR, REALIZATION DAWNED OVER HIM. HE HAD LEFT A BUNDT CAKE IN THE OVEN BACK AT BASE. SURELY IT WOULD BURN TO A CRISP."
NOTHING TO REPORT UP HERE, GUYS! JUST MORE TREES AND MUD AS FAR AS THE SQUINTY EYE CAN SEE.
I'M AFRAID WE ARE AT AN IMPASSE, MISS DINAH.
WELL THAT'S JUST GREAT. WHAT ARE WE GOING TO DO NOW?

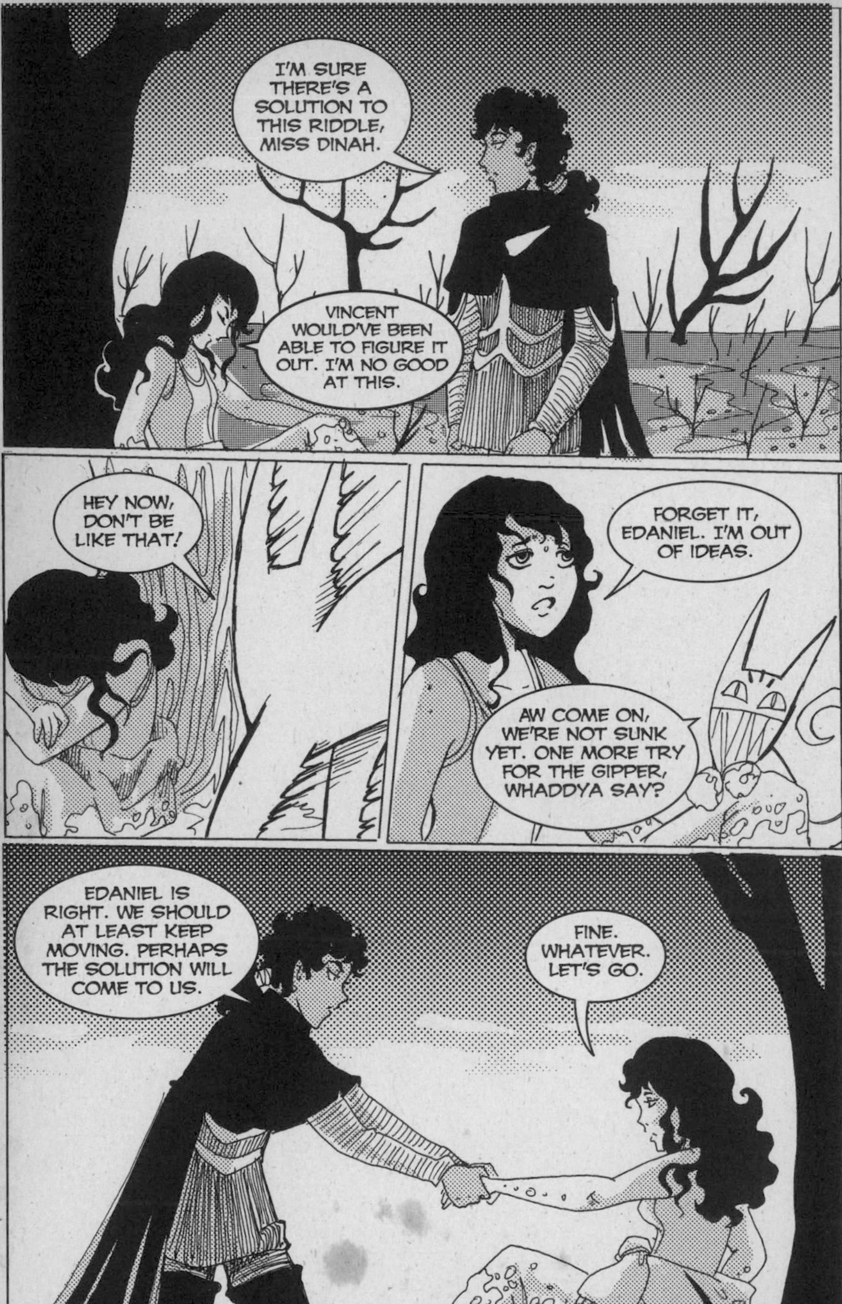
I'M SURE THERE'S A SOLUTION TO THIS RIDDLE, MISS DINAH.
VINCENT WOULD'VE BEEN ABLE TO FIGURE IT OUT. I'M NO GOOD AT THIS.
HEY NOW, DON'T BE LIKE THAT!
FORGET IT, EDANIEL. I'M OUT OF IDEAS.
AW COME ON, WE'RE NOT SUNK YET. ONE MORE TRY FOR THE GIPPER, WHADDYA SAY?
EDANIEL IS RIGHT. WE SHOULD AT LEAST KEEP MOVING. PERHAPS THE SOLUTION WILL COME TO US.
FINE. WHATEVER. LET'S GO.

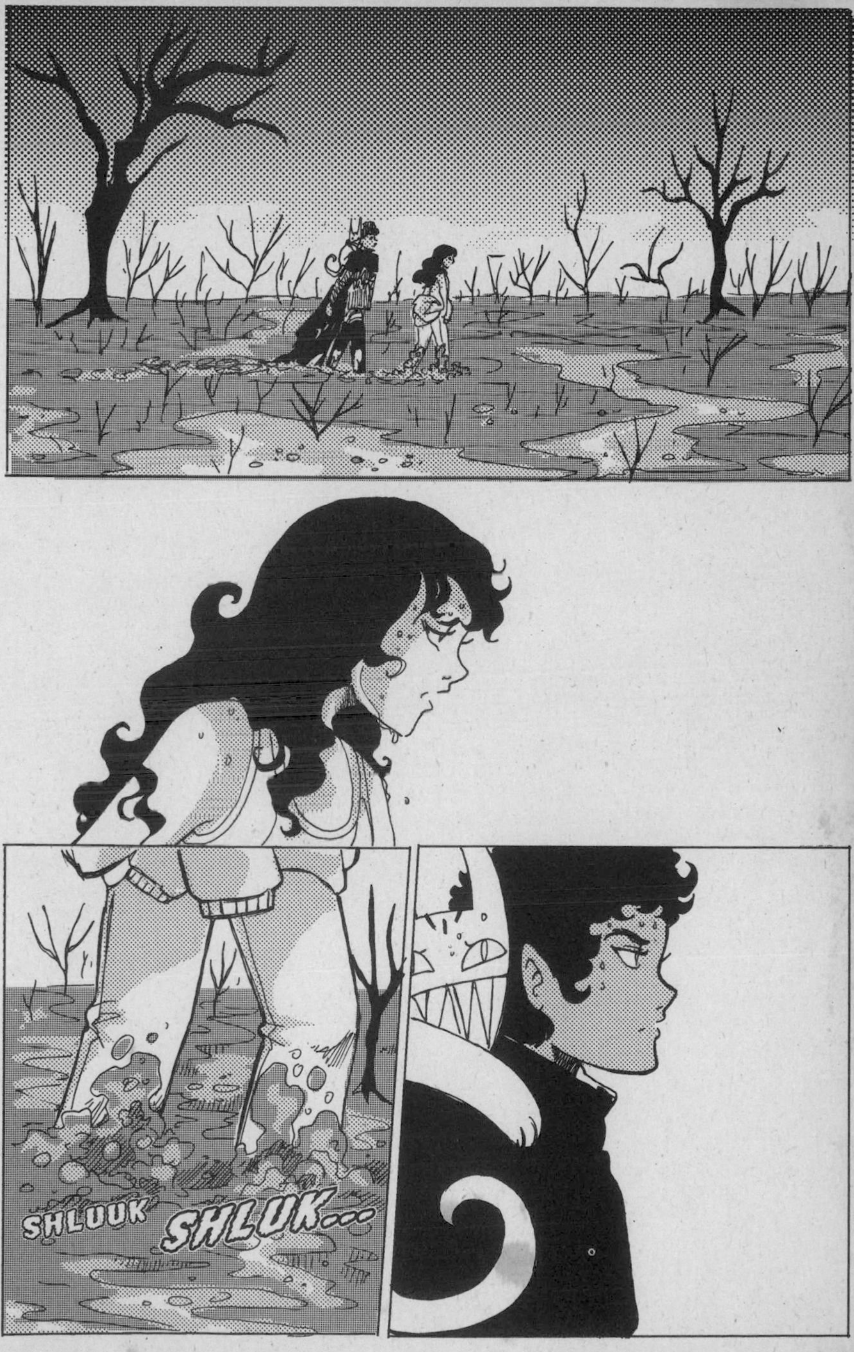
SHLUUK
SHLUK...

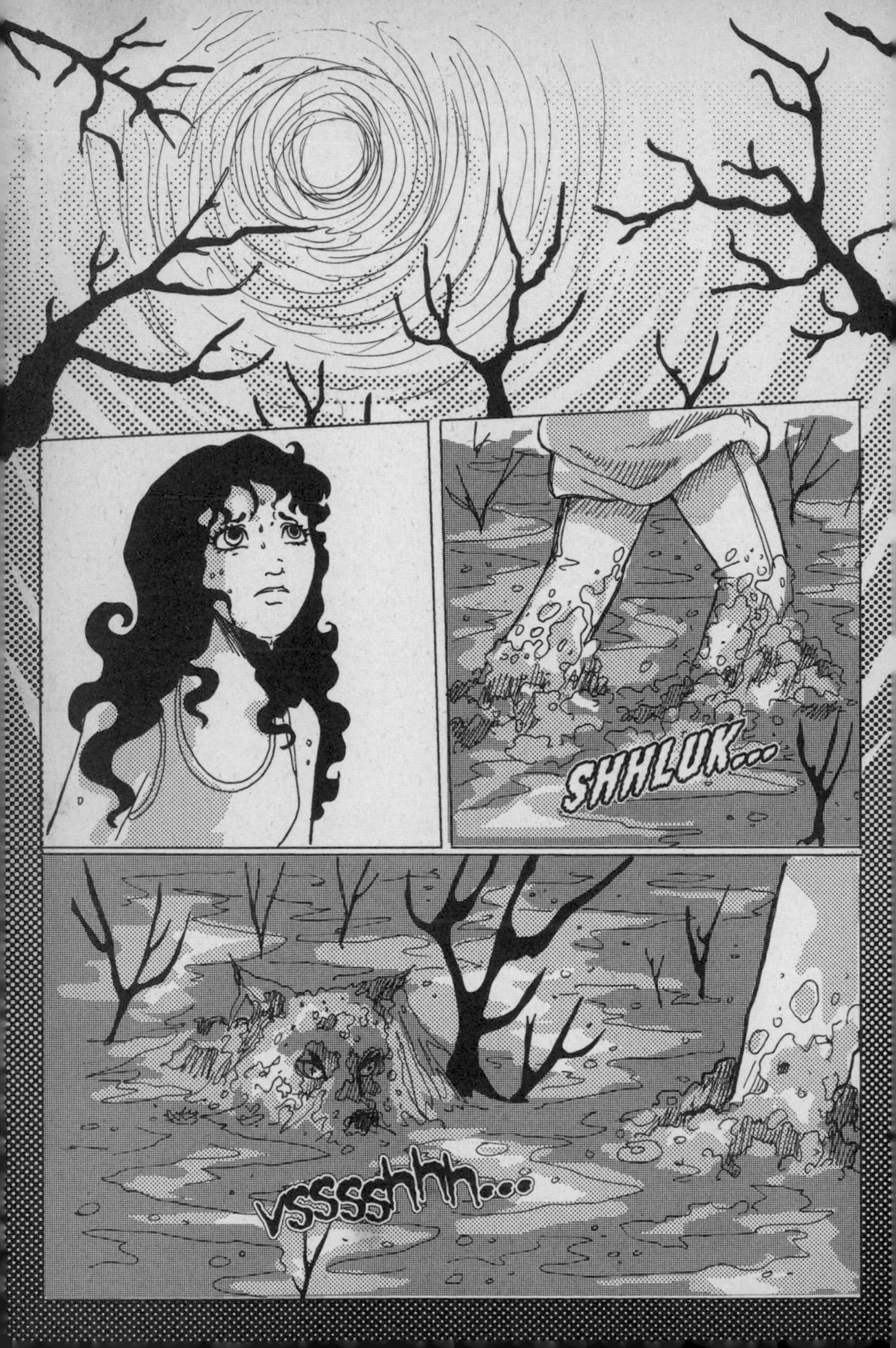
SHHLUK...
vssssshhh...

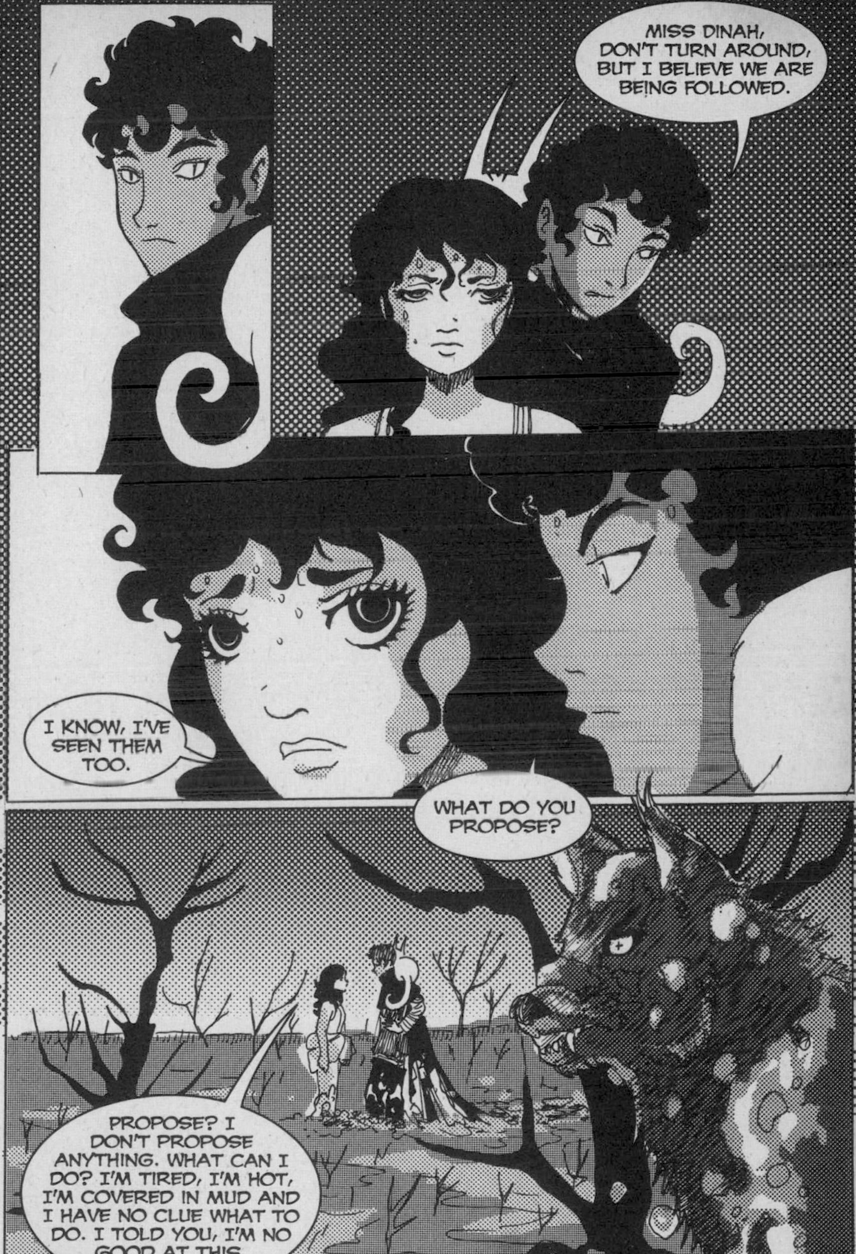
MISS DINAH, DON'T TURN AROUND, BUT I BELIEVE WE ARE BEING FOLLOWED.
I KNOW, I'VE SEEN THEM TOO.
WHAT DO YOU PROPOSE?
PROPOSE? I DON'T PROPOSE ANYTHING. WHAT CAN I DO? I'M TIRED, I'M HOT, I'M COVERED IN MUD AND I HAVE NO CLUE WHAT TO DO. I TOLD YOU, I'M NO GOOD AT THIS.

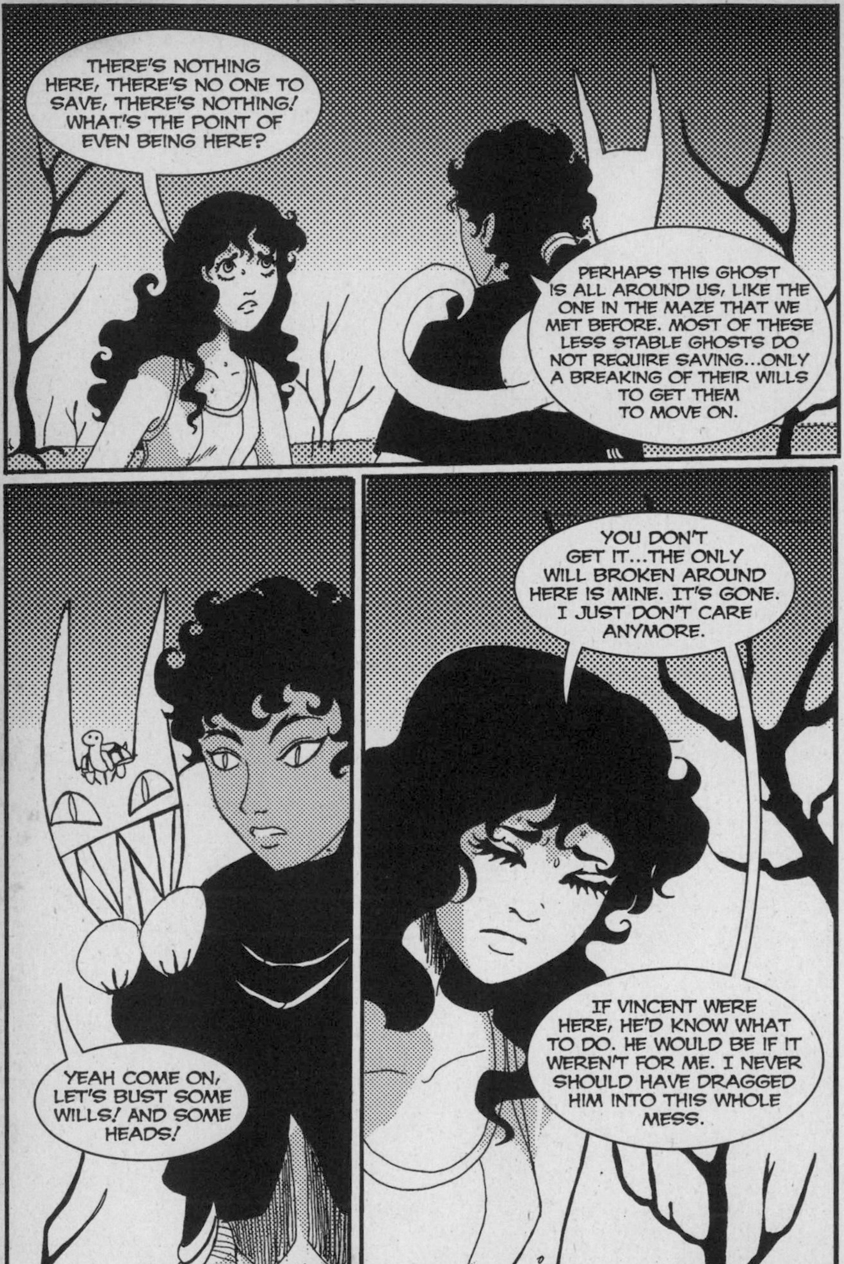
THERE'S NOTHING HERE, THERE'S NO ONE TO SAVE, THERE'S NOTHING! WHAT'S THE POINT OF EVEN BEING HERE?
PERHAPS THIS GHOST IS ALL AROUND US, LIKE THE ONE IN THE MAZE THAT WE MET BEFORE. MOST OF THESE LESS STABLE GHOSTS DO NOT REQUIRE SAVING...ONLY A BREAKING OF THEIR WILLS TO GET THEM TO MOVE ON.
YEAH COME ON, LET'S BUST SOME WILLS! AND SOME HEADS!
YOU DON'T GET IT...THE ONLY WILL BROKEN AROUND HERE IS MINE. IT'S GONE. I JUST DON'T CARE ANYMORE.
IF VINCENT WERE HERE, HE'D KNOW WHAT TO DO. HE WOULD BE IF IT WEREN'T FOR ME. I NEVER SHOULD HAVE DRAGGED HIM INTO THIS WHOLE MESS.

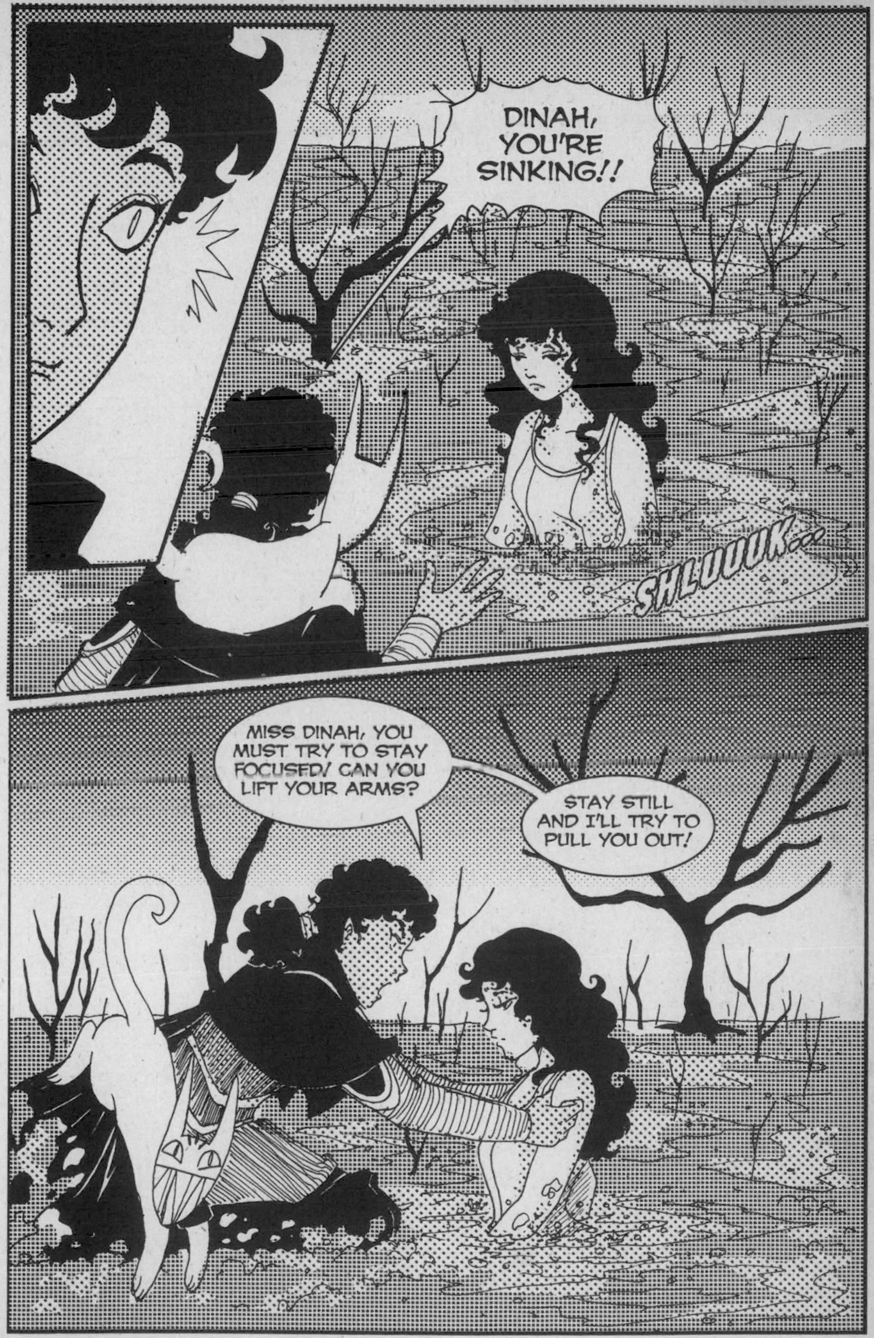
DINAH, YOU'RE SINKING!!
SHLUUUK...
MISS DINAH, YOU MUST TRY TO STAY FOCUSED! CAN YOU LIFT YOUR ARMS?
STAY STILL AND I'LL TRY TO PULL YOU OUT!

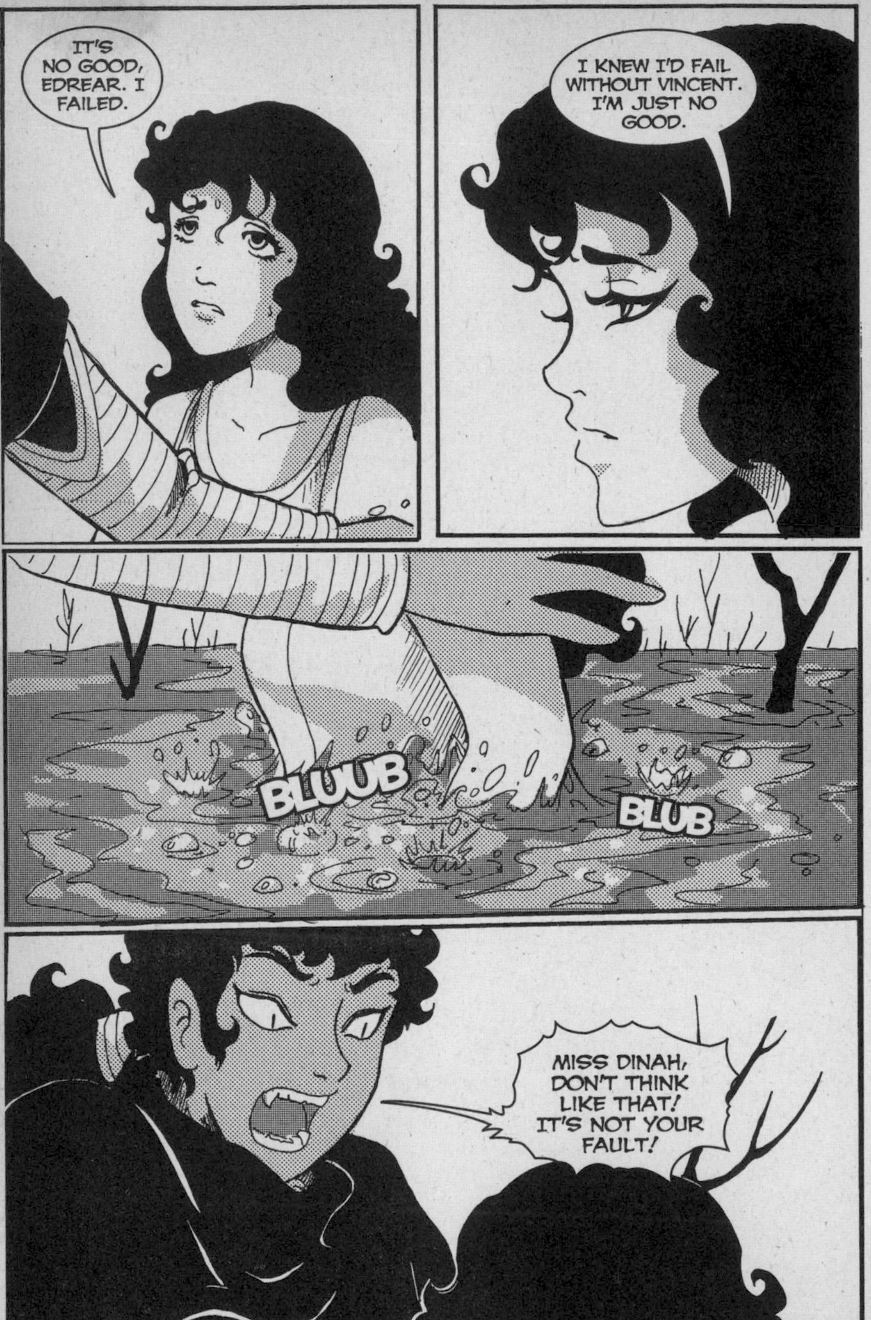
IT'S NO GOOD, EDREAR. I FAILED.
I KNEW I'D FAIL WITHOUT VINCENT. I'M JUST NO GOOD.
BLUUB
BLUB
MISS DINAH, DON'T THINK LIKE THAT! IT'S NOT YOUR FAULT!

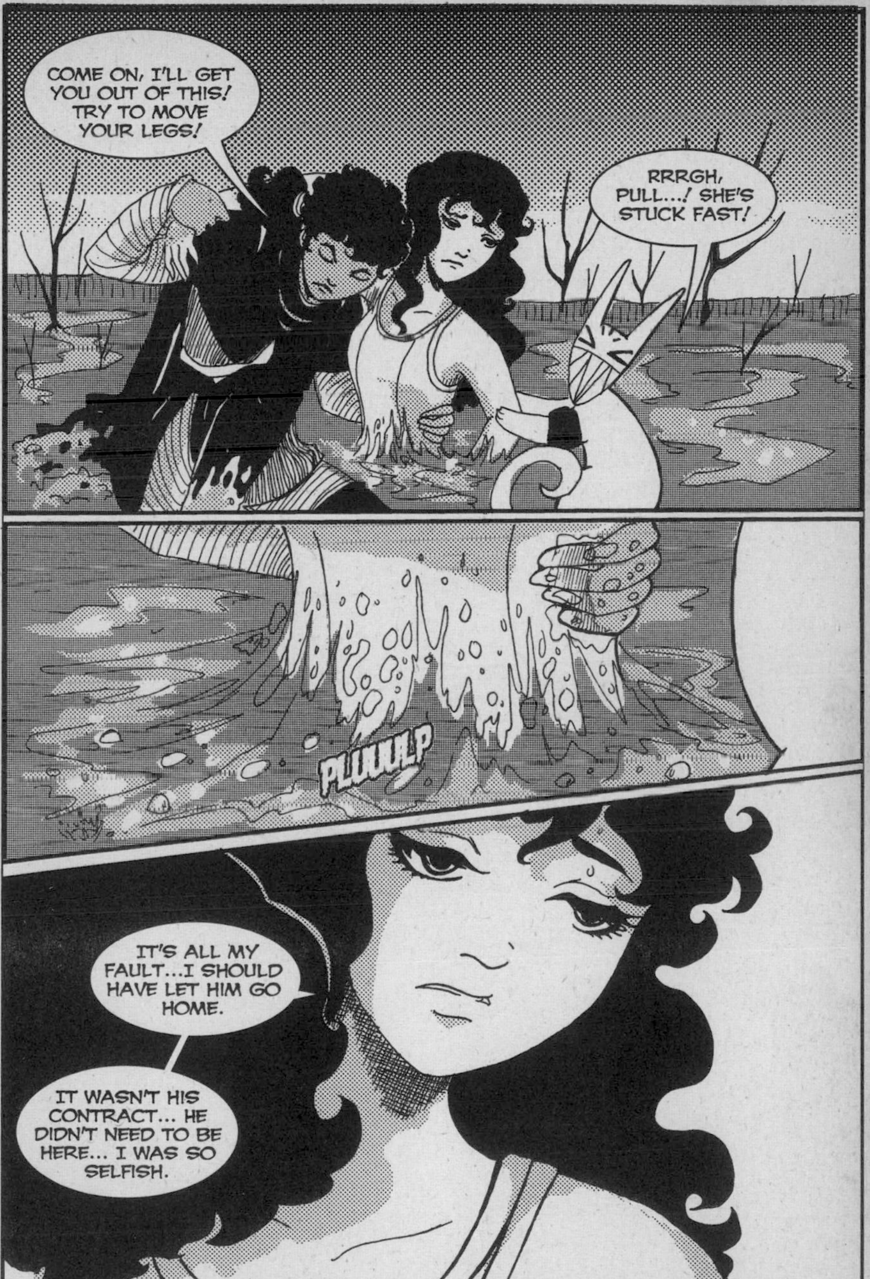
COME ON, I'LL GET YOU OUT OF THIS! TRY TO MOVE YOUR LEGS!
RRRGH, PULL...! SHE'S STUCK FAST!
PLUUULP
IT'S ALL MY FAULT...I SHOULD HAVE LET HIM GO HOME.
IT WASN'T HIS CONTRACT... HE DIDN'T NEED TO BE HERE... I WAS SO SELFISH.

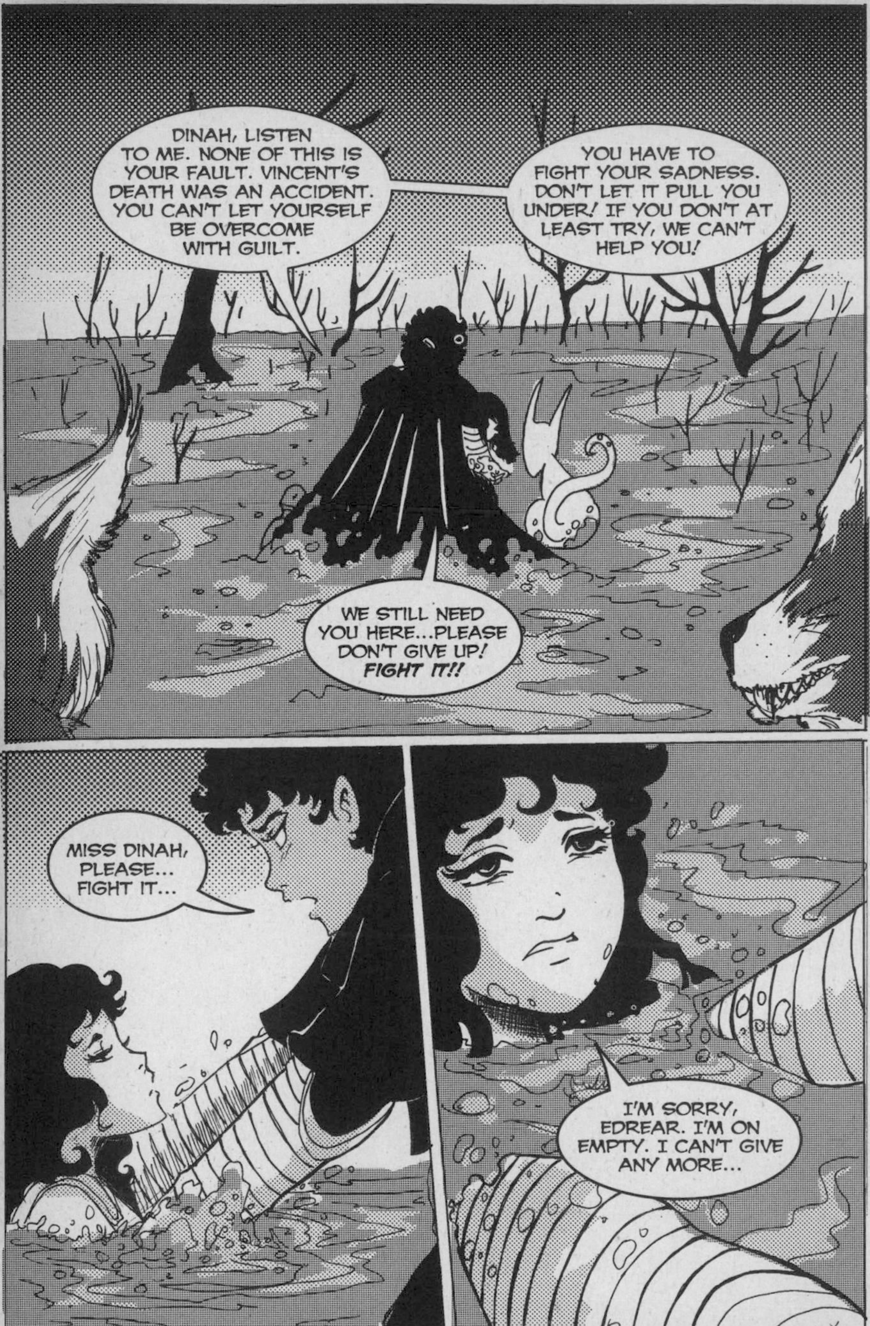
DINAH, LISTEN TO ME. NONE OF THIS IS YOUR FAULT. VINCENT'S DEATH WAS AN ACCIDENT. YOU CAN'T LET YOURSELF BE OVERCOME WITH GUILT.
YOU HAVE TO FIGHT YOUR SADNESS. DON'T LET IT PULL YOU UNDER! IF YOU DON'T AT LEAST TRY, WE CAN'T HELP YOU!
WE STILL NEED YOU HERE...PLEASE DON'T GIVE UP! *FIGHT IT!!*
MISS DINAH, PLEASE... FIGHT IT...
I'M SORRY, EDREAR. I'M ON EMPTY. I CAN'T GIVE ANY MORE...

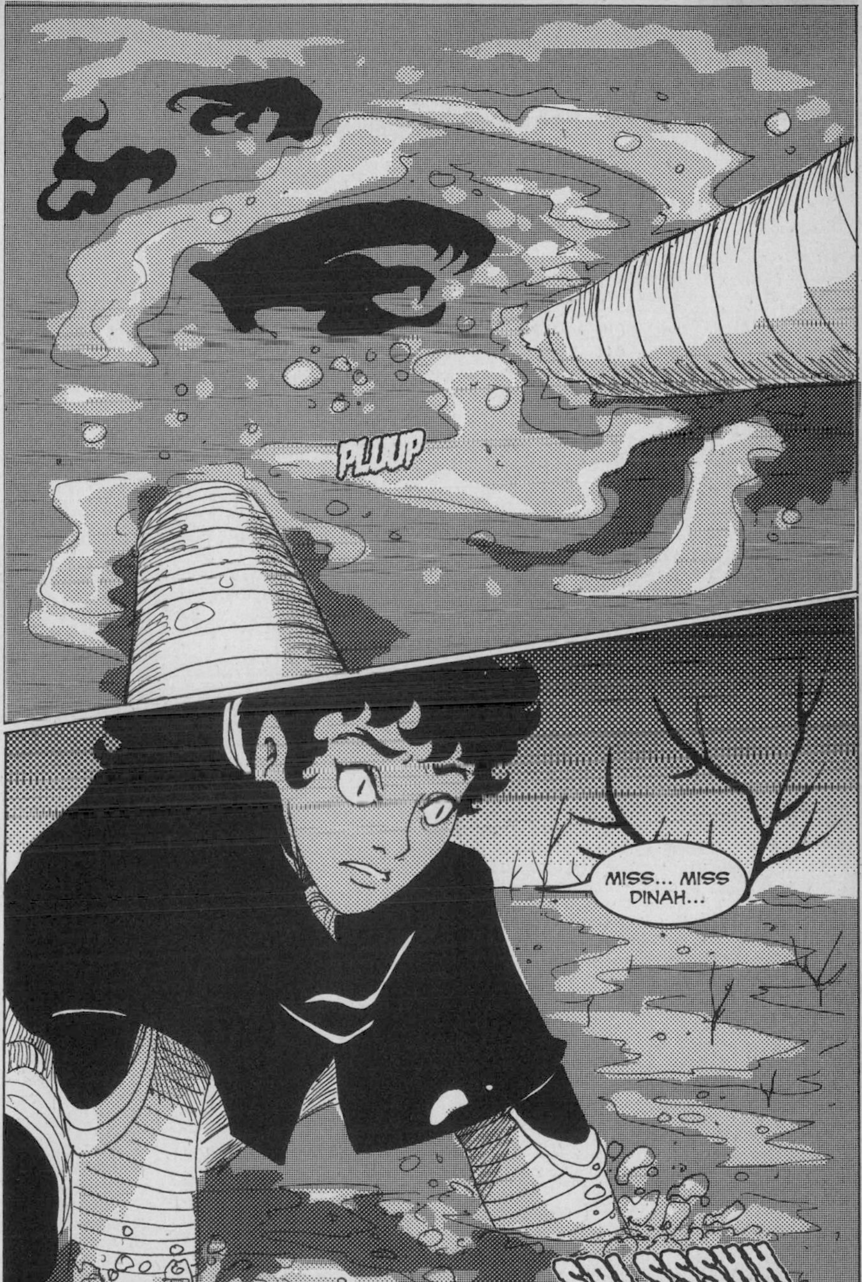
PLUUP
MISS... MISS DINAH...
SPLSSSHH

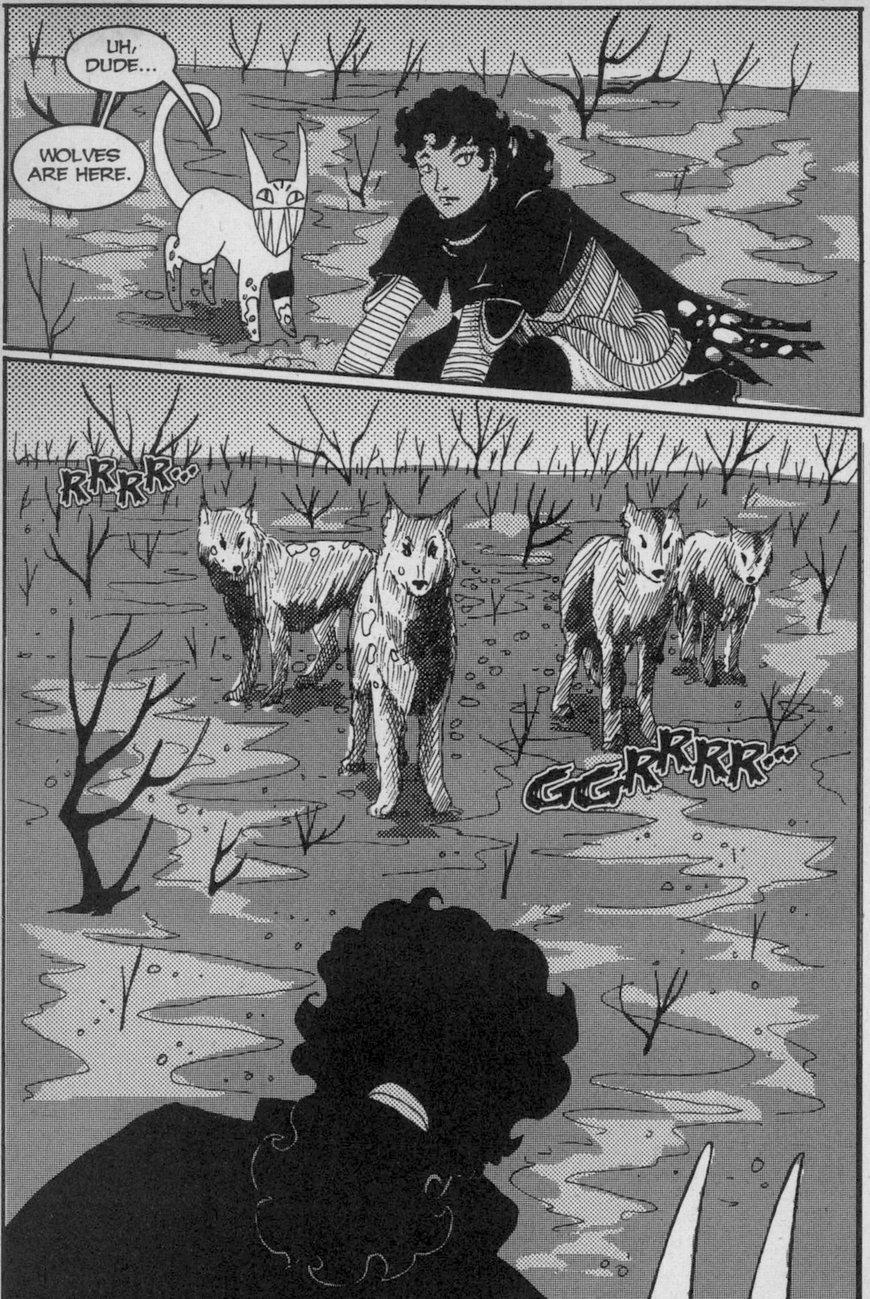
UH, DUDE...
WOLVES ARE HERE.
RRRR..
GGRRRR..

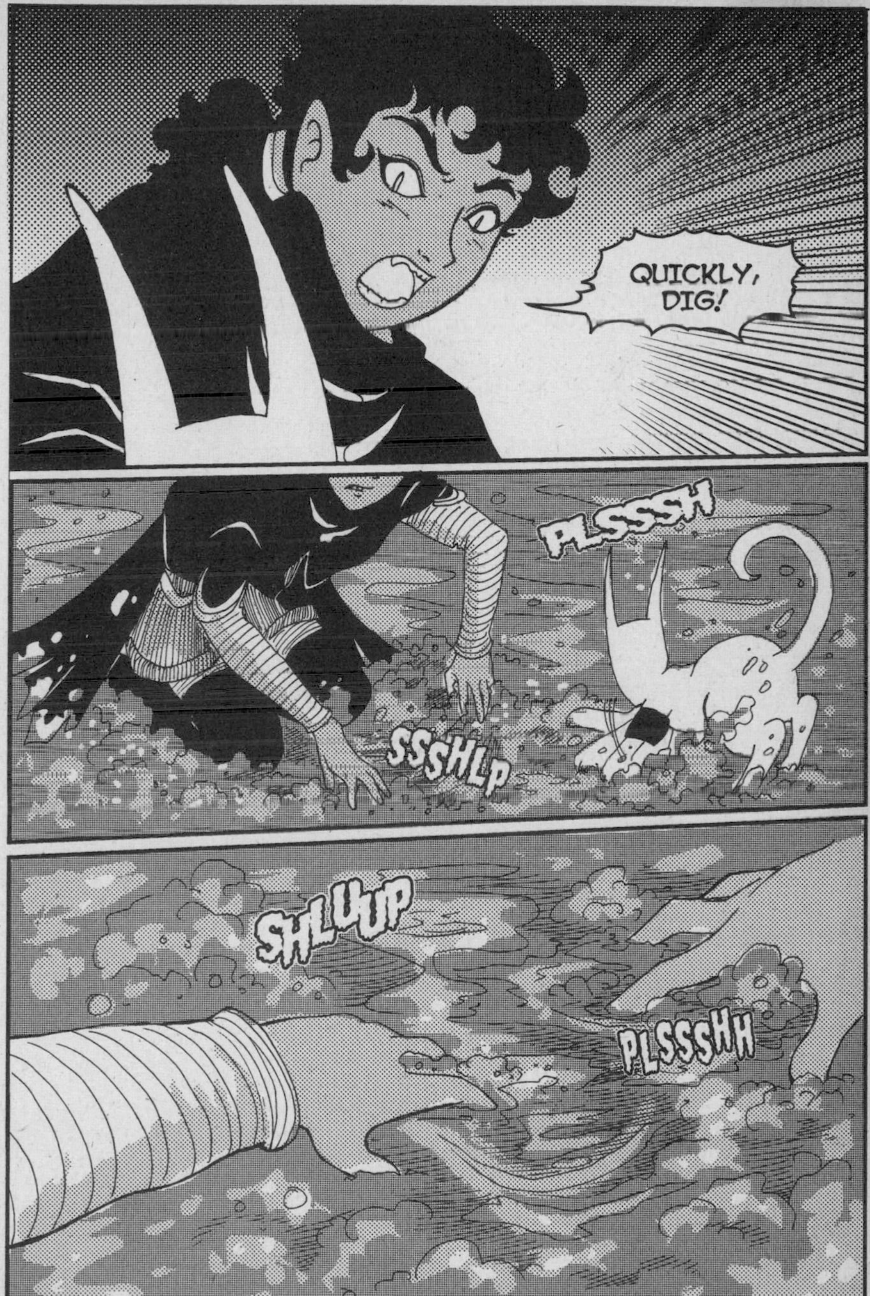
QUICKLY, DIG!
PLSSSH
SSSHLP
SHLUUP
PLSSSHH

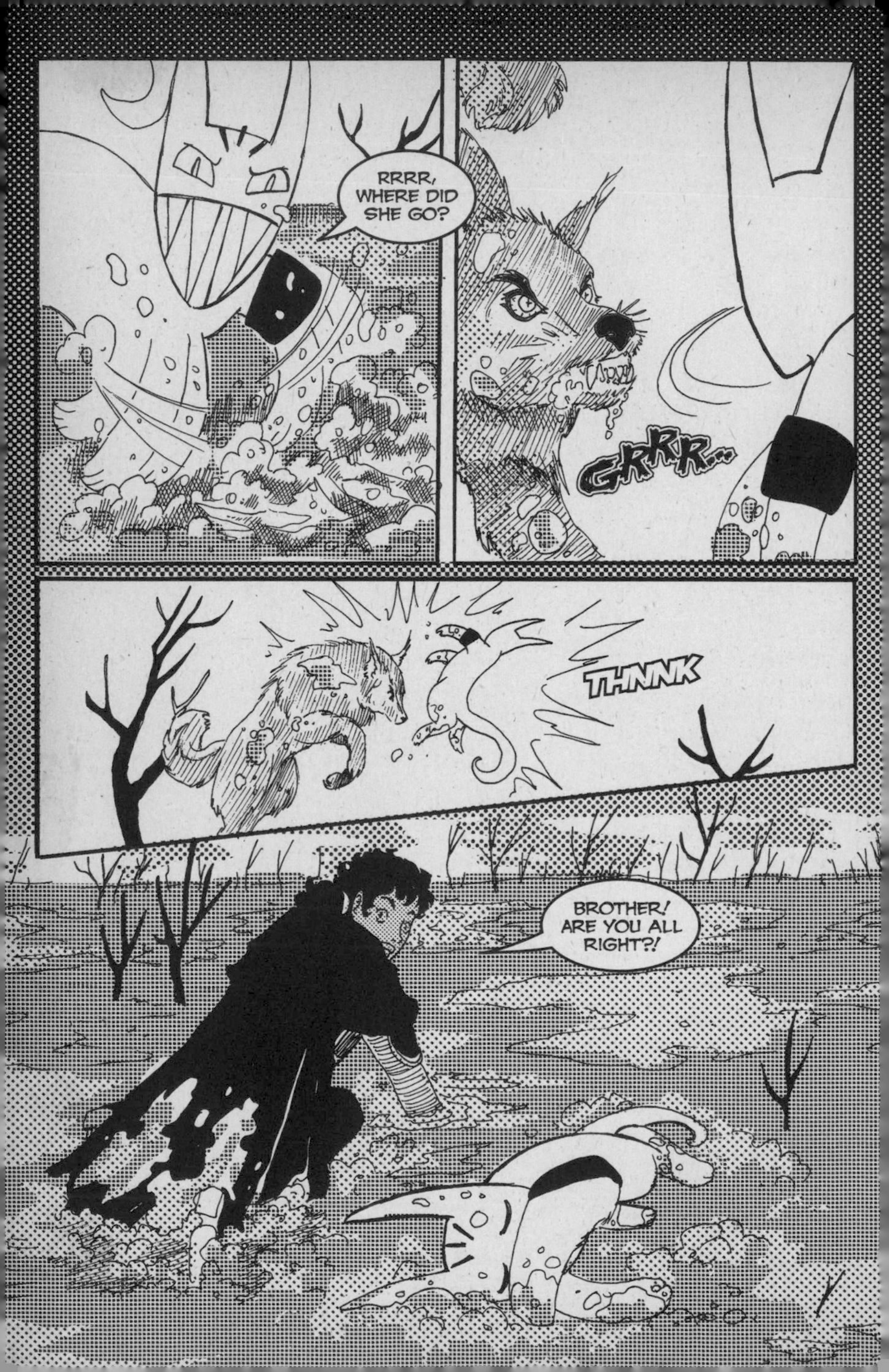
RRRR, WHERE DID SHE GO?
GRRRR...
THNNK
BROTHER! ARE YOU ALL RIGHT?!

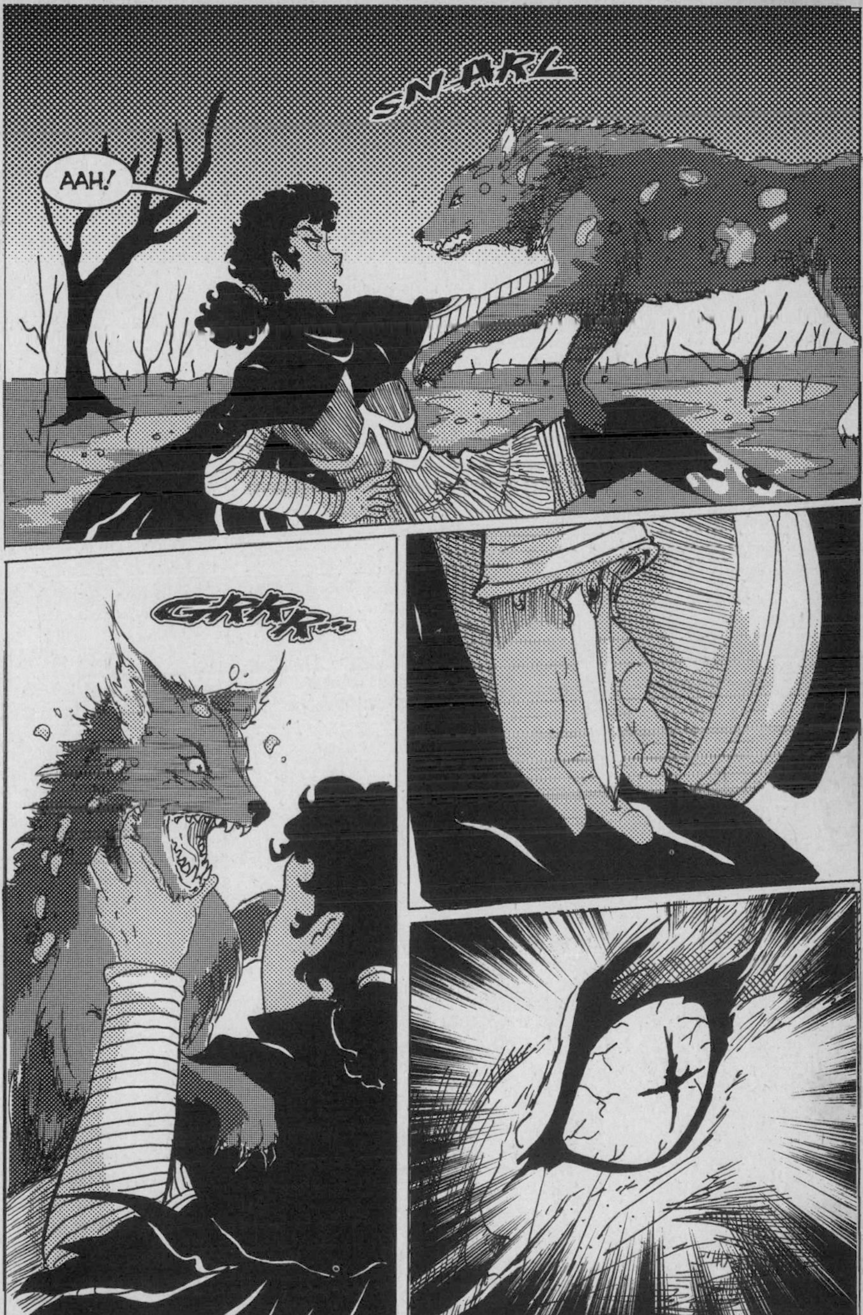
AAH!
SNARL
GRRRR...

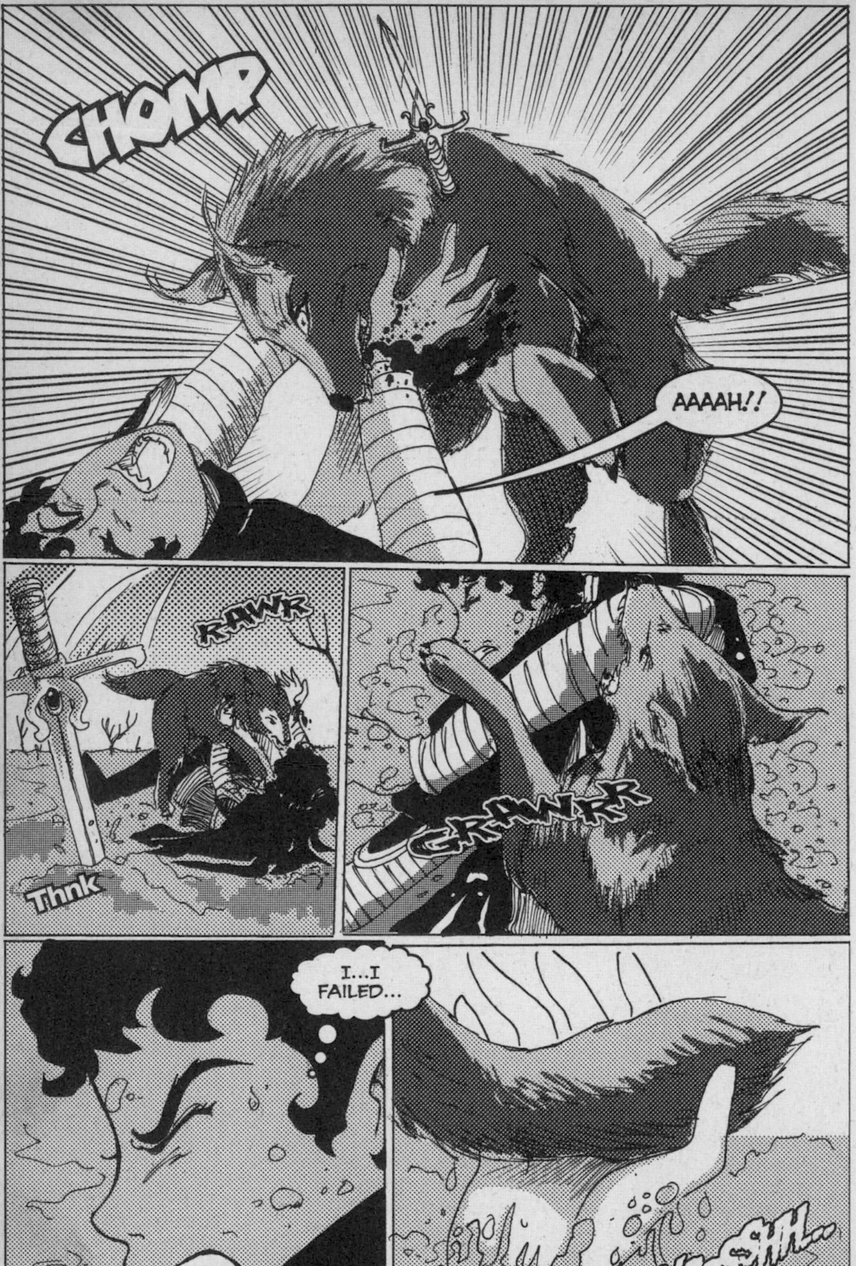
CHOMP
AAAAH!!
RAWR
Thnk
GRAWRR
I...I FAILED...
VSSSSHH...

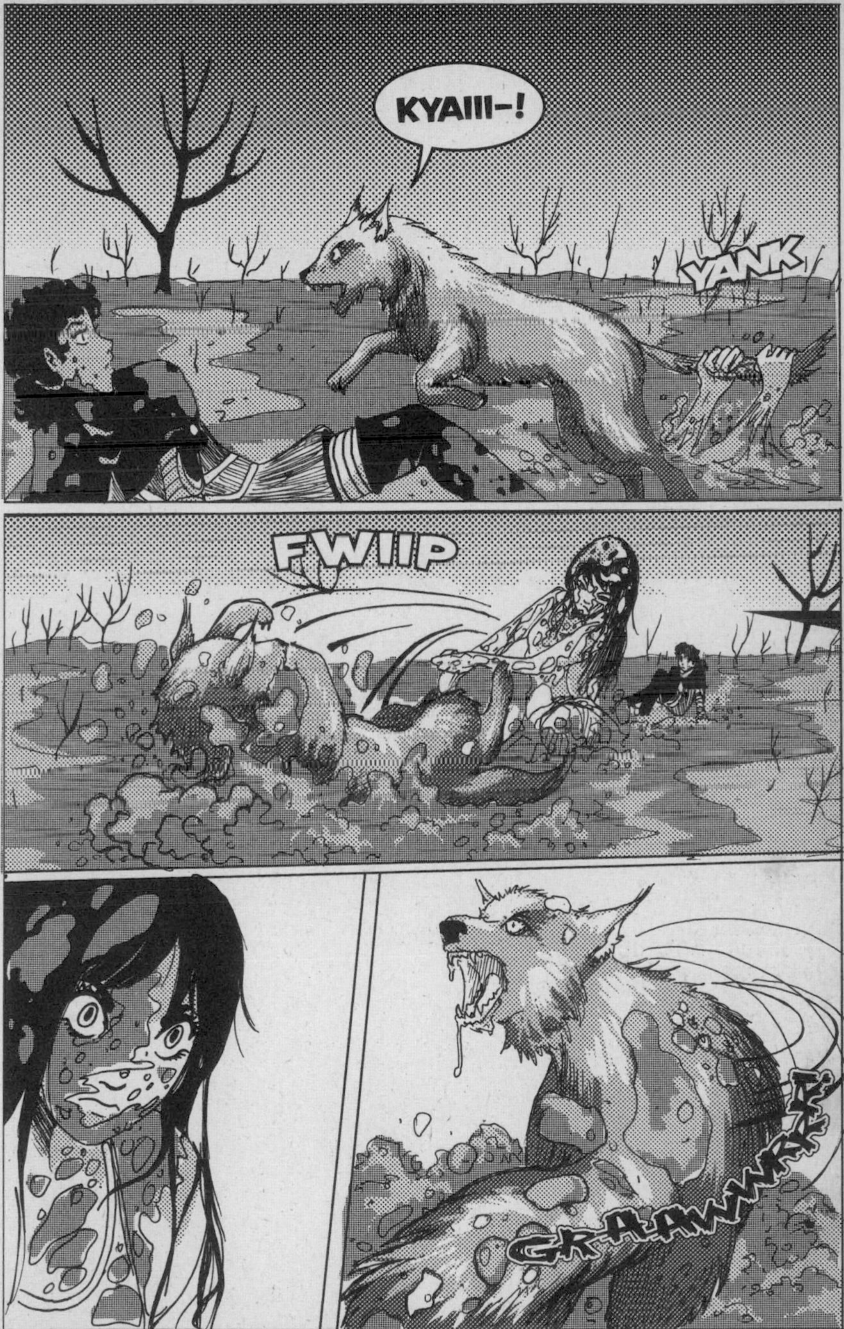
KYAIII-!
YANK
FWIIP
GRAAWWRR

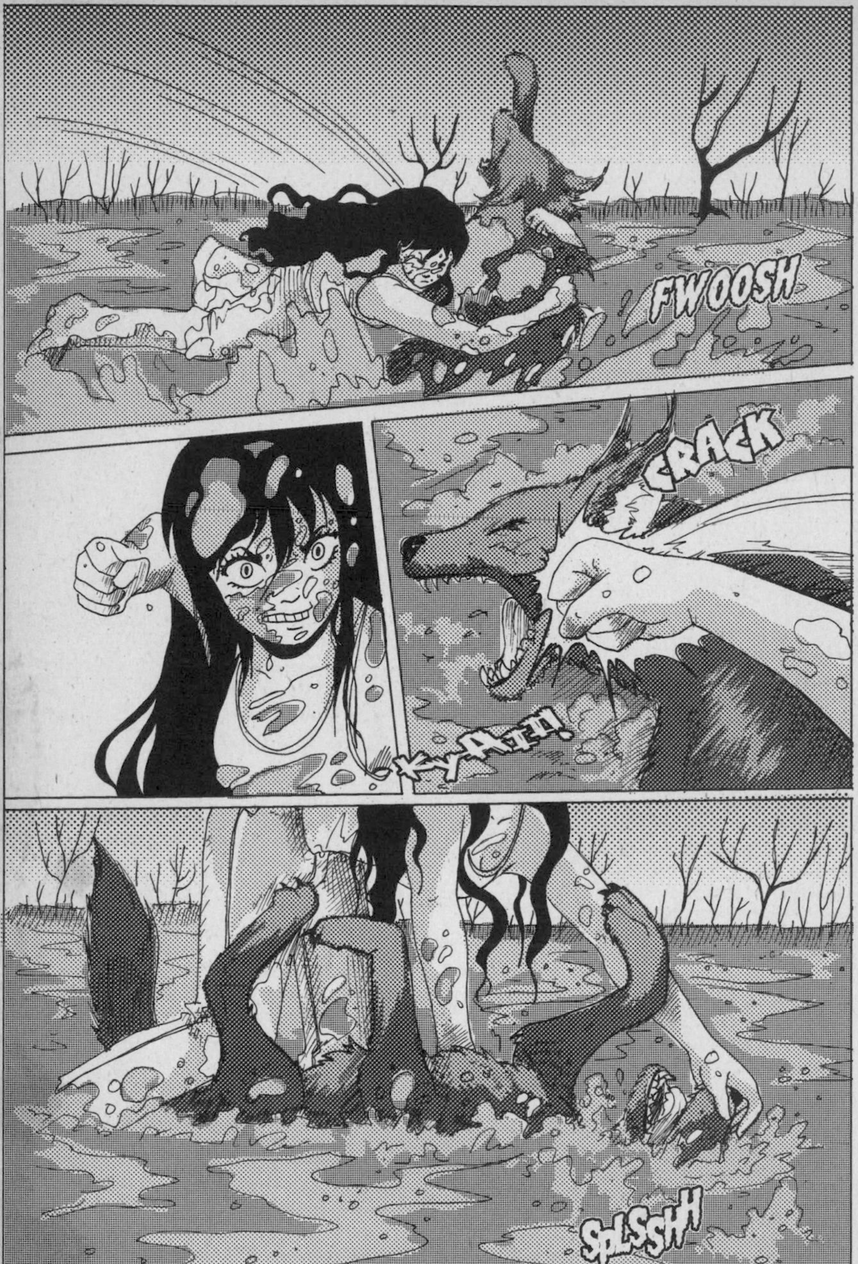
FWOOSH
CRACK
KYAII!
SPLSSHH

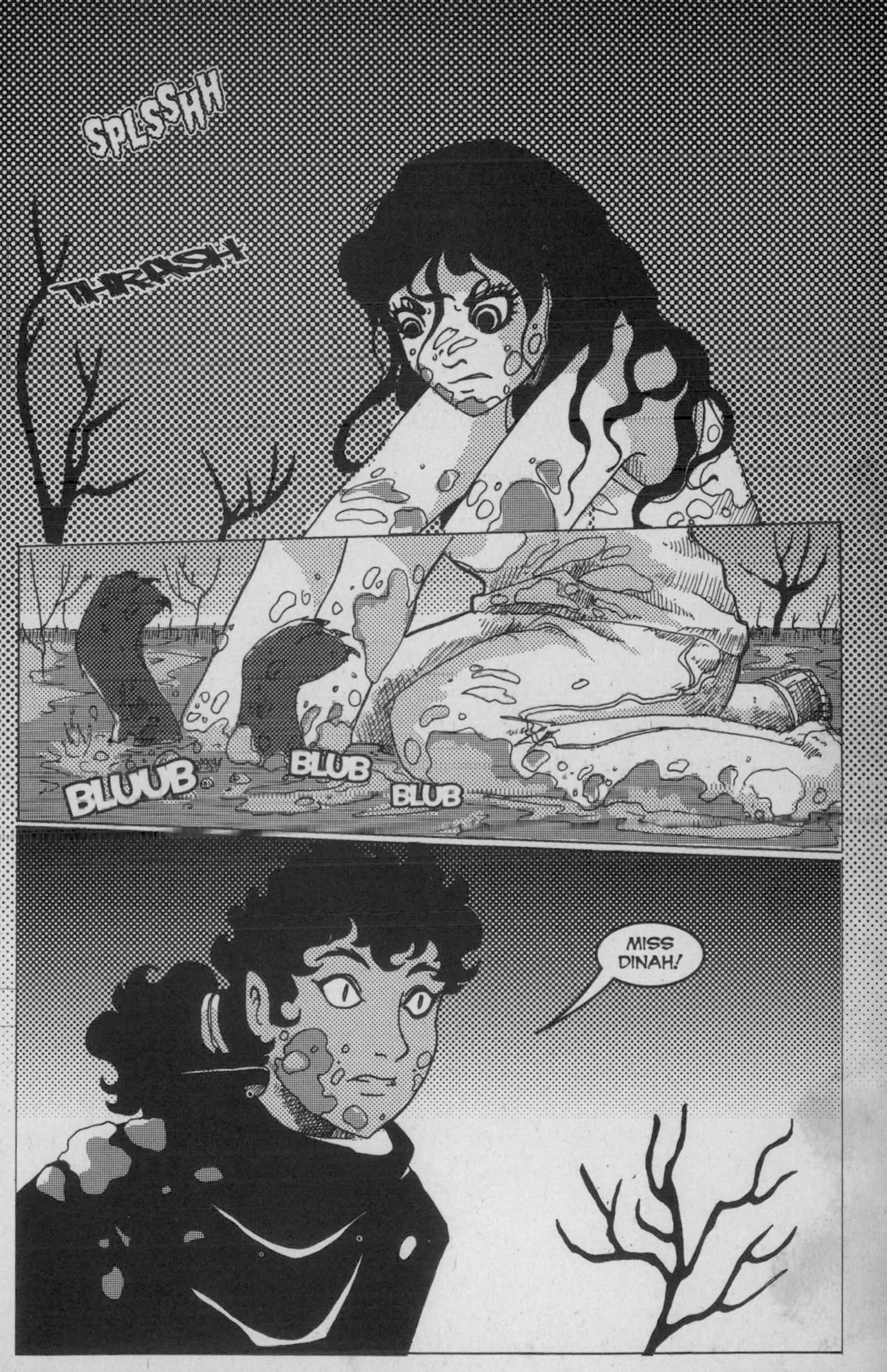
SPLSSHH
THRASH
BLUUB
BLUB
BLUB
MISS DINAH!

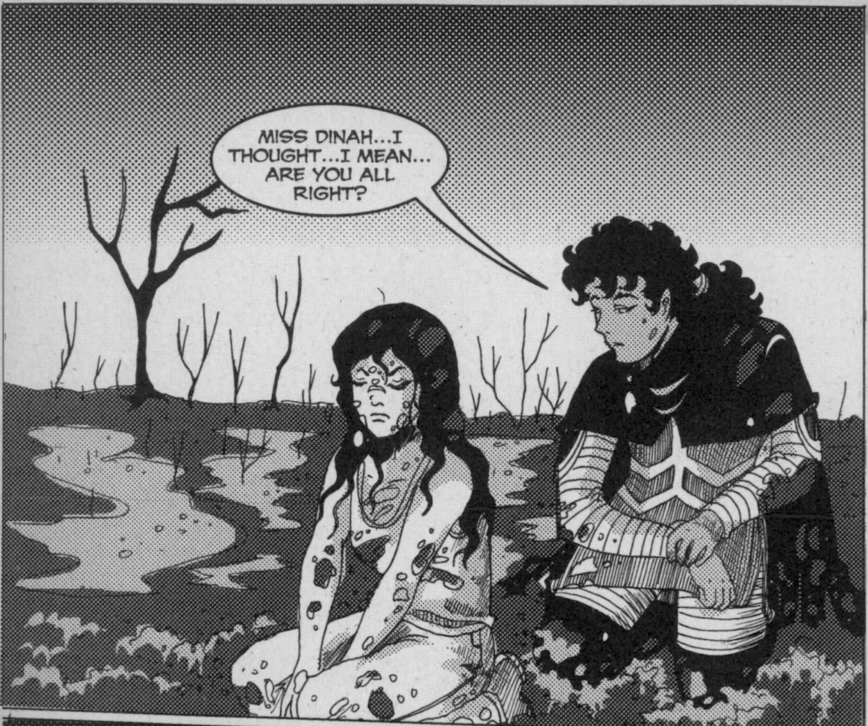
MISS DINAH...I THOUGHT...I MEAN... ARE YOU ALL RIGHT?
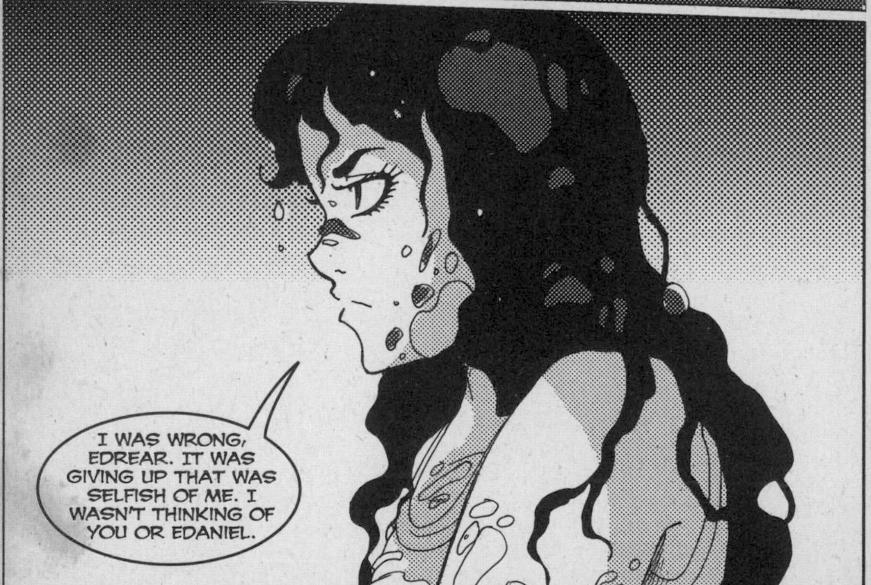
I WAS WRONG, EDREAR. IT WAS GIVING UP THAT WAS SELFISH OF ME. I WASN'T THINKING OF YOU OR EDANIEL.

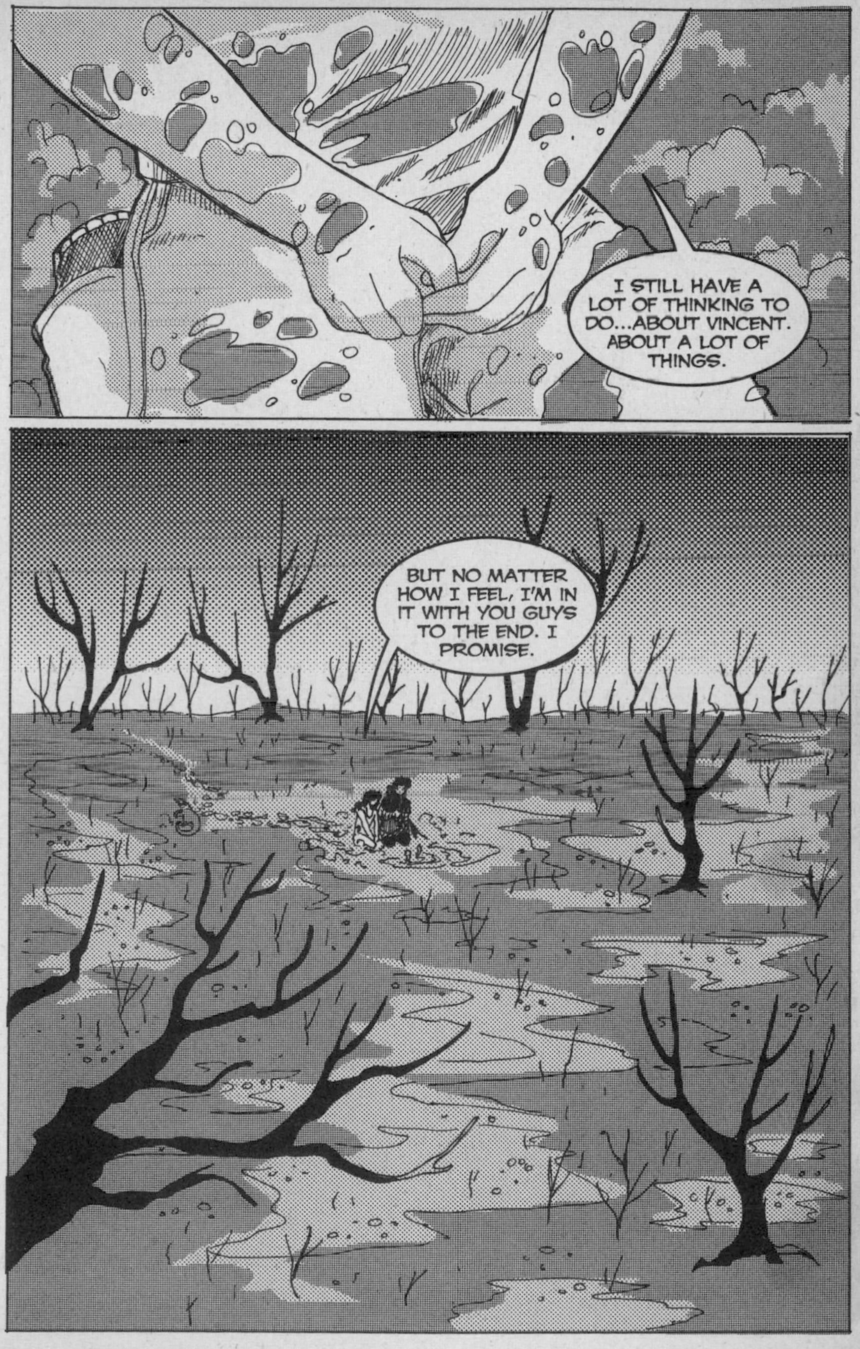
I STILL HAVE A LOT OF THINKING TO DO...ABOUT VINCENT. ABOUT A LOT OF THINGS.
BUT NO MATTER HOW I FEEL, I'M IN IT WITH YOU GUYS TO THE END. I PROMISE.

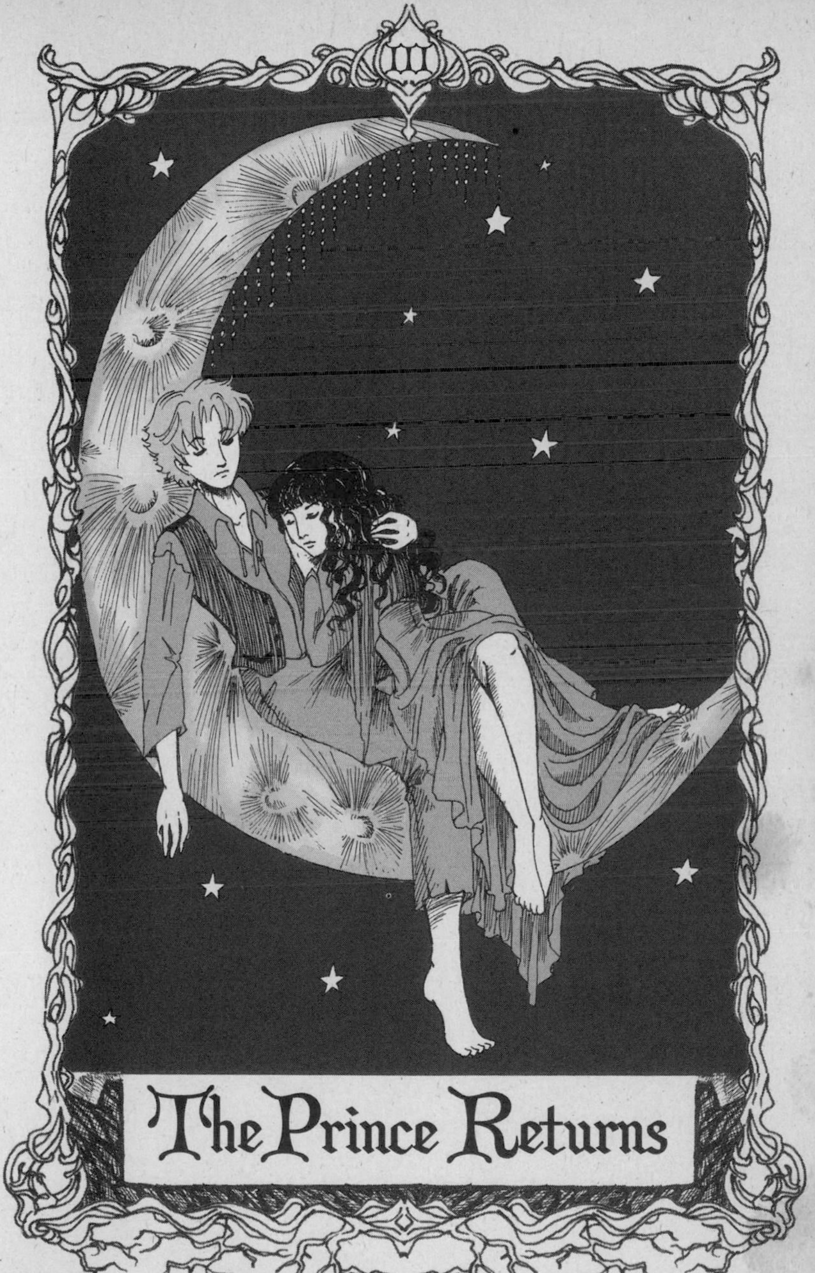
III
The Prince Returns

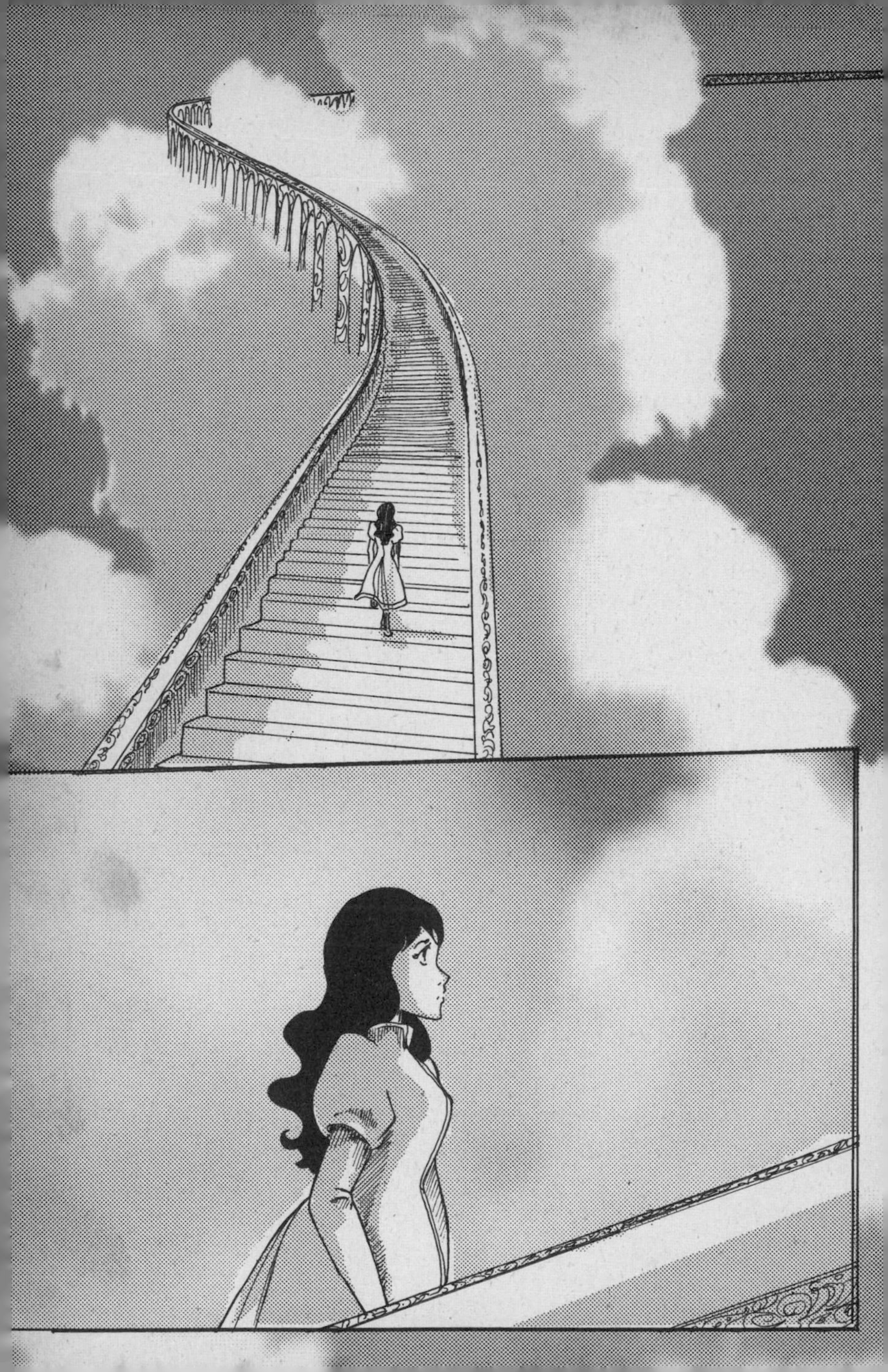

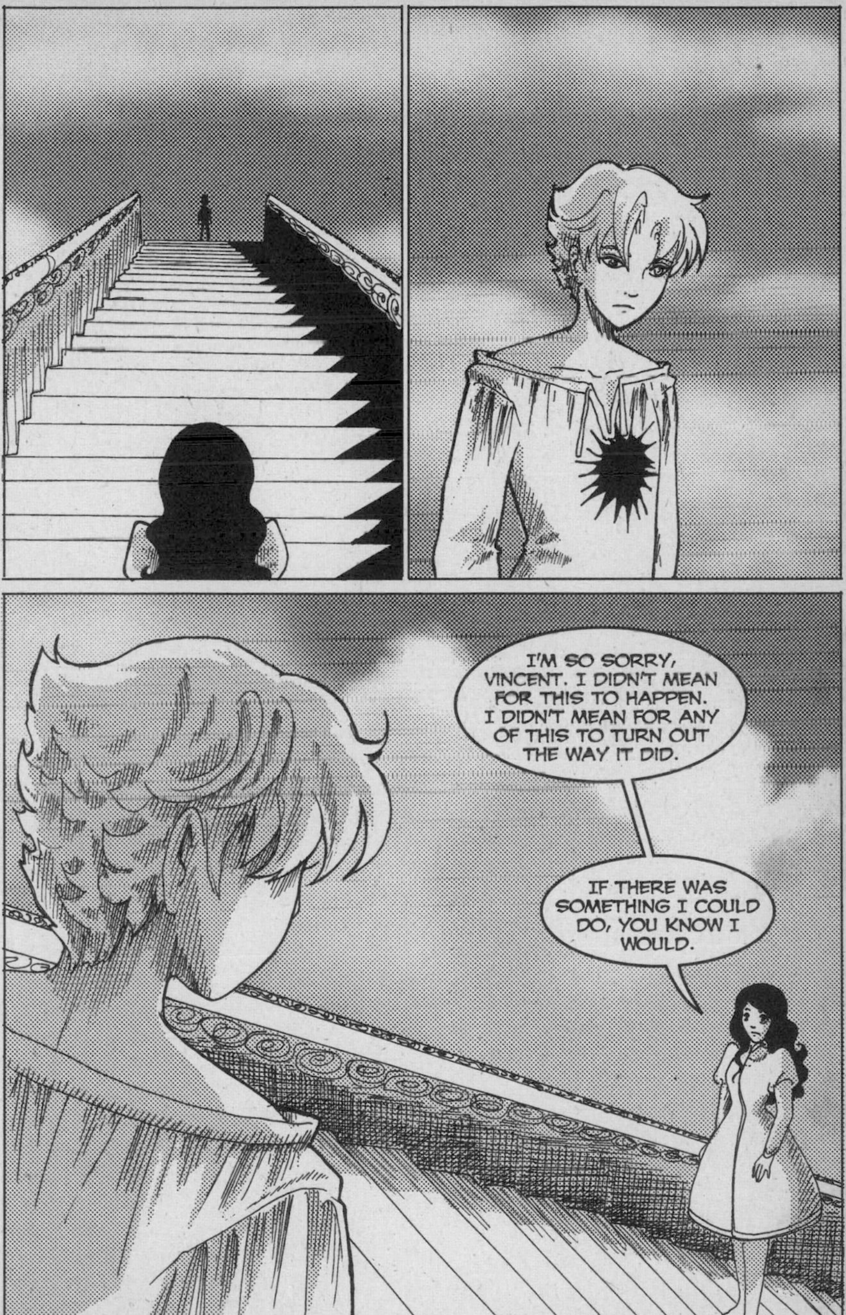
I'M SO SORRY, VINCENT. I DIDN'T MEAN FOR THIS TO HAPPEN. I DIDN'T MEAN FOR ANY OF THIS TO TURN OUT THE WAY IT DID.
IF THERE WAS SOMETHING I COULD DO, YOU KNOW I WOULD.

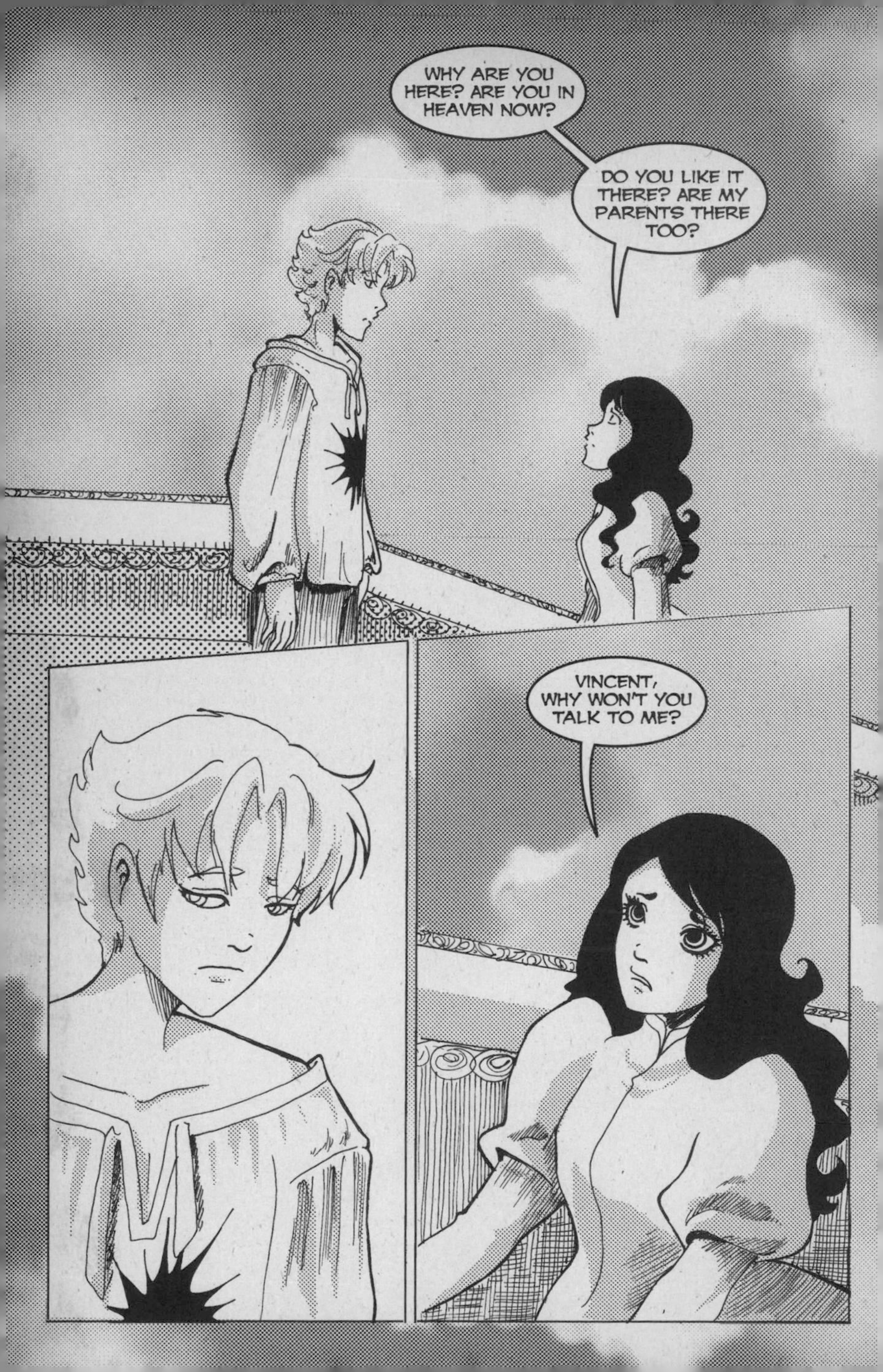
WHY ARE YOU HERE? ARE YOU IN HEAVEN NOW?
DO YOU LIKE IT THERE? ARE MY PARENTS THERE TOO?
VINCENT, WHY WON'T YOU TALK TO ME?

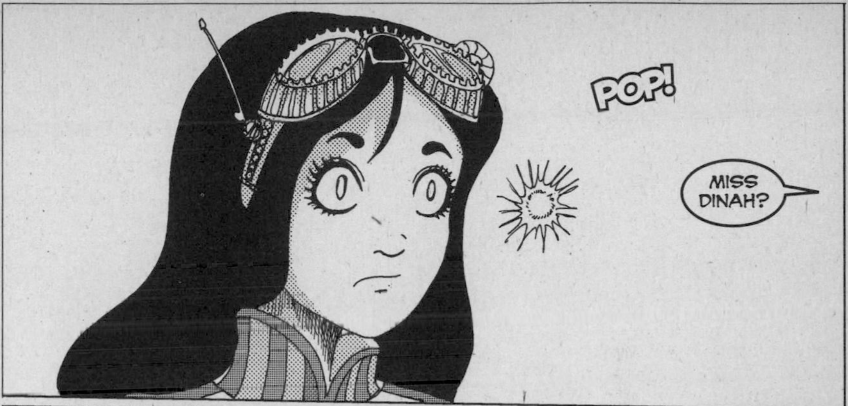
POP!
MISS DINAH?

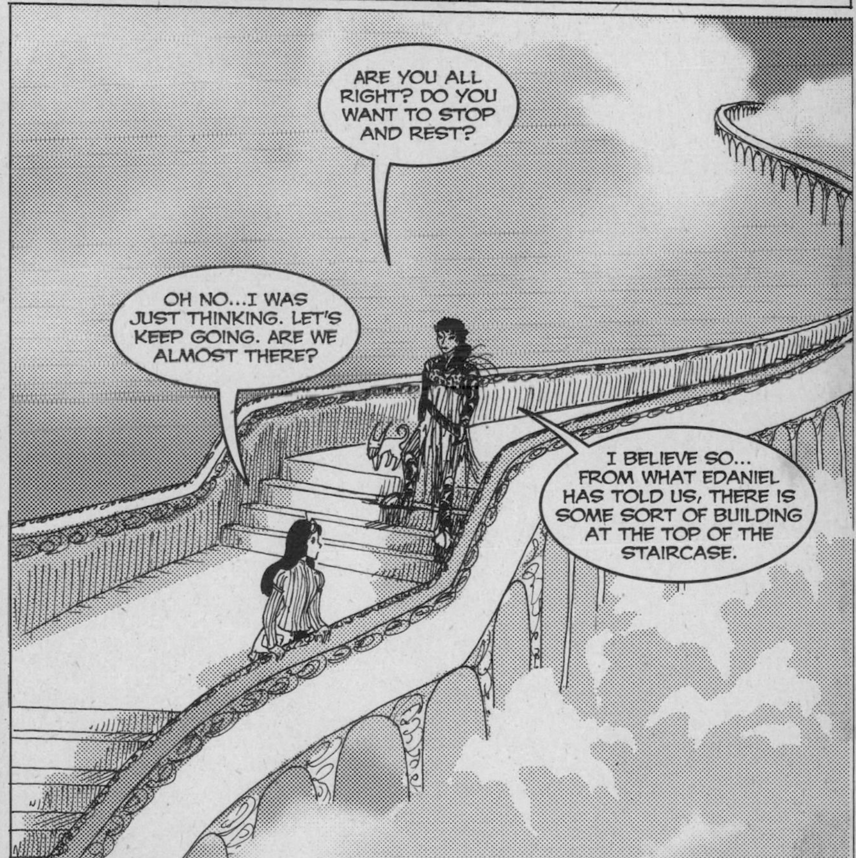
ARE YOU ALL RIGHT? DO YOU WANT TO STOP AND REST?
OH NO...I WAS JUST THINKING. LET'S KEEP GOING. ARE WE ALMOST THERE?
I BELIEVE SO... FROM WHAT EDANIEL HAS TOLD US, THERE IS SOME SORT OF BUILDING AT THE TOP OF THE STAIRCASE.

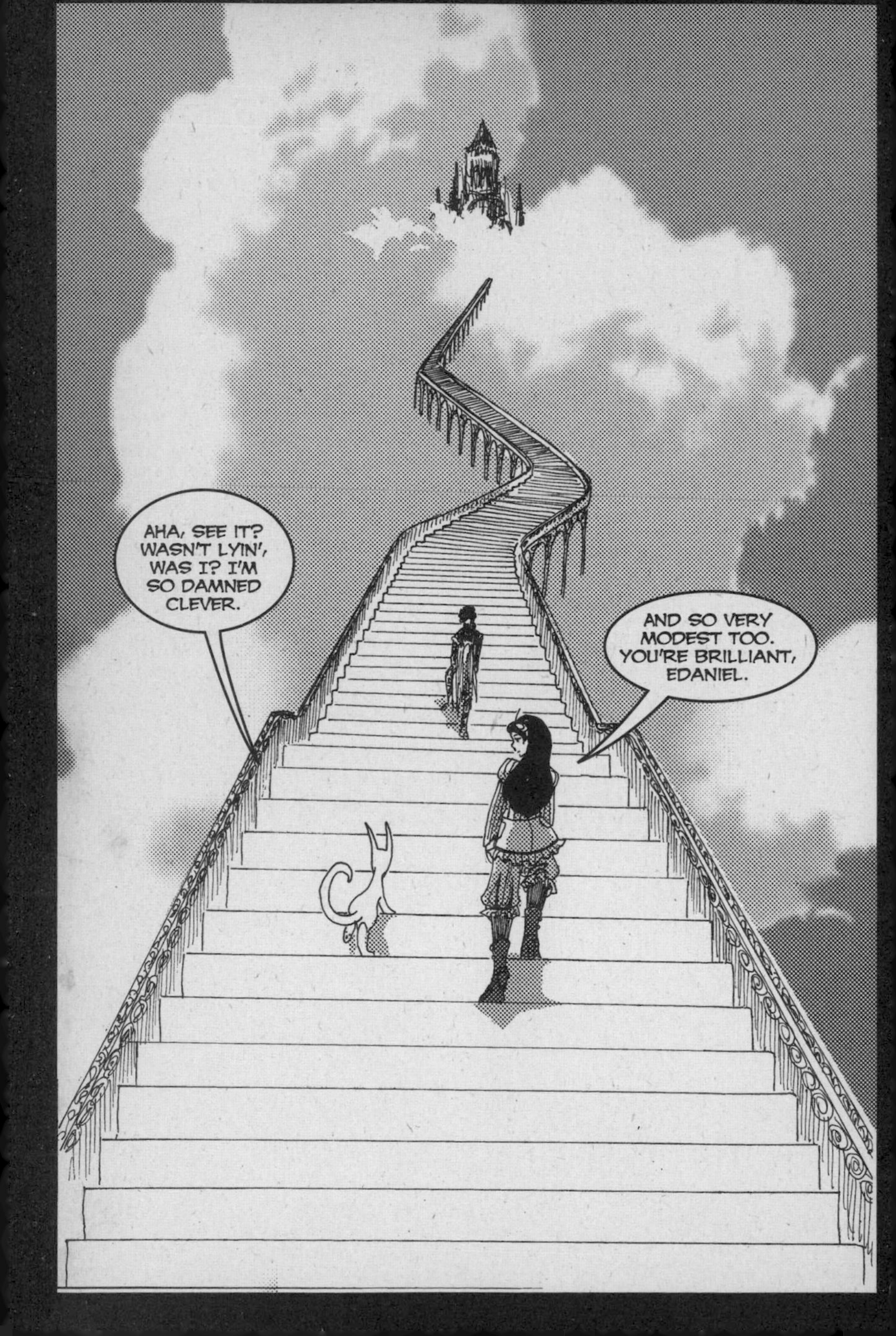
AHA, SEE IT? WASN'T LYIN', WAS I? I'M SO DAMNED CLEVER.
AND SO VERY MODEST TOO. YOU'RE BRILLIANT, EDANIEL.

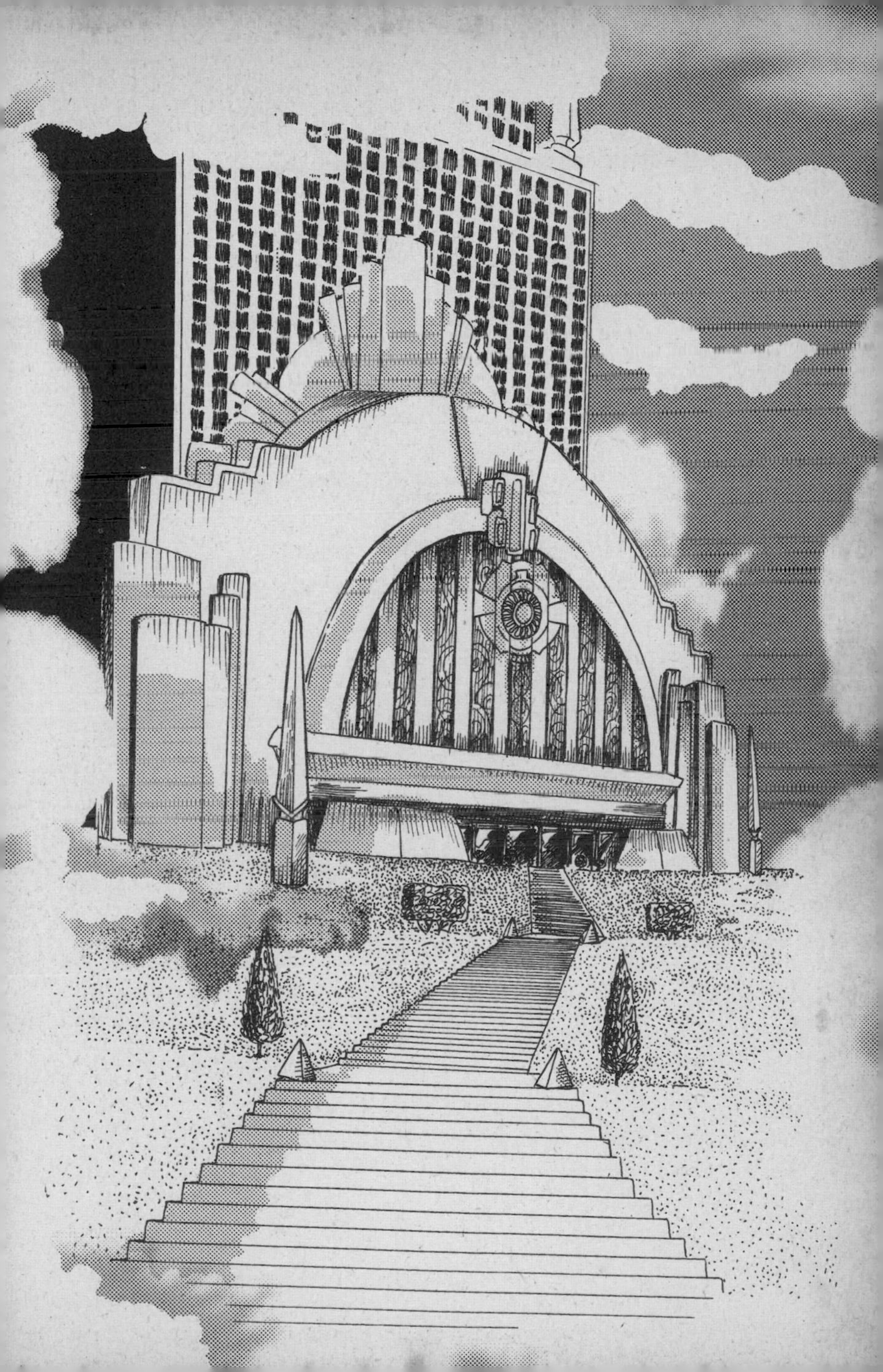

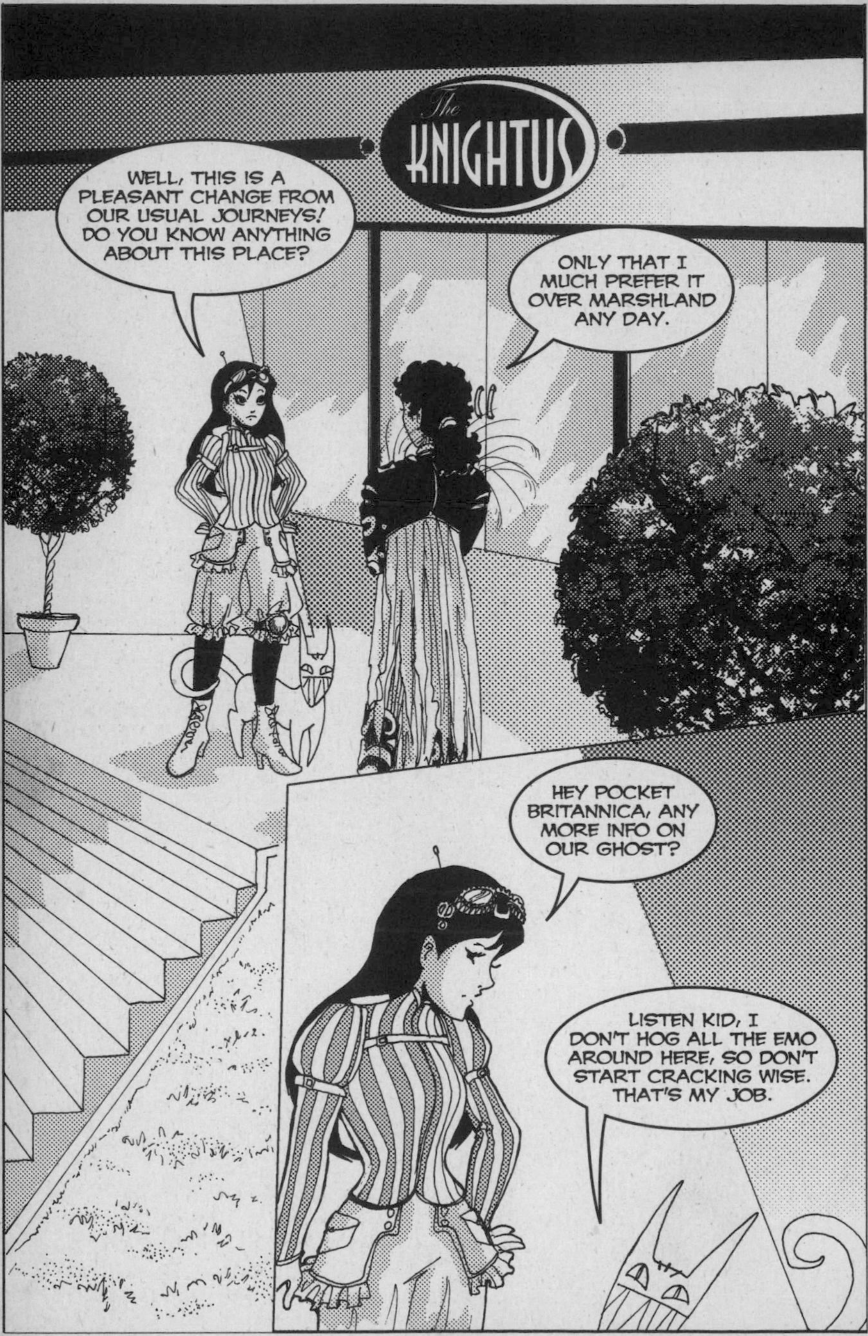
THE KNIGHTUS
WELL, THIS IS A PLEASANT CHANGE FROM OUR USUAL JOURNEYS! DO YOU KNOW ANYTHING ABOUT THIS PLACE?
ONLY THAT I MUCH PREFER IT OVER MARSHLAND ANY DAY.
HEY POCKET BRITANNICA, ANY MORE INFO ON OUR GHOST?
LISTEN KID, I DON'T HOG ALL THE EMO AROUND HERE, SO DON'T START CRACKING WISE. THAT'S MY JOB.

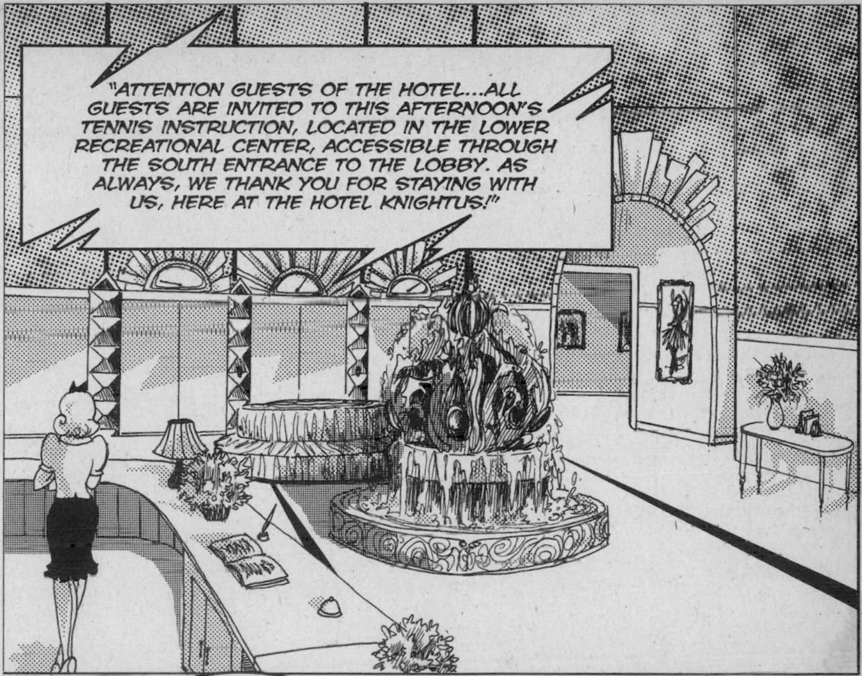
"ATTENTION GUESTS OF THE HOTEL...ALL GUESTS ARE INVITED TO THIS AFTERNOON'S TENNIS INSTRUCTION, LOCATED IN THE LOWER RECREATIONAL CENTER, ACCESSIBLE THROUGH THE SOUTH ENTRANCE TO THE LOBBY. AS ALWAYS, WE THANK YOU FOR STAYING WITH US, HERE AT THE HOTEL KNIGHTUS!"

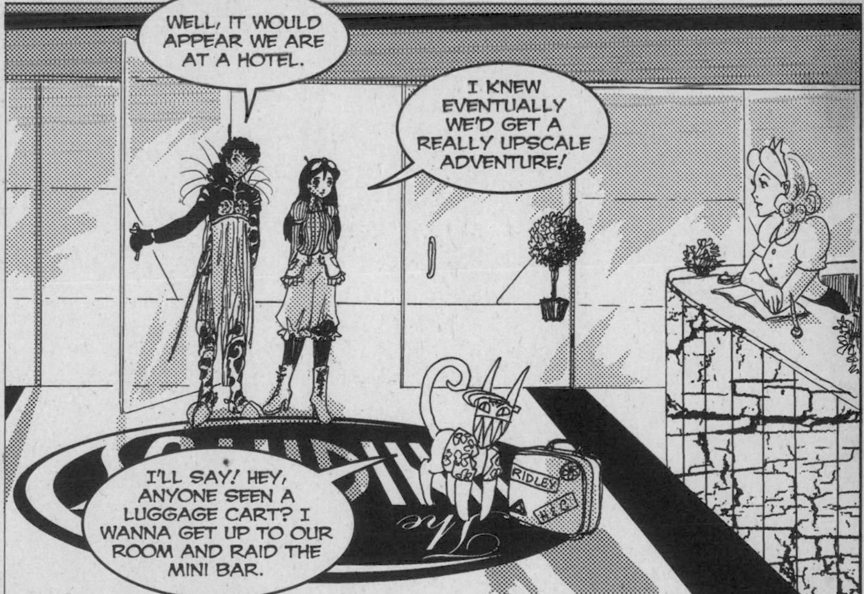
WELL, IT WOULD APPEAR WE ARE AT A HOTEL.
I KNEW EVENTUALLY WE'D GET A REALLY UPSCALE ADVENTURE!
I'LL SAY! HEY, ANYONE SEEN A LUGGAGE CART? I WANNA GET UP TO OUR ROOM AND RAID THE MINI BAR.
RIDLEY

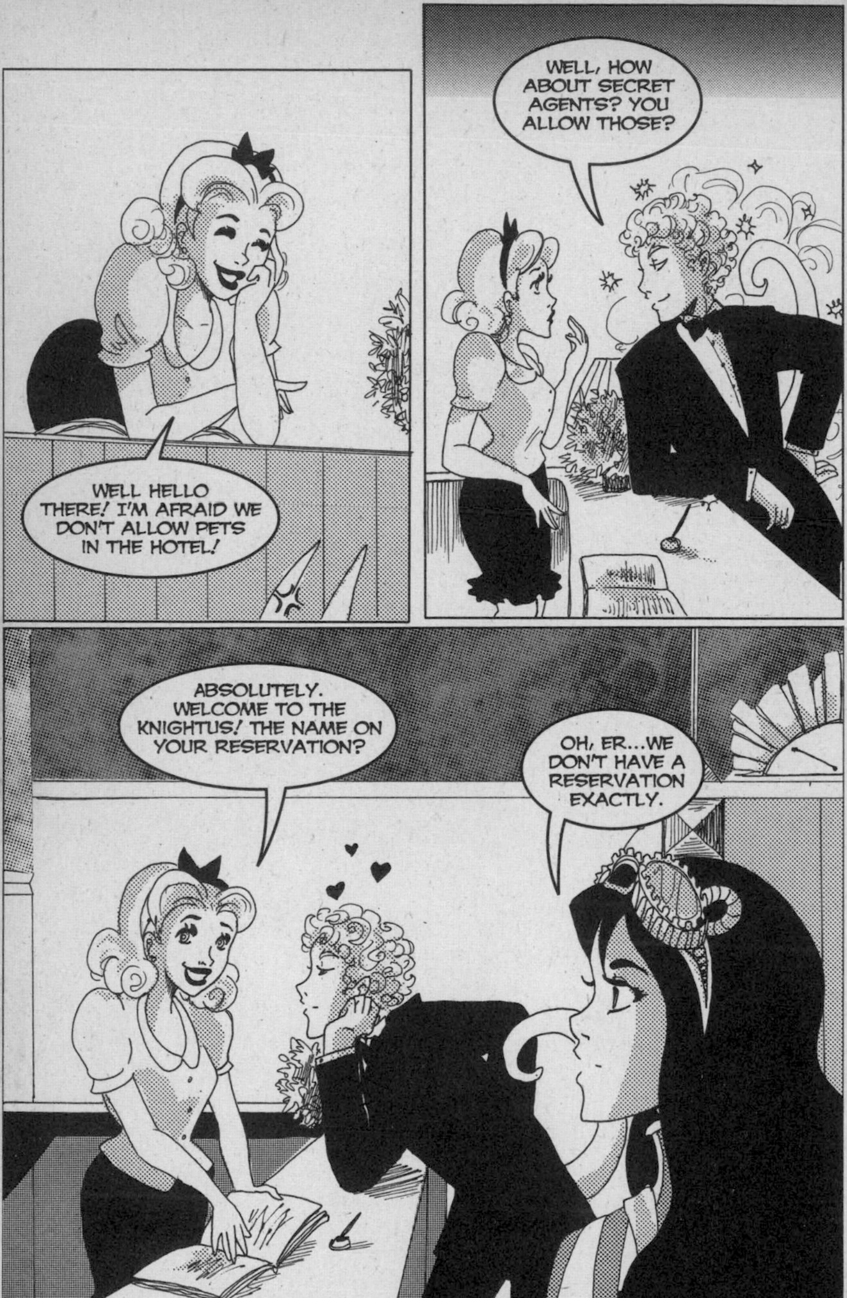
WELL HELLO THERE! I'M AFRAID WE DON'T ALLOW PETS IN THE HOTEL!
WELL, HOW ABOUT SECRET AGENTS? YOU ALLOW THOSE?
ABSOLUTELY. WELCOME TO THE KNIGHTUS! THE NAME ON YOUR RESERVATION?
OH, ER...WE DON'T HAVE A RESERVATION EXACTLY.

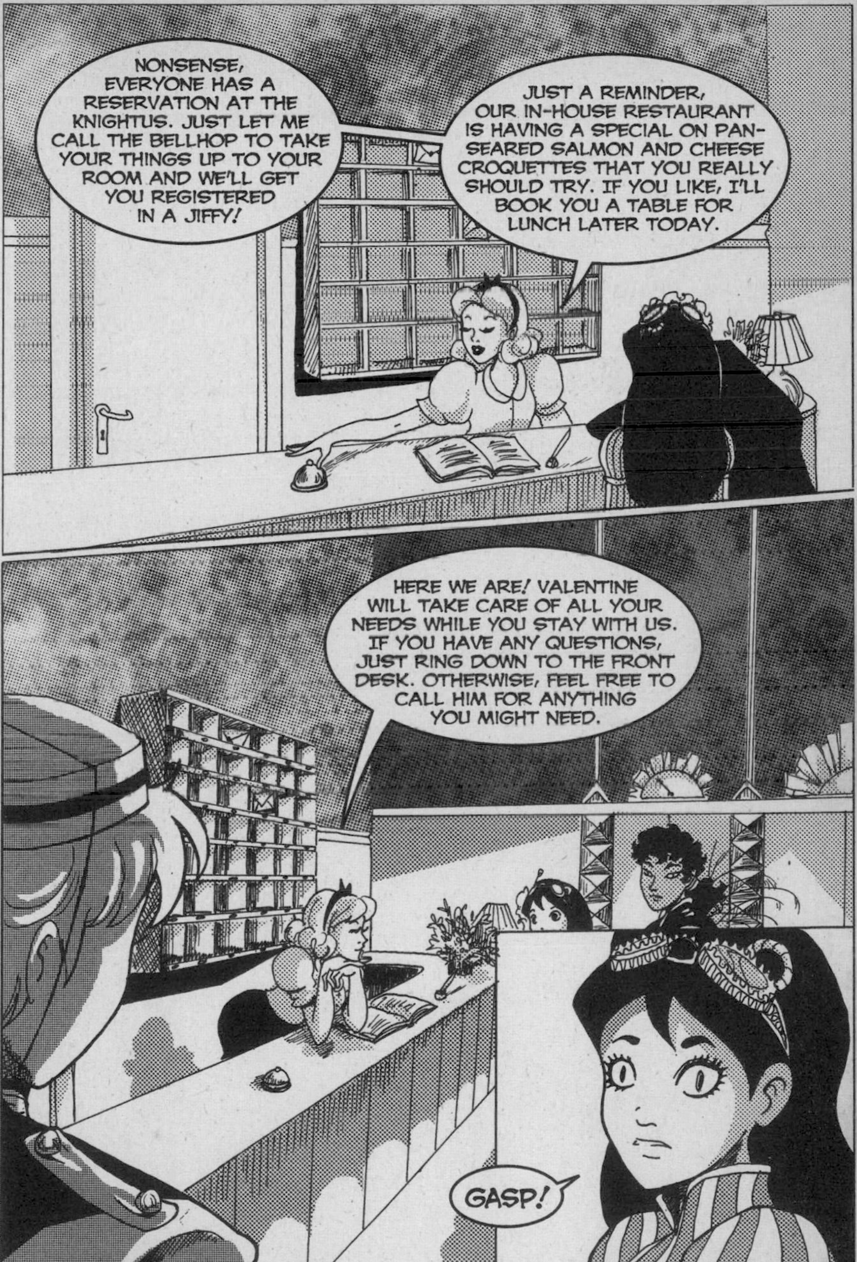
NONSENSE, EVERYONE HAS A RESERVATION AT THE KNIGHTUS. JUST LET ME CALL THE BELLHOP TO TAKE YOUR THINGS UP TO YOUR ROOM AND WE'LL GET YOU REGISTERED IN A JIFFY!
JUST A REMINDER, OUR IN-HOUSE RESTAURANT IS HAVING A SPECIAL ON PAN-SEARED SALMON AND CHEESE CROQUETTES THAT YOU REALLY SHOULD TRY. IF YOU LIKE, I'LL BOOK YOU A TABLE FOR LUNCH LATER TODAY.
HERE WE ARE! VALENTINE WILL TAKE CARE OF ALL YOUR NEEDS WHILE YOU STAY WITH US. IF YOU HAVE ANY QUESTIONS, JUST RING DOWN TO THE FRONT DESK. OTHERWISE, FEEL FREE TO CALL HIM FOR ANYTHING YOU MIGHT NEED.
GASP!

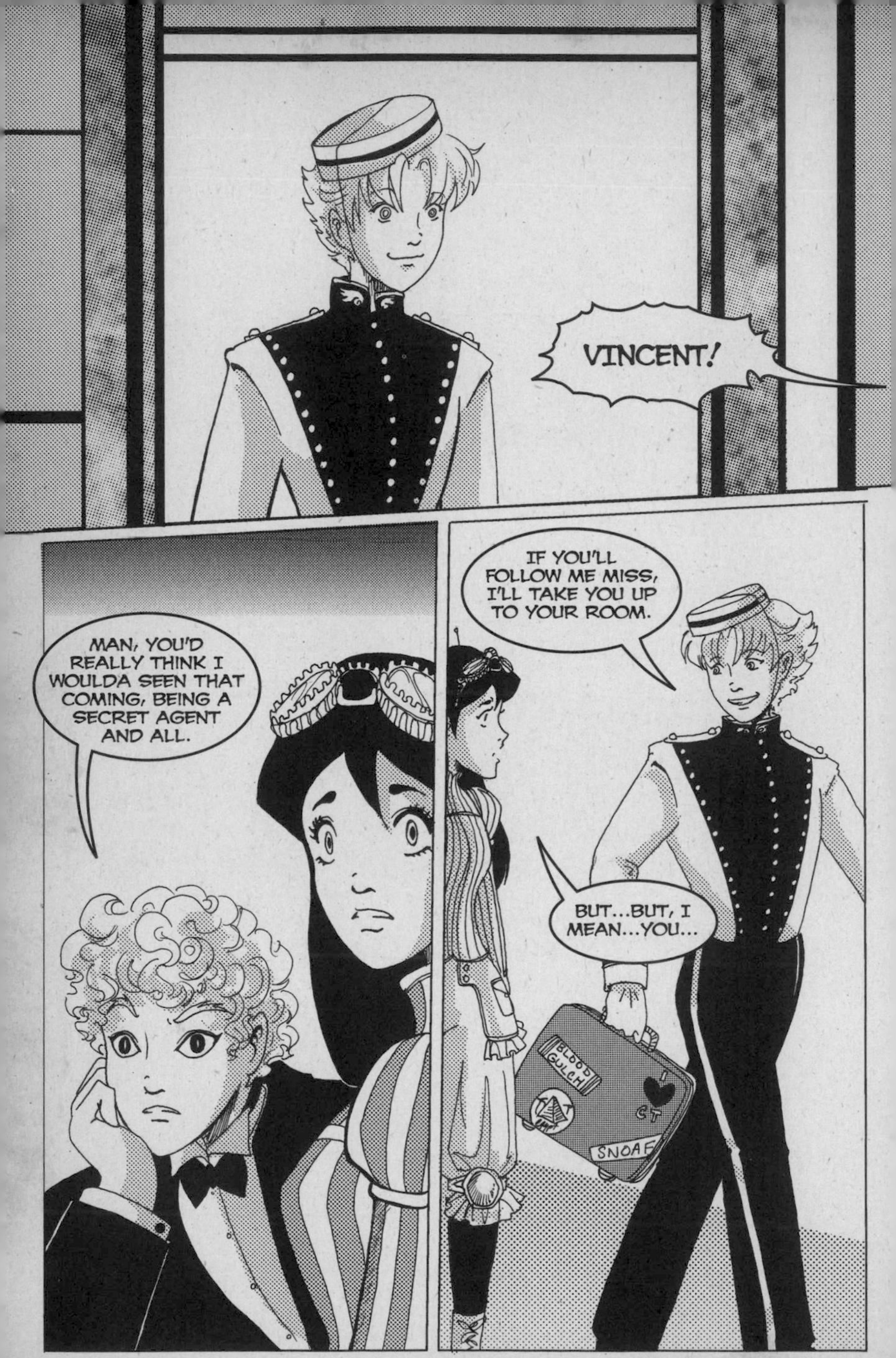
VINCENT!
MAN, YOU'D REALLY THINK I WOULDA SEEN THAT COMING, BEING A SECRET AGENT AND ALL.
IF YOU'LL FOLLOW ME MISS, I'LL TAKE YOU UP TO YOUR ROOM.
BUT...BUT, I MEAN...YOU...
BLOOD GULCH
SNOAF

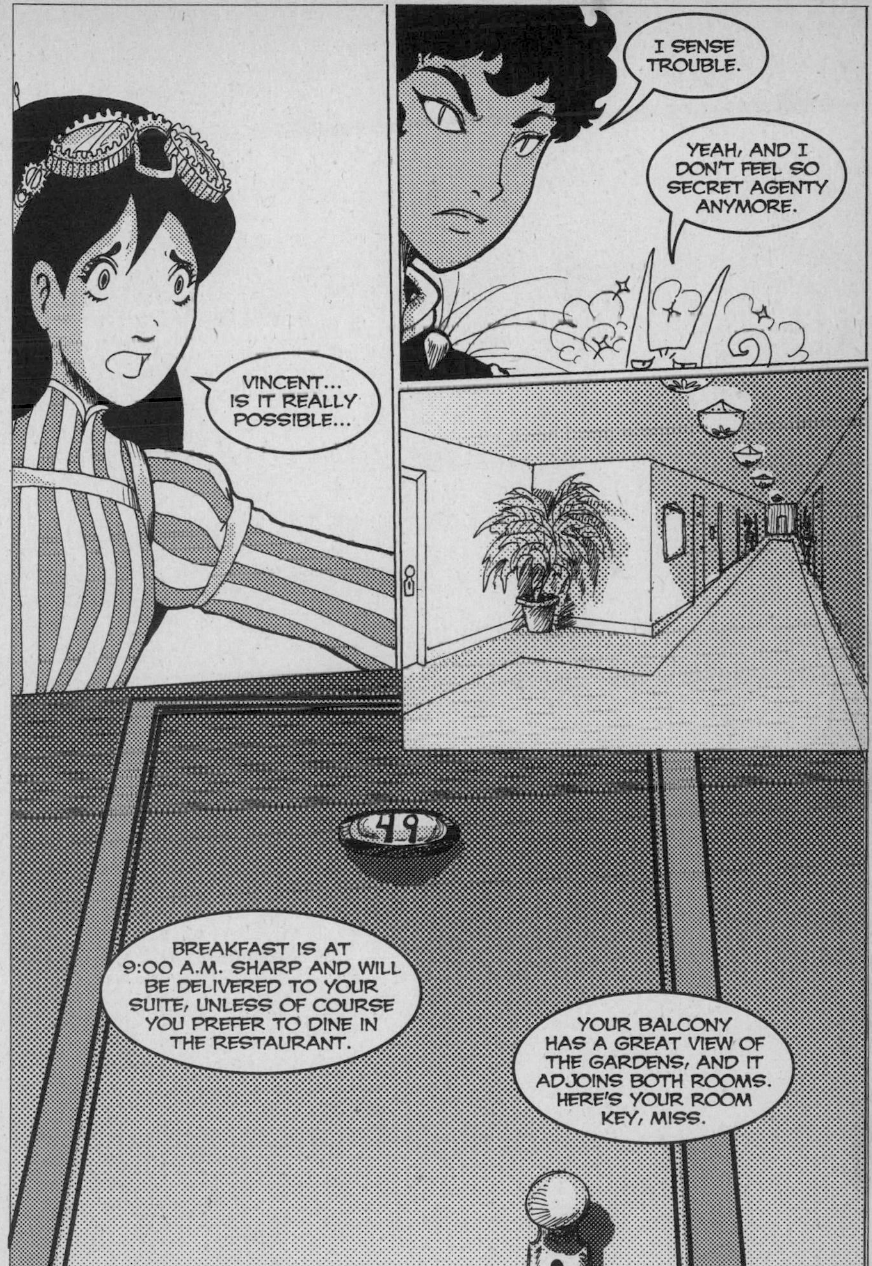
VINCENT... IS IT REALLY POSSIBLE...
I SENSE TROUBLE.
YEAH, AND I DON'T FEEL SO SECRET AGENTY ANYMORE.
49
BREAKFAST IS AT 9:00 A.M. SHARP AND WILL BE DELIVERED TO YOUR SUITE, UNLESS OF COURSE YOU PREFER TO DINE IN THE RESTAURANT.
YOUR BALCONY HAS A GREAT VIEW OF THE GARDENS, AND IT ADJOINS BOTH ROOMS. HERE'S YOUR ROOM KEY, MISS.

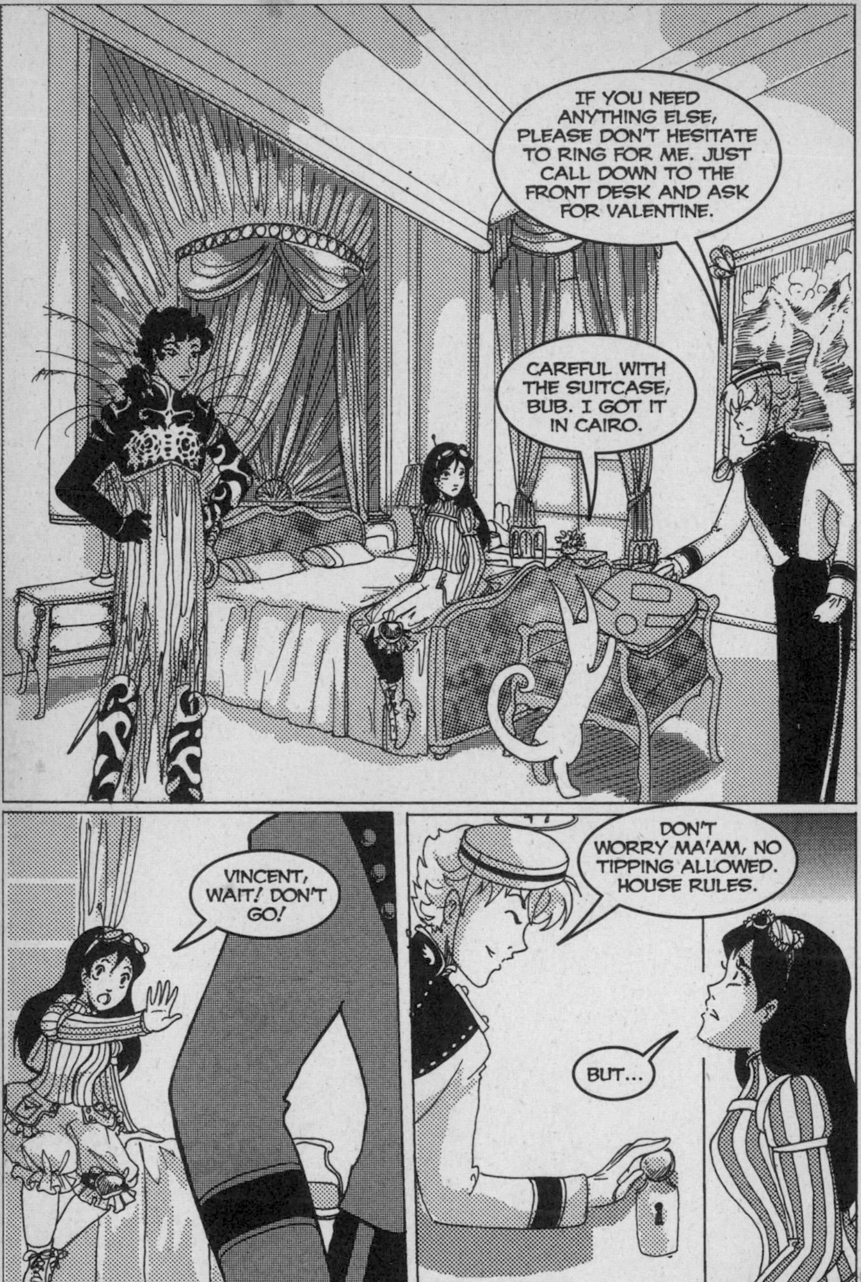
IF YOU NEED ANYTHING ELSE, PLEASE DON'T HESITATE TO RING FOR ME. JUST CALL DOWN TO THE FRONT DESK AND ASK FOR VALENTINE.
CAREFUL WITH THE SUITCASE, BUB. I GOT IT IN CAIRO.
VINCENT, WAIT! DON'T GO!
DON'T WORRY MA'AM, NO TIPPING ALLOWED. HOUSE RULES.
BUT...

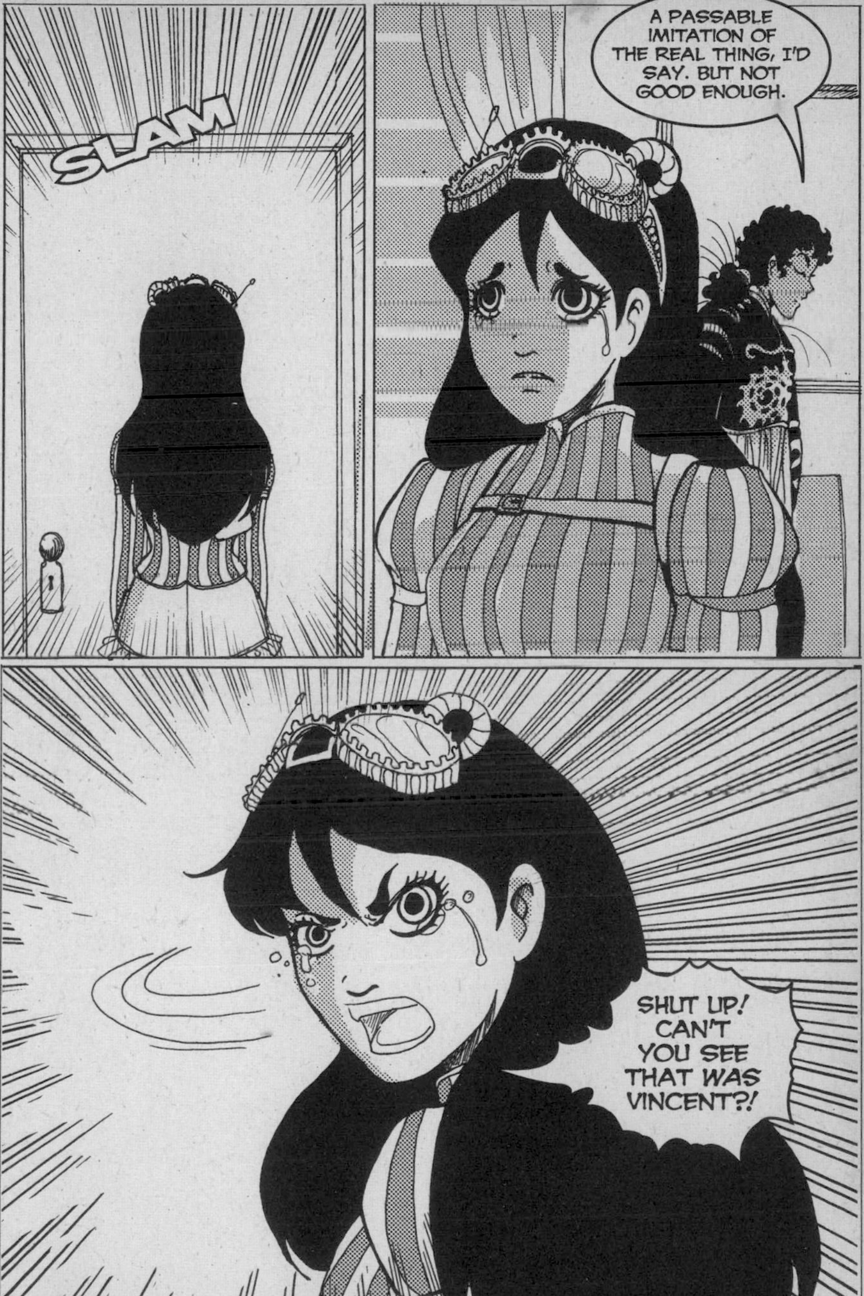
SLAM
A PASSABLE IMITATION OF THE REAL THING, I'D SAY. BUT NOT GOOD ENOUGH.
SHUT UP! CAN'T YOU SEE THAT WAS VINCENT?!

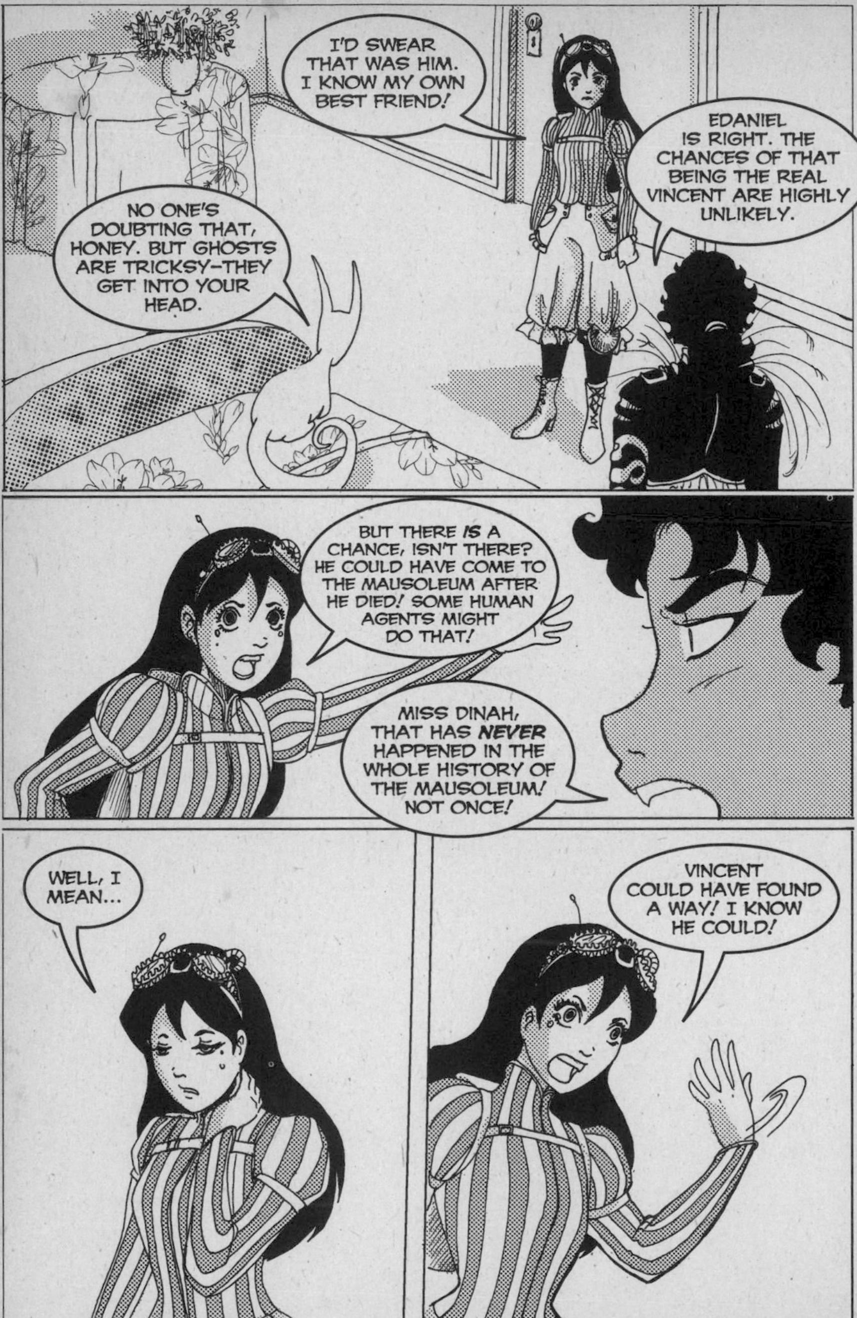
I'D SWEAR THAT WAS HIM. I KNOW MY OWN BEST FRIEND!
NO ONE'S DOUBTING THAT, HONEY. BUT GHOSTS ARE TRICKSY—THEY GET INTO YOUR HEAD.
EDANIEL IS RIGHT. THE CHANCES OF THAT BEING THE REAL VINCENT ARE HIGHLY UNLIKELY.
BUT THERE *IS* A CHANCE, ISN'T THERE? HE COULD HAVE COME TO THE MAUSOLEUM AFTER HE DIED! SOME HUMAN AGENTS MIGHT DO THAT!
MISS DINAH, THAT HAS ***NEVER*** HAPPENED IN THE WHOLE HISTORY OF THE MAUSOLEUM! NOT ONCE!
WELL, I MEAN...
VINCENT COULD HAVE FOUND A WAY! I KNOW HE COULD!

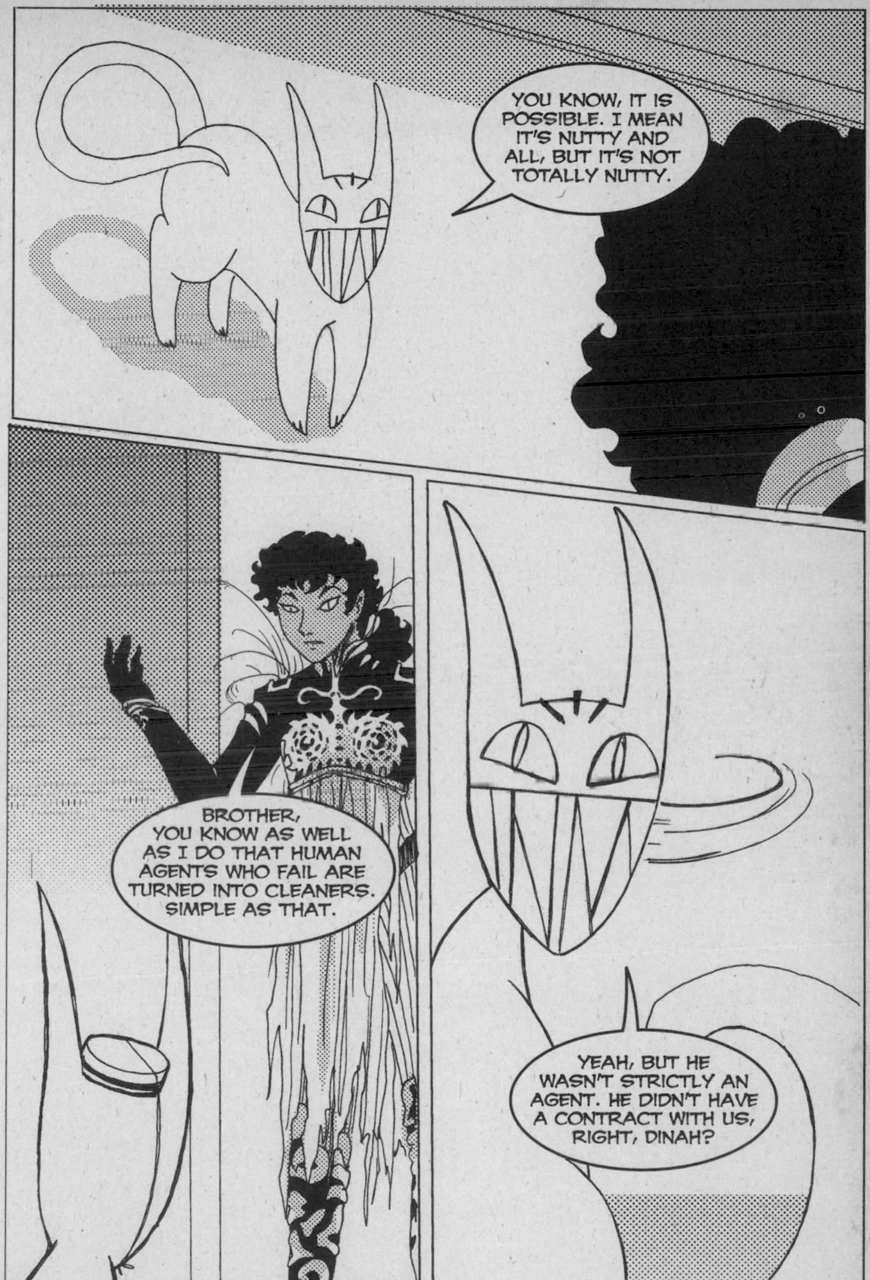
YOU KNOW, IT IS POSSIBLE. I MEAN IT'S NUTTY AND ALL, BUT IT'S NOT TOTALLY NUTTY.
BROTHER, YOU KNOW AS WELL AS I DO THAT HUMAN AGENTS WHO FAIL ARE TURNED INTO CLEANERS. SIMPLE AS THAT.
YEAH, BUT HE WASN'T STRICTLY AN AGENT. HE DIDN'T HAVE A CONTRACT WITH US, RIGHT, DINAH?

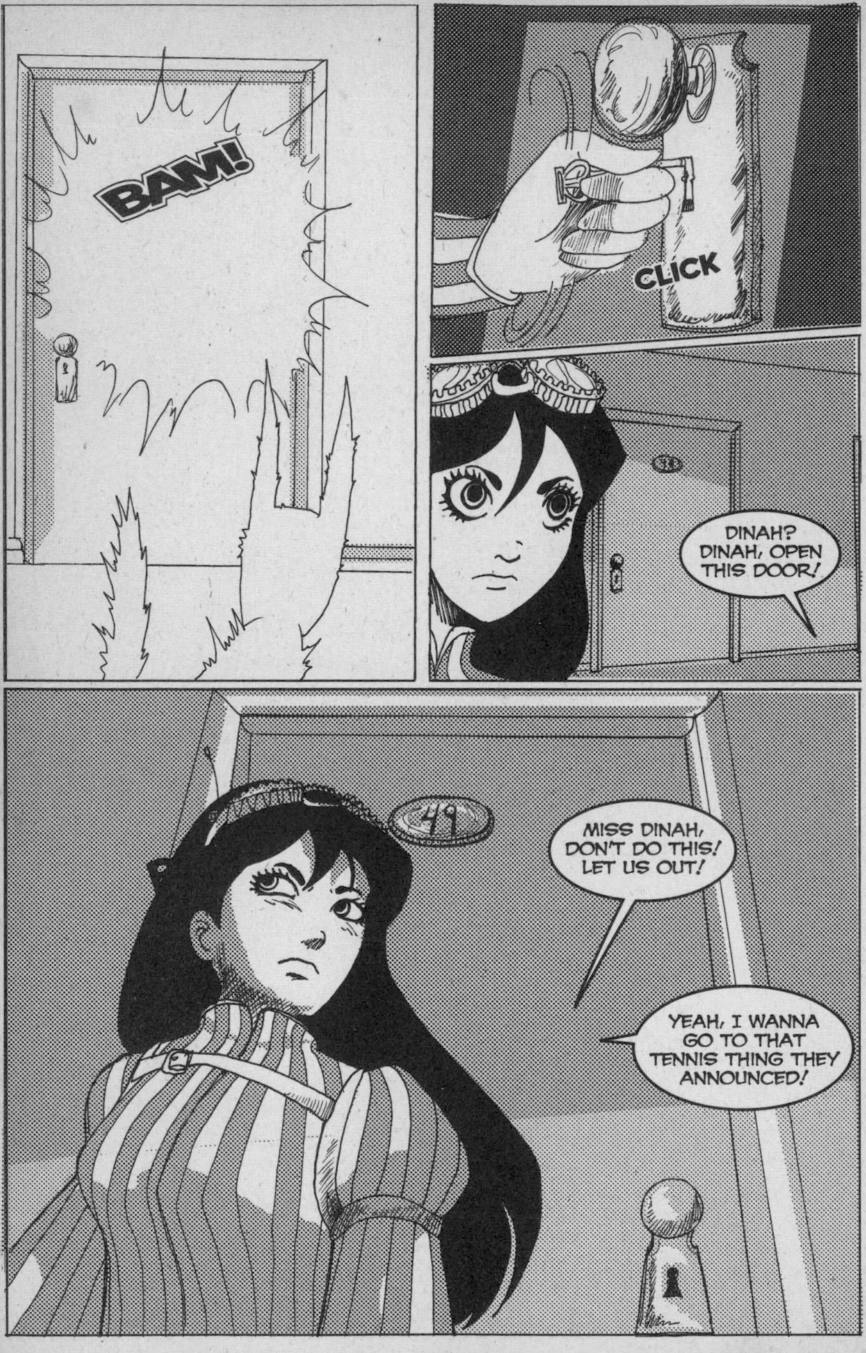
BAM!
CLICK
DINAH? DINAH, OPEN THIS DOOR!
MISS DINAH, DON'T DO THIS! LET US OUT!
YEAH, I WANNA GO TO THAT TENNIS THING THEY ANNOUNCED!

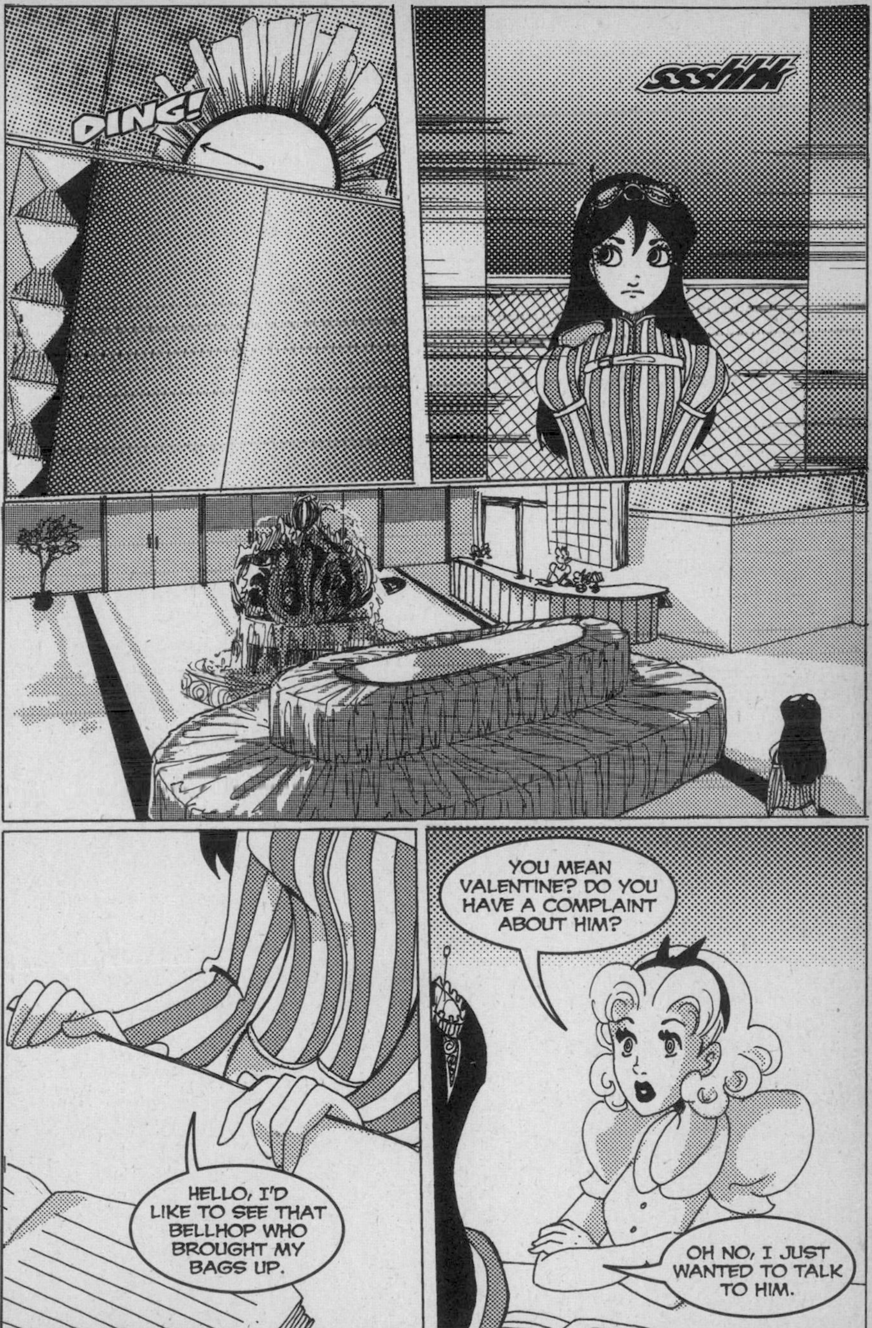
DING!
SSSHHK
HELLO, I'D LIKE TO SEE THAT BELLHOP WHO BROUGHT MY BAGS UP.
YOU MEAN VALENTINE? DO YOU HAVE A COMPLAINT ABOUT HIM?
OH NO, I JUST WANTED TO TALK TO HIM.

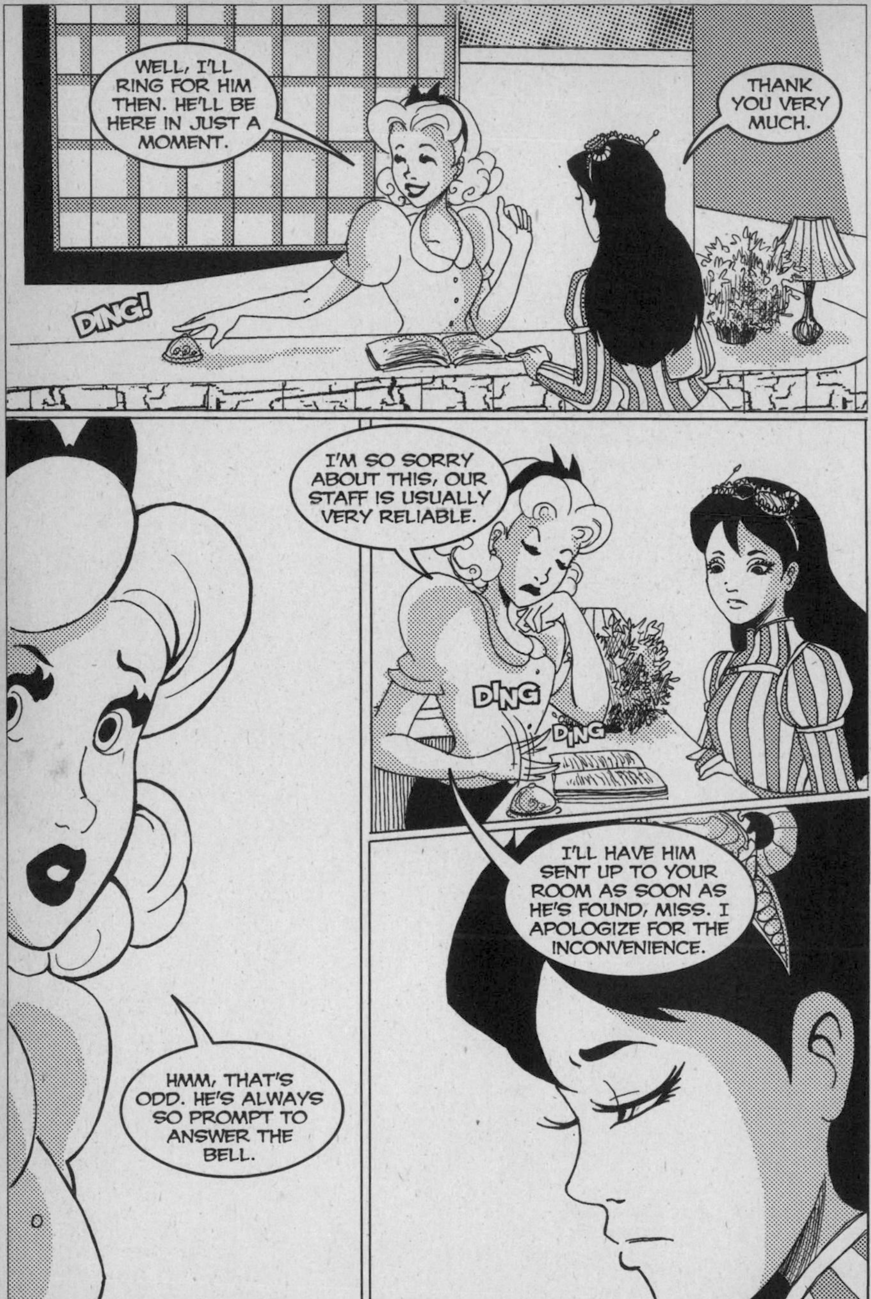
WELL, I'LL RING FOR HIM THEN. HE'LL BE HERE IN JUST A MOMENT.
THANK YOU VERY MUCH.
DING!
HMM, THAT'S ODD. HE'S ALWAYS SO PROMPT TO ANSWER THE BELL.
I'M SO SORRY ABOUT THIS, OUR STAFF IS USUALLY VERY RELIABLE.
DING
DING
I'LL HAVE HIM SENT UP TO YOUR ROOM AS SOON AS HE'S FOUND, MISS. I APOLOGIZE FOR THE INCONVENIENCE.

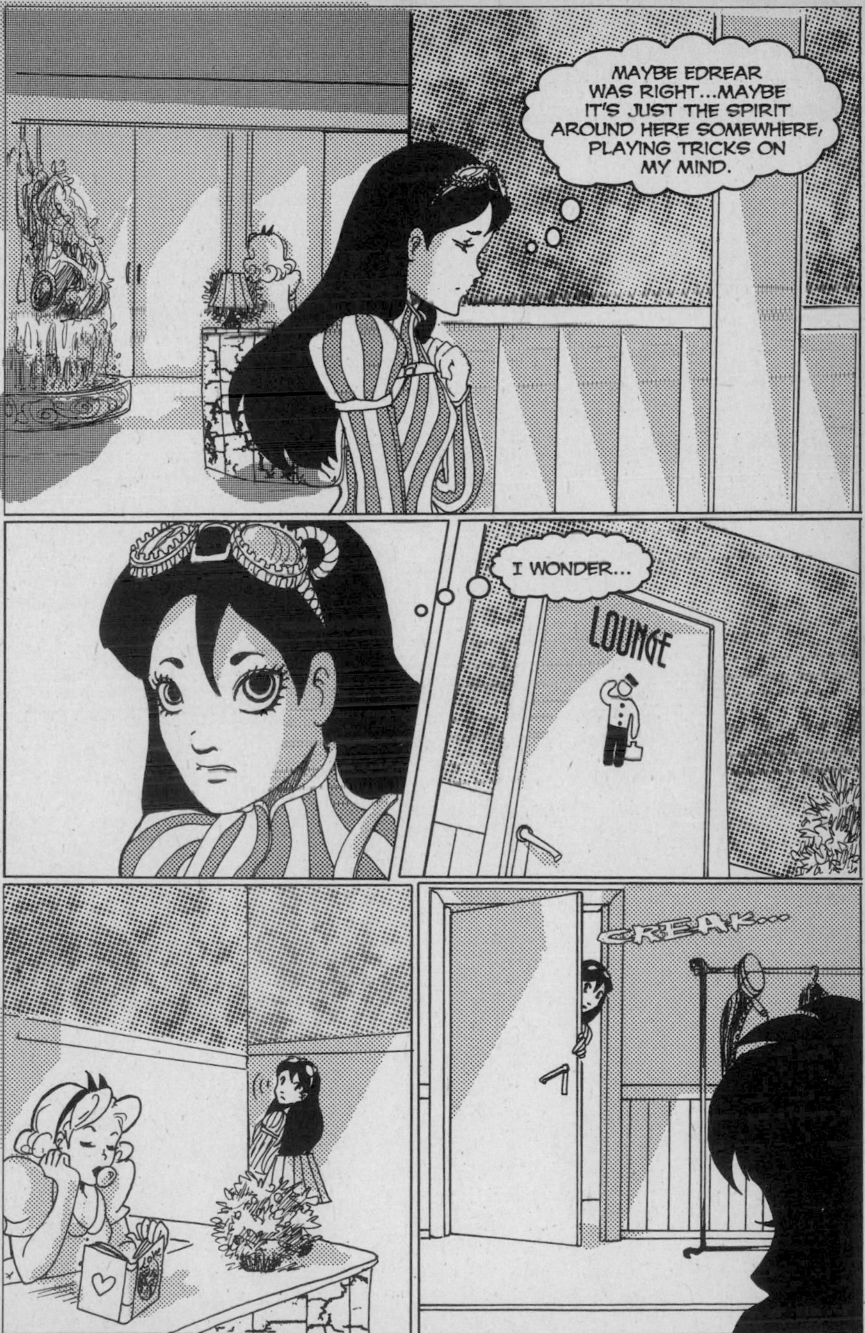
MAYBE EDREAR WAS RIGHT...MAYBE IT'S JUST THE SPIRIT AROUND HERE SOMEWHERE, PLAYING TRICKS ON MY MIND.
I WONDER...
LOUNGE
CREAK...

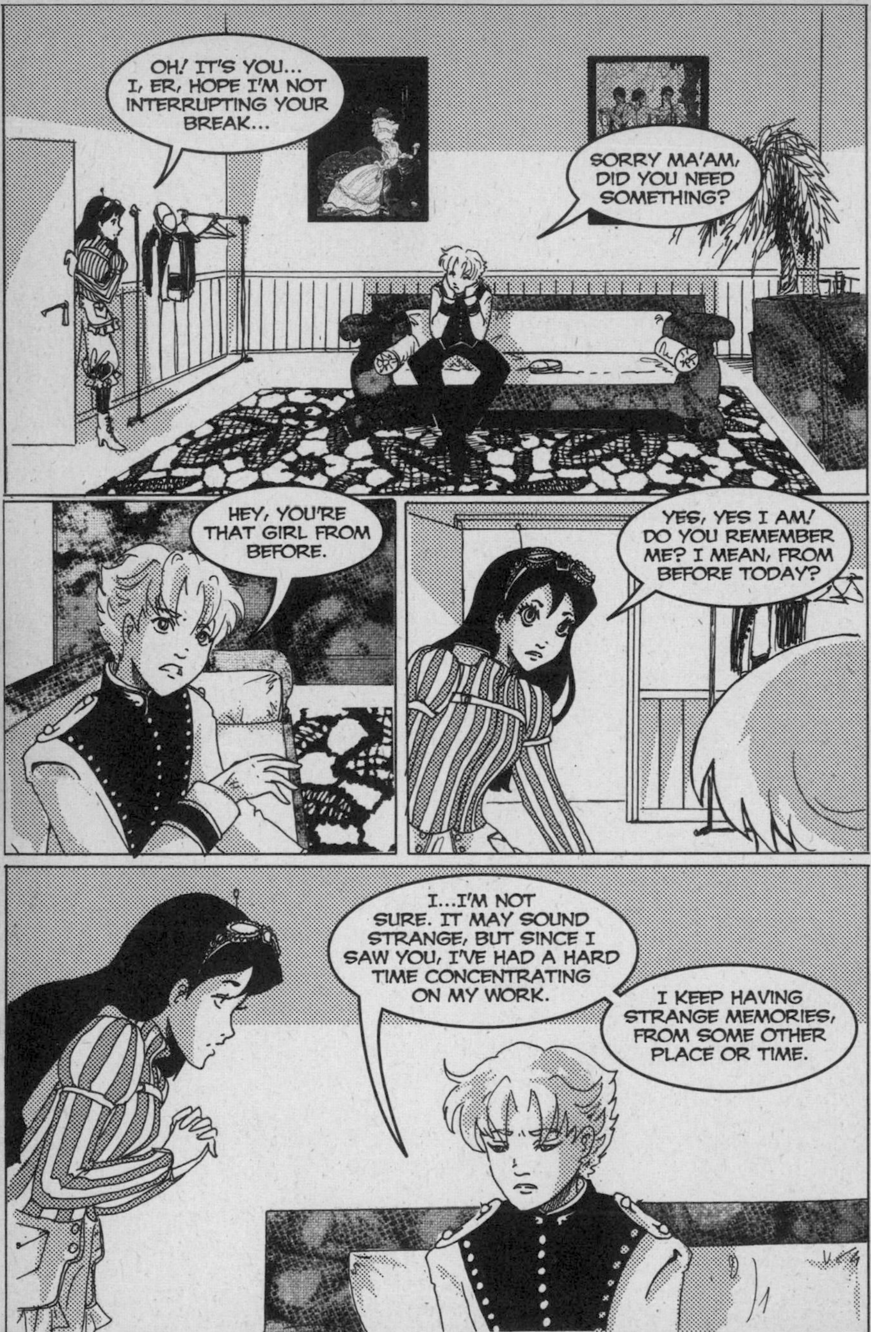
OH! IT'S YOU... I, ER, HOPE I'M NOT INTERRUPTING YOUR BREAK...
SORRY MA'AM, DID YOU NEED SOMETHING?
HEY, YOU'RE THAT GIRL FROM BEFORE.
YES, YES I AM! DO YOU REMEMBER ME? I MEAN, FROM BEFORE TODAY?
I...I'M NOT SURE. IT MAY SOUND STRANGE, BUT SINCE I SAW YOU, I'VE HAD A HARD TIME CONCENTRATING ON MY WORK.
I KEEP HAVING STRANGE MEMORIES, FROM SOME OTHER PLACE OR TIME.

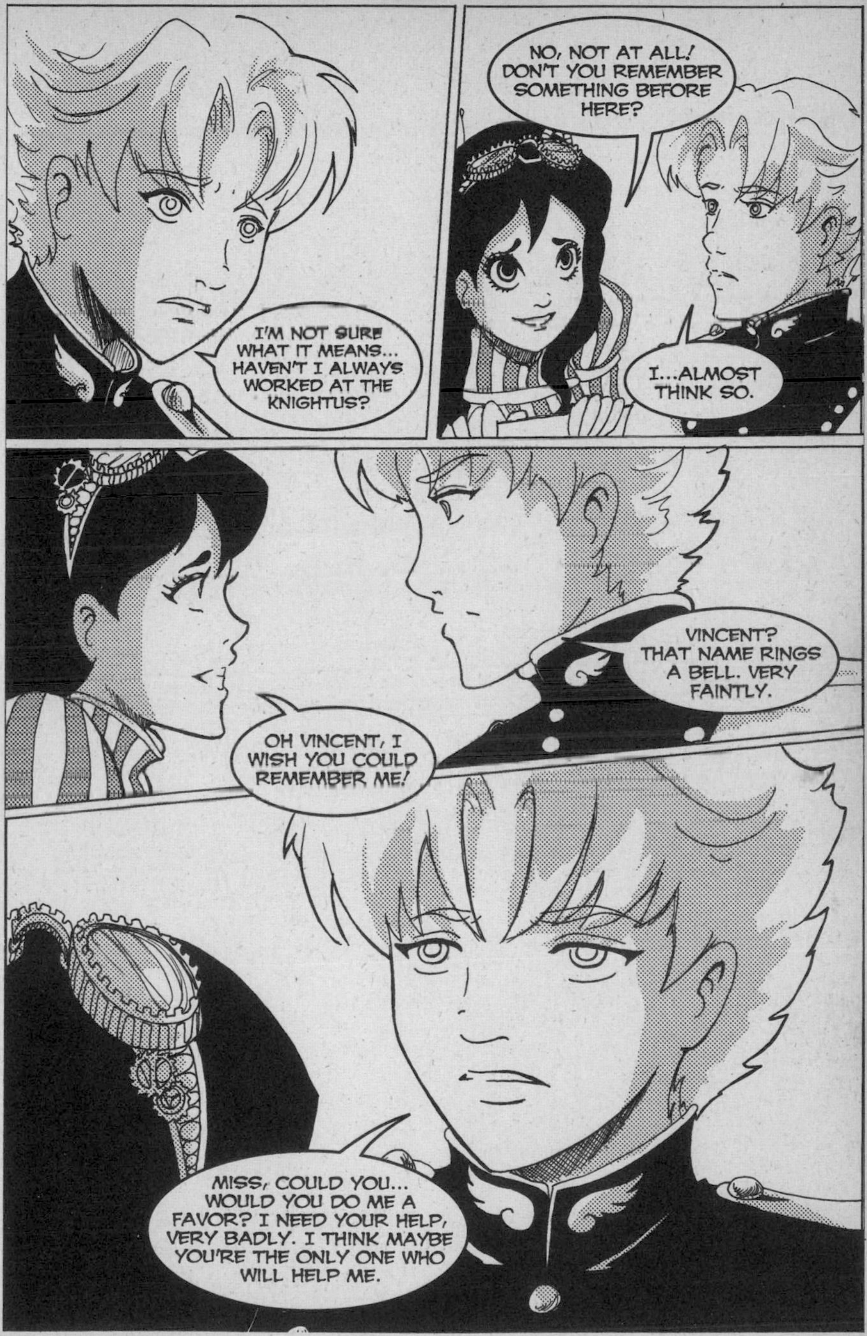
I'M NOT SURE WHAT IT MEANS... HAVEN'T I ALWAYS WORKED AT THE KNIGHTUS?
NO, NOT AT ALL! DON'T YOU REMEMBER SOMETHING BEFORE HERE?
I...ALMOST THINK SO.
VINCENT? THAT NAME RINGS A BELL. VERY FAINTLY.
OH VINCENT, I WISH YOU COULD REMEMBER ME!
MISS, COULD YOU... WOULD YOU DO ME A FAVOR? I NEED YOUR HELP, VERY BADLY. I THINK MAYBE YOU'RE THE ONLY ONE WHO WILL HELP ME.

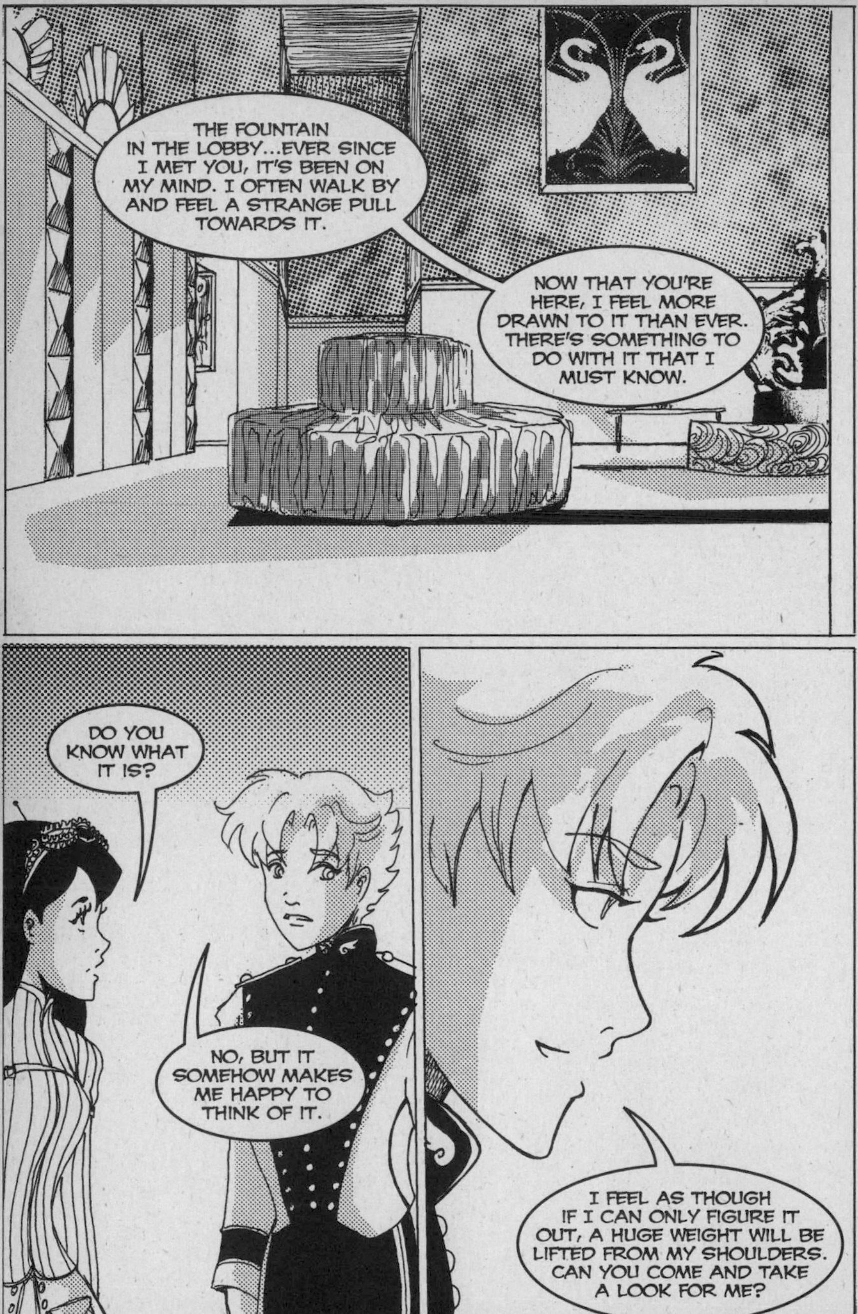
THE FOUNTAIN IN THE LOBBY...EVER SINCE I MET YOU, IT'S BEEN ON MY MIND. I OFTEN WALK BY AND FEEL A STRANGE PULL TOWARDS IT.
NOW THAT YOU'RE HERE, I FEEL MORE DRAWN TO IT THAN EVER. THERE'S SOMETHING TO DO WITH IT THAT I MUST KNOW.
DO YOU KNOW WHAT IT IS?
NO, BUT IT SOMEHOW MAKES ME HAPPY TO THINK OF IT.
I FEEL AS THOUGH IF I CAN ONLY FIGURE IT OUT, A HUGE WEIGHT WILL BE LIFTED FROM MY SHOULDERS. CAN YOU COME AND TAKE A LOOK FOR ME?

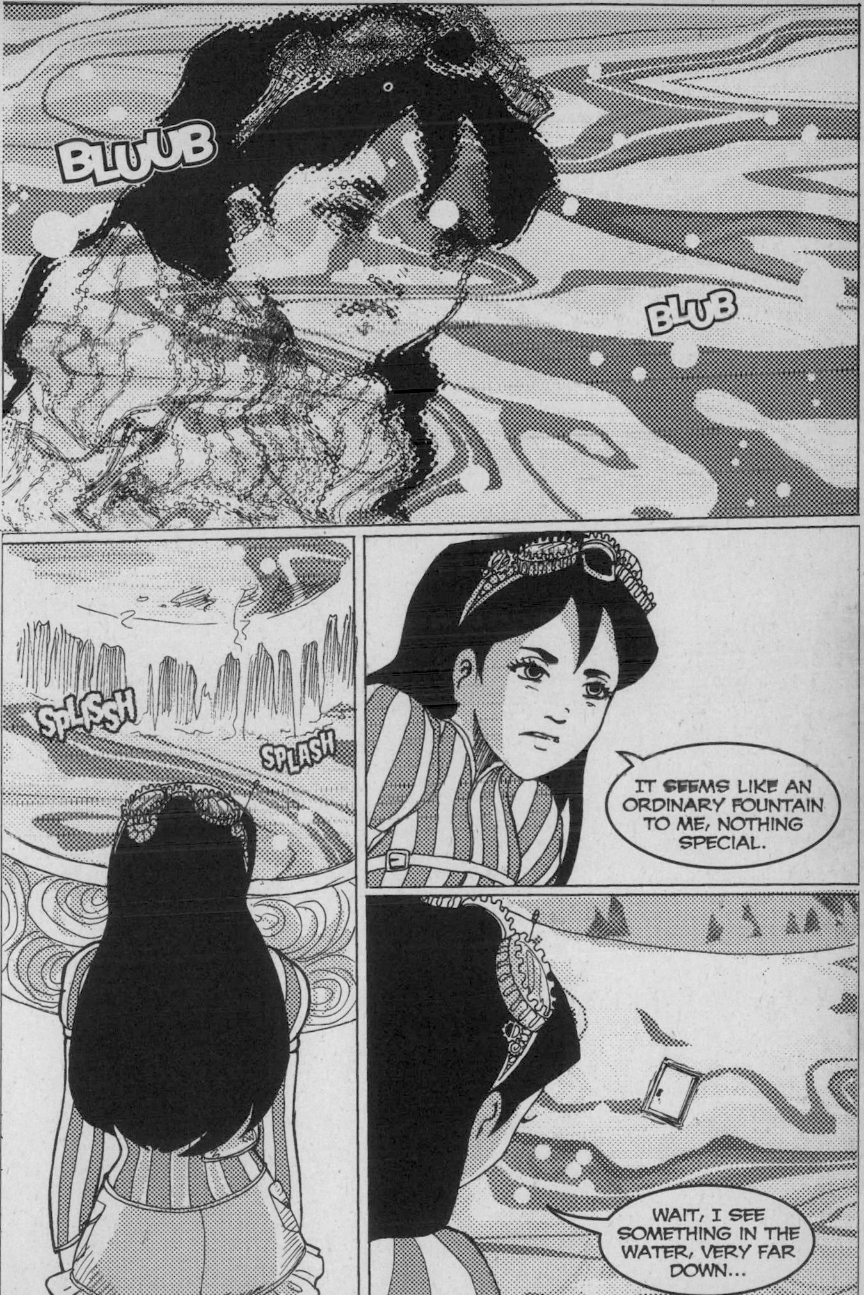
BLUUB
BLUB
SPLISSH
SPLASH
IT SEEMS LIKE AN ORDINARY FOUNTAIN TO ME, NOTHING SPECIAL.
WAIT, I SEE SOMETHING IN THE WATER, VERY FAR DOWN...

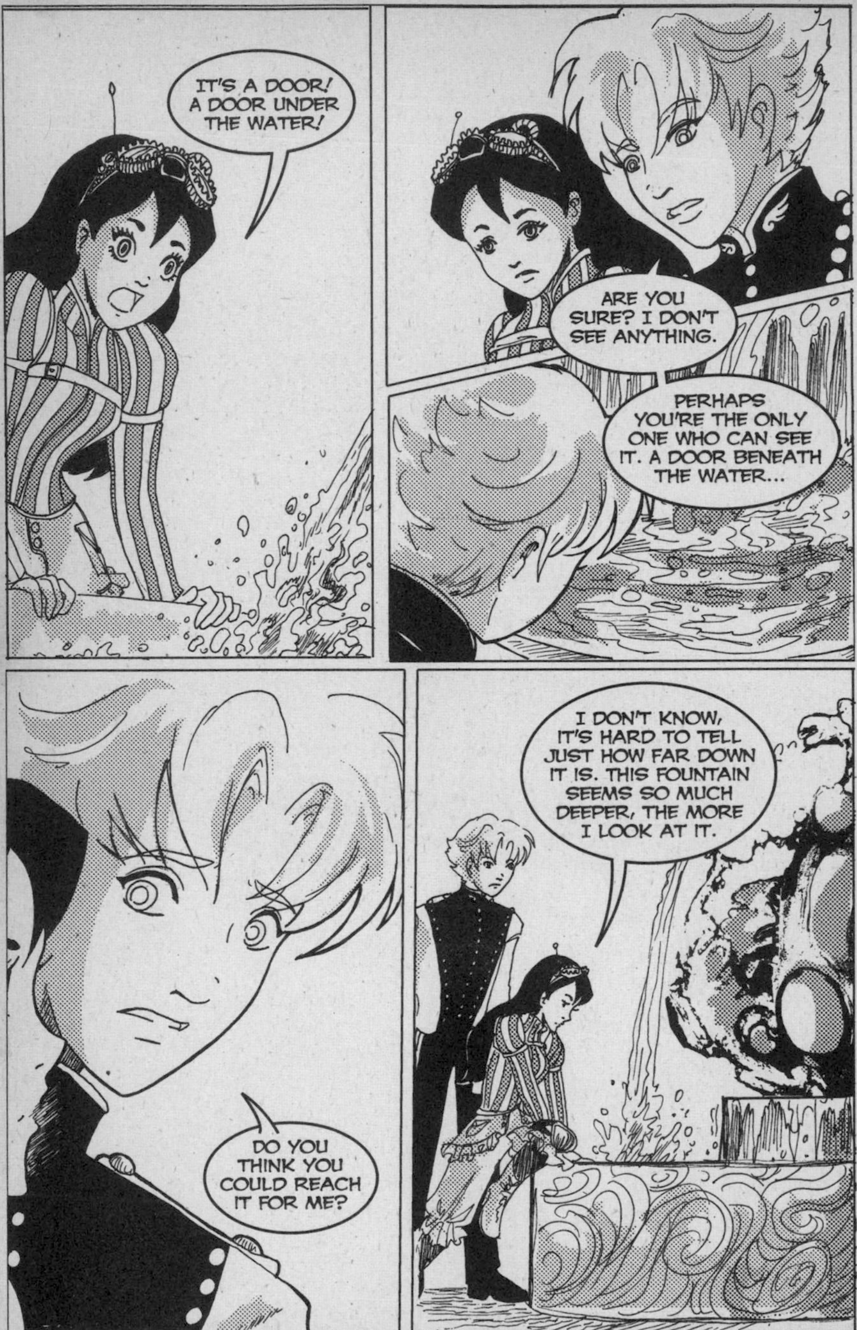
IT'S A DOOR! A DOOR UNDER THE WATER!
ARE YOU SURE? I DON'T SEE ANYTHING.
PERHAPS YOU'RE THE ONLY ONE WHO CAN SEE IT. A DOOR BENEATH THE WATER...
DO YOU THINK YOU COULD REACH IT FOR ME?
I DON'T KNOW, IT'S HARD TO TELL JUST HOW FAR DOWN IT IS. THIS FOUNTAIN SEEMS SO MUCH DEEPER, THE MORE I LOOK AT IT.

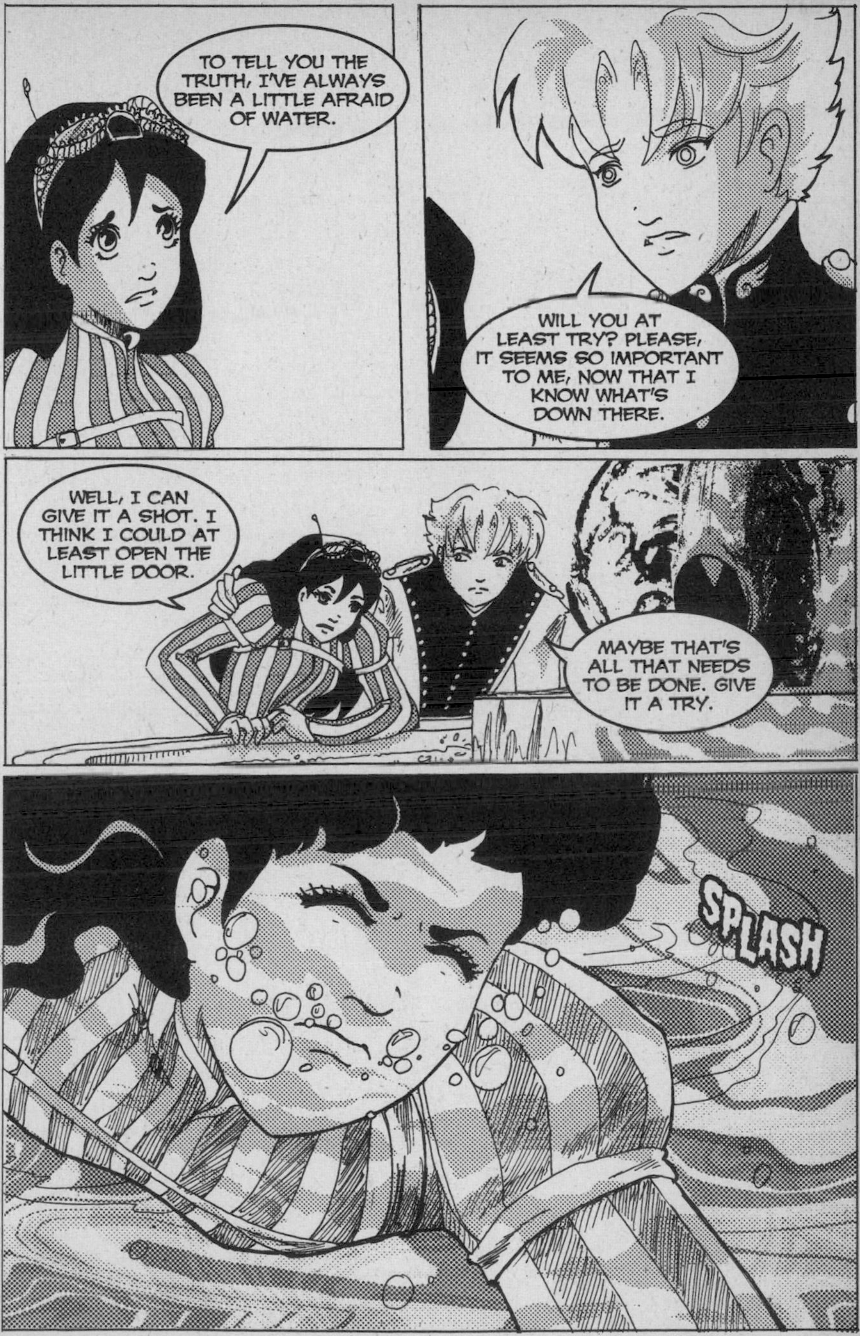
TO TELL YOU THE TRUTH, I'VE ALWAYS BEEN A LITTLE AFRAID OF WATER.
WILL YOU AT LEAST TRY? PLEASE, IT SEEMS SO IMPORTANT TO ME, NOW THAT I KNOW WHAT'S DOWN THERE.
WELL, I CAN GIVE IT A SHOT. I THINK I COULD AT LEAST OPEN THE LITTLE DOOR.
MAYBE THAT'S ALL THAT NEEDS TO BE DONE. GIVE IT A TRY.
SPLASH

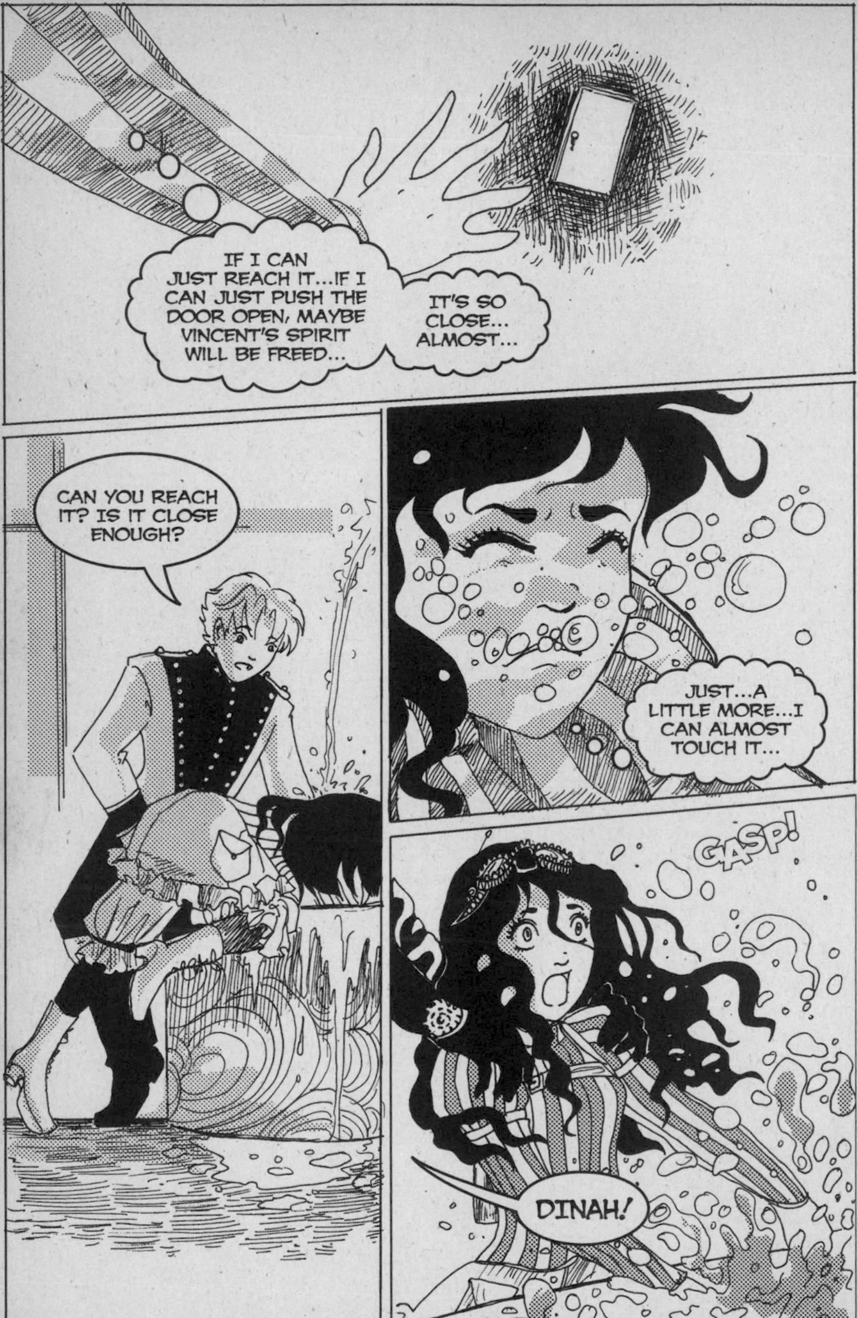
IF I CAN JUST REACH IT...IF I CAN JUST PUSH THE DOOR OPEN, MAYBE VINCENT'S SPIRIT WILL BE FREED...
IT'S SO CLOSE... ALMOST...
CAN YOU REACH IT? IS IT CLOSE ENOUGH?
JUST...A LITTLE MORE...I CAN ALMOST TOUCH IT...
GASP!
DINAH!

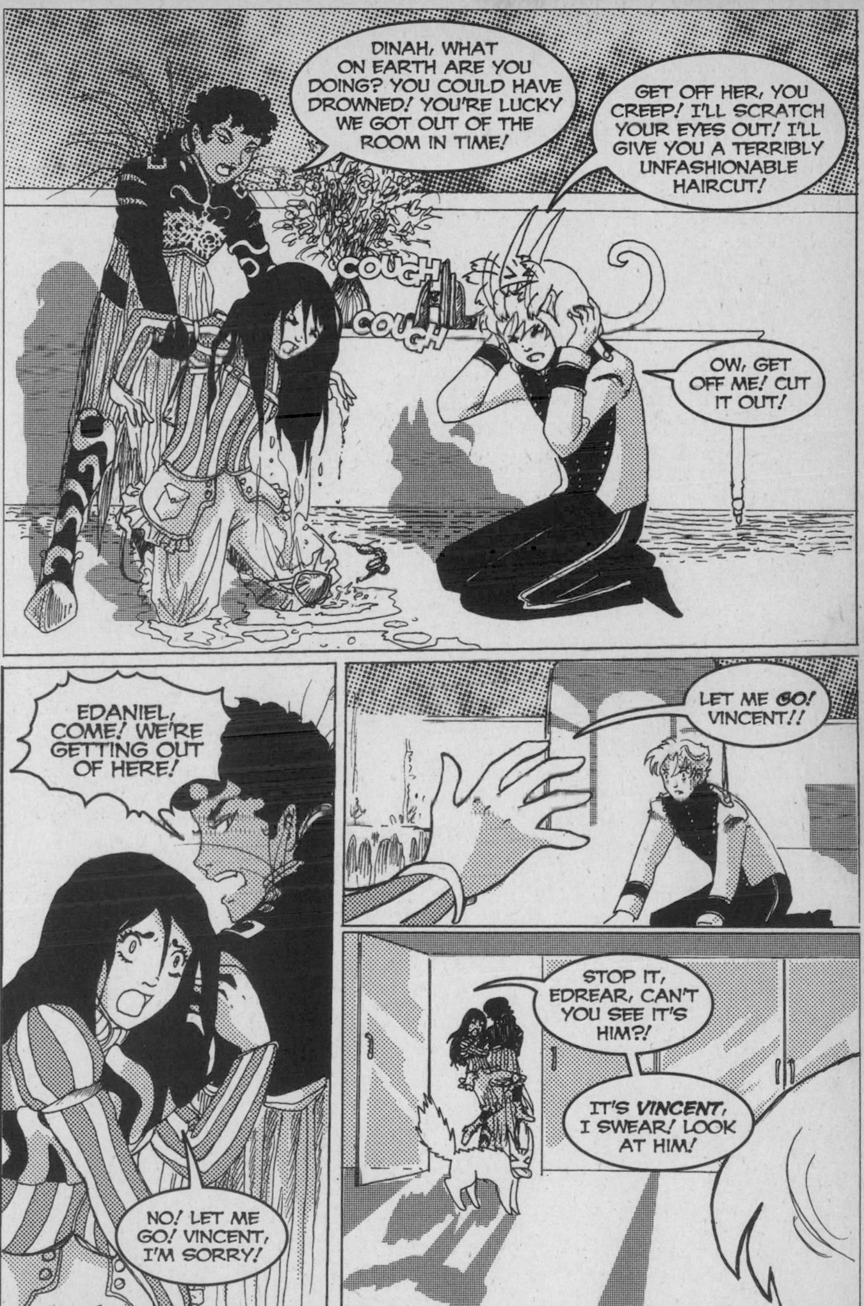
DINAH, WHAT ON EARTH ARE YOU DOING? YOU COULD HAVE DROWNED! YOU'RE LUCKY WE GOT OUT OF THE ROOM IN TIME!
GET OFF HER, YOU CREEP! I'LL SCRATCH YOUR EYES OUT! I'LL GIVE YOU A TERRIBLY UNFASHIONABLE HAIRCUT!
COUGH
COUGH
OW, GET OFF ME! CUT IT OUT!
EDANIEL, COME! WE'RE GETTING OUT OF HERE!
NO! LET ME GO! VINCENT, I'M SORRY!
LET ME *GO*! VINCENT!!
STOP IT, EDREAR, CAN'T YOU SEE IT'S HIM?!
IT'S ***VINCENT***, I SWEAR! LOOK AT HIM!

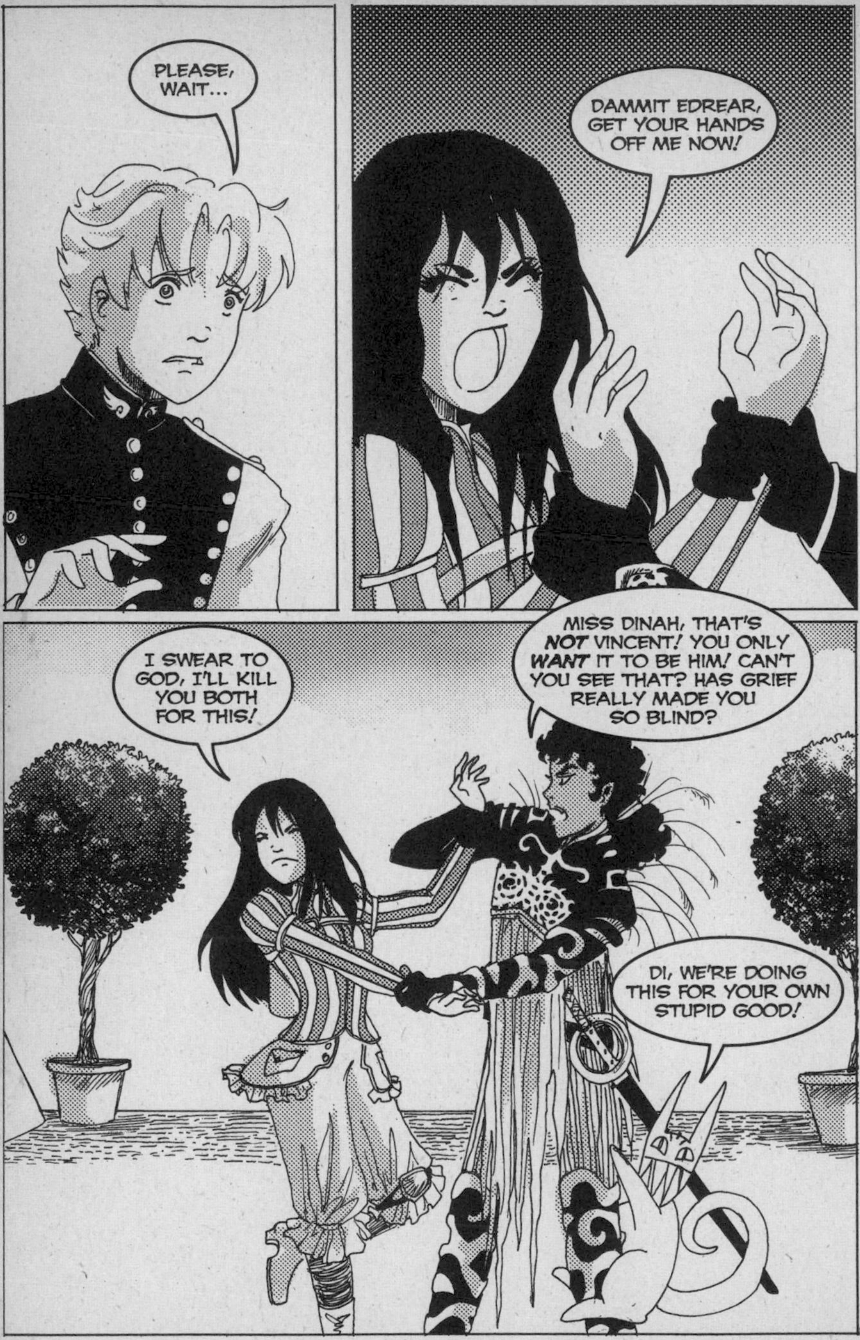
PLEASE, WAIT...
DAMMIT EDREAR, GET YOUR HANDS OFF ME NOW!
I SWEAR TO GOD, I'LL KILL YOU BOTH FOR THIS!
MISS DINAH, THAT'S NOT VINCENT! YOU ONLY WANT IT TO BE HIM! CAN'T YOU SEE THAT? HAS GRIEF REALLY MADE YOU SO BLIND?
DI, WE'RE DOING THIS FOR YOUR OWN STUPID GOOD!

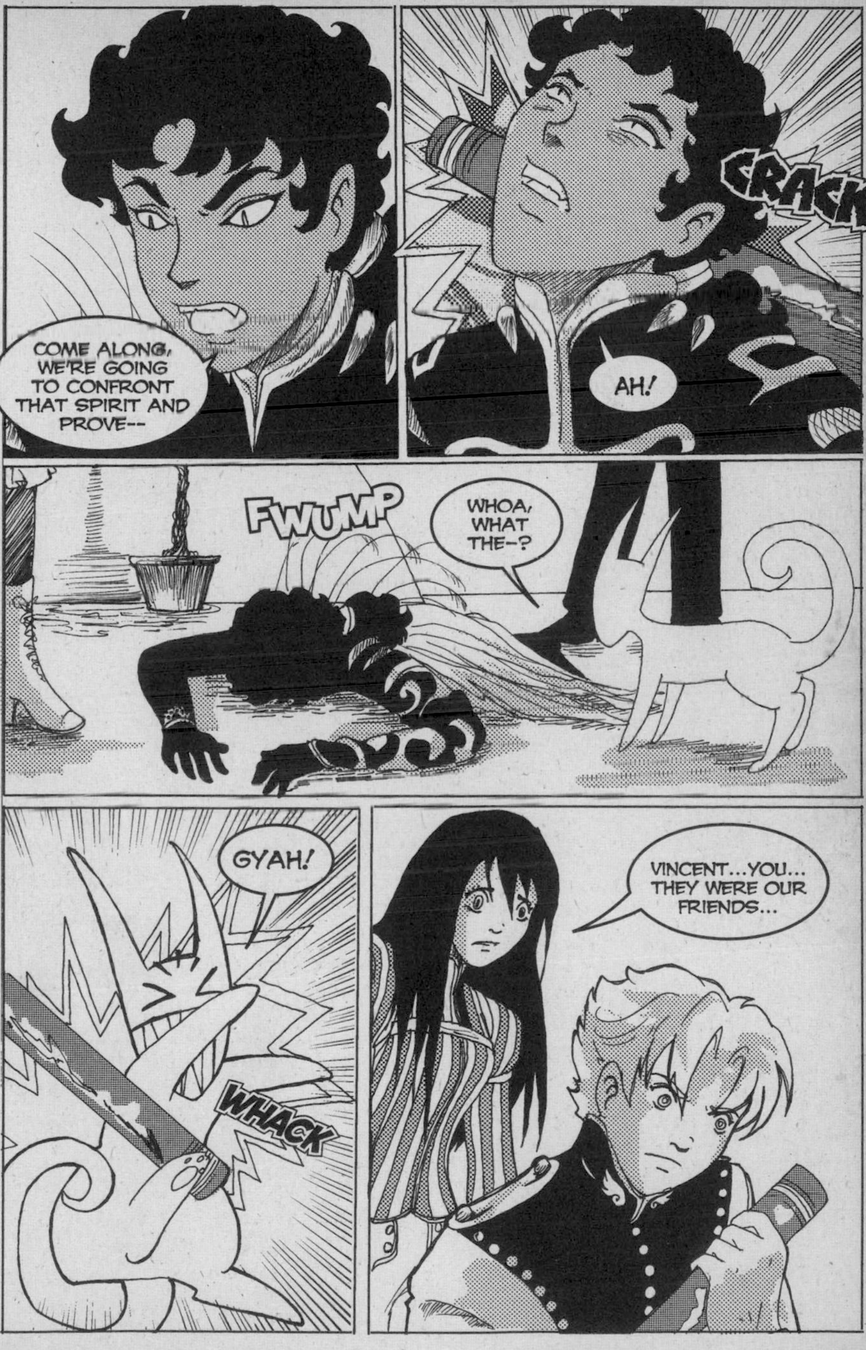
COME ALONG, WE'RE GOING TO CONFRONT THAT SPIRIT AND PROVE--
CRACK
AH!
FWUMP
WHOA, WHAT THE-?
GYAH!
WHACK
VINCENT...YOU... THEY WERE OUR FRIENDS...

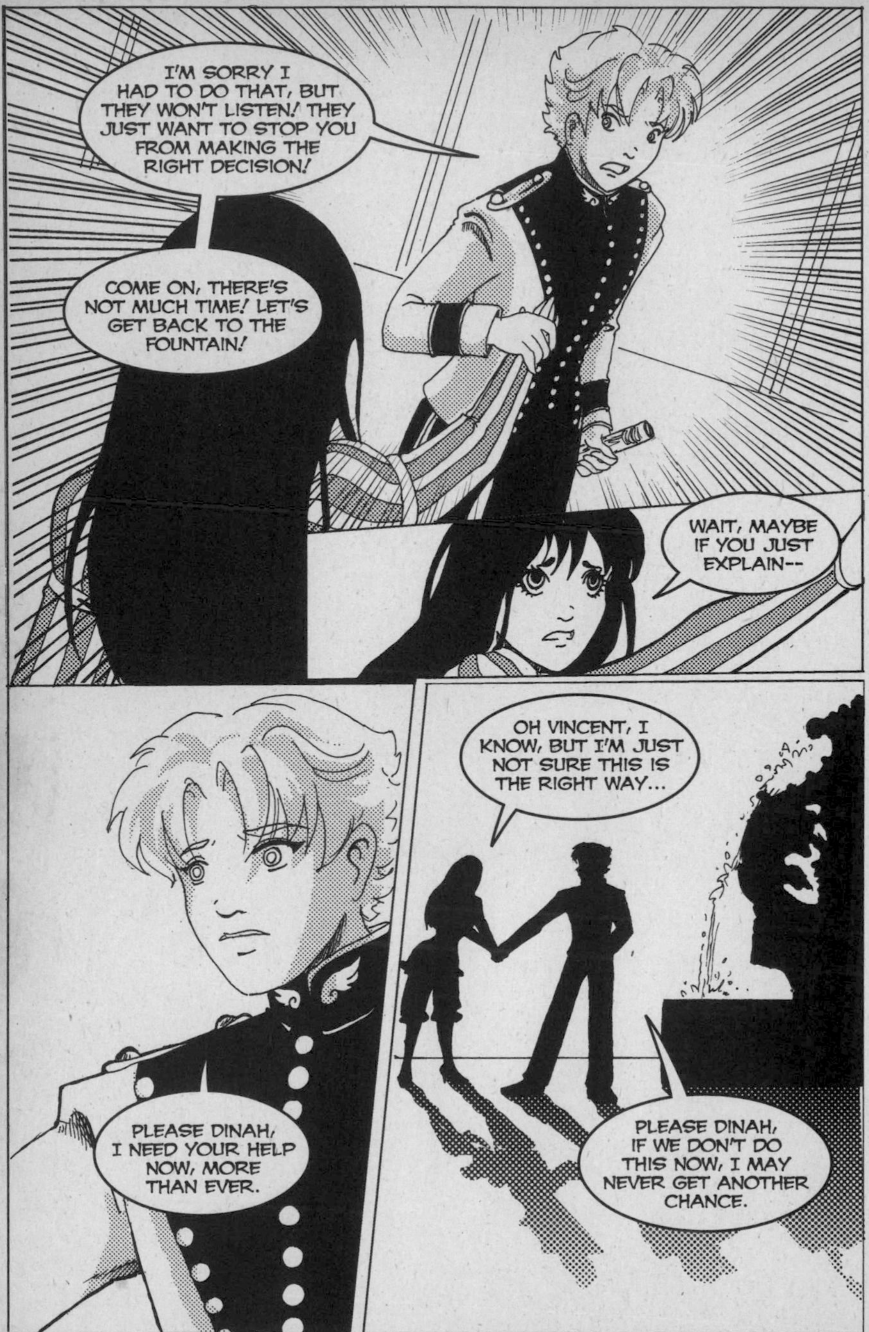
I'M SORRY I HAD TO DO THAT, BUT THEY WON'T LISTEN! THEY JUST WANT TO STOP YOU FROM MAKING THE RIGHT DECISION!
COME ON, THERE'S NOT MUCH TIME! LET'S GET BACK TO THE FOUNTAIN!
WAIT, MAYBE IF YOU JUST EXPLAIN--
PLEASE DINAH, I NEED YOUR HELP NOW, MORE THAN EVER.
OH VINCENT, I KNOW, BUT I'M JUST NOT SURE THIS IS THE RIGHT WAY...
PLEASE DINAH, IF WE DON'T DO THIS NOW, I MAY NEVER GET ANOTHER CHANCE.

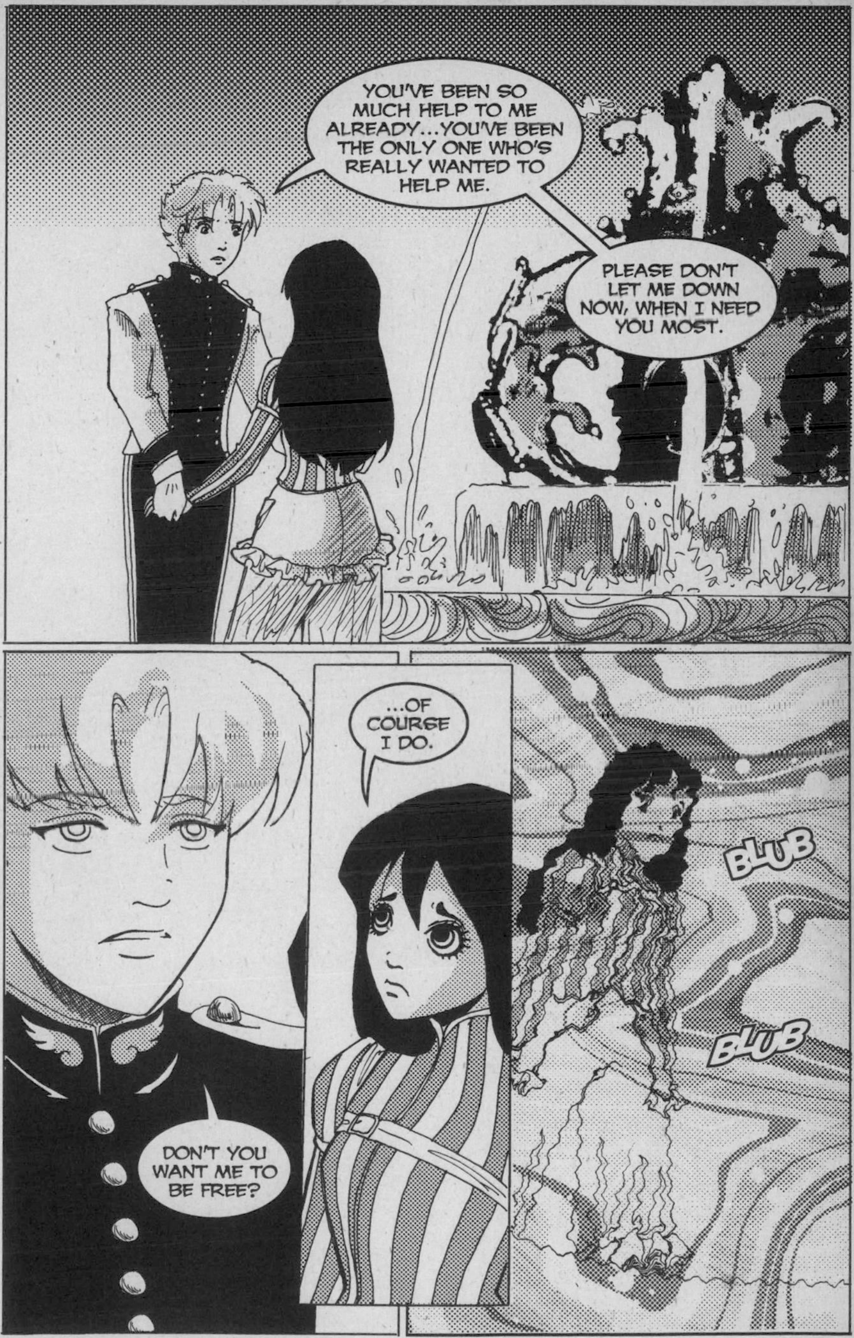
YOU'VE BEEN SO MUCH HELP TO ME ALREADY...YOU'VE BEEN THE ONLY ONE WHO'S REALLY WANTED TO HELP ME.
PLEASE DON'T LET ME DOWN NOW, WHEN I NEED YOU MOST.
DON'T YOU WANT ME TO BE FREE?
...OF COURSE I DO.
BLUB
BLUB

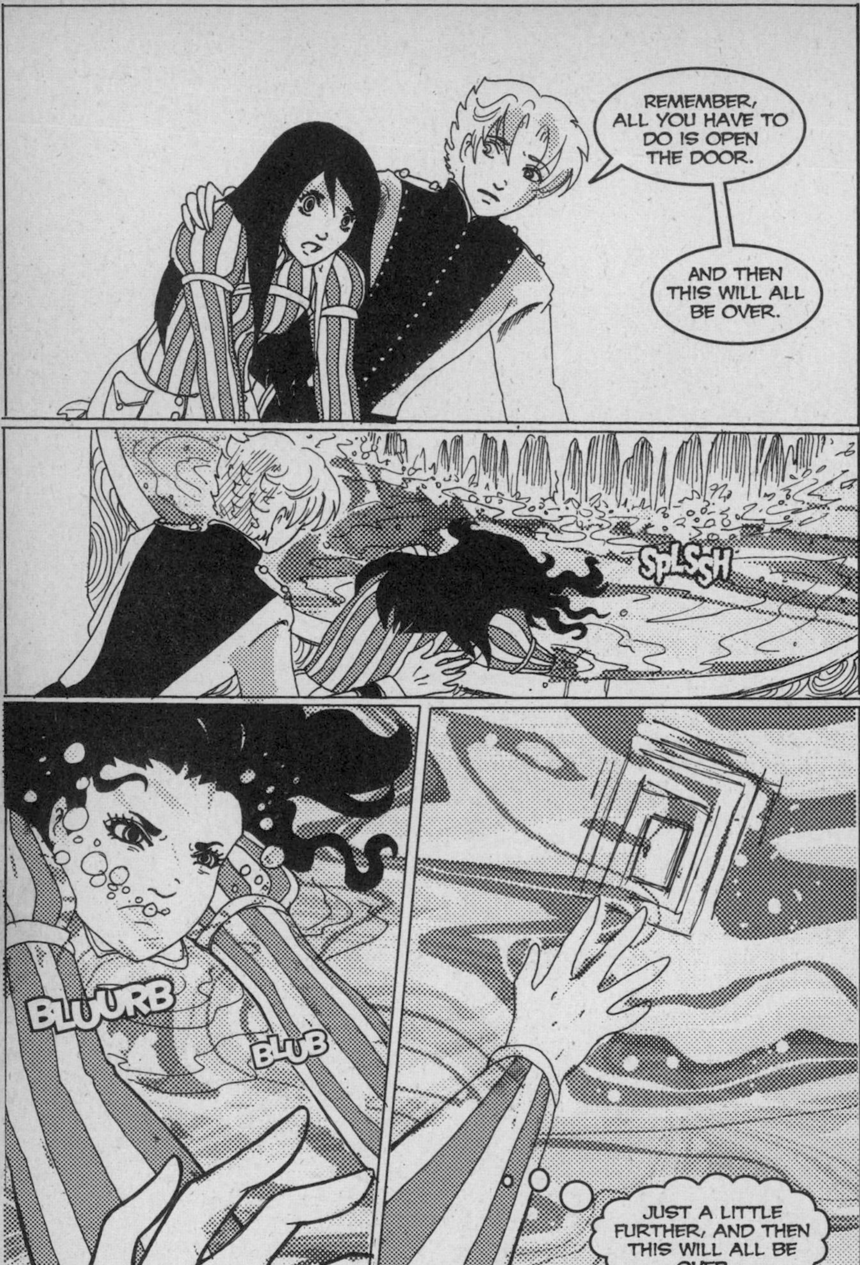
REMEMBER, ALL YOU HAVE TO DO IS OPEN THE DOOR.
AND THEN THIS WILL ALL BE OVER.
SPLSSH
BLUURB
BLUB
JUST A LITTLE FURTHER, AND THEN THIS WILL ALL BE OVER...

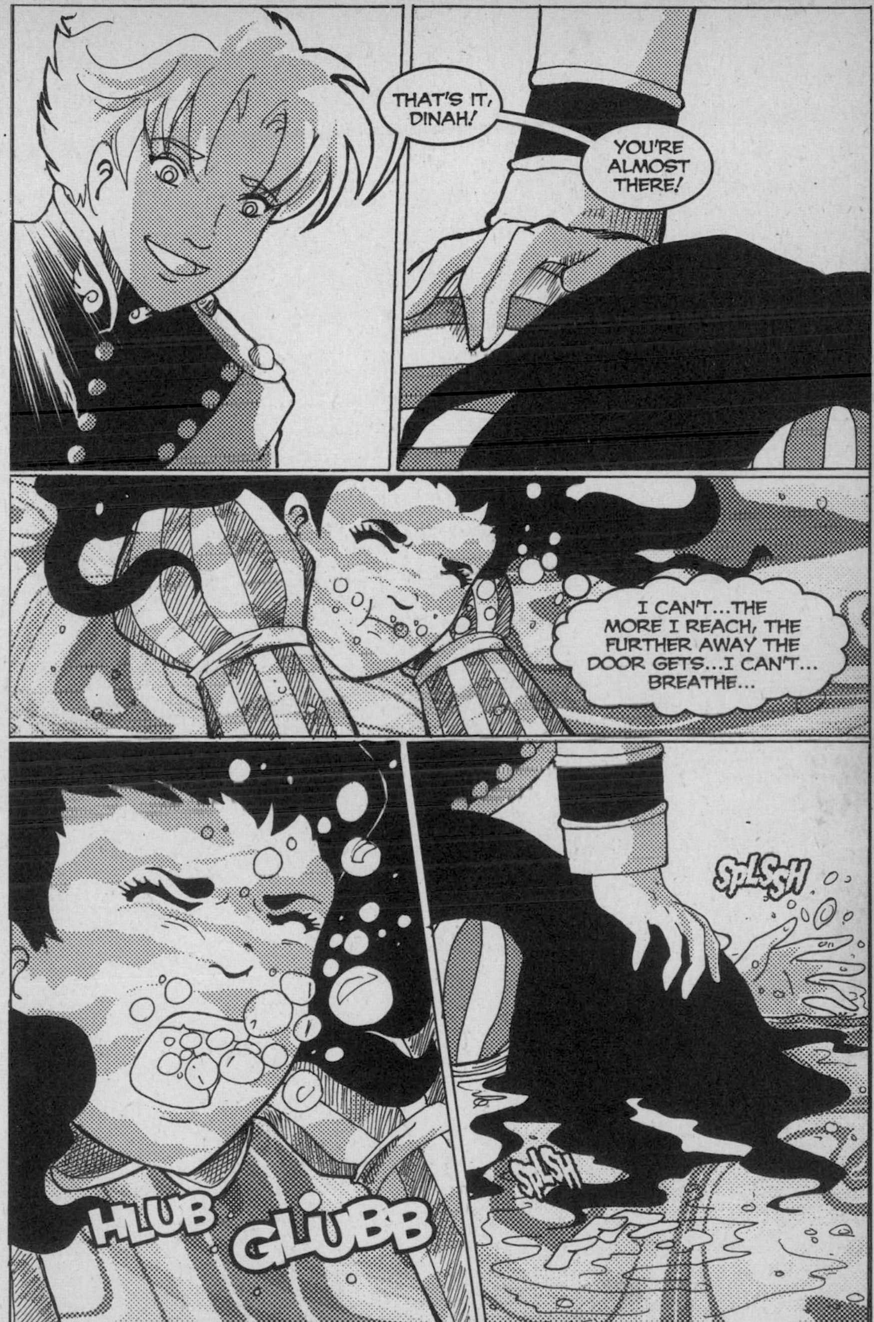
THAT'S IT, DINAH!
YOU'RE ALMOST THERE!
I CAN'T...THE MORE I REACH, THE FURTHER AWAY THE DOOR GETS...I CAN'T... BREATHE...
HLUB
GLUBB
SPLSSH
SPLSH

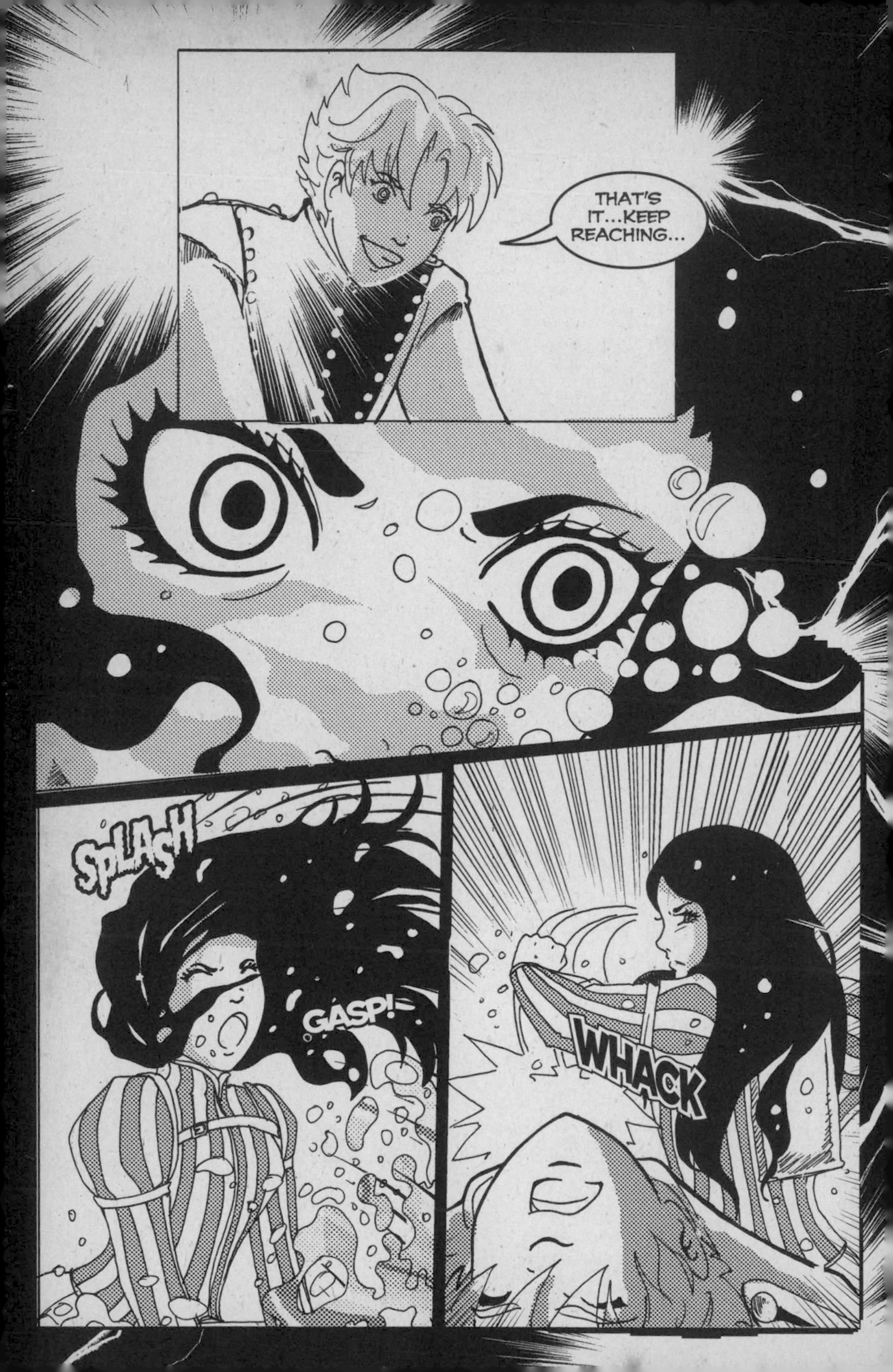
THAT'S IT...KEEP REACHING...
SPLASH
GASP!
WHACK

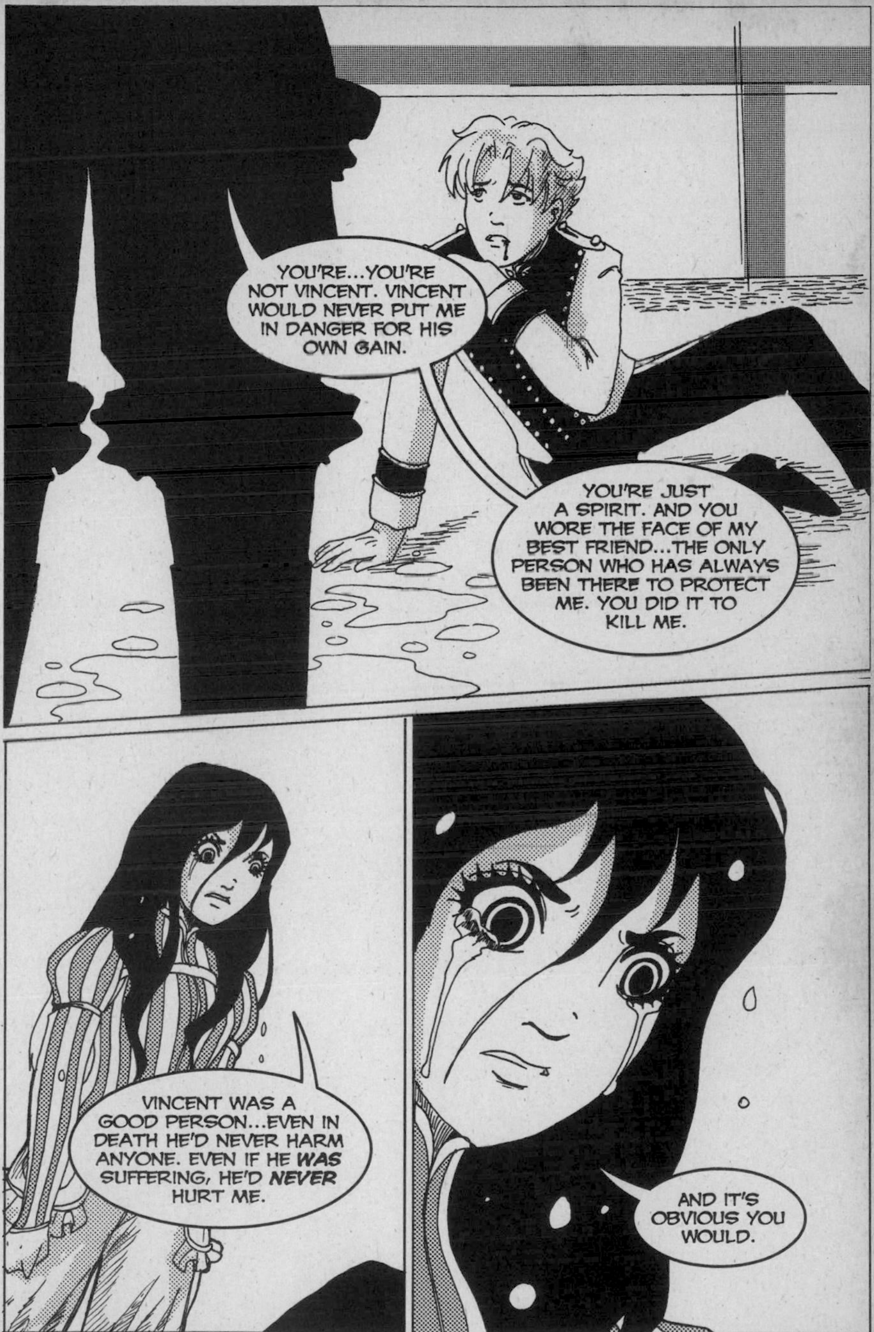
YOU'RE...YOU'RE NOT VINCENT. VINCENT WOULD NEVER PUT ME IN DANGER FOR HIS OWN GAIN.
YOU'RE JUST A SPIRIT. AND YOU WORE THE FACE OF MY BEST FRIEND...THE ONLY PERSON WHO HAS ALWAYS BEEN THERE TO PROTECT ME. YOU DID IT TO KILL ME.
VINCENT WAS A GOOD PERSON...EVEN IN DEATH HE'D NEVER HARM ANYONE. EVEN IF HE *WAS* SUFFERING, HE'D *NEVER* HURT ME.
AND IT'S OBVIOUS YOU WOULD.

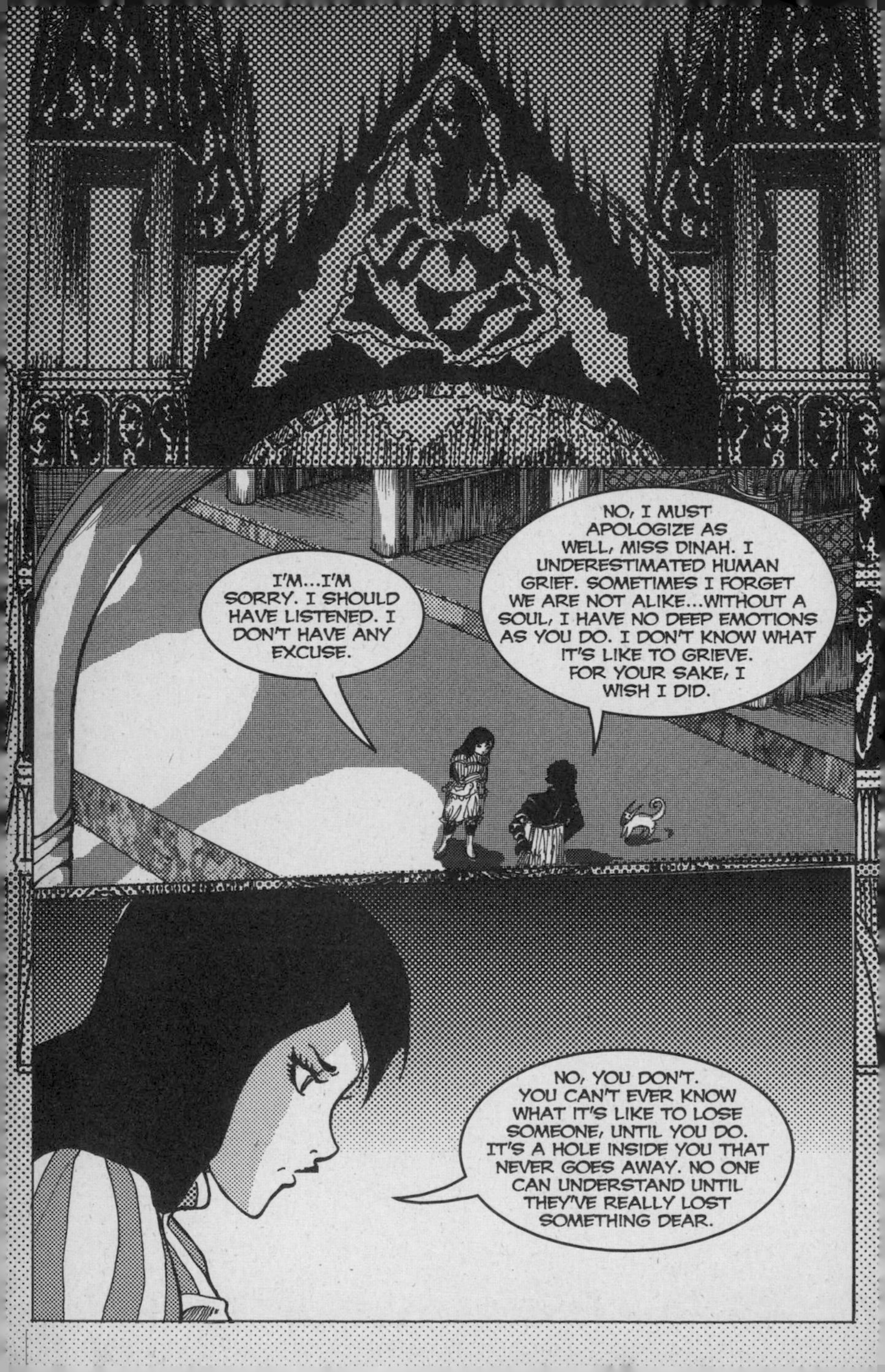
I'M...I'M SORRY. I SHOULD HAVE LISTENED. I DON'T HAVE ANY EXCUSE.
NO, I MUST APOLOGIZE AS WELL, MISS DINAH. I UNDERESTIMATED HUMAN GRIEF. SOMETIMES I FORGET WE ARE NOT ALIKE...WITHOUT A SOUL, I HAVE NO DEEP EMOTIONS AS YOU DO. I DON'T KNOW WHAT IT'S LIKE TO GRIEVE. FOR YOUR SAKE, I WISH I DID.
NO, YOU DON'T. YOU CAN'T EVER KNOW WHAT IT'S LIKE TO LOSE SOMEONE, UNTIL YOU DO. IT'S A HOLE INSIDE YOU THAT NEVER GOES AWAY. NO ONE CAN UNDERSTAND UNTIL THEY'VE REALLY LOST SOMETHING DEAR.

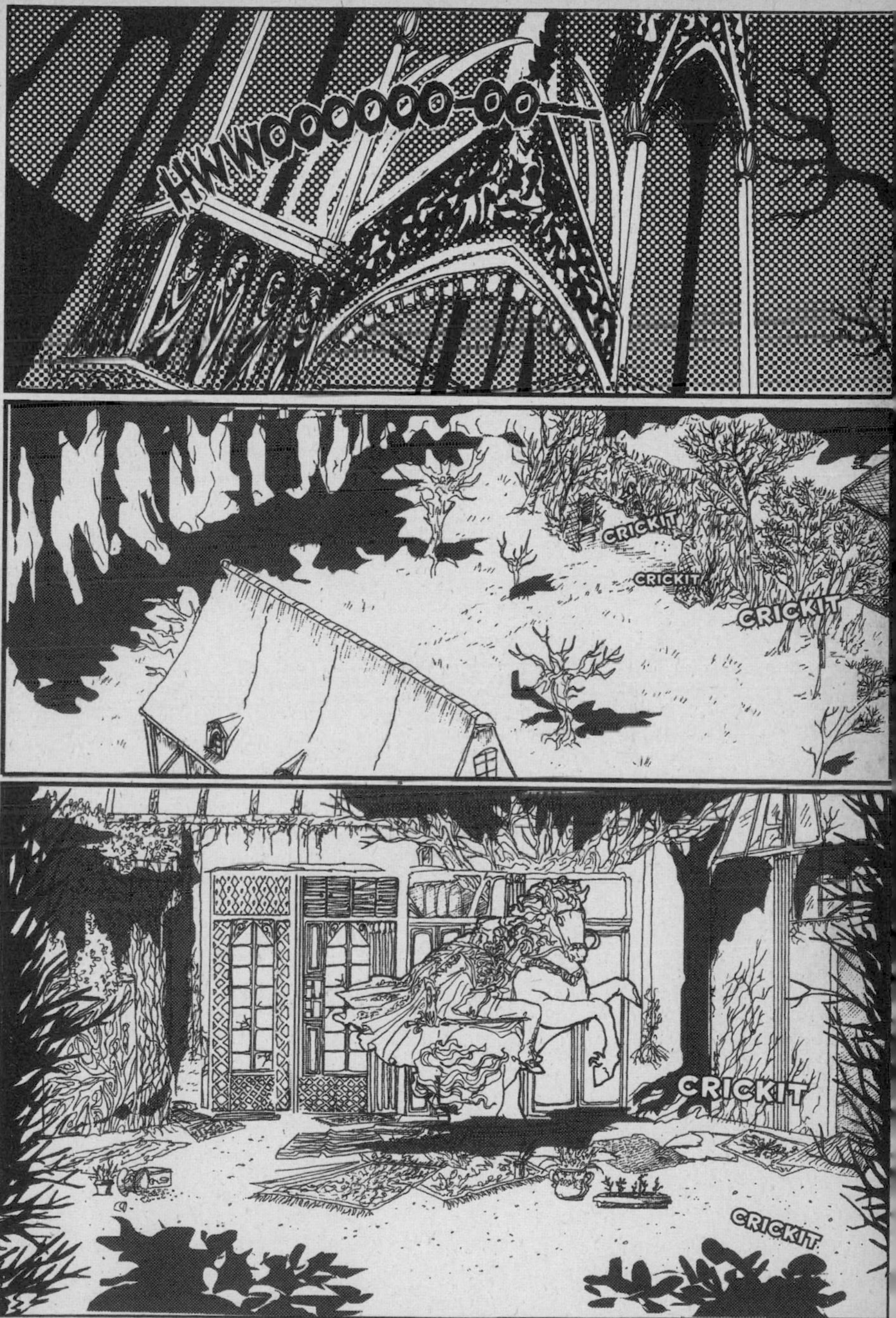
HWWOOOOOO-OO
CRICKIT
CRICKIT
CRICKIT
CRICKIT
CRICKIT

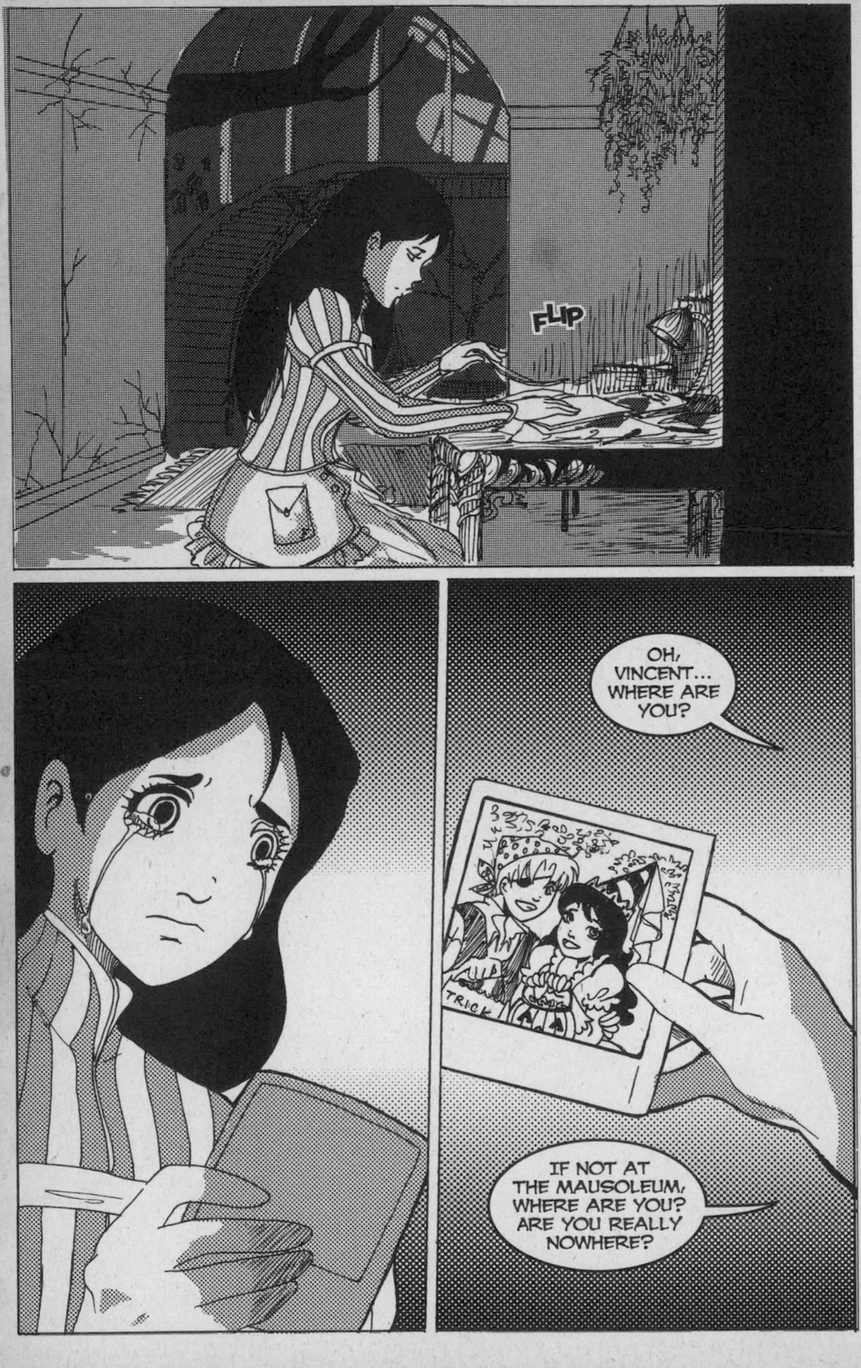
FLIP
OH, VINCENT... WHERE ARE YOU?
TRICK
IF NOT AT THE MAUSOLEUM, WHERE ARE YOU? ARE YOU REALLY NOWHERE?

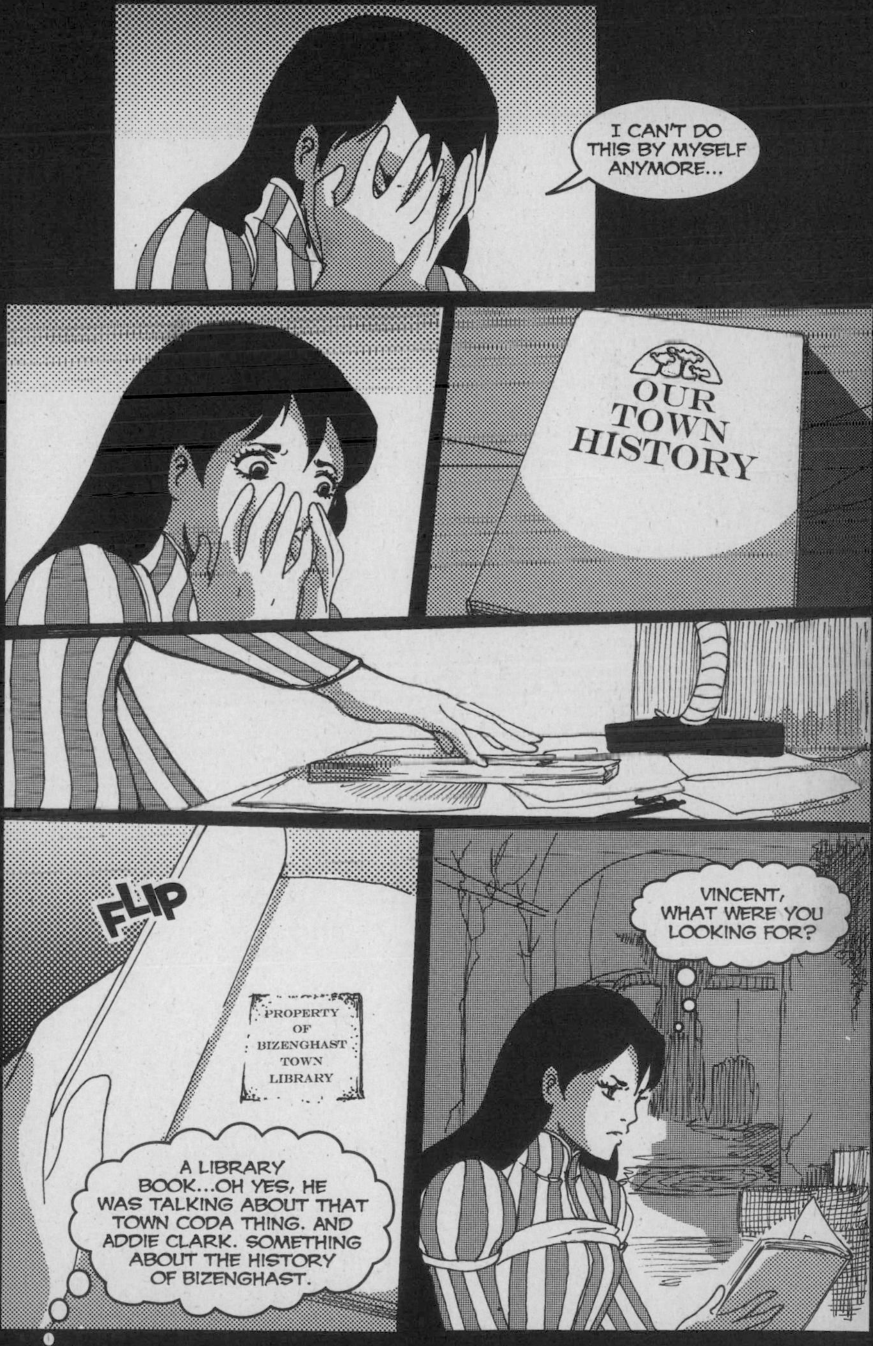
I CAN'T DO THIS BY MYSELF ANYMORE...
OUR TOWN HISTORY
FLIP
PROPERTY OF BIZENGHAST TOWN LIBRARY
A LIBRARY BOOK...OH YES, HE WAS TALKING ABOUT THAT TOWN CODA THING. AND ADDIE CLARK. SOMETHING ABOUT THE HISTORY OF BIZENGHAST.
VINCENT, WHAT WERE YOU LOOKING FOR?

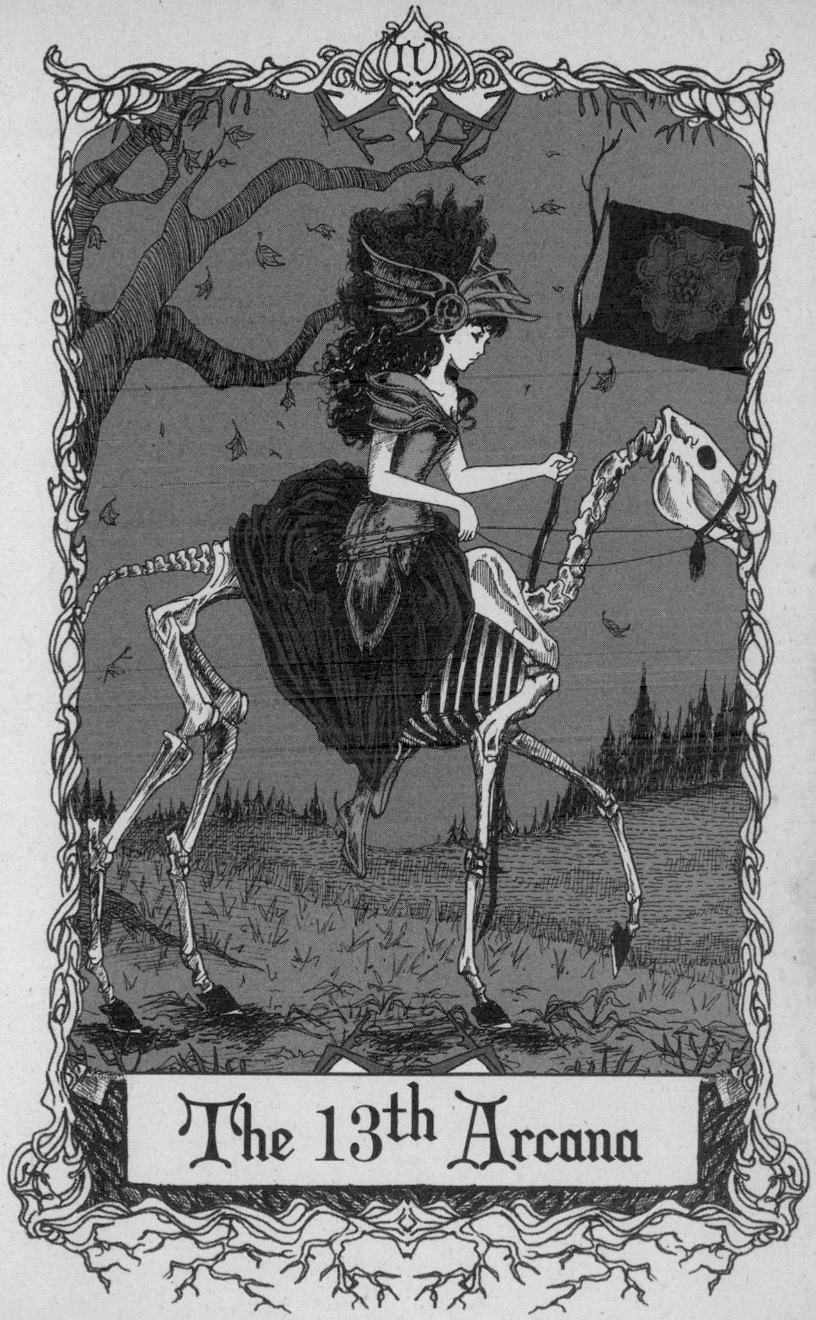
IV
The 13th Arcana

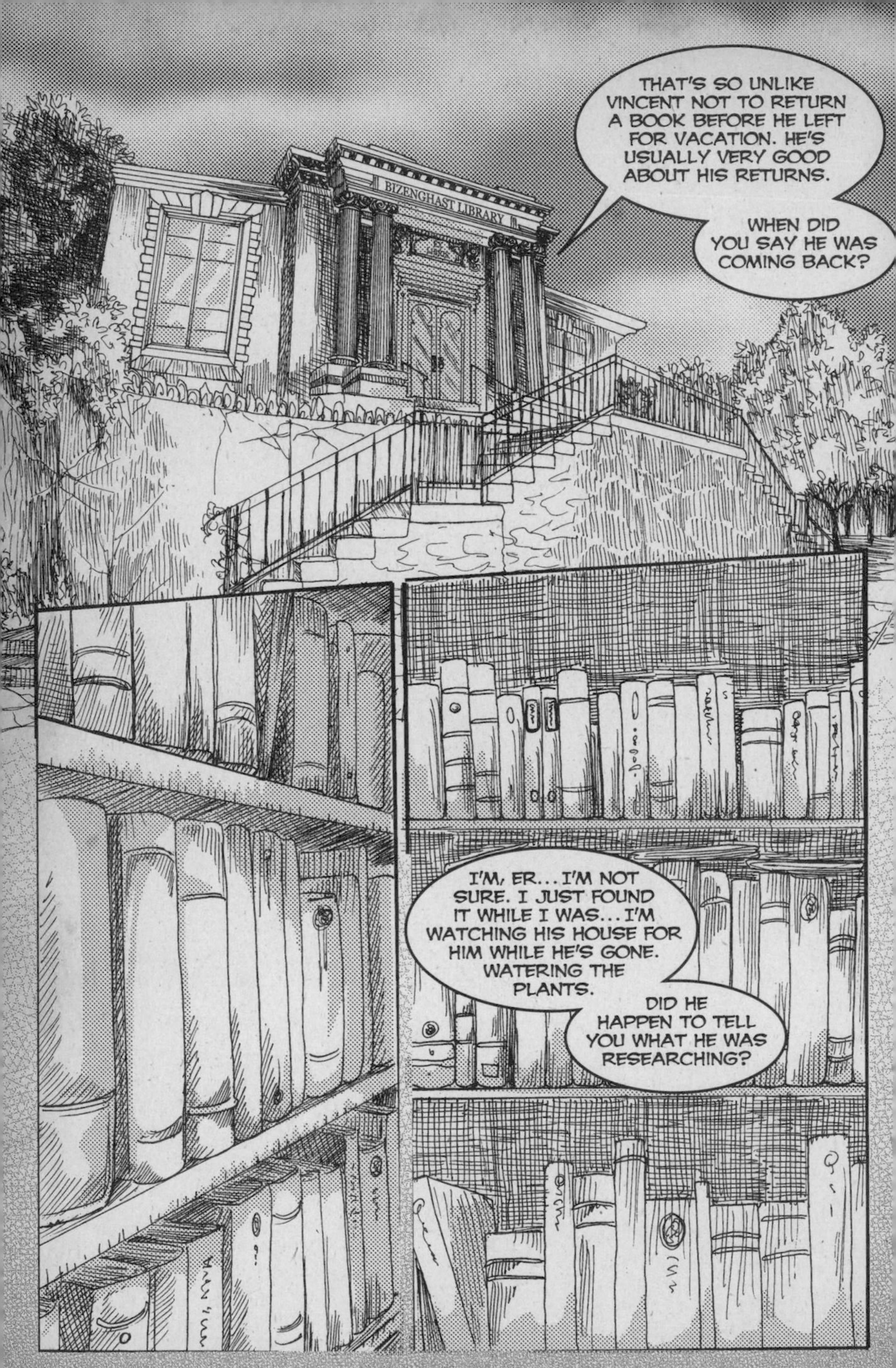
BIZENGHAST LIBRARY
THAT'S SO UNLIKE VINCENT NOT TO RETURN A BOOK BEFORE HE LEFT FOR VACATION. HE'S USUALLY VERY GOOD ABOUT HIS RETURNS.
WHEN DID YOU SAY HE WAS COMING BACK?
I'M, ER... I'M NOT SURE. I JUST FOUND IT WHILE I WAS... I'M WATCHING HIS HOUSE FOR HIM WHILE HE'S GONE. WATERING THE PLANTS.
DID HE HAPPEN TO TELL YOU WHAT HE WAS RESEARCHING?

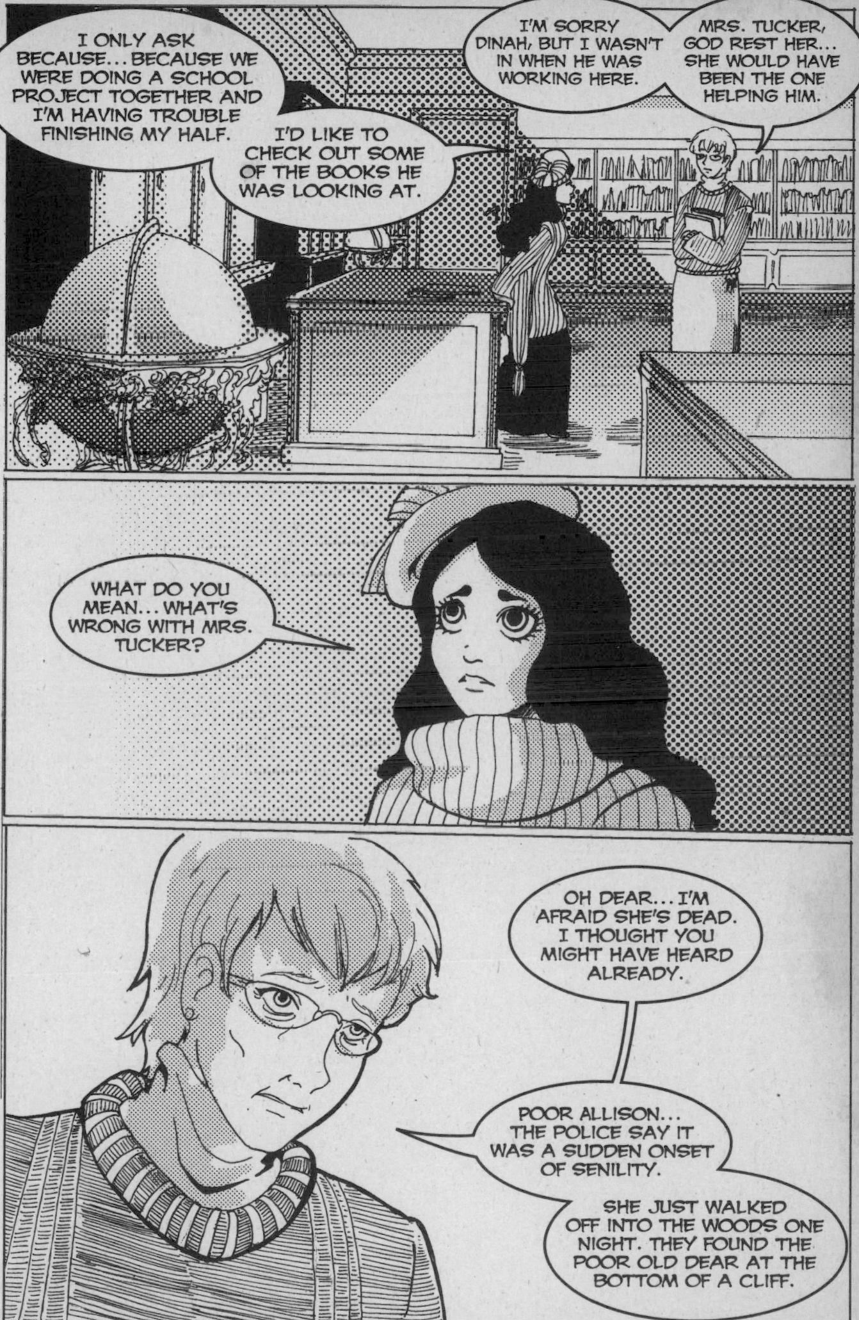
I ONLY ASK BECAUSE... BECAUSE WE WERE DOING A SCHOOL PROJECT TOGETHER AND I'M HAVING TROUBLE FINISHING MY HALF.
I'D LIKE TO CHECK OUT SOME OF THE BOOKS HE WAS LOOKING AT.
I'M SORRY DINAH, BUT I WASN'T IN WHEN HE WAS WORKING HERE.
MRS. TUCKER, GOD REST HER... SHE WOULD HAVE BEEN THE ONE HELPING HIM.
WHAT DO YOU MEAN... WHAT'S WRONG WITH MRS. TUCKER?
OH DEAR... I'M AFRAID SHE'S DEAD. I THOUGHT YOU MIGHT HAVE HEARD ALREADY.
POOR ALLISON... THE POLICE SAY IT WAS A SUDDEN ONSET OF SENILITY.
SHE JUST WALKED OFF INTO THE WOODS ONE NIGHT. THEY FOUND THE POOR OLD DEAR AT THE BOTTOM OF A CLIFF.

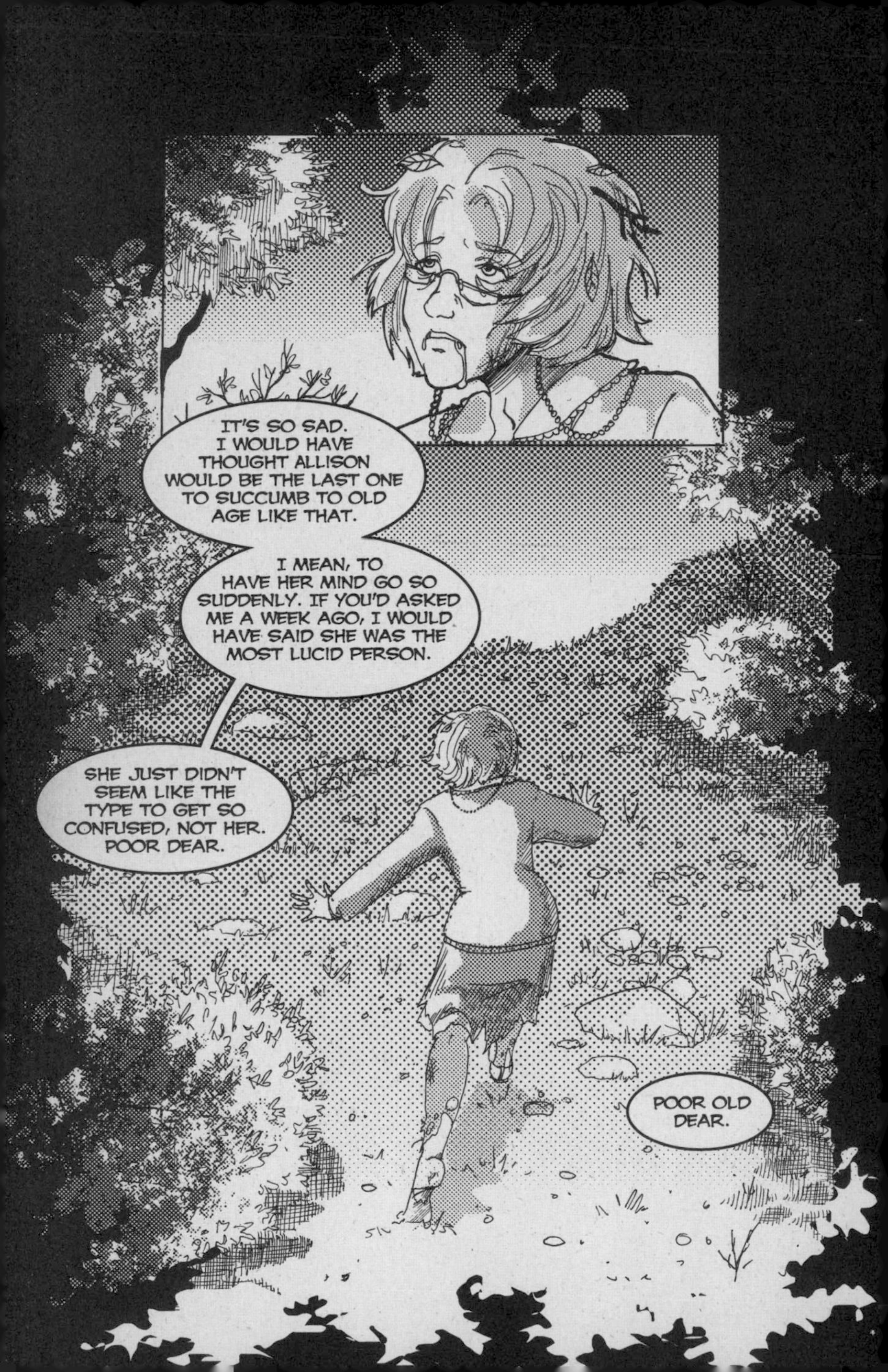
IT'S SO SAD. I WOULD HAVE THOUGHT ALLISON WOULD BE THE LAST ONE TO SUCCUMB TO OLD AGE LIKE THAT.
I MEAN, TO HAVE HER MIND GO SO SUDDENLY. IF YOU'D ASKED ME A WEEK AGO, I WOULD HAVE SAID SHE WAS THE MOST LUCID PERSON.
SHE JUST DIDN'T SEEM LIKE THE TYPE TO GET SO CONFUSED, NOT HER. POOR DEAR.
POOR OLD DEAR.

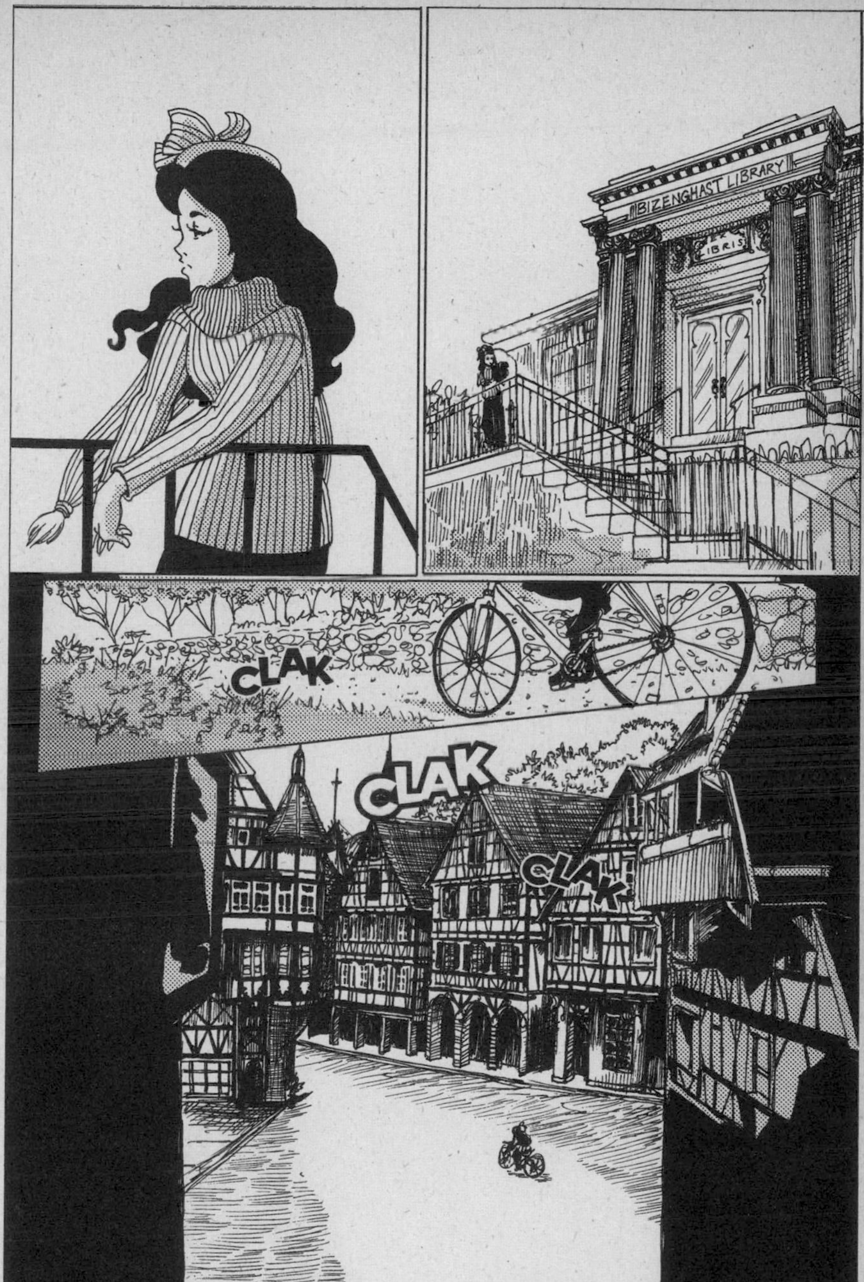
BIZENGHAST LIBRARY
LIBRIS
CLAK
CLAK
CLAK

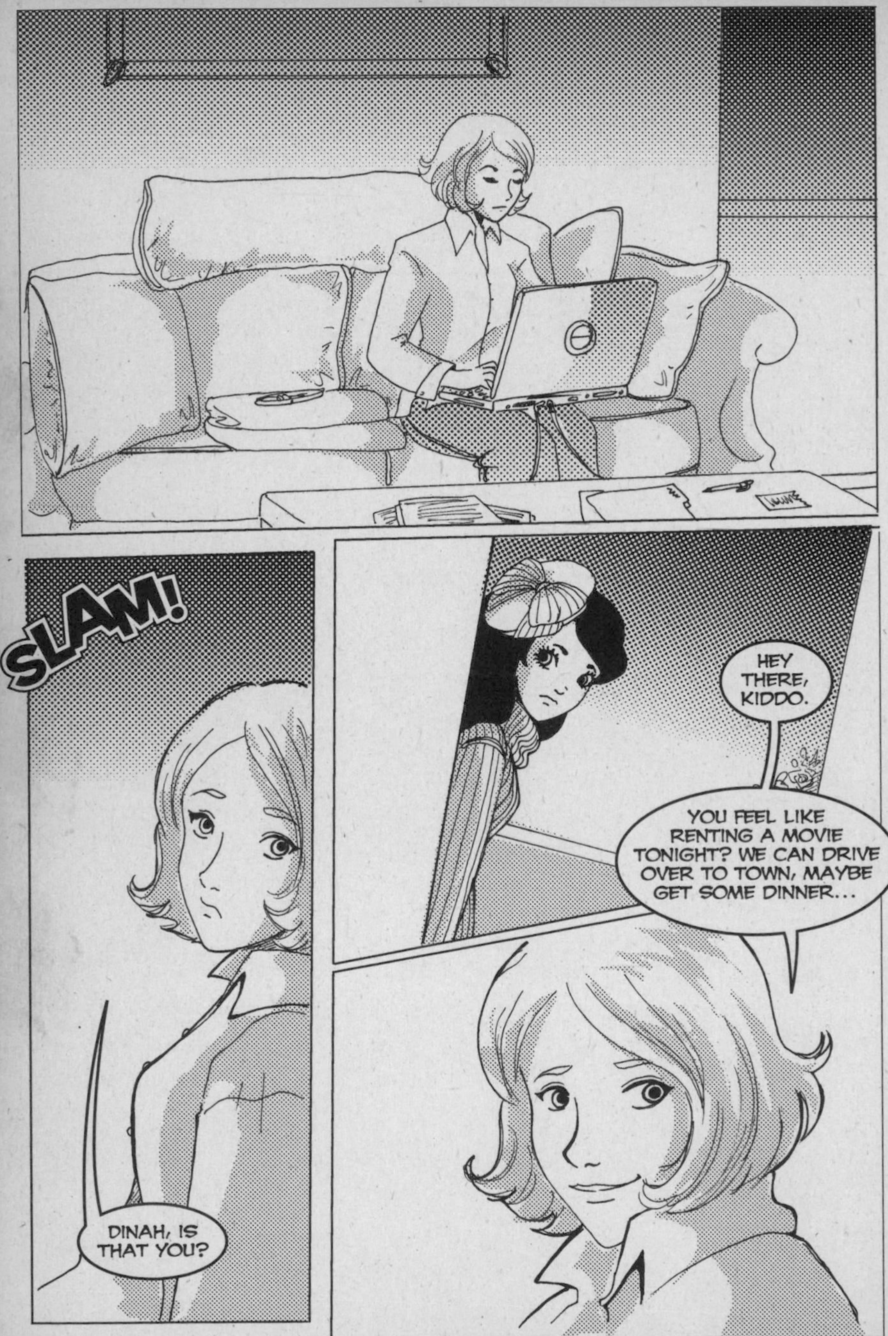
SLAM!
DINAH, IS THAT YOU?
HEY THERE, KIDDO.
YOU FEEL LIKE RENTING A MOVIE TONIGHT? WE CAN DRIVE OVER TO TOWN, MAYBE GET SOME DINNER...

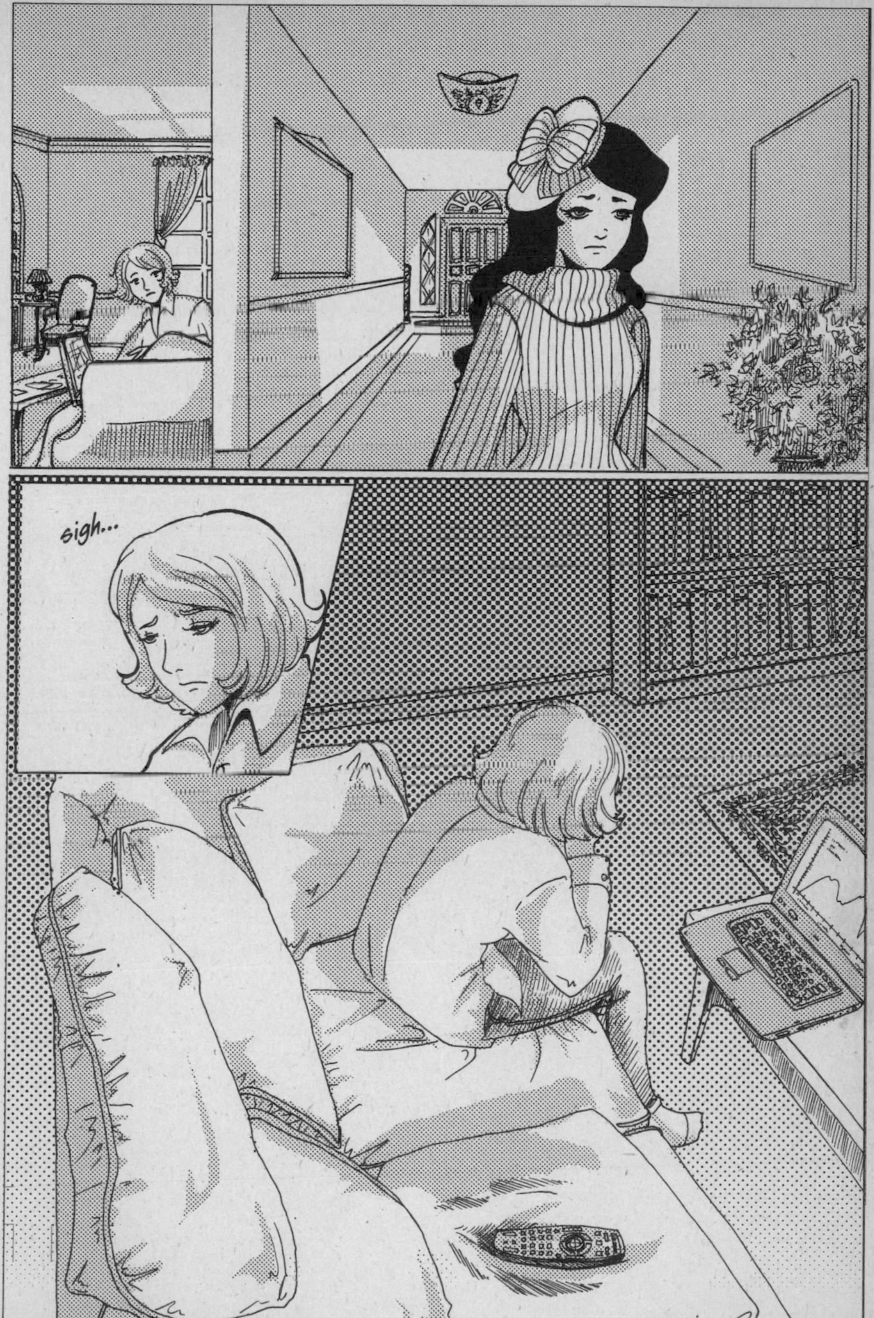
sigh...

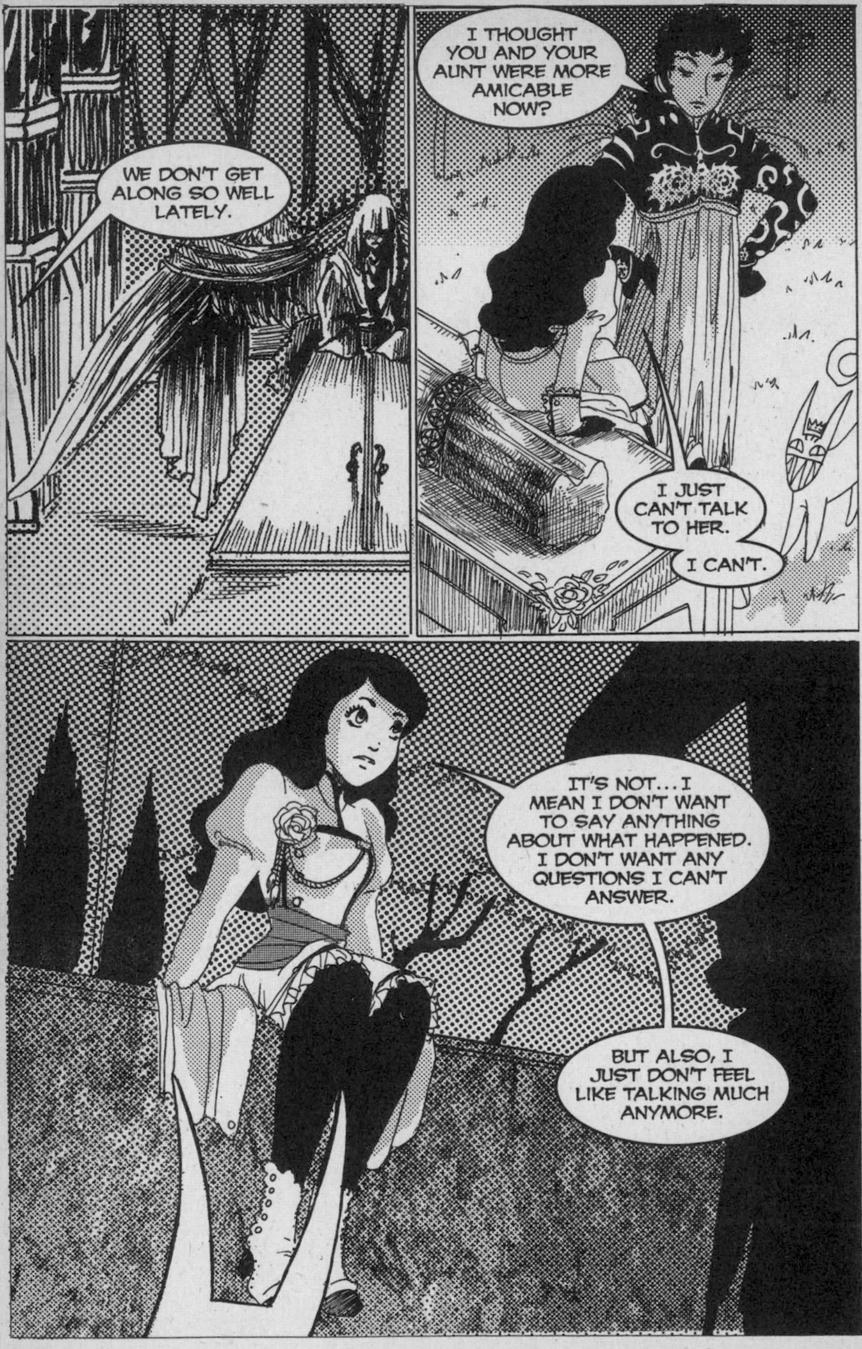
WE DON'T GET ALONG SO WELL LATELY.
I THOUGHT YOU AND YOUR AUNT WERE MORE AMICABLE NOW?
I JUST CAN'T TALK TO HER.
I CAN'T.
IT'S NOT... I MEAN I DON'T WANT TO SAY ANYTHING ABOUT WHAT HAPPENED. I DON'T WANT ANY QUESTIONS I CAN'T ANSWER.
BUT ALSO, I JUST DON'T FEEL LIKE TALKING MUCH ANYMORE.

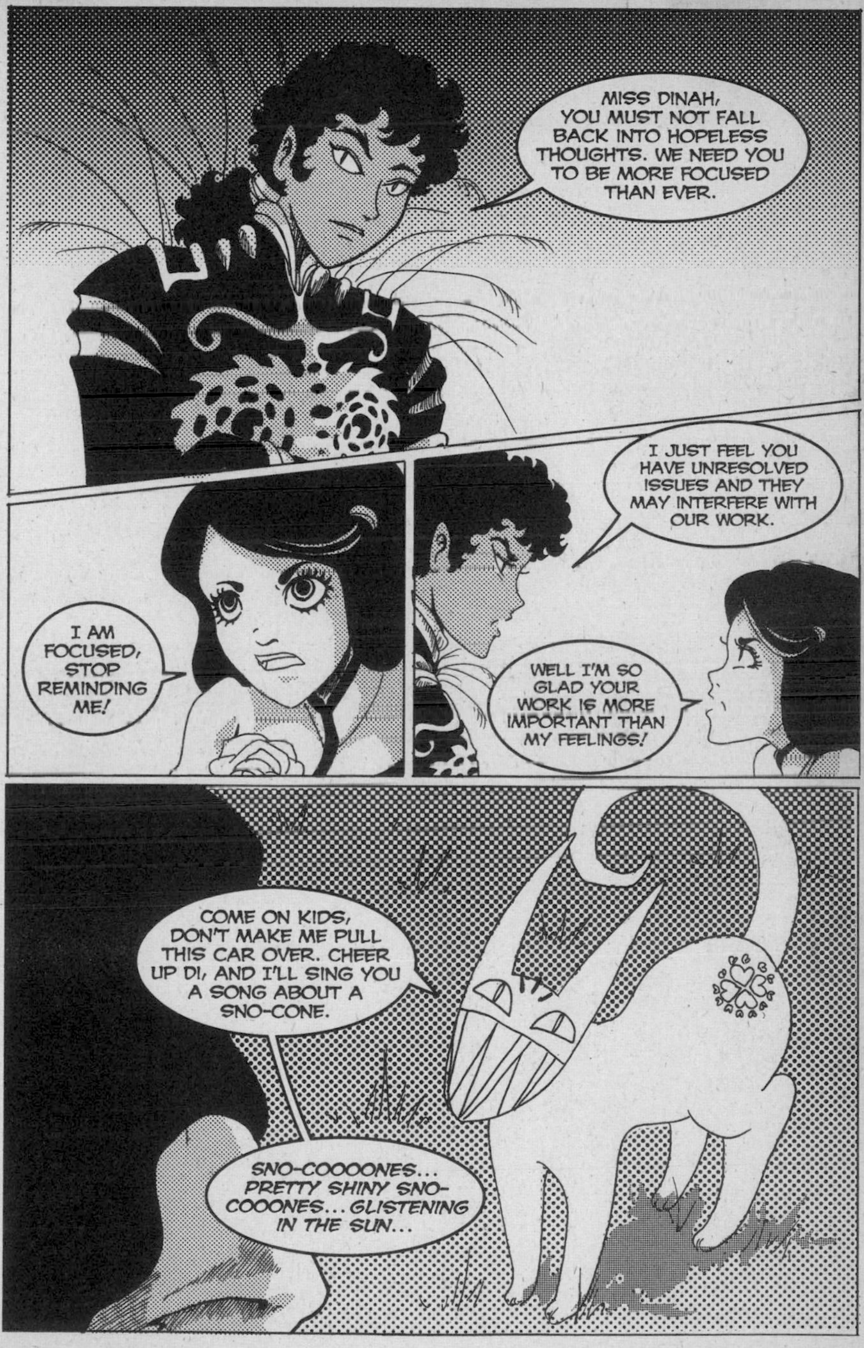
MISS DINAH, YOU MUST NOT FALL BACK INTO HOPELESS THOUGHTS. WE NEED YOU TO BE MORE FOCUSED THAN EVER.
I AM FOCUSED, STOP REMINDING ME!
I JUST FEEL YOU HAVE UNRESOLVED ISSUES AND THEY MAY INTERFERE WITH OUR WORK.
WELL I'M SO GLAD YOUR WORK IS MORE IMPORTANT THAN MY FEELINGS!
COME ON KIDS, DON'T MAKE ME PULL THIS CAR OVER. CHEER UP DI, AND I'LL SING YOU A SONG ABOUT A SNO-CONE.
SNO-COOOONES... PRETTY SHINY SNO-COOONES... GLISTENING IN THE SUN...

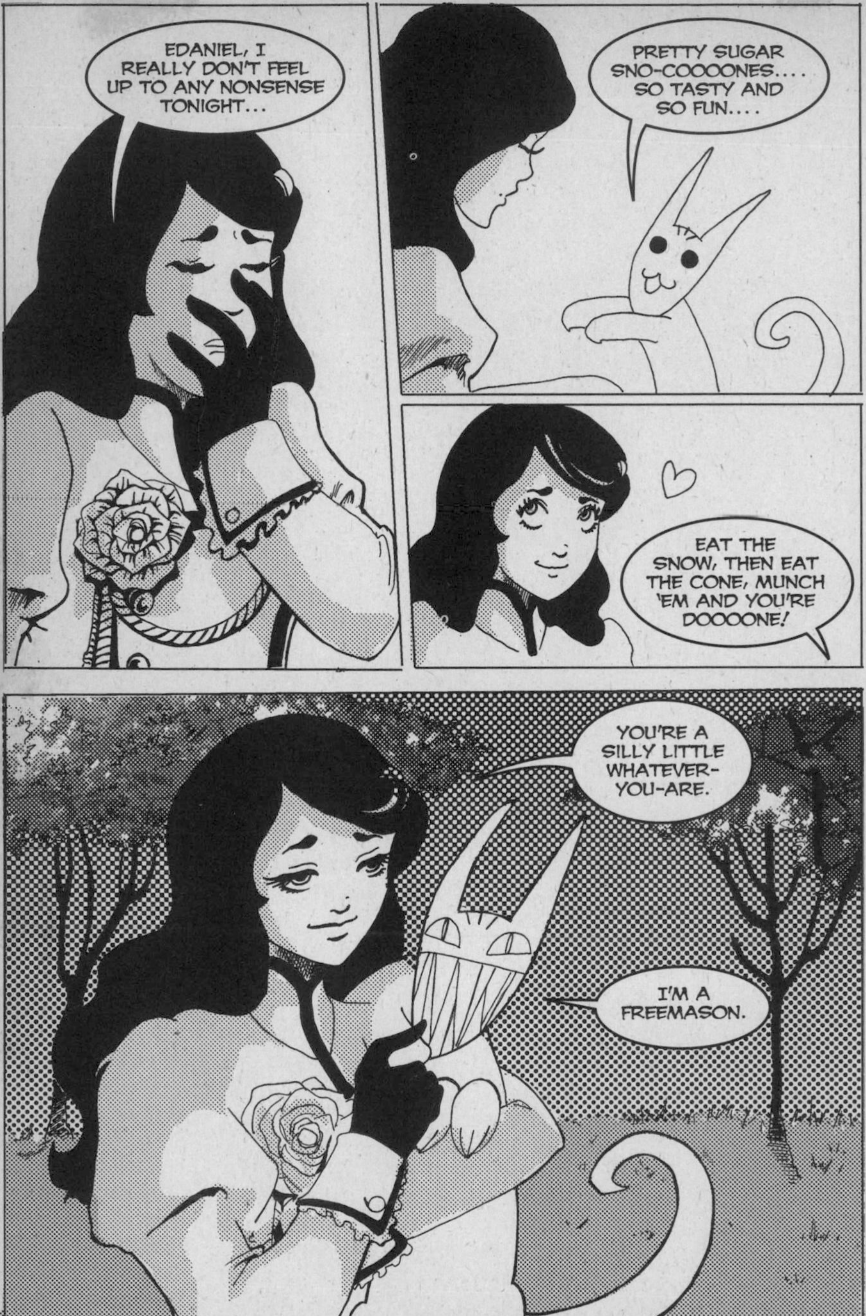
EDANIEL, I REALLY DON'T FEEL UP TO ANY NONSENSE TONIGHT...
PRETTY SUGAR SNO-COOOONES.... SO TASTY AND SO FUN....
EAT THE SNOW, THEN EAT THE CONE, MUNCH 'EM AND YOU'RE DOOOONE!
YOU'RE A SILLY LITTLE WHATEVER-YOU-ARE.
I'M A FREEMASON.

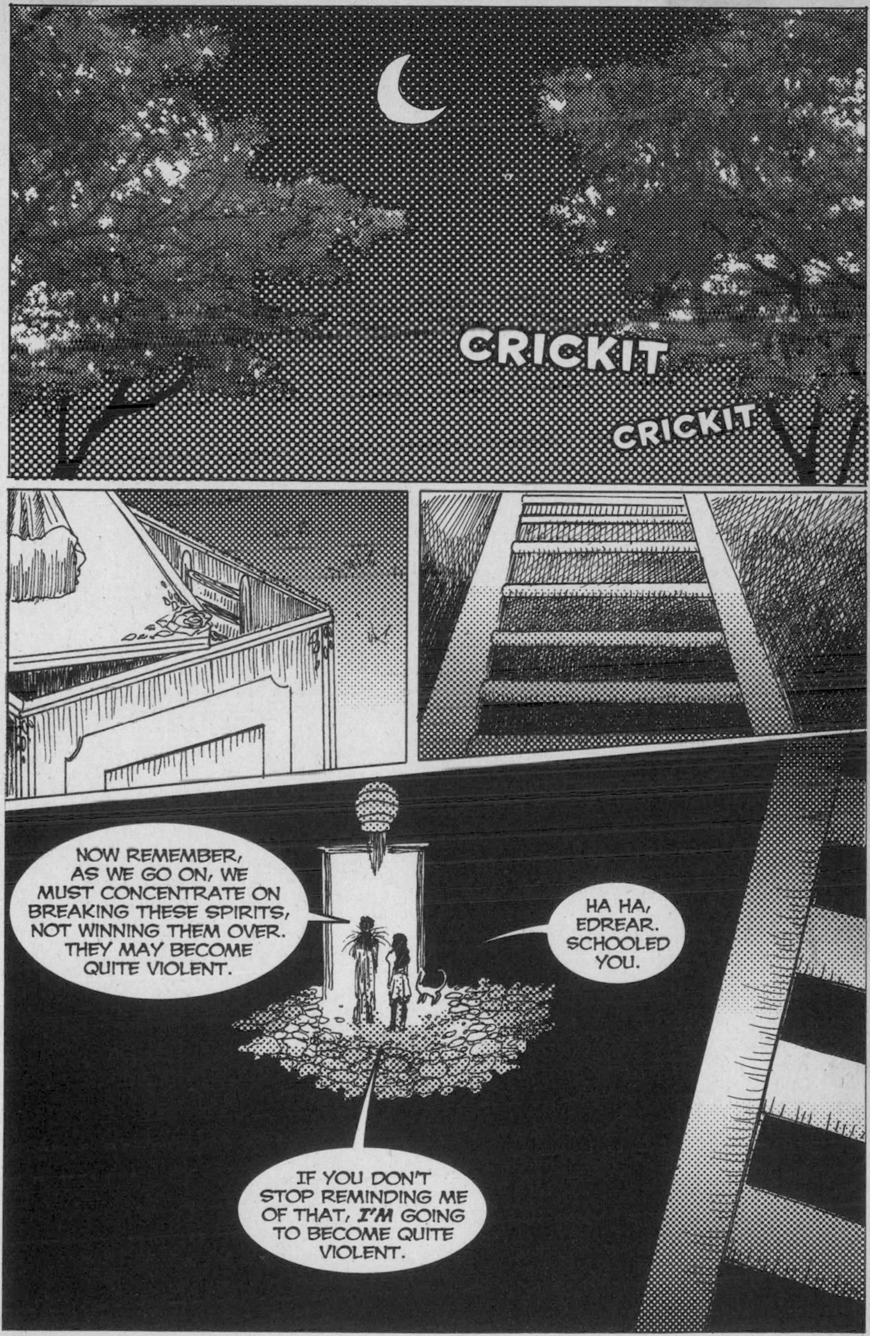
CRICKIT
CRICKIT
NOW REMEMBER, AS WE GO ON, WE MUST CONCENTRATE ON BREAKING THESE SPIRITS, NOT WINNING THEM OVER. THEY MAY BECOME QUITE VIOLENT.
HA HA, EDREAR. SCHOOLED YOU.
IF YOU DON'T STOP REMINDING ME OF THAT, *I'M* GOING TO BECOME QUITE VIOLENT.

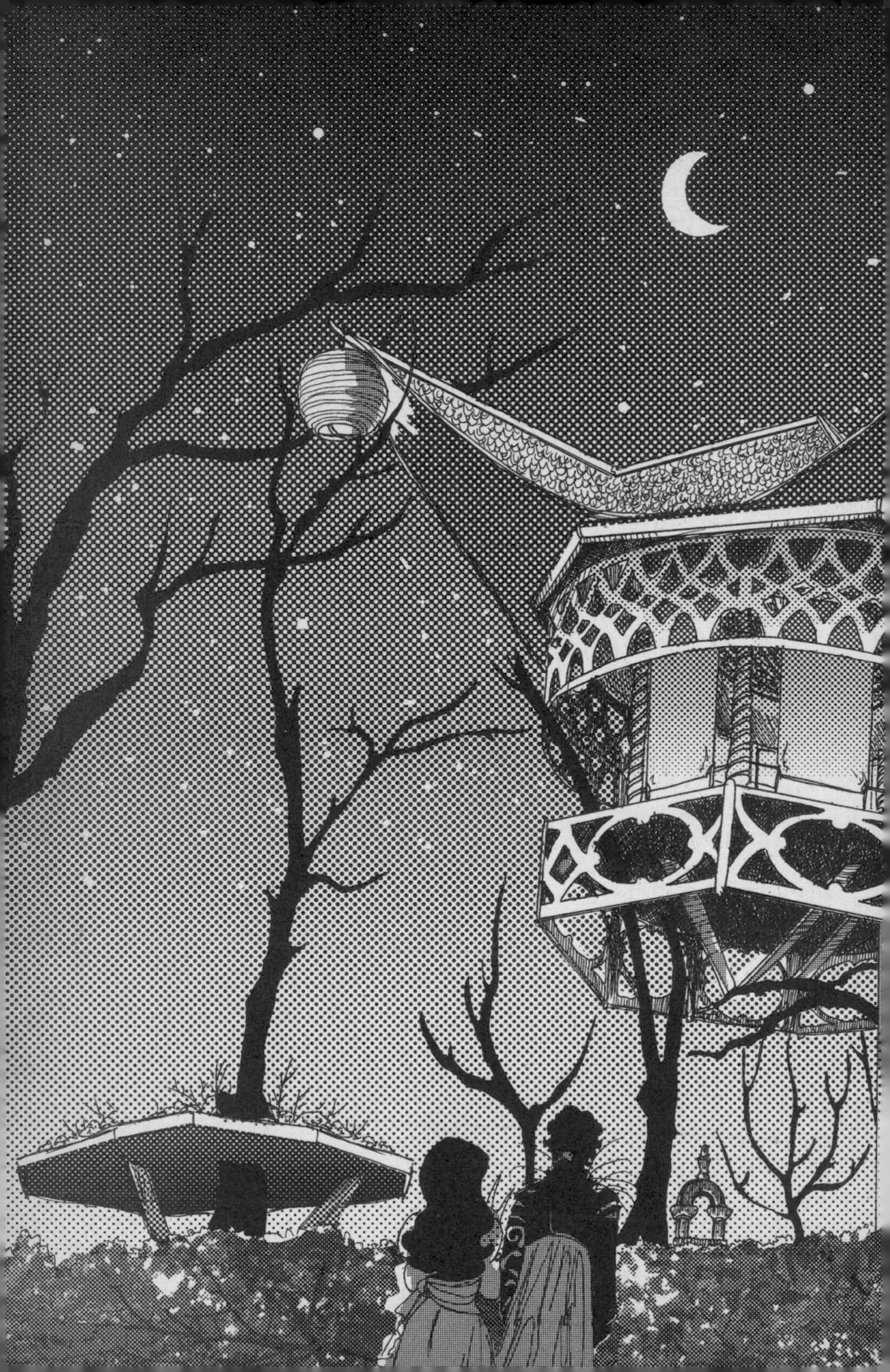

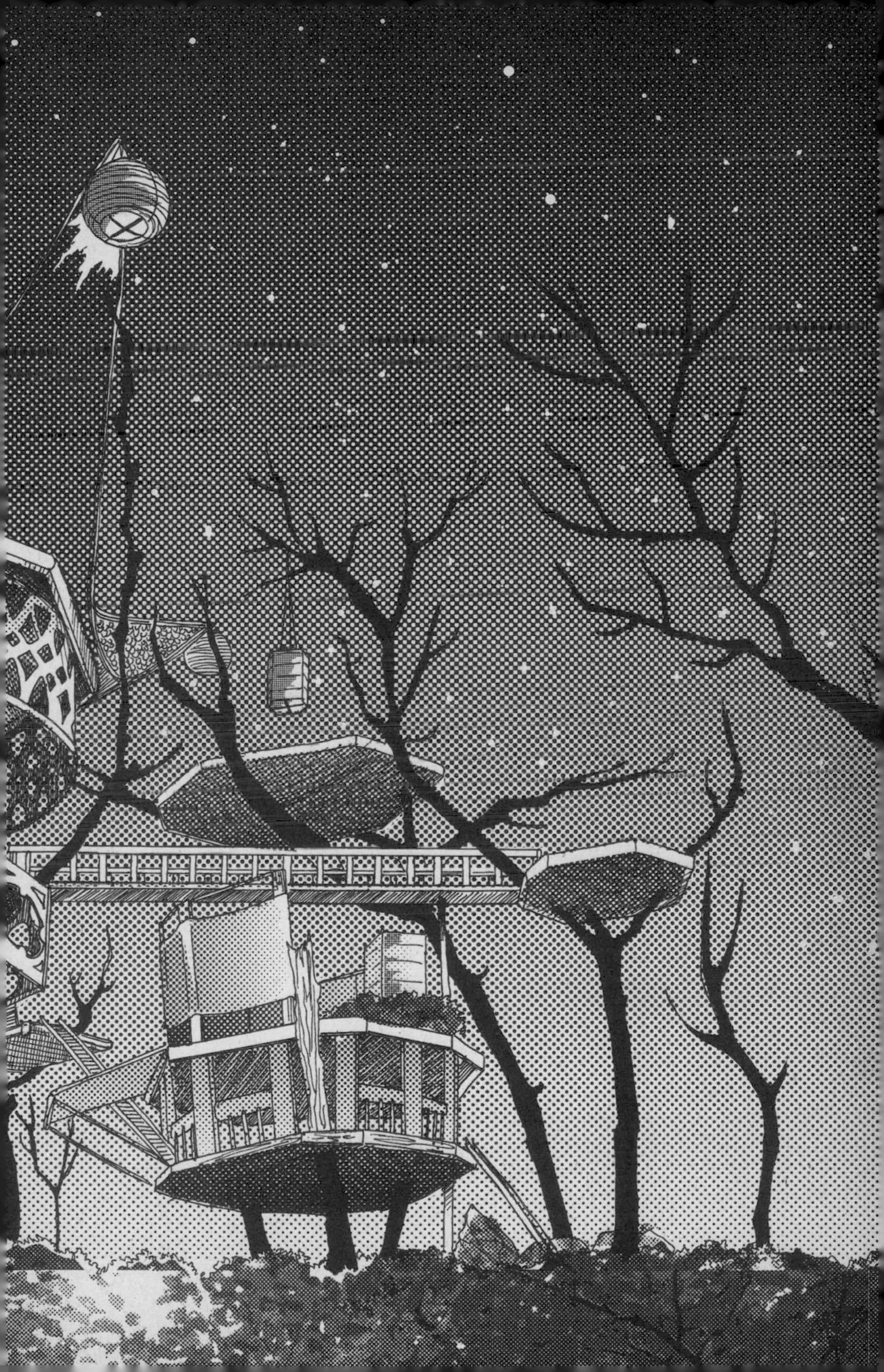

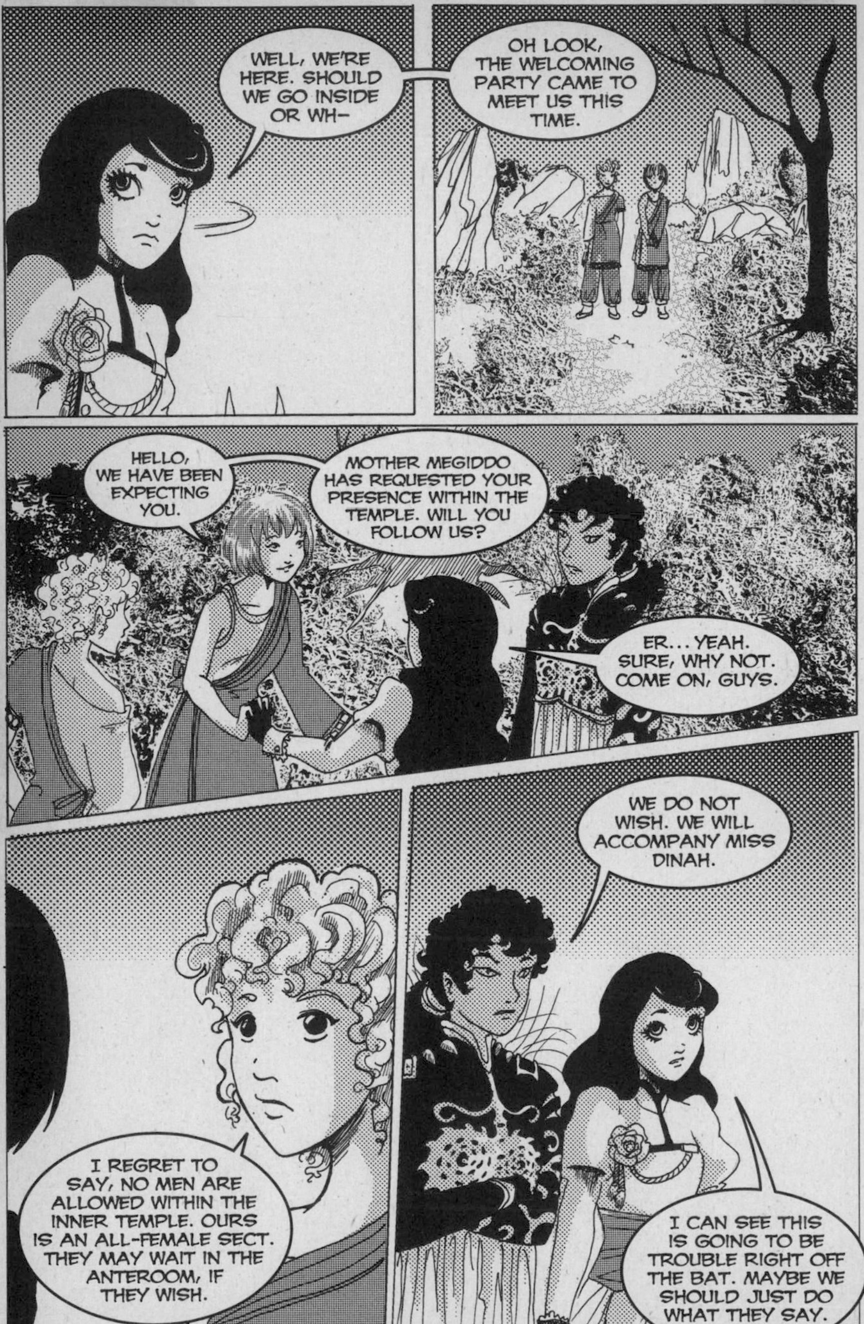
WELL, WE'RE HERE. SHOULD WE GO INSIDE OR WH-
OH LOOK, THE WELCOMING PARTY CAME TO MEET US THIS TIME.
HELLO, WE HAVE BEEN EXPECTING YOU.
MOTHER MEGIDDO HAS REQUESTED YOUR PRESENCE WITHIN THE TEMPLE. WILL YOU FOLLOW US?
ER... YEAH. SURE, WHY NOT. COME ON, GUYS.
I REGRET TO SAY, NO MEN ARE ALLOWED WITHIN THE INNER TEMPLE. OURS IS AN ALL-FEMALE SECT. THEY MAY WAIT IN THE ANTEROOM, IF THEY WISH.
WE DO NOT WISH. WE WILL ACCOMPANY MISS DINAH.
I CAN SEE THIS IS GOING TO BE TROUBLE RIGHT OFF THE BAT. MAYBE WE SHOULD JUST DO WHAT THEY SAY.

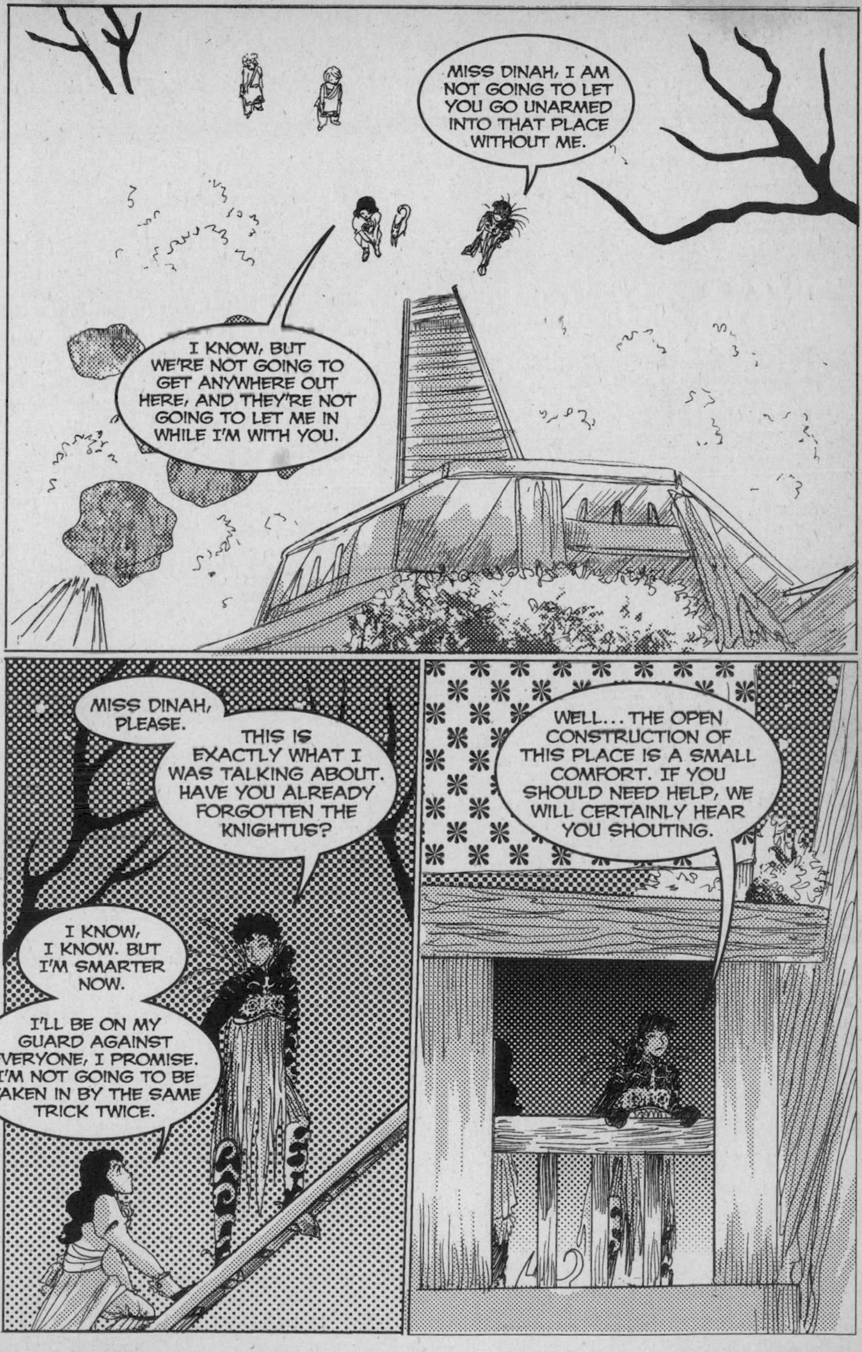
MISS DINAH, I AM NOT GOING TO LET YOU GO UNARMED INTO THAT PLACE WITHOUT ME.
I KNOW, BUT WE'RE NOT GOING TO GET ANYWHERE OUT HERE, AND THEY'RE NOT GOING TO LET ME IN WHILE I'M WITH YOU.
MISS DINAH, PLEASE.
THIS IS EXACTLY WHAT I WAS TALKING ABOUT. HAVE YOU ALREADY FORGOTTEN THE KNIGHTUS?
I KNOW, I KNOW. BUT I'M SMARTER NOW.
I'LL BE ON MY GUARD AGAINST EVERYONE, I PROMISE. I'M NOT GOING TO BE TAKEN IN BY THE SAME TRICK TWICE.
WELL... THE OPEN CONSTRUCTION OF THIS PLACE IS A SMALL COMFORT. IF YOU SHOULD NEED HELP, WE WILL CERTAINLY HEAR YOU SHOUTING.

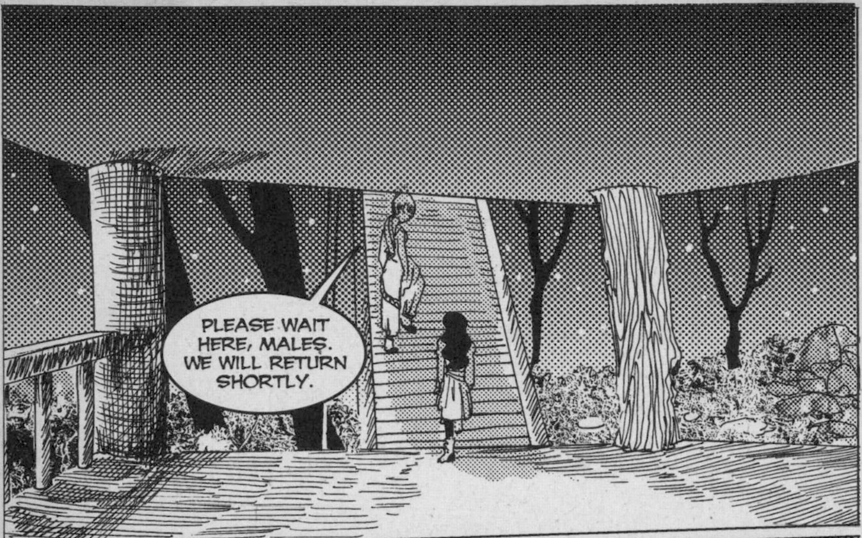
PLEASE WAIT HERE, MALEŞ. WE WILL RETURN SHORTLY.

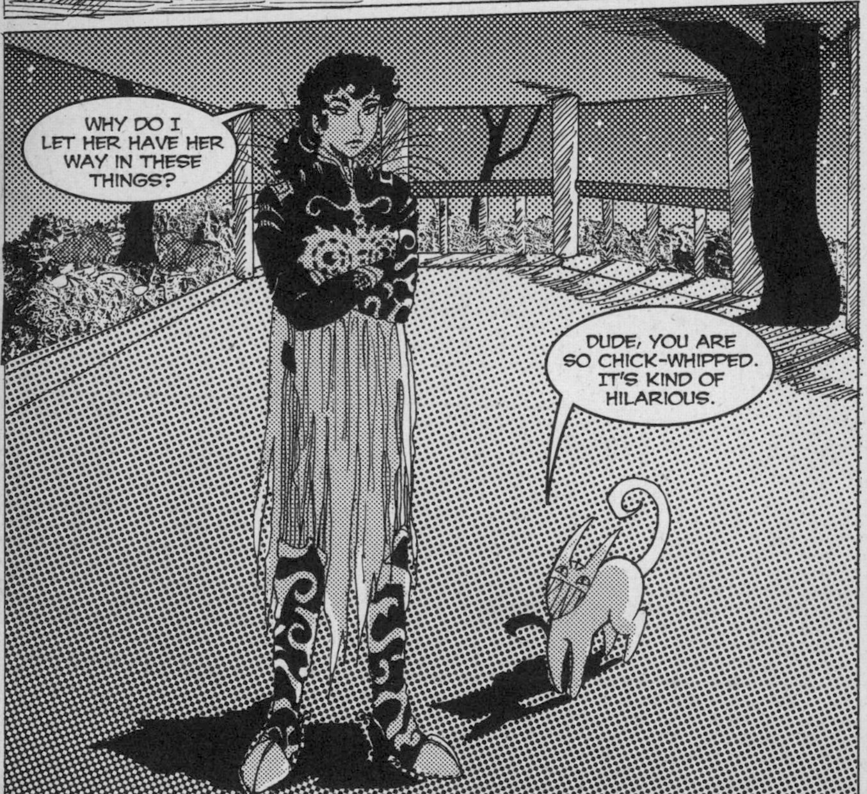
WHY DO I LET HER HAVE HER WAY IN THESE THINGS?
DUDE, YOU ARE SO CHICK-WHIPPED. IT'S KIND OF HILARIOUS.

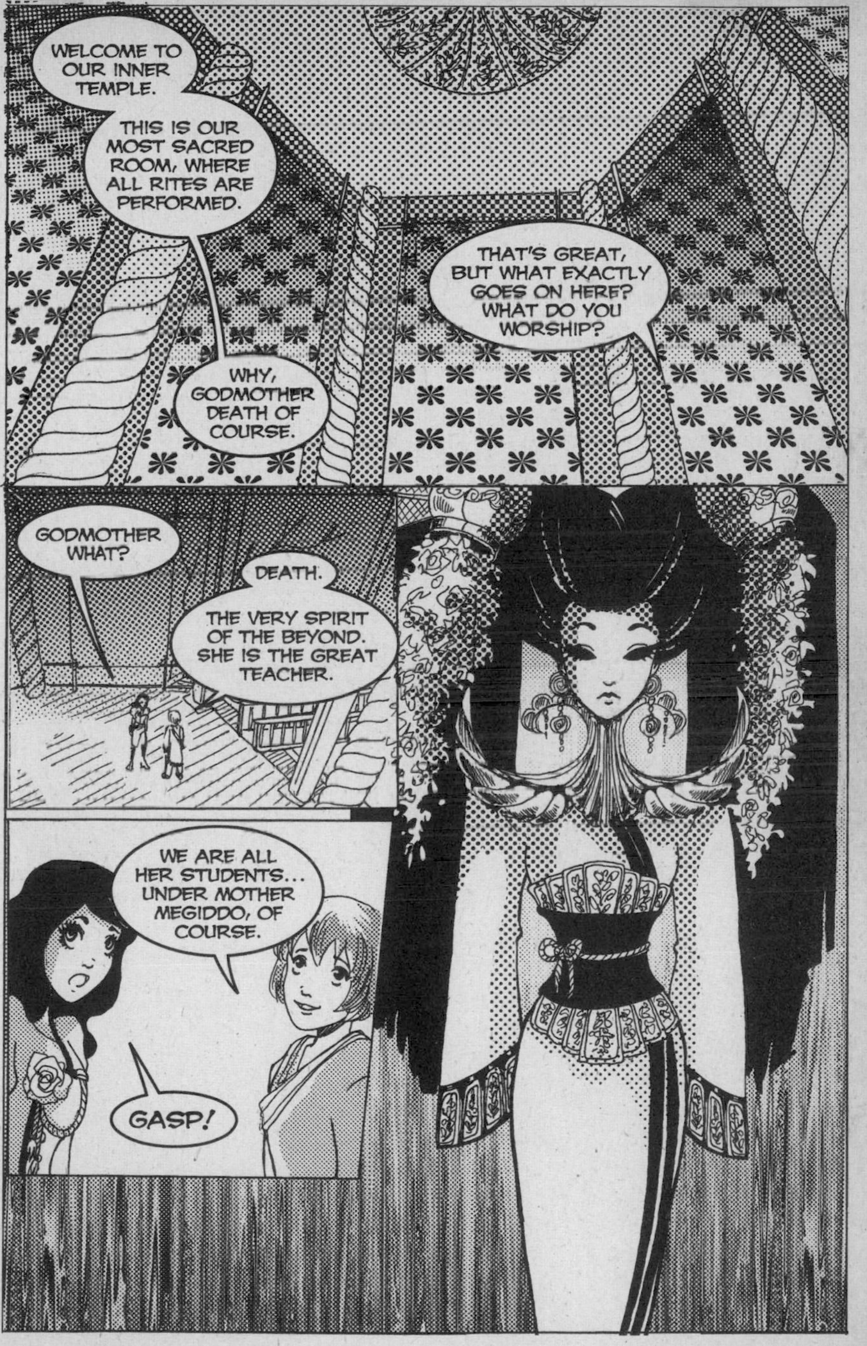
WELCOME TO OUR INNER TEMPLE.
THIS IS OUR MOST SACRED ROOM, WHERE ALL RITES ARE PERFORMED.
THAT'S GREAT, BUT WHAT EXACTLY GOES ON HERE? WHAT DO YOU WORSHIP?
WHY, GODMOTHER DEATH OF COURSE.
GODMOTHER WHAT?
DEATH.
THE VERY SPIRIT OF THE BEYOND. SHE IS THE GREAT TEACHER.
WE ARE ALL HER STUDENTS... UNDER MOTHER MEGIDDO, OF COURSE.
GASP!

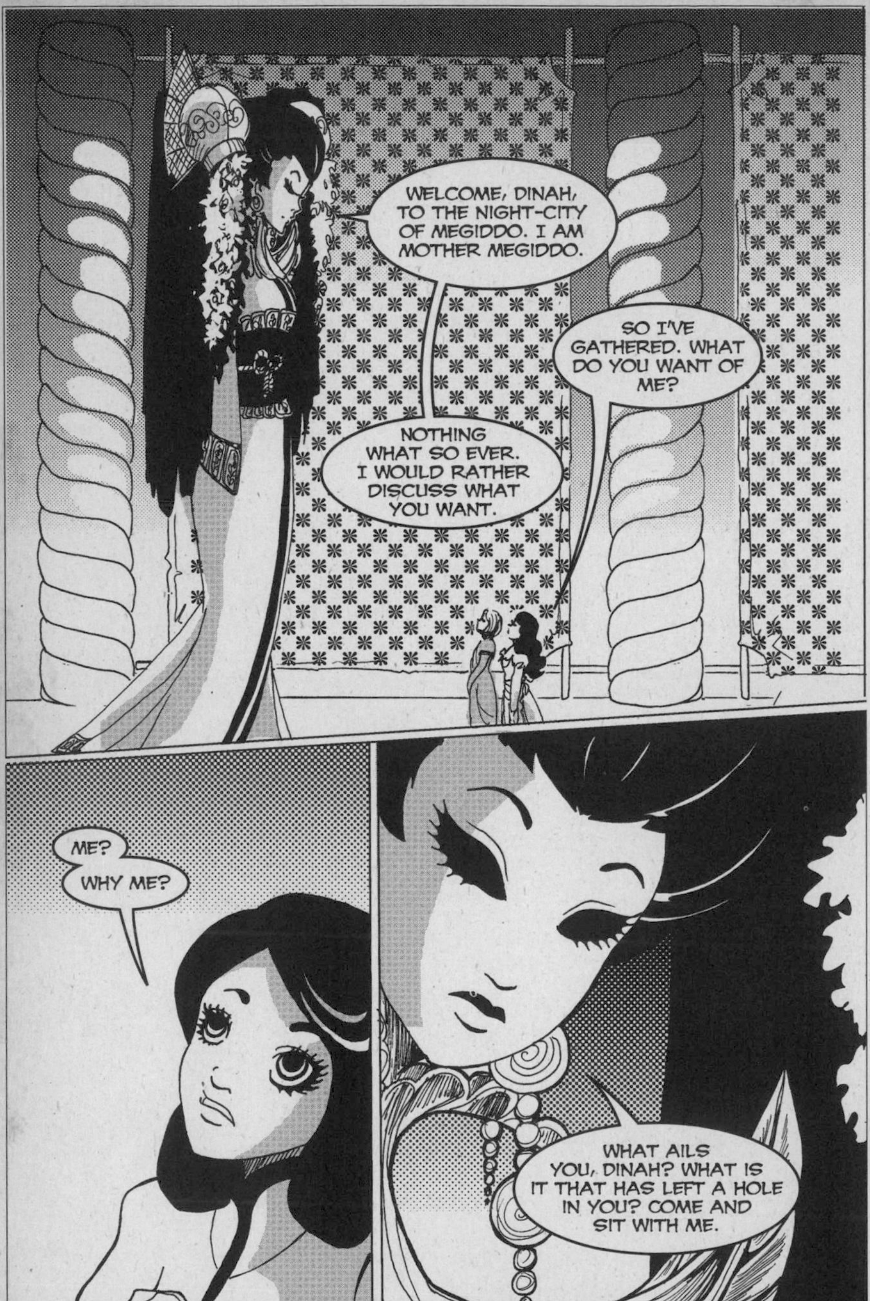
WELCOME, DINAH, TO THE NIGHT-CITY OF MEGIDDO. I AM MOTHER MEGIDDO.
SO I'VE GATHERED. WHAT DO YOU WANT OF ME?
NOTHING WHAT SO EVER. I WOULD RATHER DISCUSS WHAT YOU WANT.
ME?
WHY ME?
WHAT AILS YOU, DINAH? WHAT IS IT THAT HAS LEFT A HOLE IN YOU? COME AND SIT WITH ME.

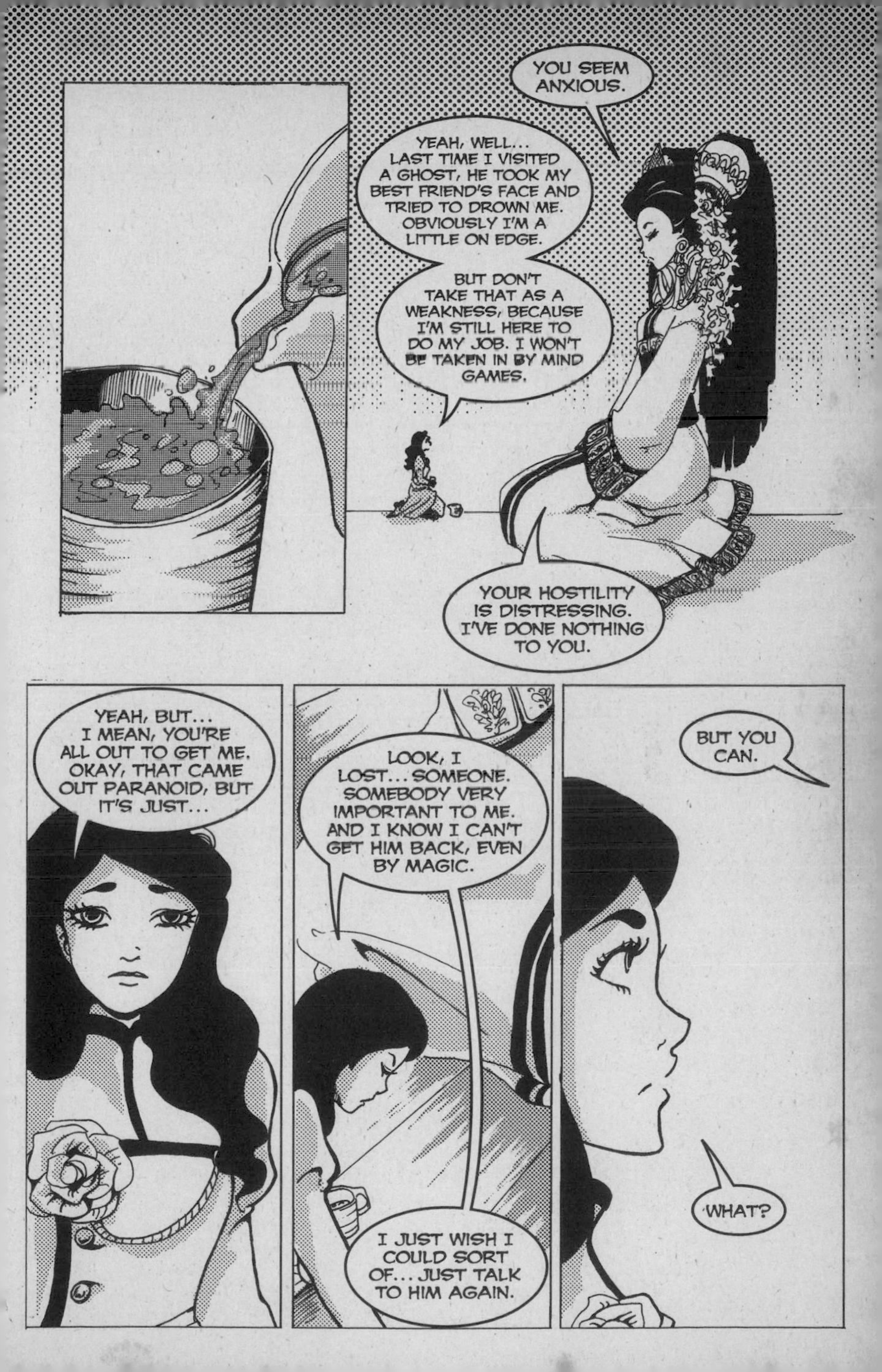
YOU SEEM ANXIOUS.
YEAH, WELL... LAST TIME I VISITED A GHOST, HE TOOK MY BEST FRIEND'S FACE AND TRIED TO DROWN ME. OBVIOUSLY I'M A LITTLE ON EDGE.
BUT DON'T TAKE THAT AS A WEAKNESS, BECAUSE I'M STILL HERE TO DO MY JOB. I WON'T BE TAKEN IN BY MIND GAMES.
YOUR HOSTILITY IS DISTRESSING. I'VE DONE NOTHING TO YOU.
YEAH, BUT... I MEAN, YOU'RE ALL OUT TO GET ME. OKAY, THAT CAME OUT PARANOID, BUT IT'S JUST...
LOOK, I LOST... SOMEONE. SOMEBODY VERY IMPORTANT TO ME. AND I KNOW I CAN'T GET HIM BACK, EVEN BY MAGIC.
I JUST WISH I COULD SORT OF... JUST TALK TO HIM AGAIN.
BUT YOU CAN.
WHAT?

WE HERE IN MEGIDDO ARE LIKE YOU, DINAH. WE HAVE ALL LOST SOMEONE. I HAVE LOST SOMEONE. WHO I HAVE LOST IS NOT IMPORTANT, BUT MY PURPOSE HERE IS.

LIKE YOU, I WAS LOST FOR A LONG TIME. I FELT WITHOUT DIRECTION, WITHOUT GUIDANCE. I WAS LESS THAN WHOLE.

WHEN MY LIFE SEEMED DARKEST, I WAS WITHOUT REASON TO LIVE. IT WAS THEN THAT GODMOTHER DEATH SPOKE TO ME.

SHE CAME TO ME, WRAPPED IN COLDEST NIGHT, WITH THE MOON IN HER HAIR AND STARS IN HER EYES.

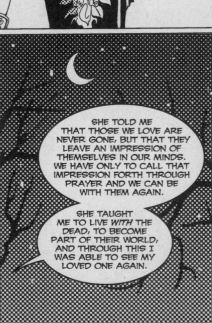

SHE TOLD ME THAT THOSE WE LOVE ARE NEVER GONE, BUT THAT THEY LEAVE AN IMPRESSION OF THEMSELVES IN OUR MINDS. WE HAVE ONLY TO CALL THAT IMPRESSION FORTH THROUGH PRAYER AND WE CAN BE WITH THEM AGAIN.

SHE TAUGHT ME TO LIVE *WITH* THE DEAD, TO BECOME PART OF THEIR WORLD, AND THROUGH THIS I WAS ABLE TO SEE MY LOVED ONE AGAIN.

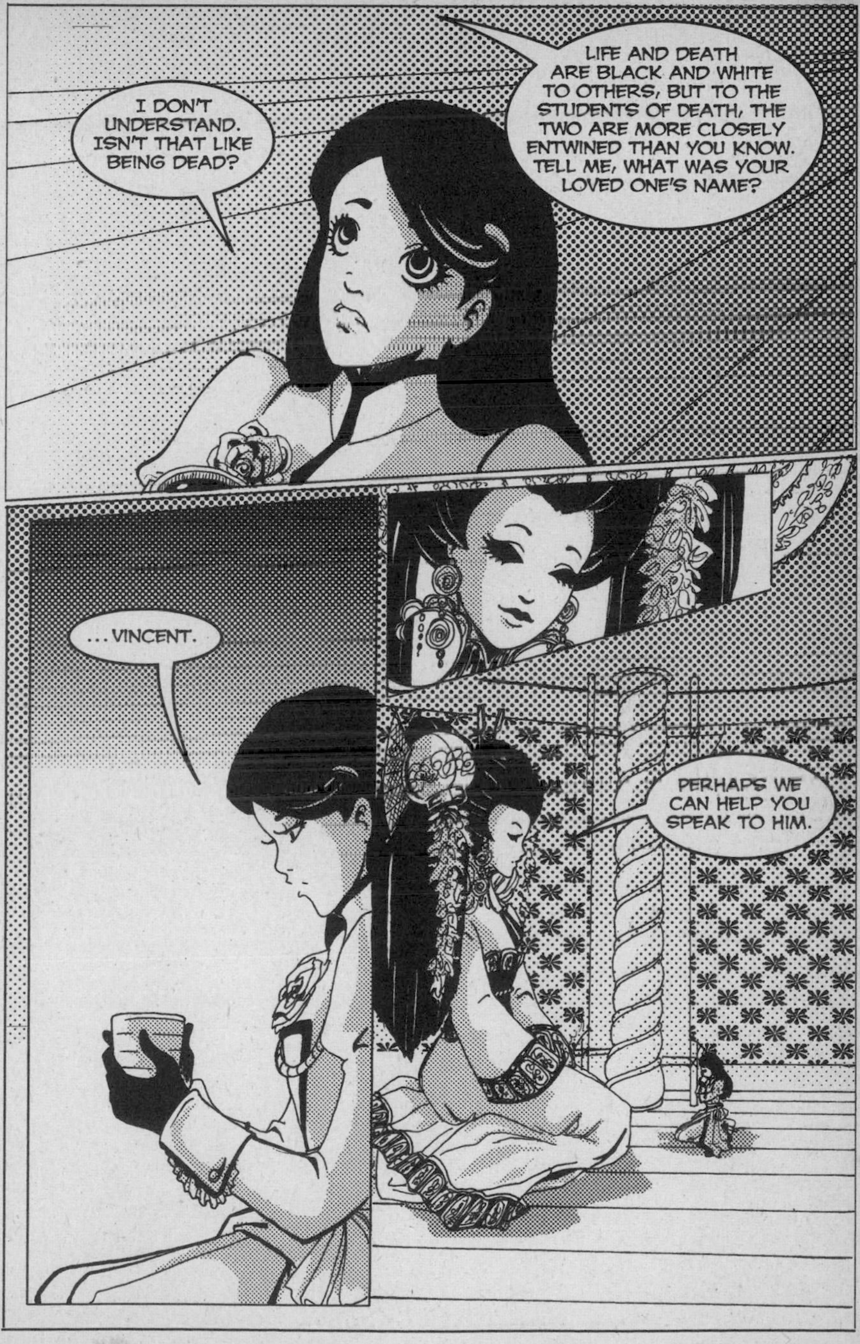
I DON'T UNDERSTAND. ISN'T THAT LIKE BEING DEAD?
LIFE AND DEATH ARE BLACK AND WHITE TO OTHERS, BUT TO THE STUDENTS OF DEATH, THE TWO ARE MORE CLOSELY ENTWINED THAN YOU KNOW. TELL ME, WHAT WAS YOUR LOVED ONE'S NAME?
...VINCENT.
PERHAPS WE CAN HELP YOU SPEAK TO HIM.

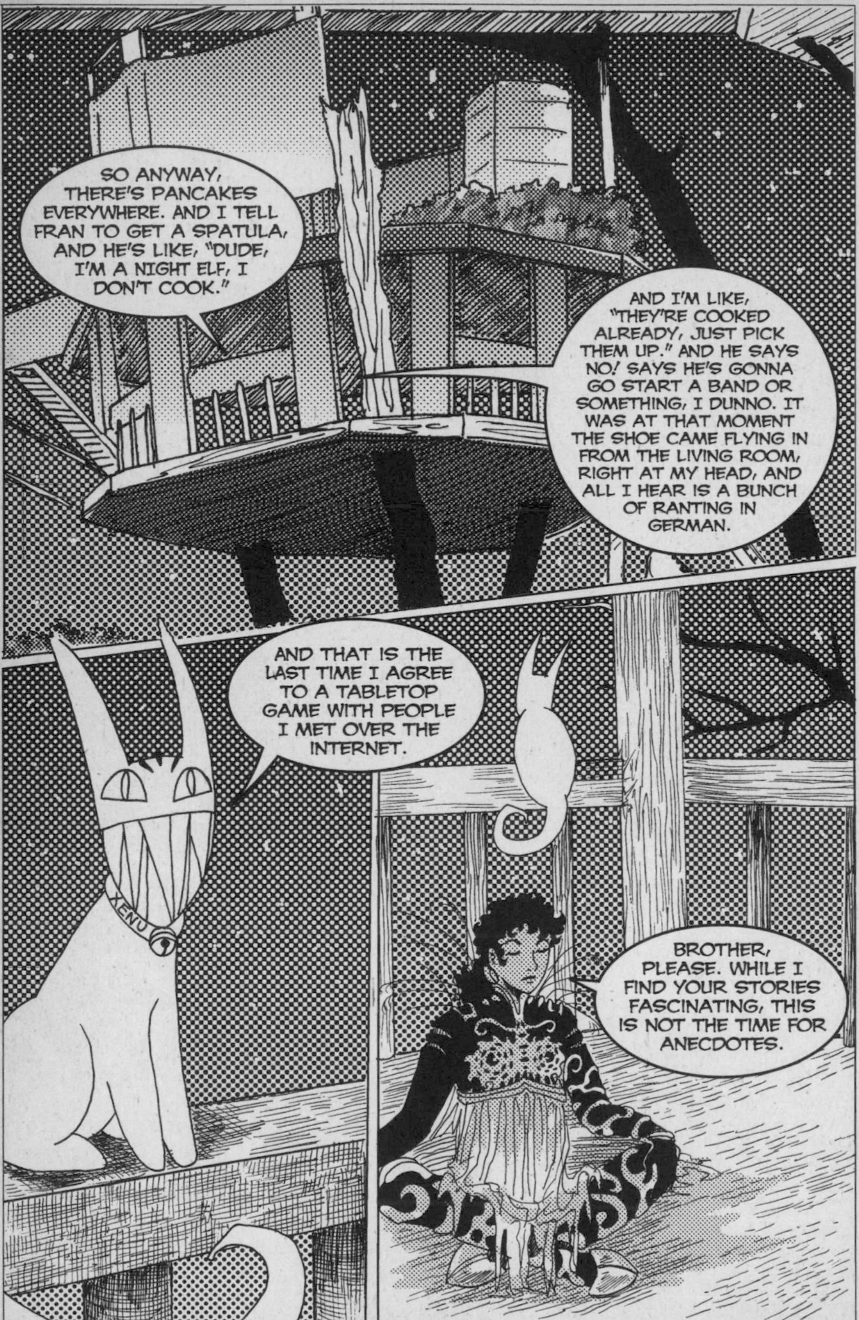
SO ANYWAY, THERE'S PANCAKES EVERYWHERE. AND I TELL FRAN TO GET A SPATULA, AND HE'S LIKE, "DUDE, I'M A NIGHT ELF, I DON'T COOK."
AND I'M LIKE, "THEY'RE COOKED ALREADY, JUST PICK THEM UP." AND HE SAYS NO! SAYS HE'S GONNA GO START A BAND OR SOMETHING, I DUNNO. IT WAS AT THAT MOMENT THE SHOE CAME FLYING IN FROM THE LIVING ROOM, RIGHT AT MY HEAD, AND ALL I HEAR IS A BUNCH OF RANTING IN GERMAN.
AND THAT IS THE LAST TIME I AGREE TO A TABLETOP GAME WITH PEOPLE I MET OVER THE INTERNET.
XENU
BROTHER, PLEASE. WHILE I FIND YOUR STORIES FASCINATING, THIS IS NOT THE TIME FOR ANECDOTES.

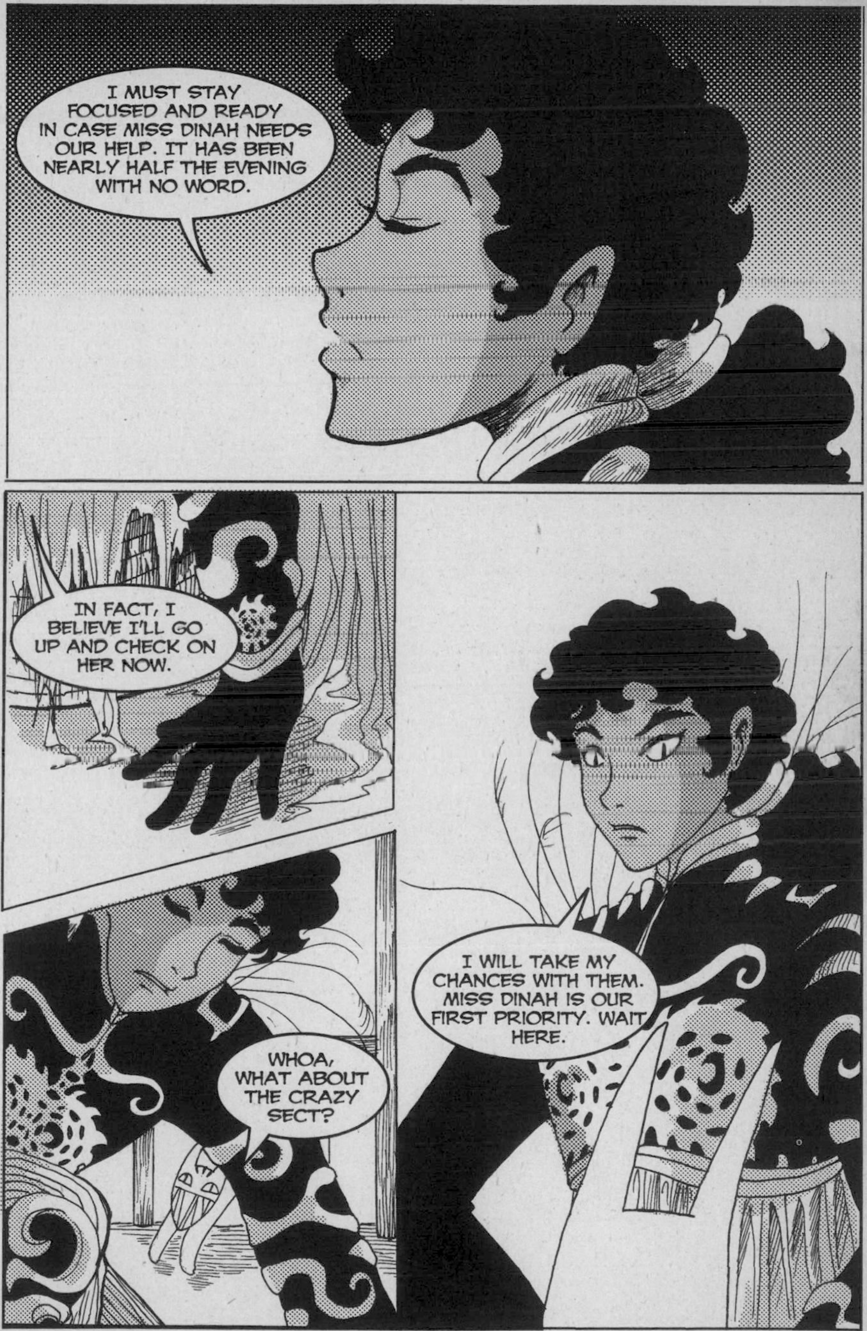
I MUST STAY FOCUSED AND READY IN CASE MISS DINAH NEEDS OUR HELP. IT HAS BEEN NEARLY HALF THE EVENING WITH NO WORD.
IN FACT, I BELIEVE I'LL GO UP AND CHECK ON HER NOW.
WHOA, WHAT ABOUT THE CRAZY SECT?
I WILL TAKE MY CHANCES WITH THEM. MISS DINAH IS OUR FIRST PRIORITY. WAIT HERE.

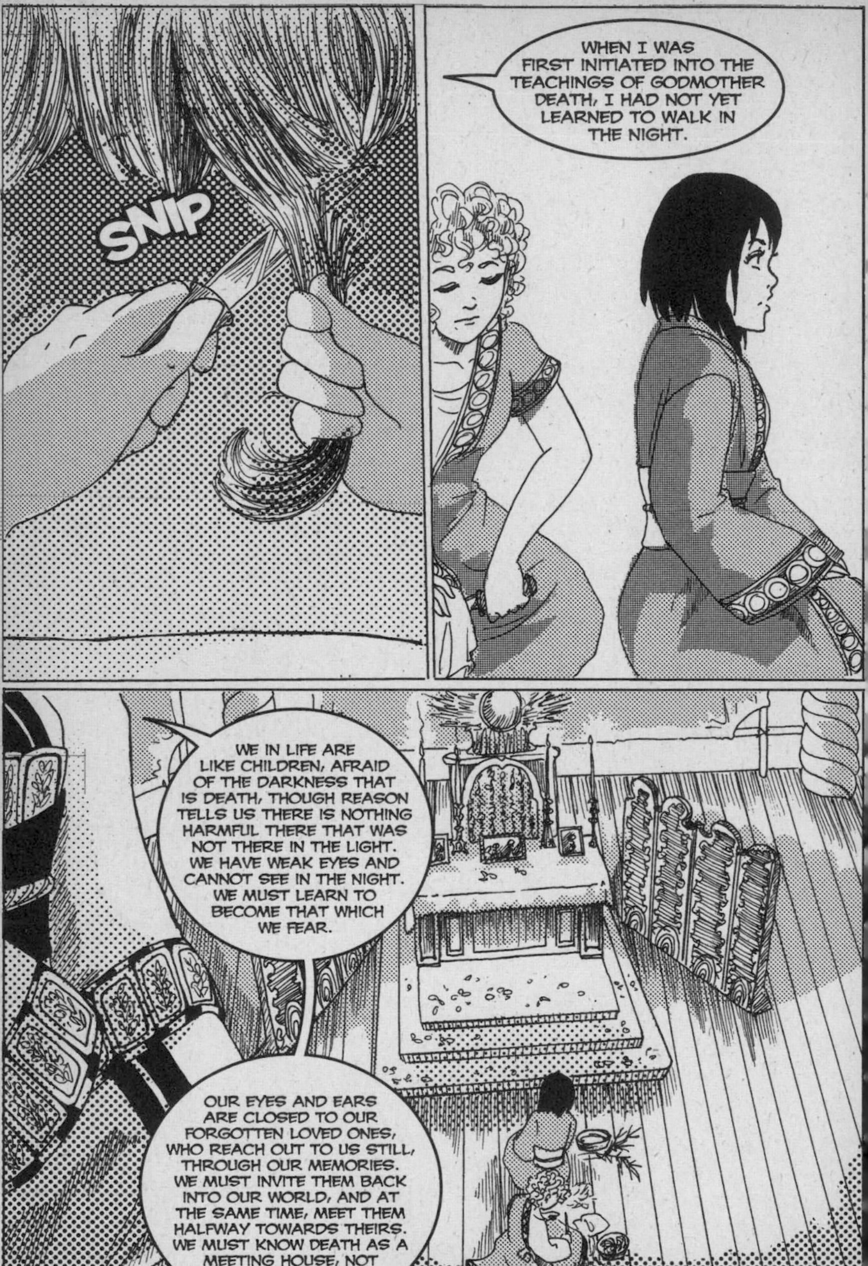
SNIP
WHEN I WAS FIRST INITIATED INTO THE TEACHINGS OF GODMOTHER DEATH, I HAD NOT YET LEARNED TO WALK IN THE NIGHT.
WE IN LIFE ARE LIKE CHILDREN, AFRAID OF THE DARKNESS THAT IS DEATH, THOUGH REASON TELLS US THERE IS NOTHING HARMFUL THERE THAT WAS NOT THERE IN THE LIGHT. WE HAVE WEAK EYES AND CANNOT SEE IN THE NIGHT. WE MUST LEARN TO BECOME THAT WHICH WE FEAR.
OUR EYES AND EARS ARE CLOSED TO OUR FORGOTTEN LOVED ONES, WHO REACH OUT TO US STILL, THROUGH OUR MEMORIES. WE MUST INVITE THEM BACK INTO OUR WORLD, AND AT THE SAME TIME, MEET THEM HALFWAY TOWARDS THEIRS. WE MUST KNOW DEATH AS A MEETING HOUSE, NOT AS A RAVENOUS MONSTER.

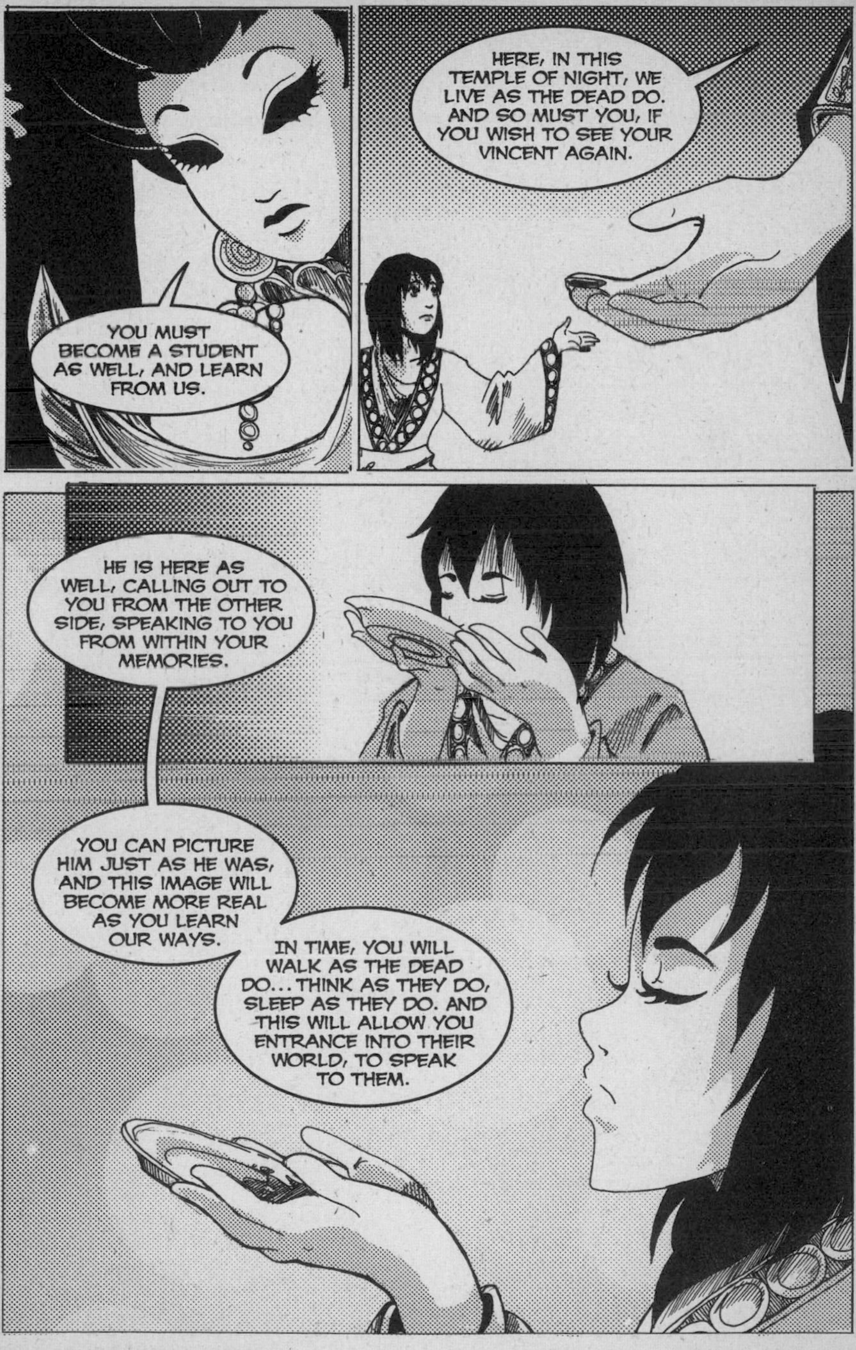
YOU MUST BECOME A STUDENT AS WELL, AND LEARN FROM US.
HERE, IN THIS TEMPLE OF NIGHT, WE LIVE AS THE DEAD DO. AND SO MUST YOU, IF YOU WISH TO SEE YOUR VINCENT AGAIN.
HE IS HERE AS WELL, CALLING OUT TO YOU FROM THE OTHER SIDE, SPEAKING TO YOU FROM WITHIN YOUR MEMORIES.
YOU CAN PICTURE HIM JUST AS HE WAS, AND THIS IMAGE WILL BECOME MORE REAL AS YOU LEARN OUR WAYS.
IN TIME, YOU WILL WALK AS THE DEAD DO... THINK AS THEY DO, SLEEP AS THEY DO. AND THIS WILL ALLOW YOU ENTRANCE INTO THEIR WORLD, TO SPEAK TO THEM.

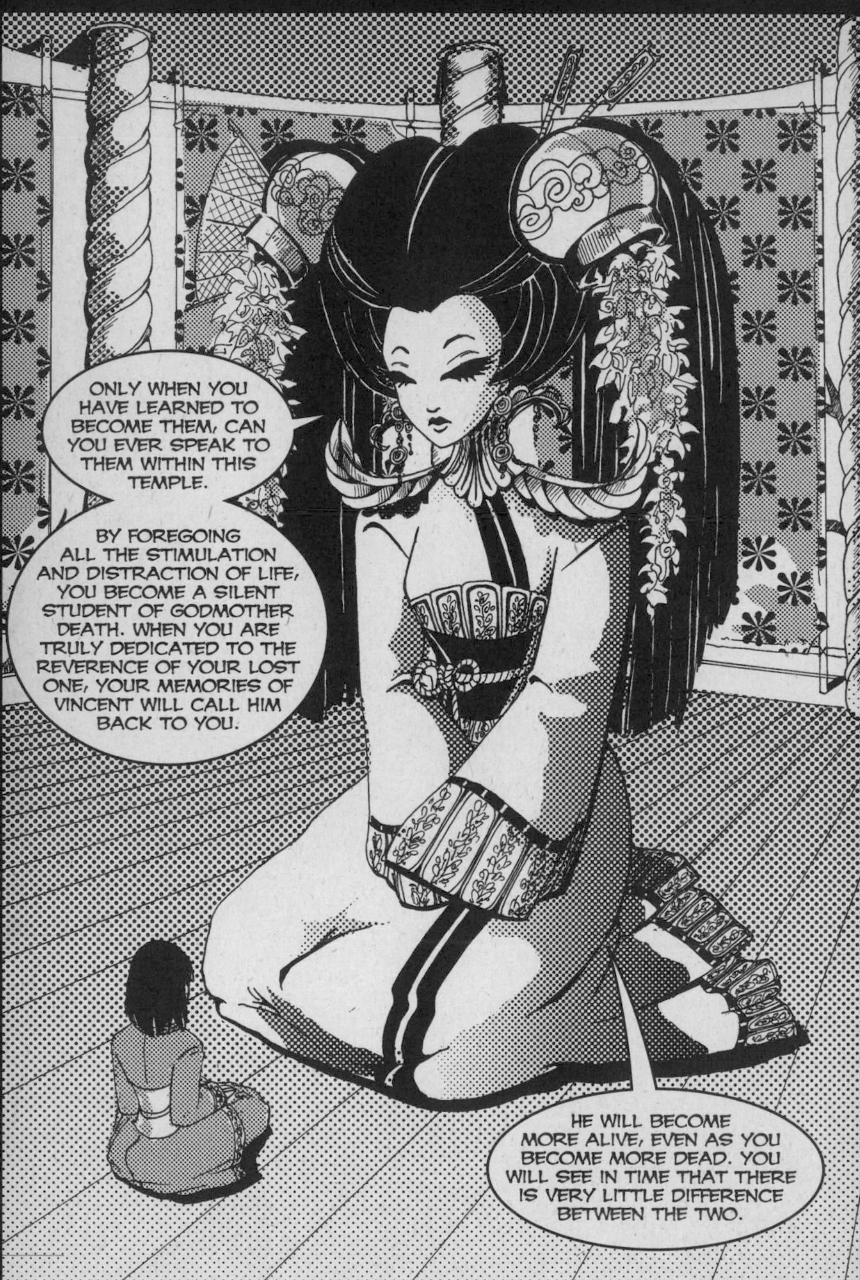
ONLY WHEN YOU HAVE LEARNED TO BECOME THEM, CAN YOU EVER SPEAK TO THEM WITHIN THIS TEMPLE.
BY FOREGOING ALL THE STIMULATION AND DISTRACTION OF LIFE, YOU BECOME A SILENT STUDENT OF GODMOTHER DEATH. WHEN YOU ARE TRULY DEDICATED TO THE REVERENCE OF YOUR LOST ONE, YOUR MEMORIES OF VINCENT WILL CALL HIM BACK TO YOU.
HE WILL BECOME MORE ALIVE, EVEN AS YOU BECOME MORE DEAD. YOU WILL SEE IN TIME THAT THERE IS VERY LITTLE DIFFERENCE BETWEEN THE TWO.

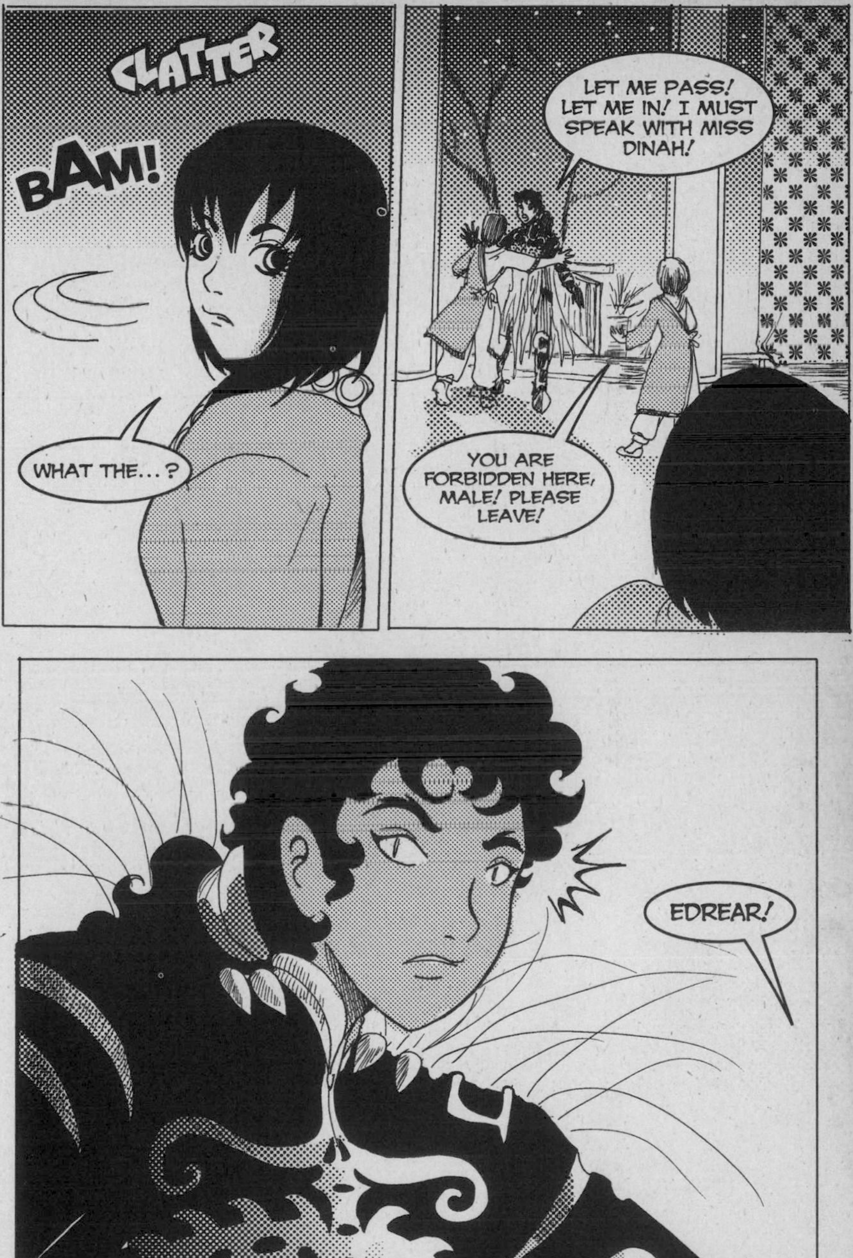
CLATTER
BAM!
WHAT THE...?
LET ME PASS! LET ME IN! I MUST SPEAK WITH MISS DINAH!
YOU ARE FORBIDDEN HERE, MALE! PLEASE LEAVE!
EDREAR!

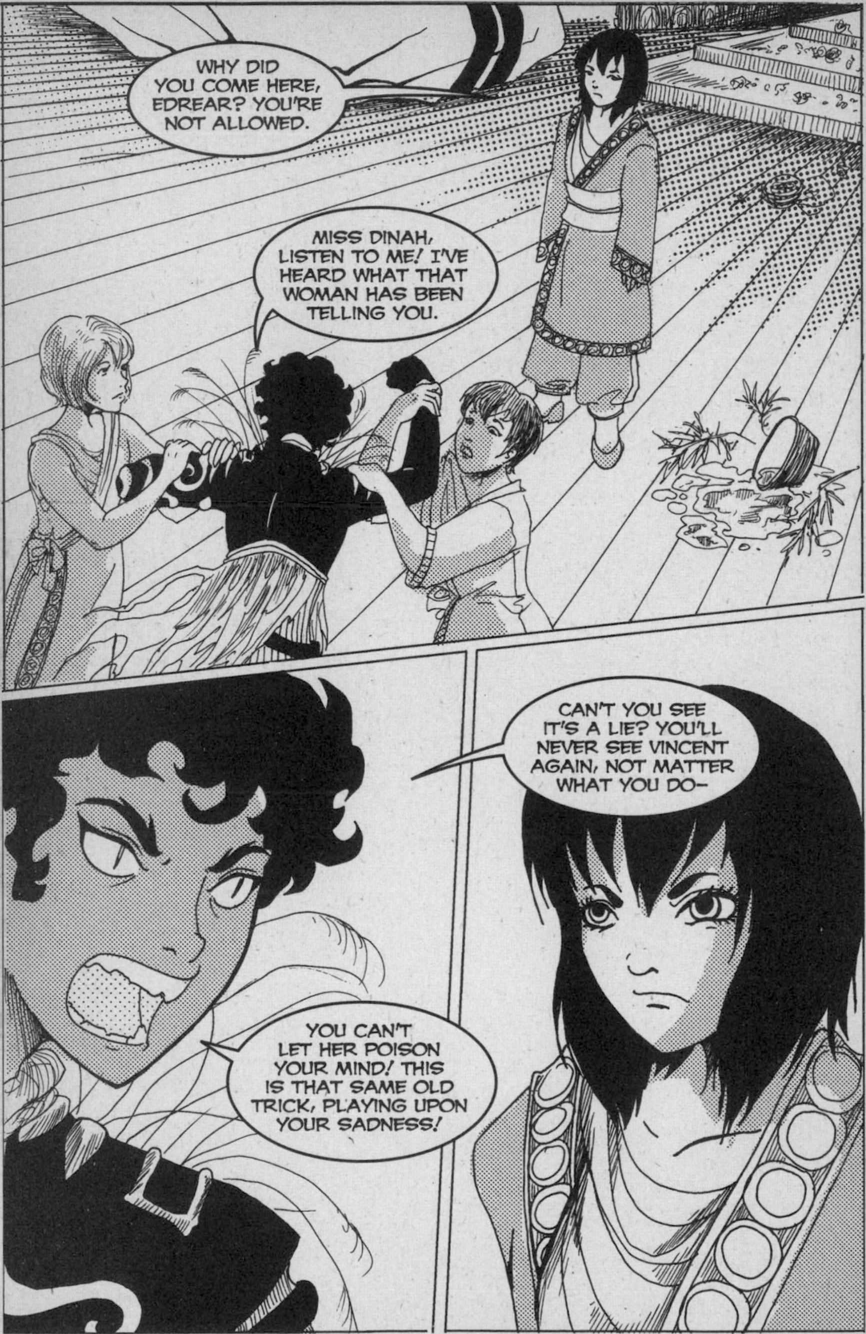
WHY DID YOU COME HERE, EDREAR? YOU'RE NOT ALLOWED.
MISS DINAH, LISTEN TO ME! I'VE HEARD WHAT THAT WOMAN HAS BEEN TELLING YOU.
CAN'T YOU SEE IT'S A LIE? YOU'LL NEVER SEE VINCENT AGAIN, NOT MATTER WHAT YOU DO–
YOU CAN'T LET HER POISON YOUR MIND! THIS IS THAT SAME OLD TRICK, PLAYING UPON YOUR SADNESS!

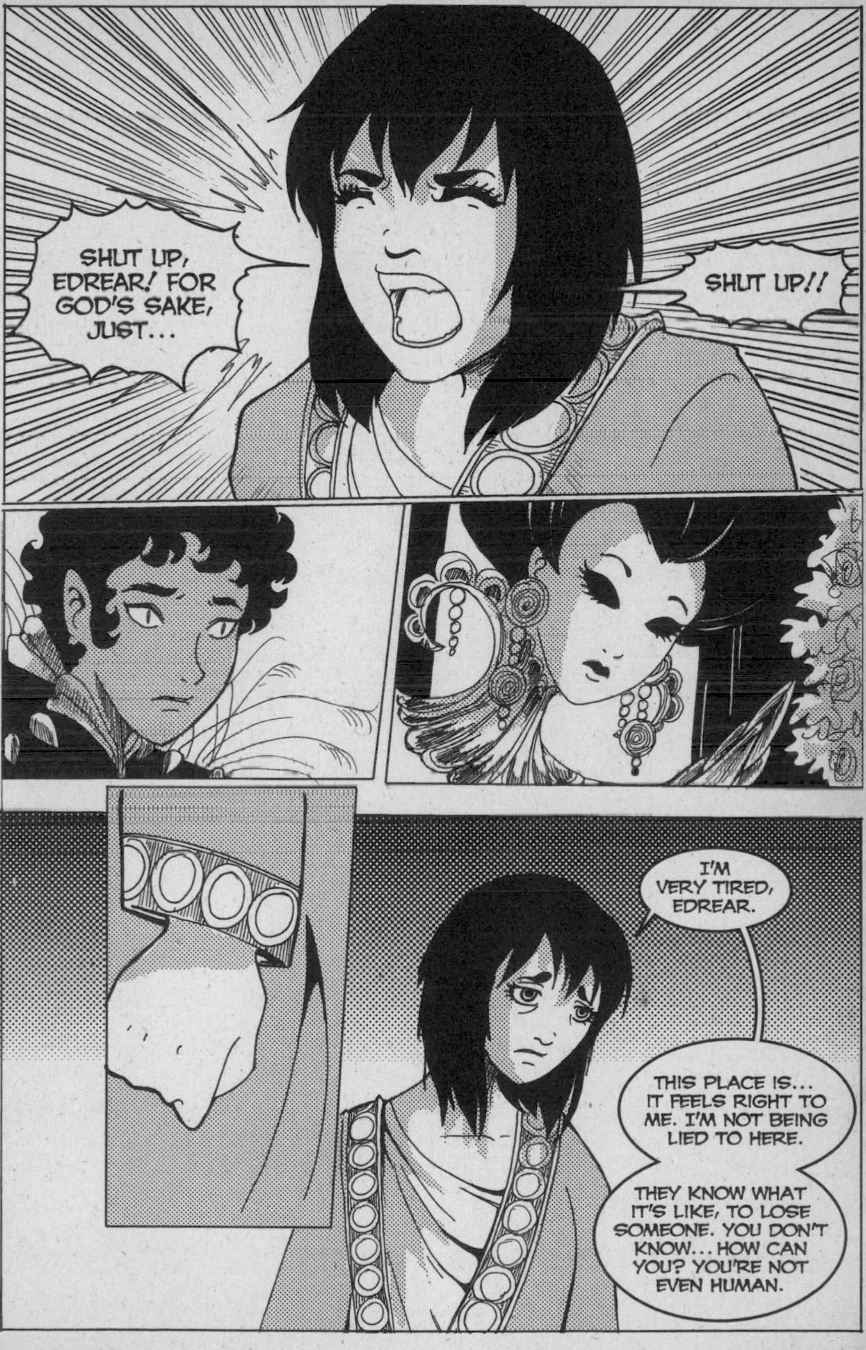
SHUT UP, EDREAR! FOR GOD'S SAKE, JUST...
SHUT UP!!
I'M VERY TIRED, EDREAR.
THIS PLACE IS... IT FEELS RIGHT TO ME. I'M NOT BEING LIED TO HERE.
THEY KNOW WHAT IT'S LIKE, TO LOSE SOMEONE. YOU DON'T KNOW... HOW CAN YOU? YOU'RE NOT EVEN HUMAN.

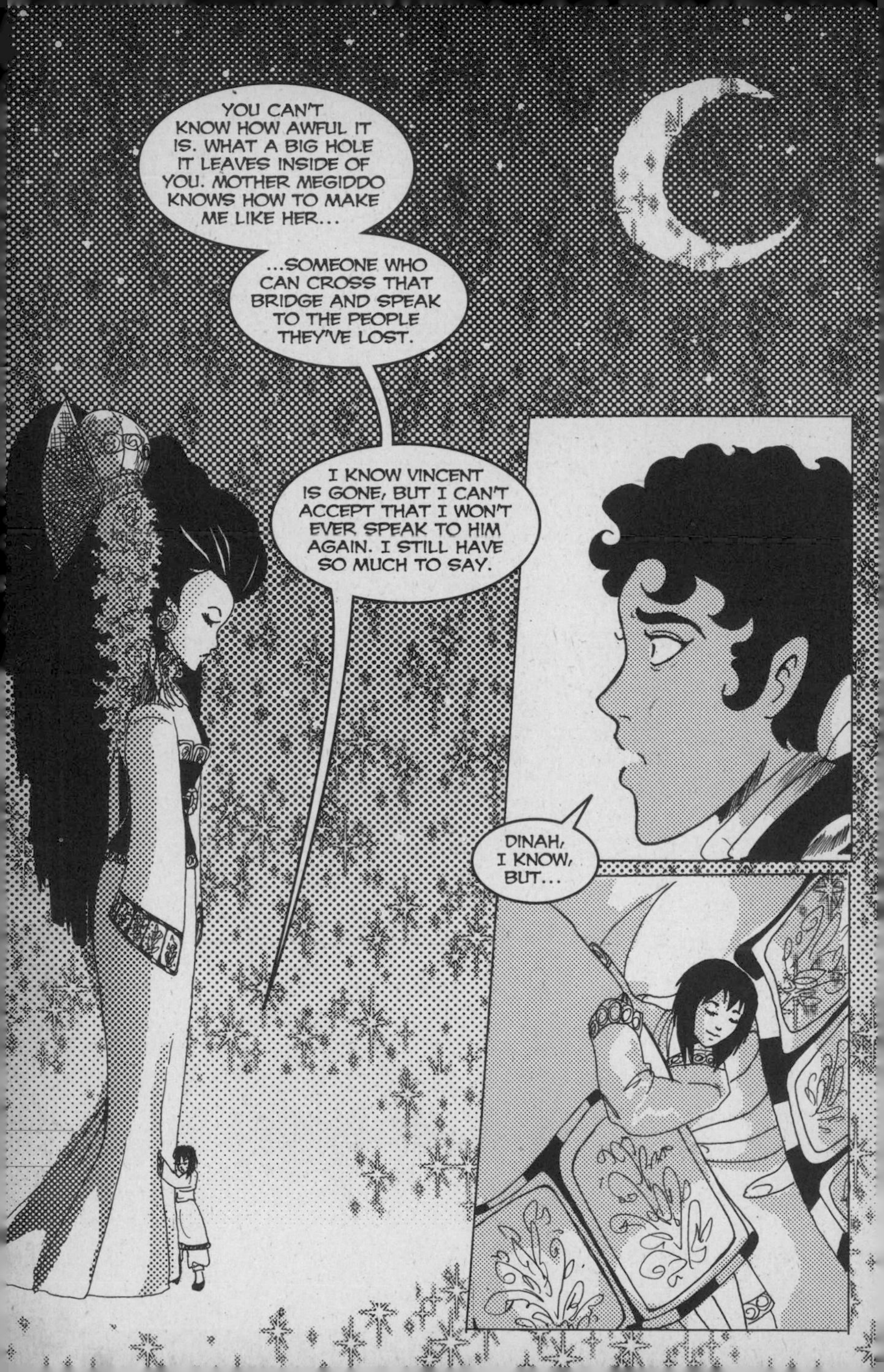
YOU CAN'T KNOW HOW AWFUL IT IS. WHAT A BIG HOLE IT LEAVES INSIDE OF YOU. MOTHER MEGIDDO KNOWS HOW TO MAKE ME LIKE HER...
...SOMEONE WHO CAN CROSS THAT BRIDGE AND SPEAK TO THE PEOPLE THEY'VE LOST.
I KNOW VINCENT IS GONE, BUT I CAN'T ACCEPT THAT I WON'T EVER SPEAK TO HIM AGAIN. I STILL HAVE SO MUCH TO SAY.
DINAH, I KNOW, BUT...

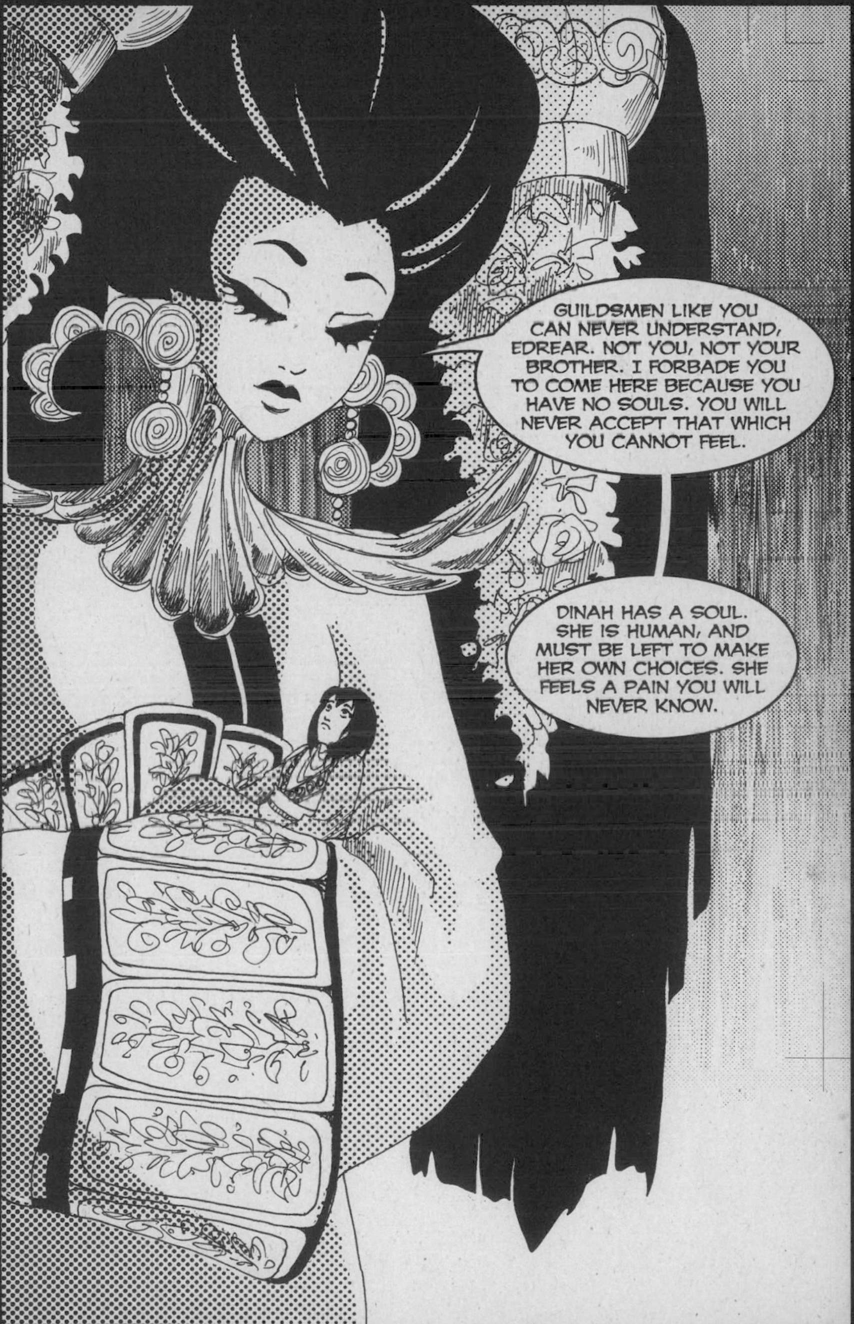
GUILDSMEN LIKE YOU CAN NEVER UNDERSTAND, EDREAR. NOT YOU, NOT YOUR BROTHER. I FORBADE YOU TO COME HERE BECAUSE YOU HAVE NO SOULS. YOU WILL NEVER ACCEPT THAT WHICH YOU CANNOT FEEL.
DINAH HAS A SOUL. SHE IS HUMAN, AND MUST BE LEFT TO MAKE HER OWN CHOICES. SHE FEELS A PAIN YOU WILL NEVER KNOW.

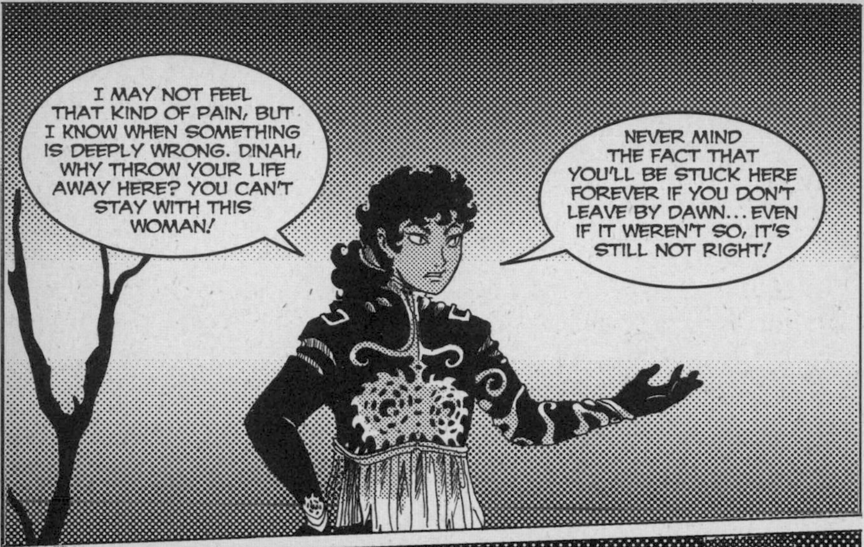
I MAY NOT FEEL THAT KIND OF PAIN, BUT I KNOW WHEN SOMETHING IS DEEPLY WRONG. DINAH, WHY THROW YOUR LIFE AWAY HERE? YOU CAN'T STAY WITH THIS WOMAN!
NEVER MIND THE FACT THAT YOU'LL BE STUCK HERE FOREVER IF YOU DON'T LEAVE BY DAWN... EVEN IF IT WEREN'T SO, IT'S STILL NOT RIGHT!

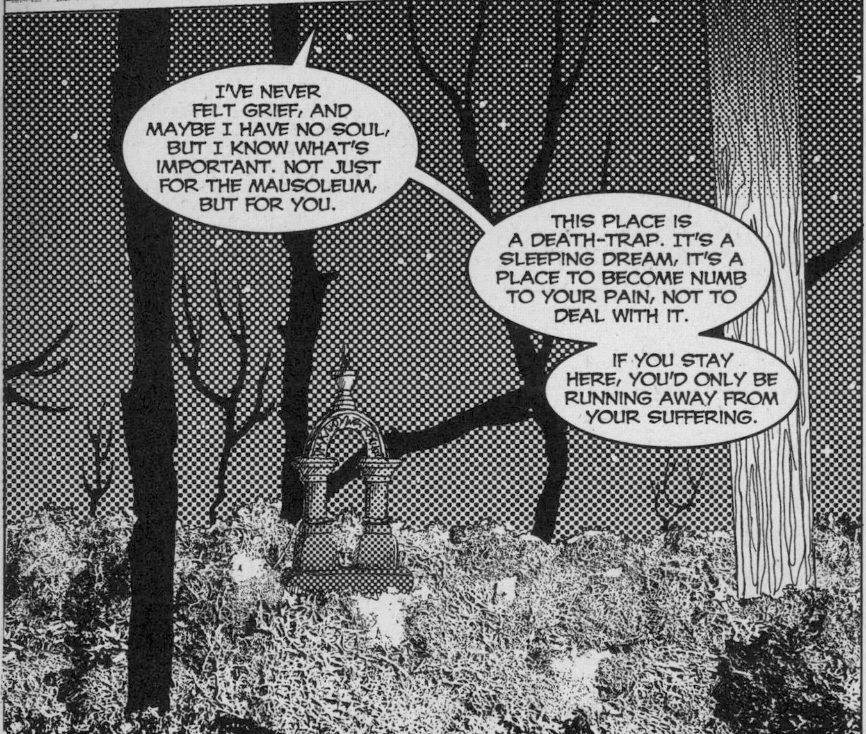
I'VE NEVER FELT GRIEF, AND MAYBE I HAVE NO SOUL, BUT I KNOW WHAT'S IMPORTANT. NOT JUST FOR THE MAUSOLEUM, BUT FOR YOU.
THIS PLACE IS A DEATH-TRAP. IT'S A SLEEPING DREAM, IT'S A PLACE TO BECOME NUMB TO YOUR PAIN, NOT TO DEAL WITH IT.
IF YOU STAY HERE, YOU'D ONLY BE RUNNING AWAY FROM YOUR SUFFERING.

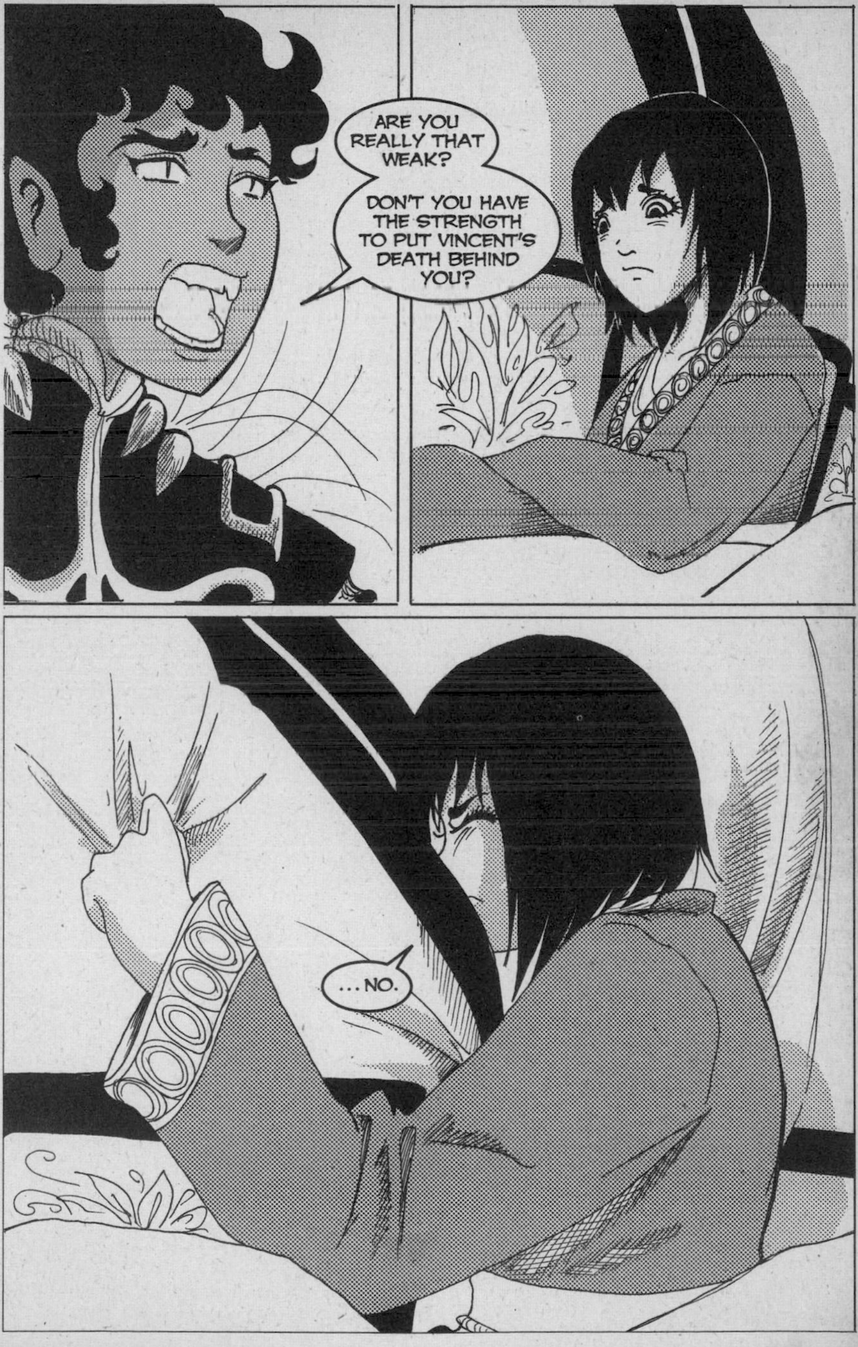
ARE YOU REALLY THAT WEAK?
DON'T YOU HAVE THE STRENGTH TO PUT VINCENT'S DEATH BEHIND YOU?
...NO.

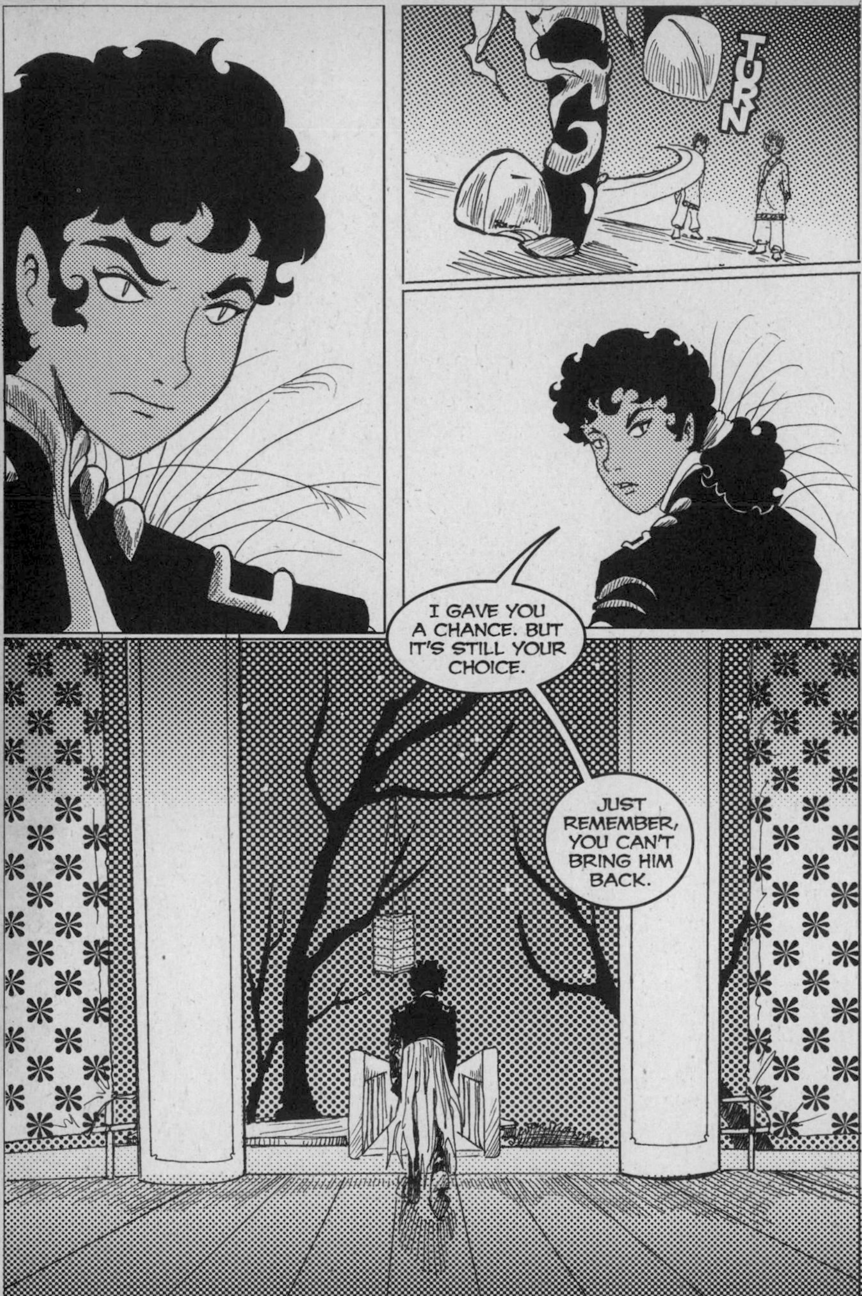
TURN
I GAVE YOU A CHANCE. BUT IT'S STILL YOUR CHOICE.
JUST REMEMBER, YOU CAN'T BRING HIM BACK.

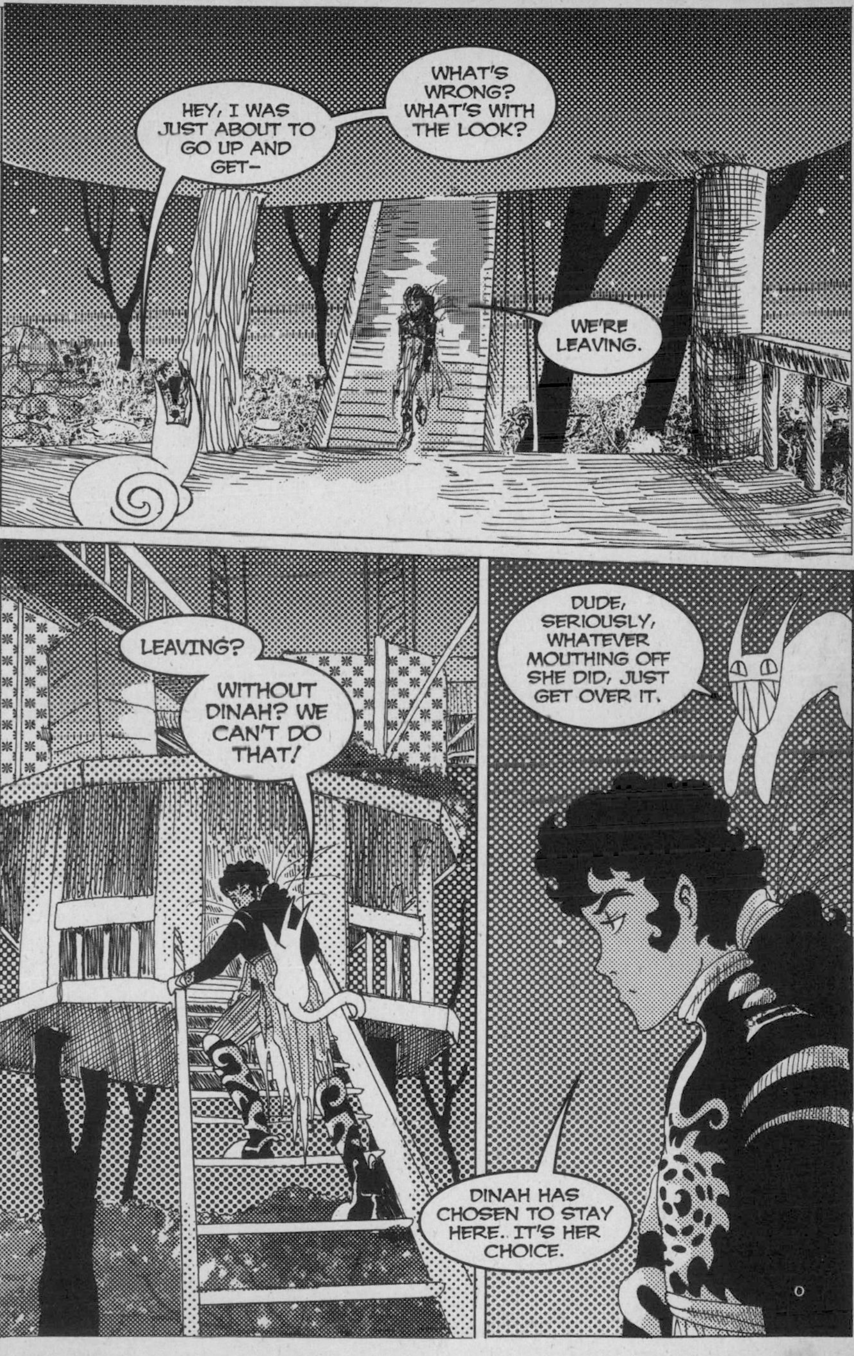
HEY, I WAS JUST ABOUT TO GO UP AND GET-
WHAT'S WRONG? WHAT'S WITH THE LOOK?
WE'RE LEAVING.
LEAVING?
WITHOUT DINAH? WE CAN'T DO THAT!
DUDE, SERIOUSLY, WHATEVER MOUTHING OFF SHE DID, JUST GET OVER IT.
DINAH HAS CHOSEN TO STAY HERE.. IT'S HER CHOICE.

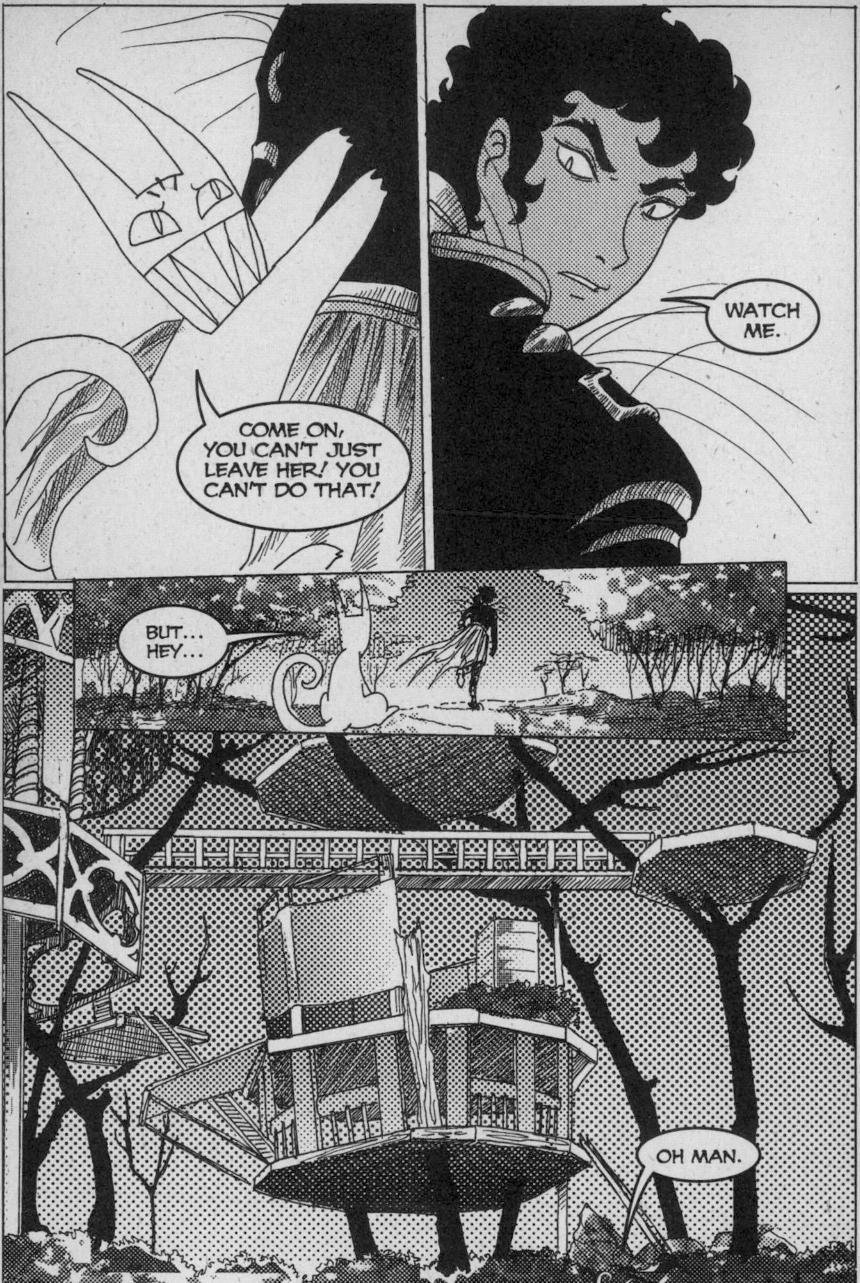
COME ON, YOU CAN'T JUST LEAVE HER! YOU CAN'T DO THAT!
WATCH ME.
BUT... HEY...
OH MAN.

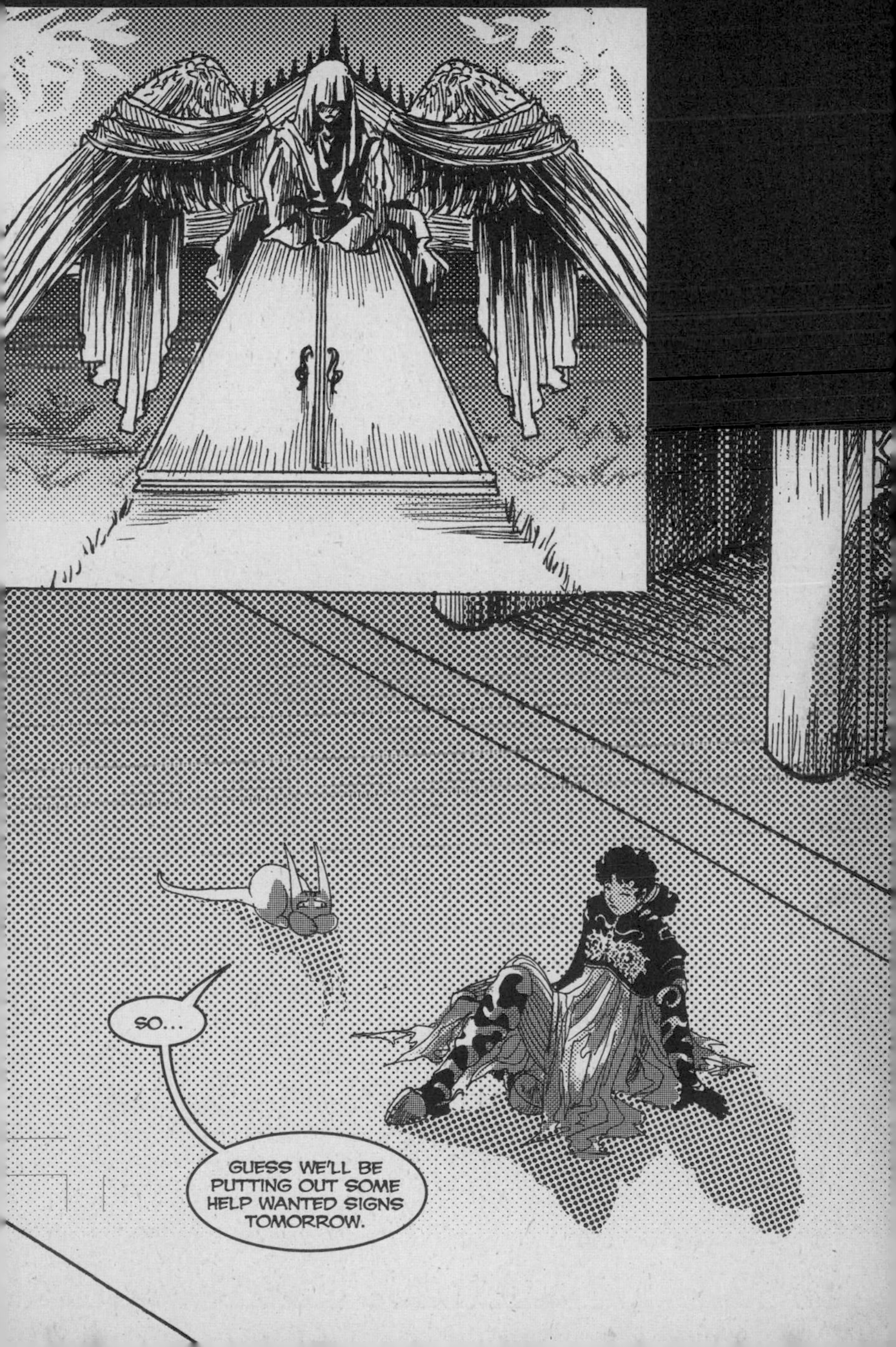
SO...
GUESS WE'LL BE PUTTING OUT SOME HELP WANTED SIGNS TOMORROW.

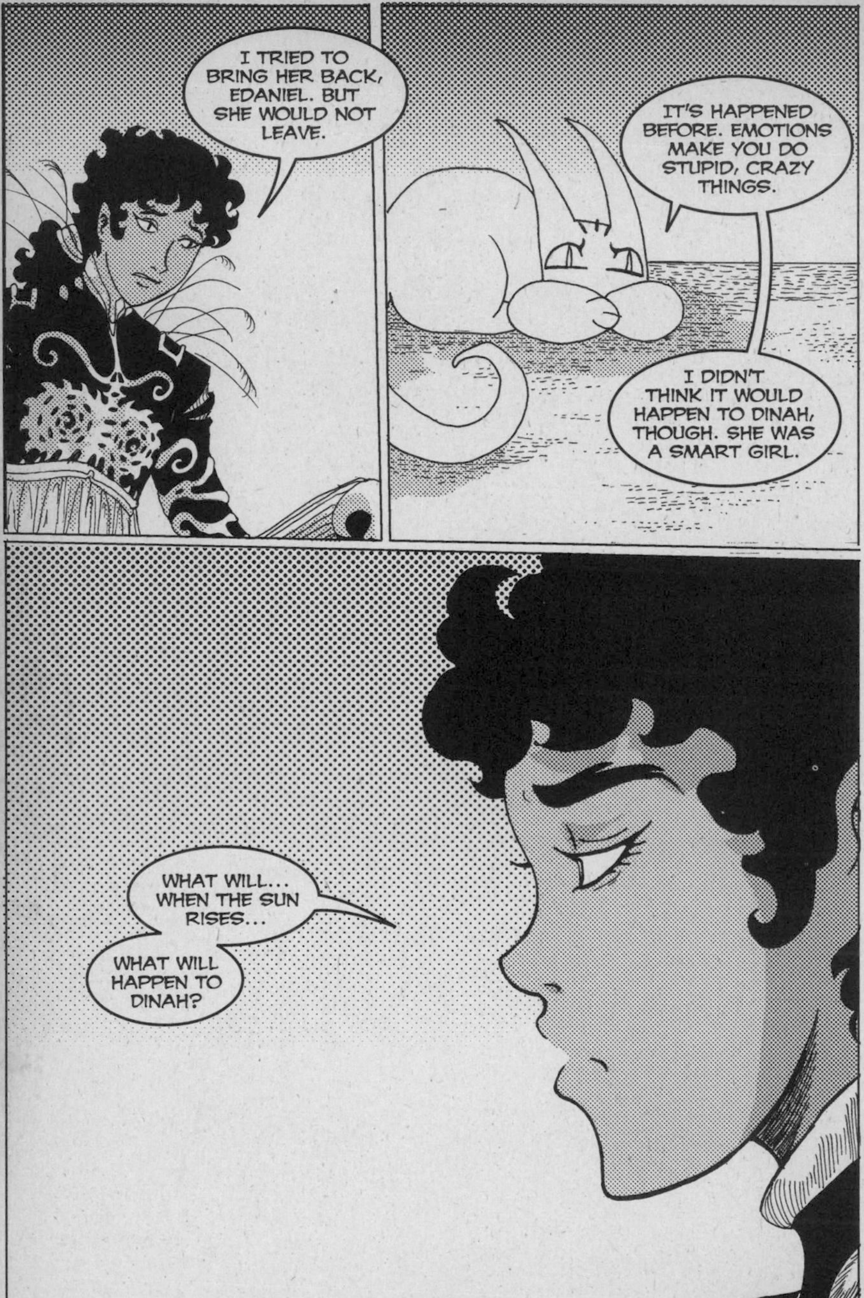
I TRIED TO BRING HER BACK, EDANIEL. BUT SHE WOULD NOT LEAVE.
IT'S HAPPENED BEFORE. EMOTIONS MAKE YOU DO STUPID, CRAZY THINGS.
I DIDN'T THINK IT WOULD HAPPEN TO DINAH, THOUGH. SHE WAS A SMART GIRL.
WHAT WILL... WHEN THE SUN RISES...
WHAT WILL HAPPEN TO DINAH?

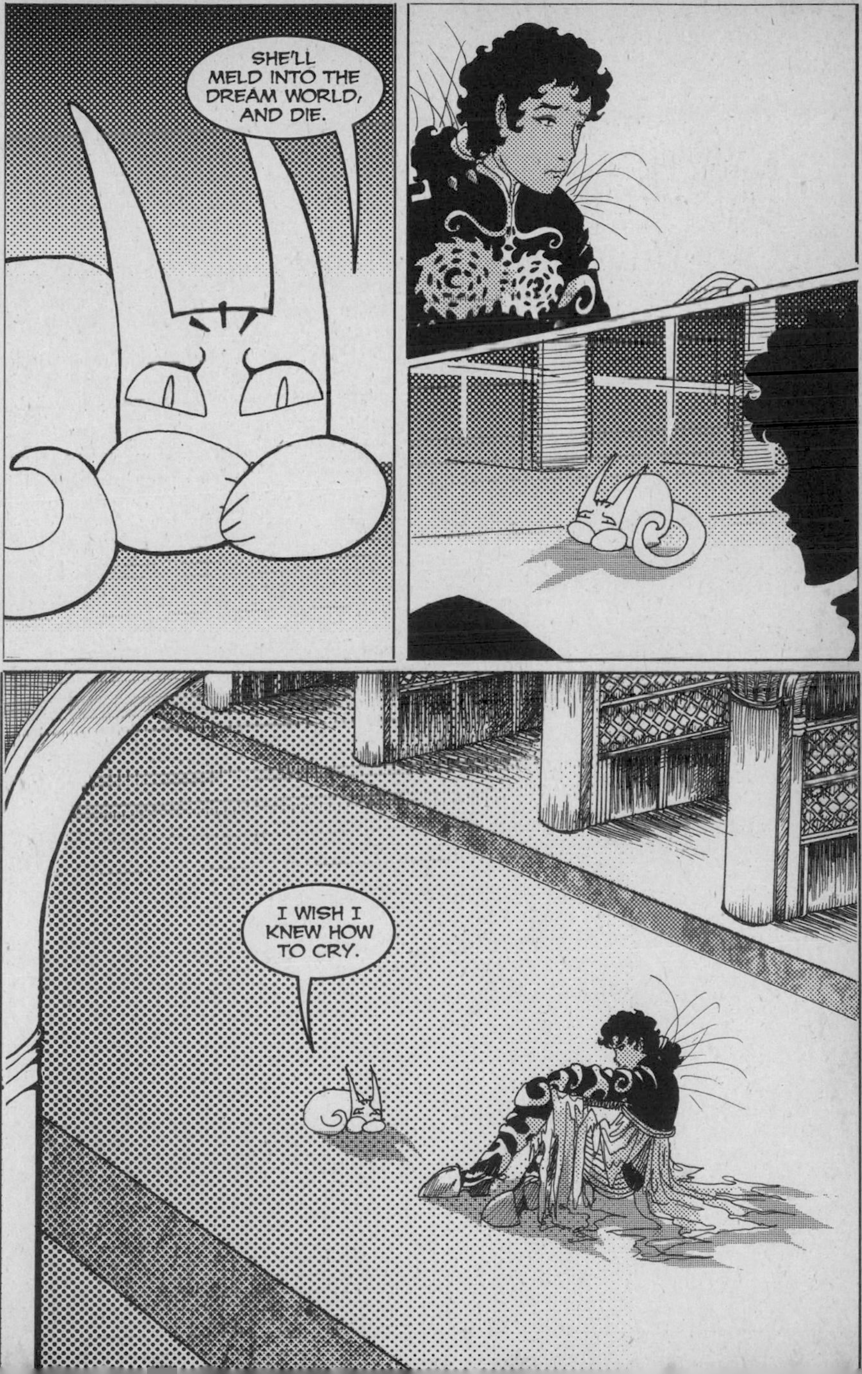
SHE'LL MELD INTO THE DREAM WORLD, AND DIE.
I WISH I KNEW HOW TO CRY.

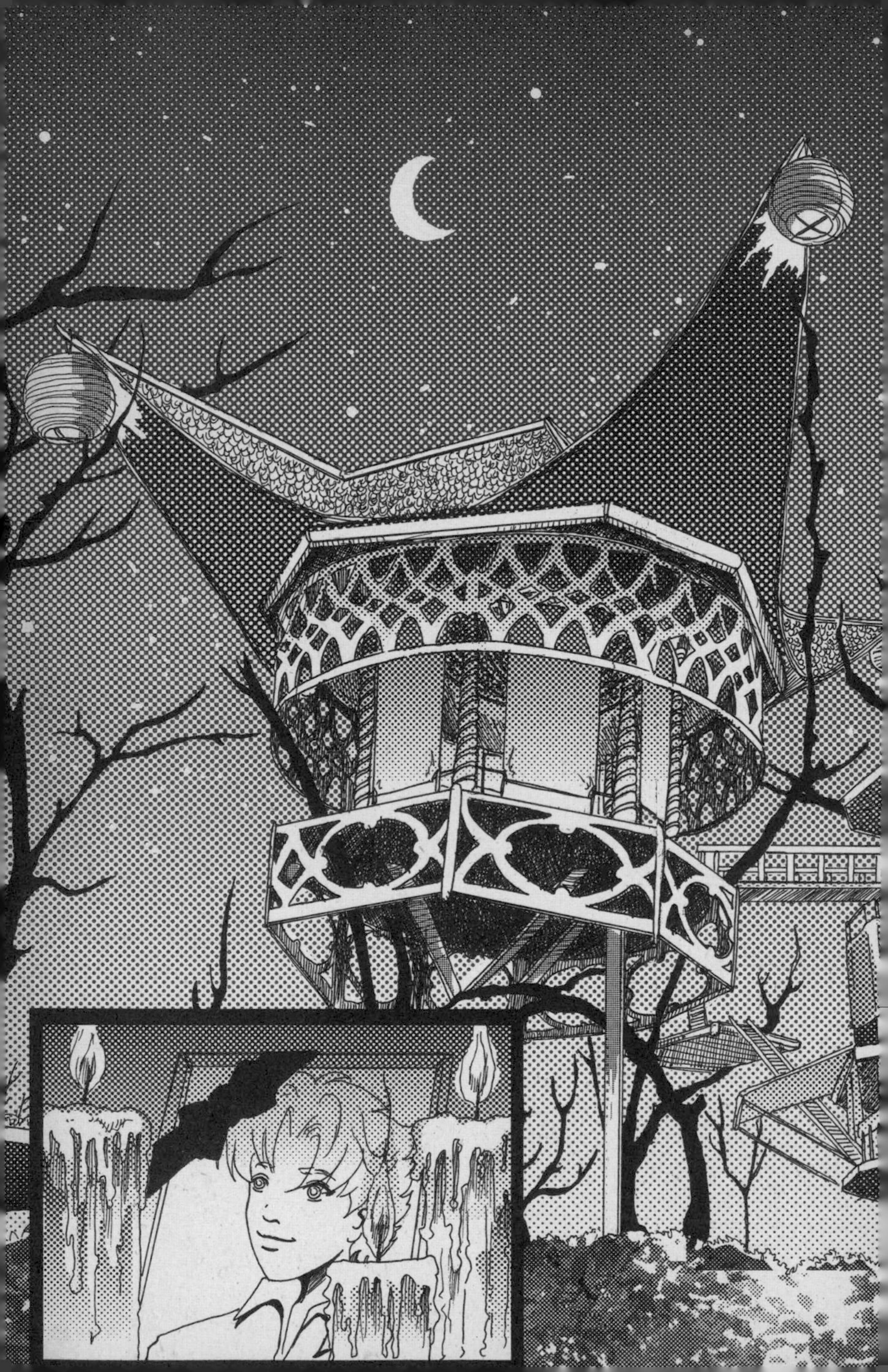

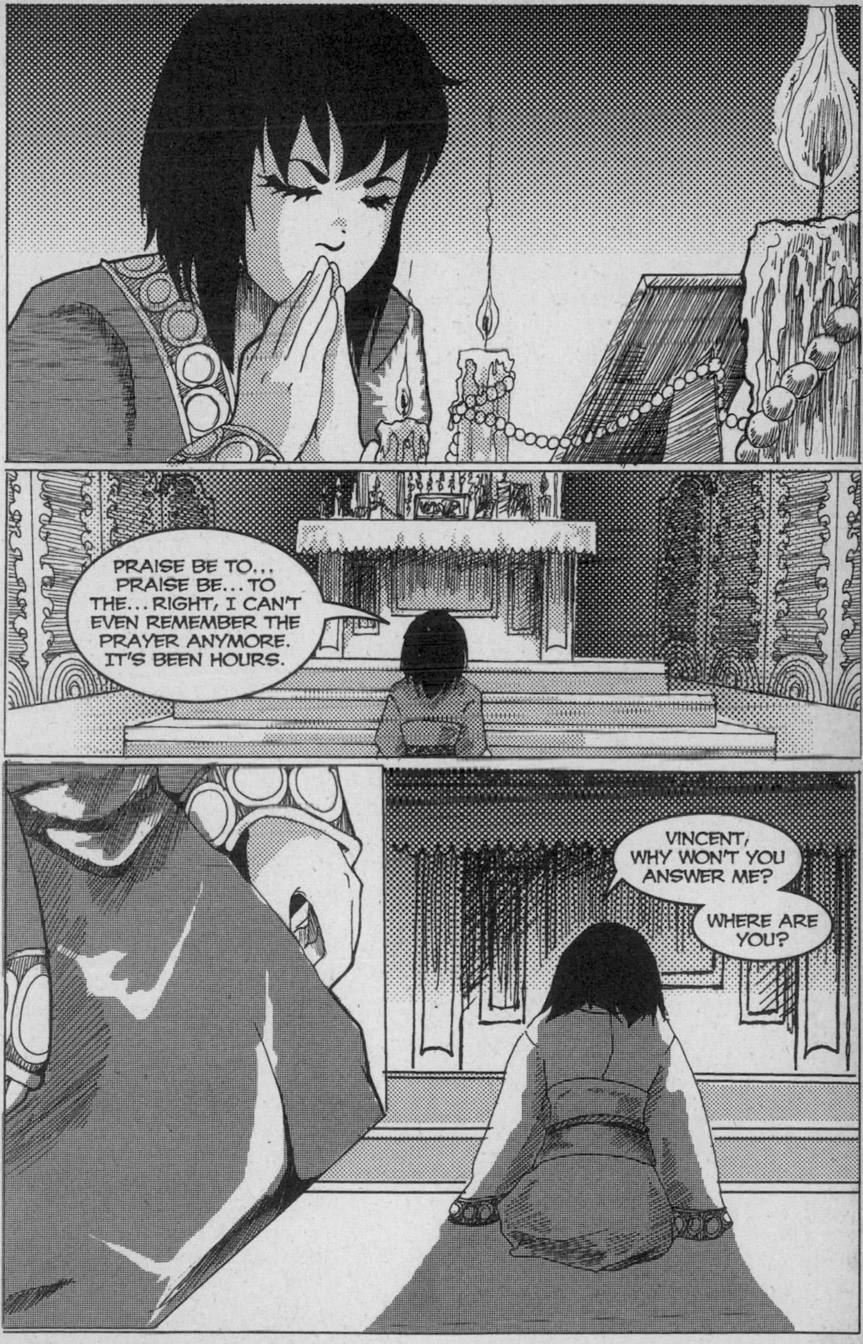
PRAISE BE TO... PRAISE BE... TO THE... RIGHT, I CAN'T EVEN REMEMBER THE PRAYER ANYMORE. IT'S BEEN HOURS.
VINCENT, WHY WON'T YOU ANSWER ME?
WHERE ARE YOU?

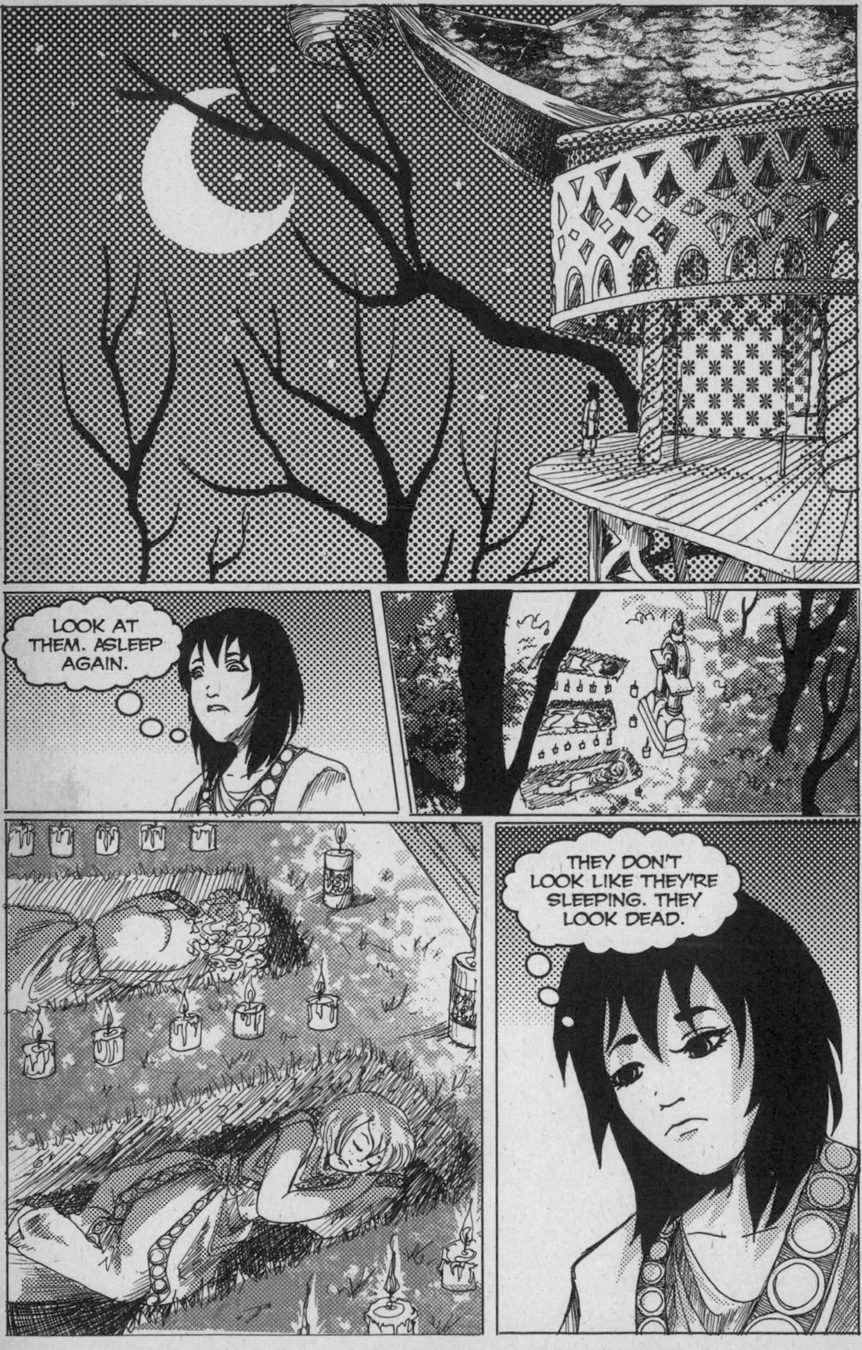
LOOK AT THEM. ASLEEP AGAIN.
THEY DON'T LOOK LIKE THEY'RE SLEEPING. THEY LOOK DEAD.

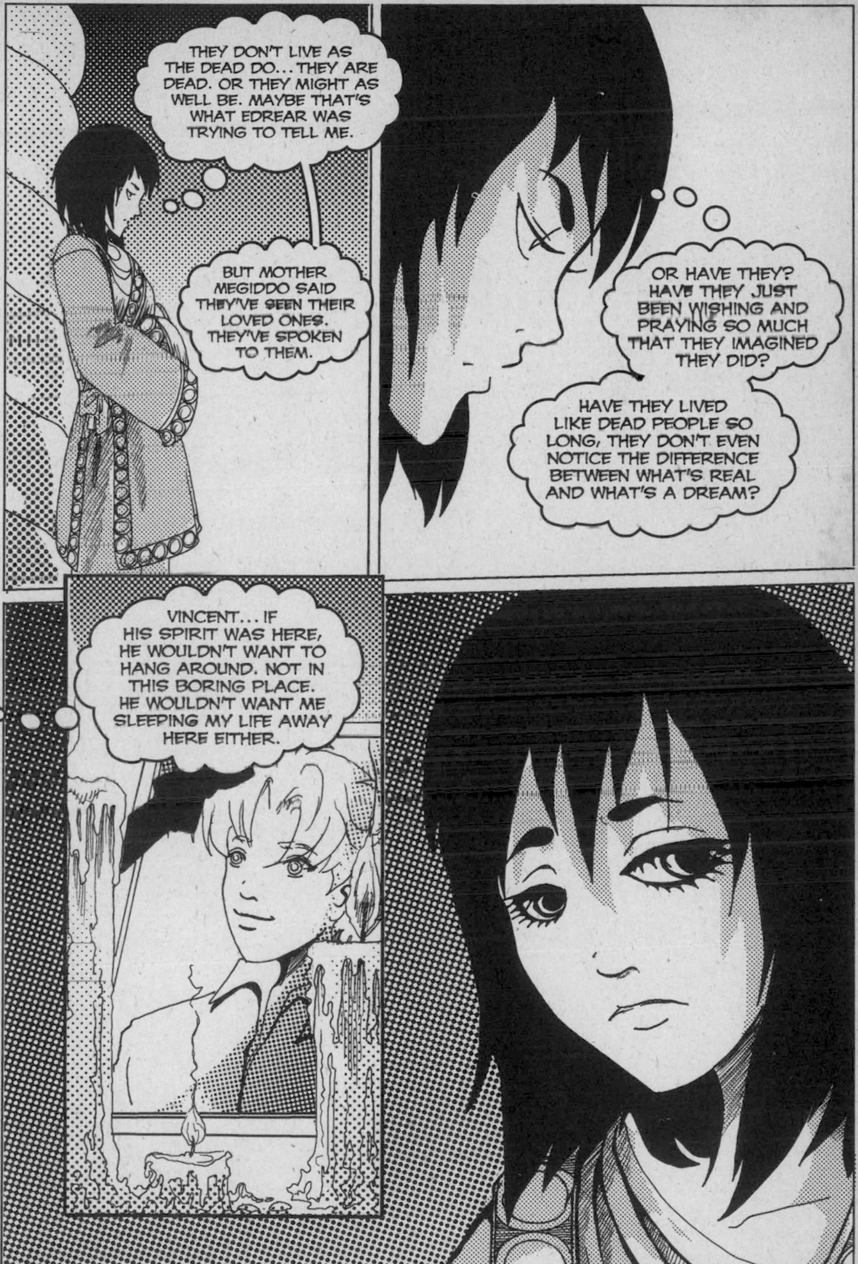
THEY DON'T LIVE AS THE DEAD DO... THEY ARE DEAD. OR THEY MIGHT AS WELL BE. MAYBE THAT'S WHAT EDREAR WAS TRYING TO TELL ME.
BUT MOTHER MEGIDDO SAID THEY'VE SEEN THEIR LOVED ONES. THEY'VE SPOKEN TO THEM.
OR HAVE THEY? HAVE THEY JUST BEEN WISHING AND PRAYING SO MUCH THAT THEY IMAGINED THEY DID?
HAVE THEY LIVED LIKE DEAD PEOPLE SO LONG, THEY DON'T EVEN NOTICE THE DIFFERENCE BETWEEN WHAT'S REAL AND WHAT'S A DREAM?
VINCENT... IF HIS SPIRIT WAS HERE, HE WOULDN'T WANT TO HANG AROUND. NOT IN THIS BORING PLACE. HE WOULDN'T WANT ME SLEEPING MY LIFE AWAY HERE EITHER.

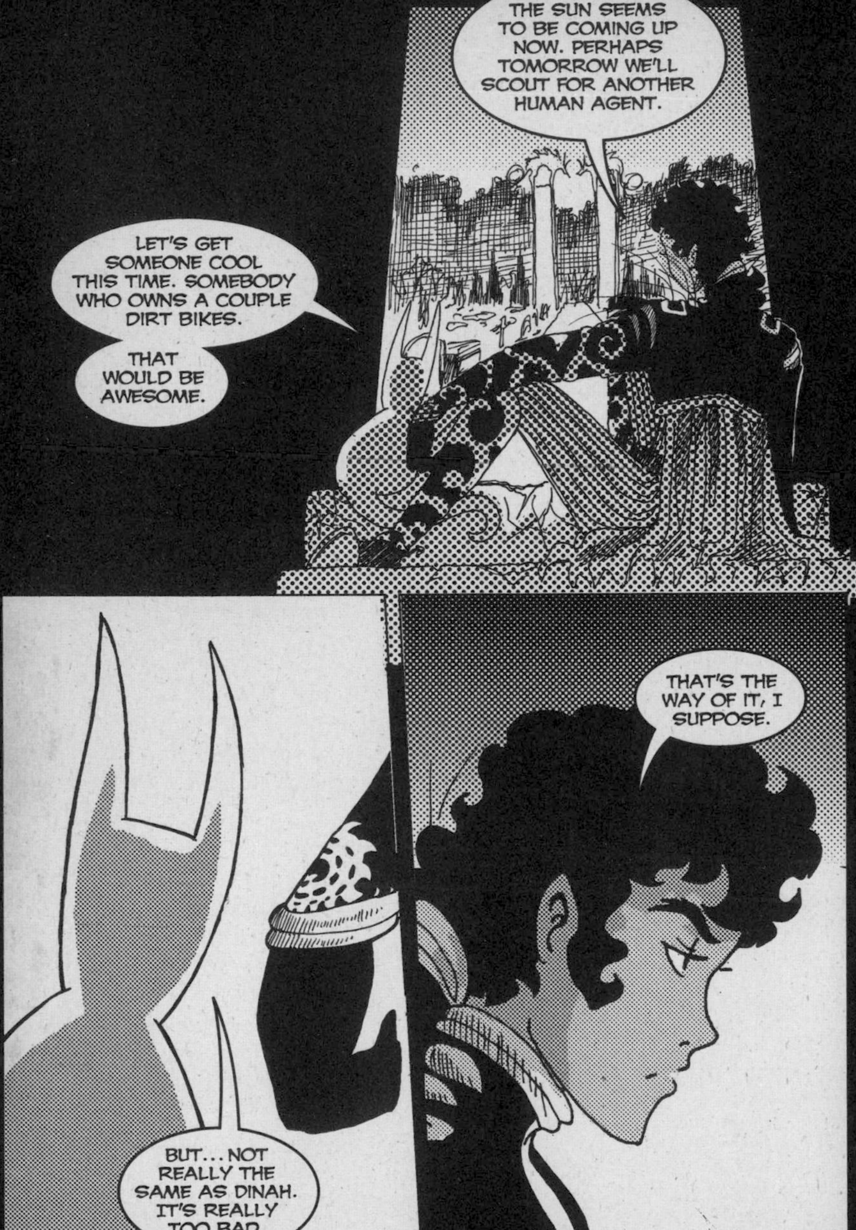
THE SUN SEEMS TO BE COMING UP NOW. PERHAPS TOMORROW WE'LL SCOUT FOR ANOTHER HUMAN AGENT.
LET'S GET SOMEONE COOL THIS TIME. SOMEBODY WHO OWNS A COUPLE DIRT BIKES.
THAT WOULD BE AWESOME.
BUT... NOT REALLY THE SAME AS DINAH. IT'S REALLY TOO BAD.
THAT'S THE WAY OF IT, I SUPPOSE.

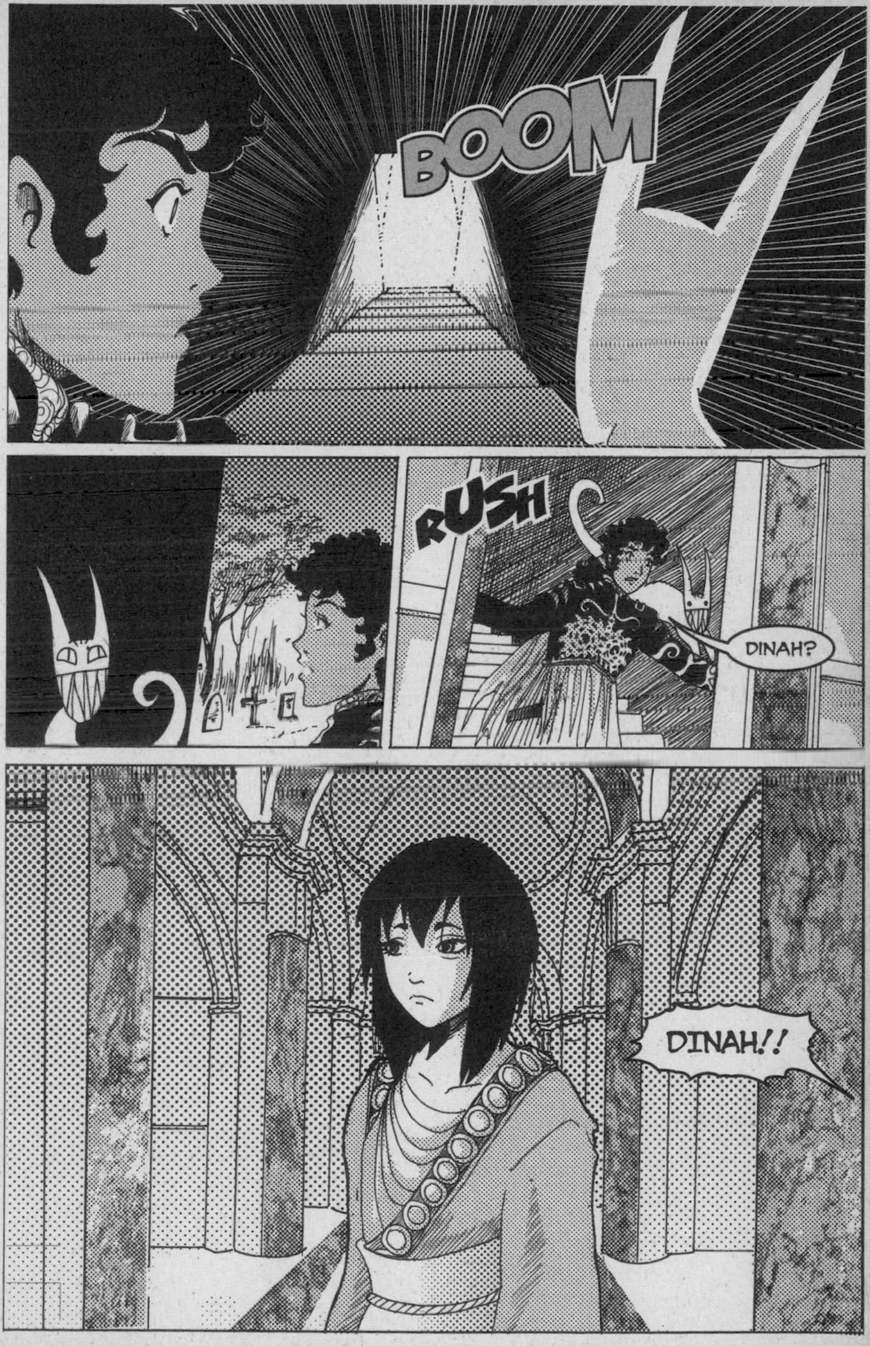
BOOM
RUSH
DINAH?
DINAH!!

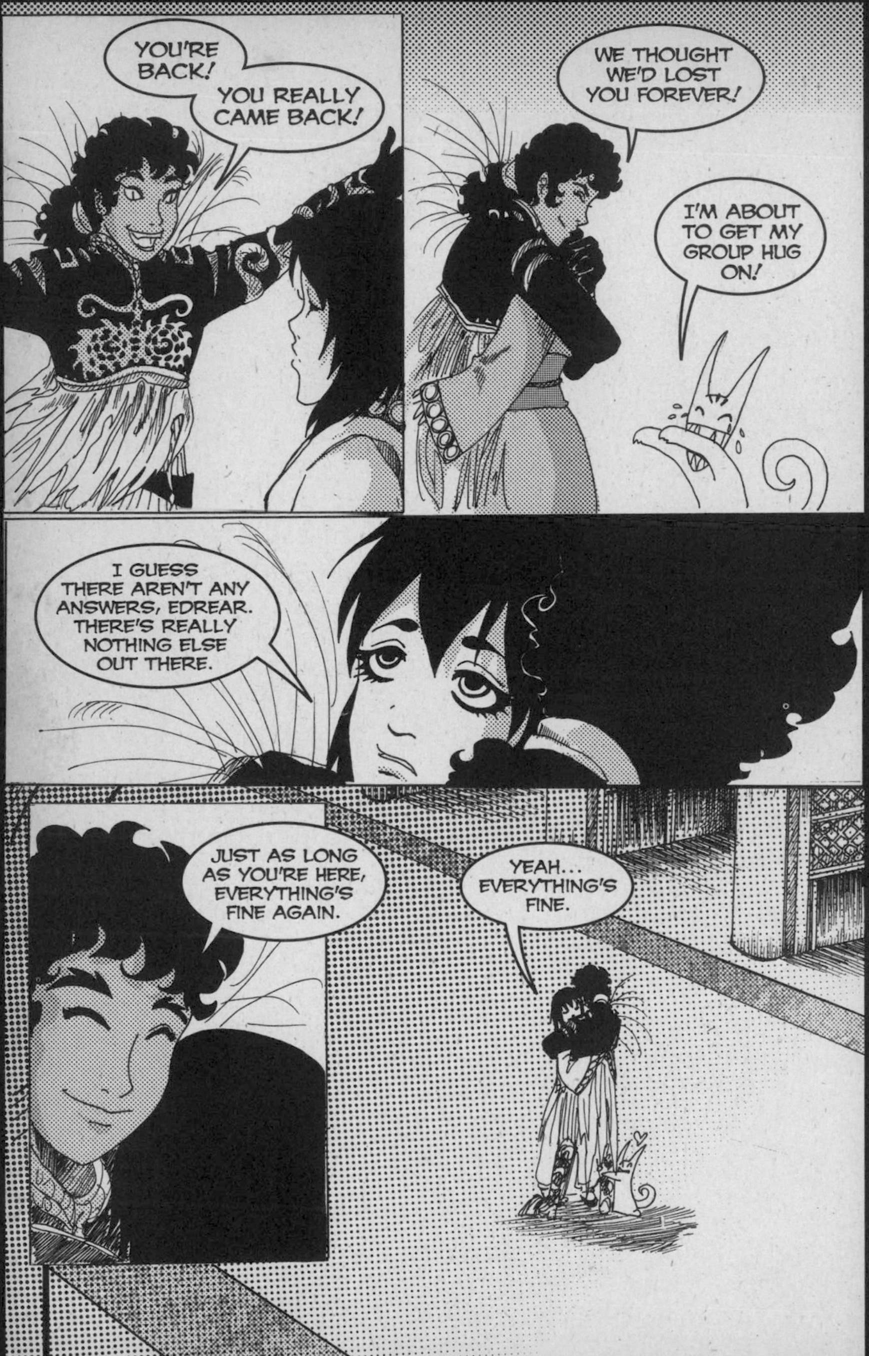
YOU'RE BACK!
YOU REALLY CAME BACK!
WE THOUGHT WE'D LOST YOU FOREVER!
I'M ABOUT TO GET MY GROUP HUG ON!
I GUESS THERE AREN'T ANY ANSWERS, EDREAR. THERE'S REALLY NOTHING ELSE OUT THERE.
JUST AS LONG AS YOU'RE HERE, EVERYTHING'S FINE AGAIN.
YEAH... EVERYTHING'S FINE.

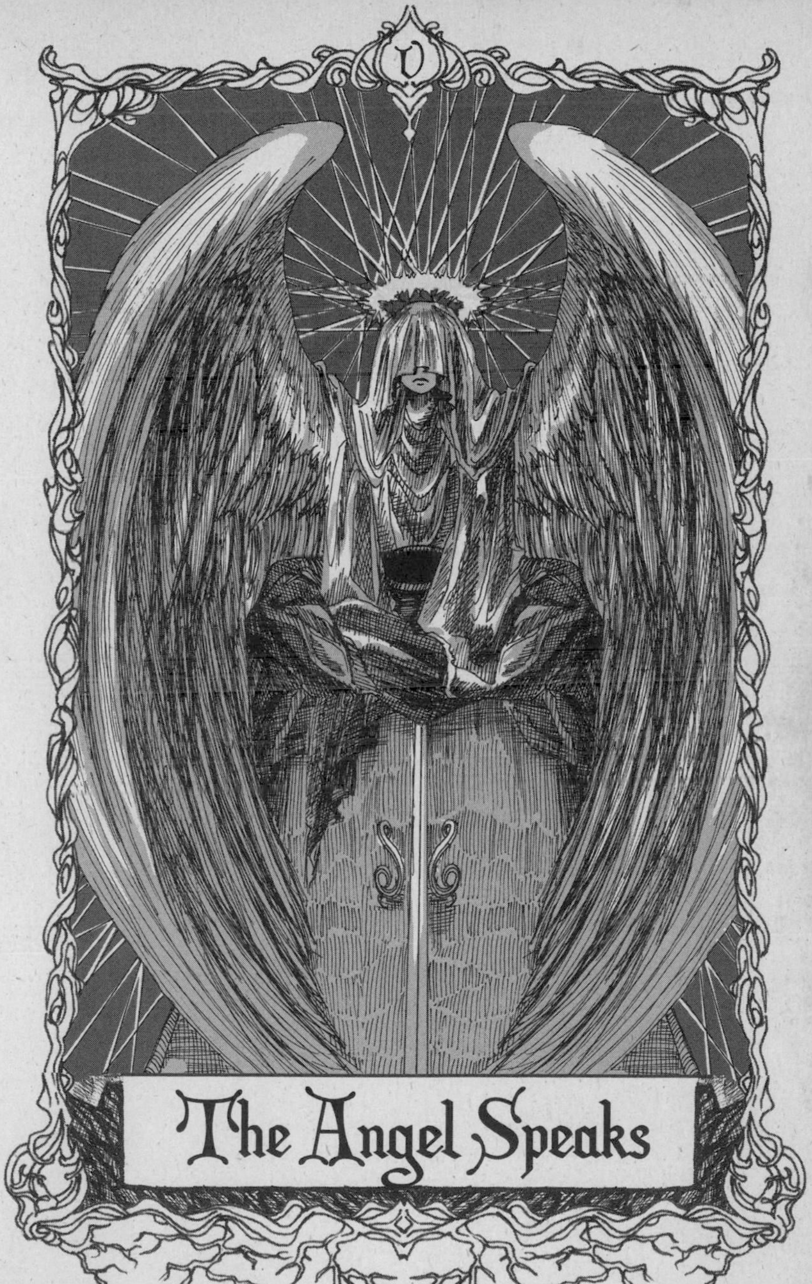
V
The Angel Speaks

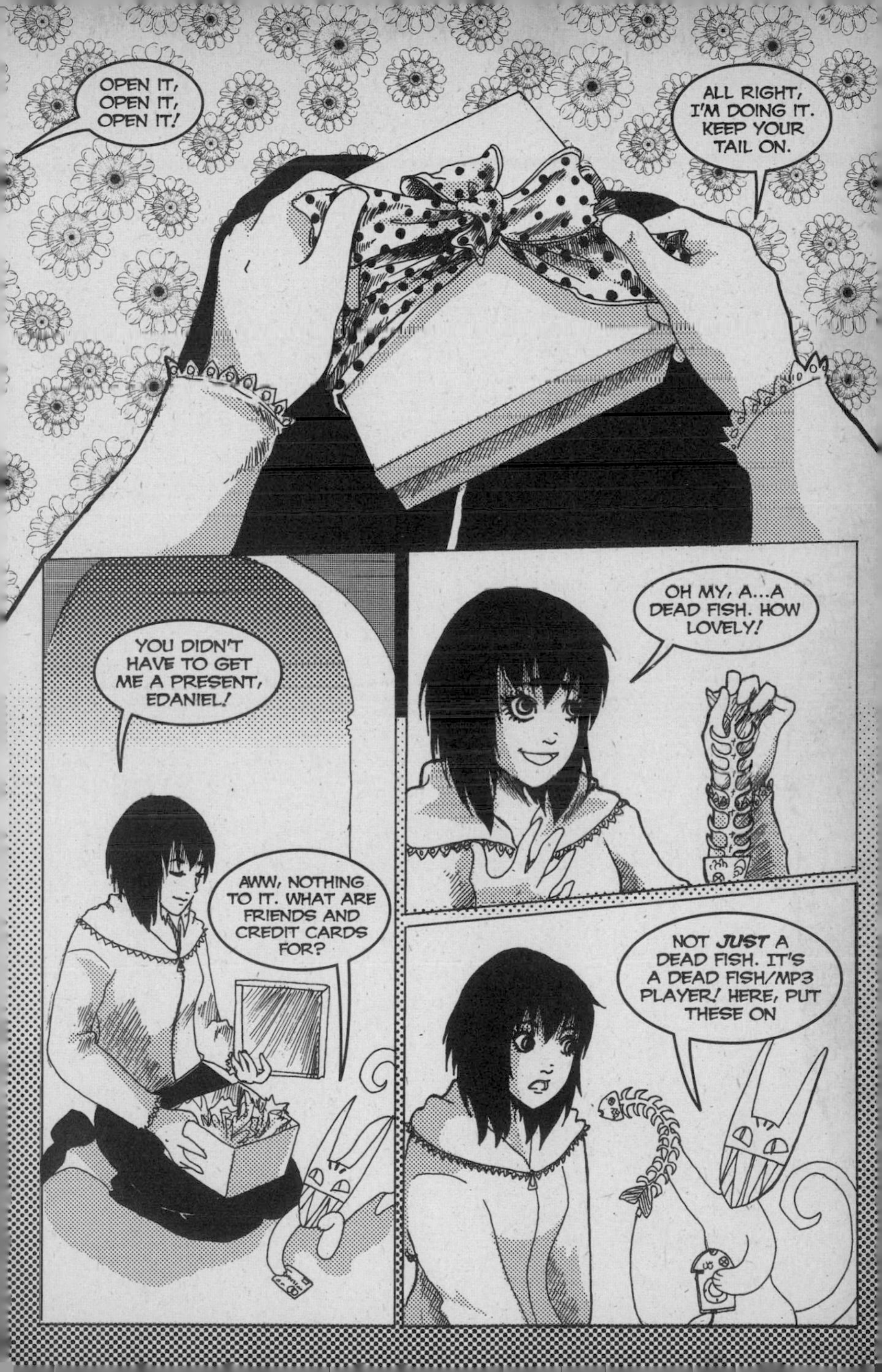
OPEN IT, OPEN IT, OPEN IT!
ALL RIGHT, I'M DOING IT. KEEP YOUR TAIL ON.
YOU DIDN'T HAVE TO GET ME A PRESENT, EDANIEL!
AWW, NOTHING TO IT. WHAT ARE FRIENDS AND CREDIT CARDS FOR?
OH MY, A...A DEAD FISH. HOW LOVELY!
NOT *JUST* A DEAD FISH. IT'S A DEAD FISH/MP3 PLAYER! HERE, PUT THESE ON

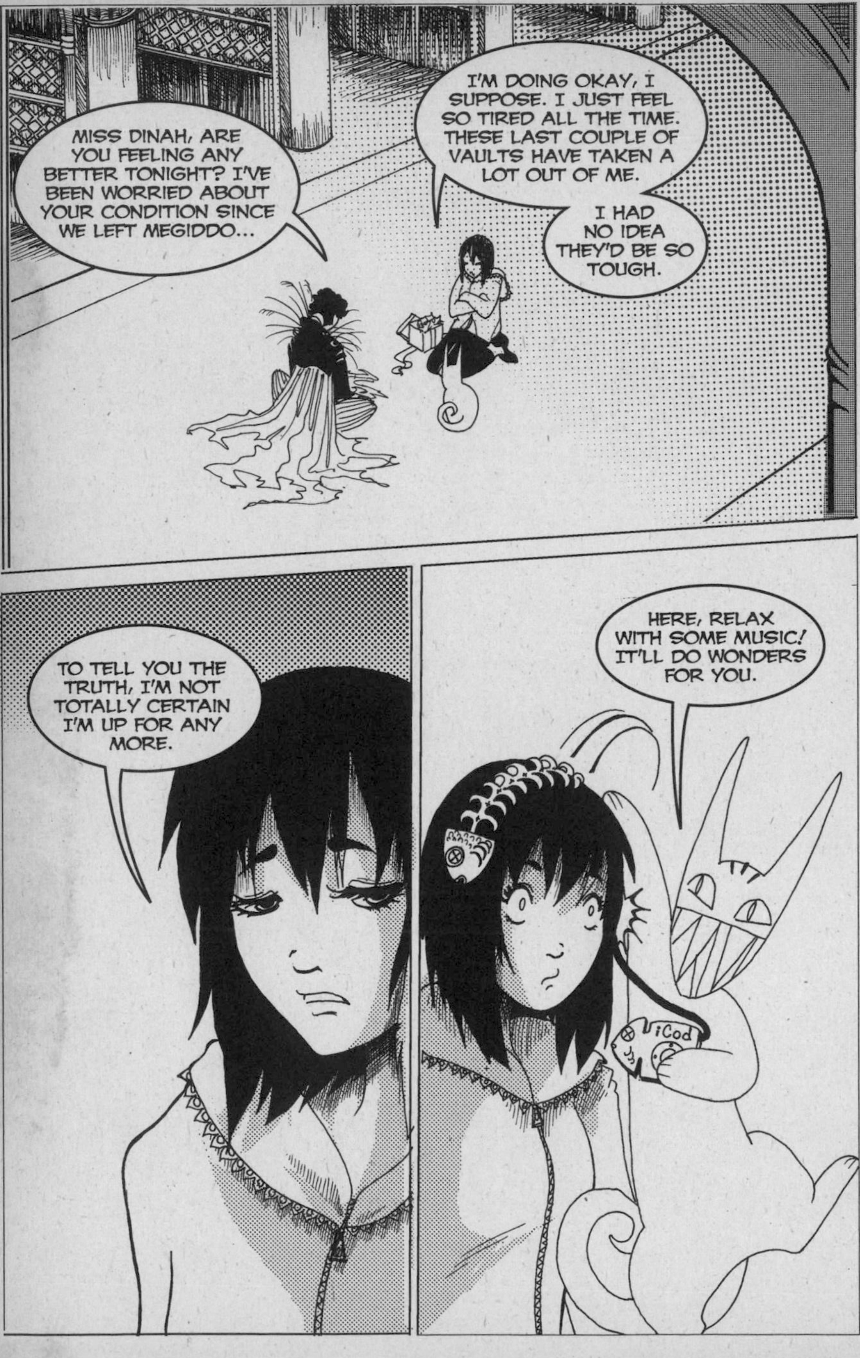
MISS DINAH, ARE YOU FEELING ANY BETTER TONIGHT? I'VE BEEN WORRIED ABOUT YOUR CONDITION SINCE WE LEFT MEGIDDO...
I'M DOING OKAY, I SUPPOSE. I JUST FEEL SO TIRED ALL THE TIME. THESE LAST COUPLE OF VAULTS HAVE TAKEN A LOT OUT OF ME.
I HAD NO IDEA THEY'D BE SO TOUGH.
TO TELL YOU THE TRUTH, I'M NOT TOTALLY CERTAIN I'M UP FOR ANY MORE.
HERE, RELAX WITH SOME MUSIC! IT'LL DO WONDERS FOR YOU.
iCod

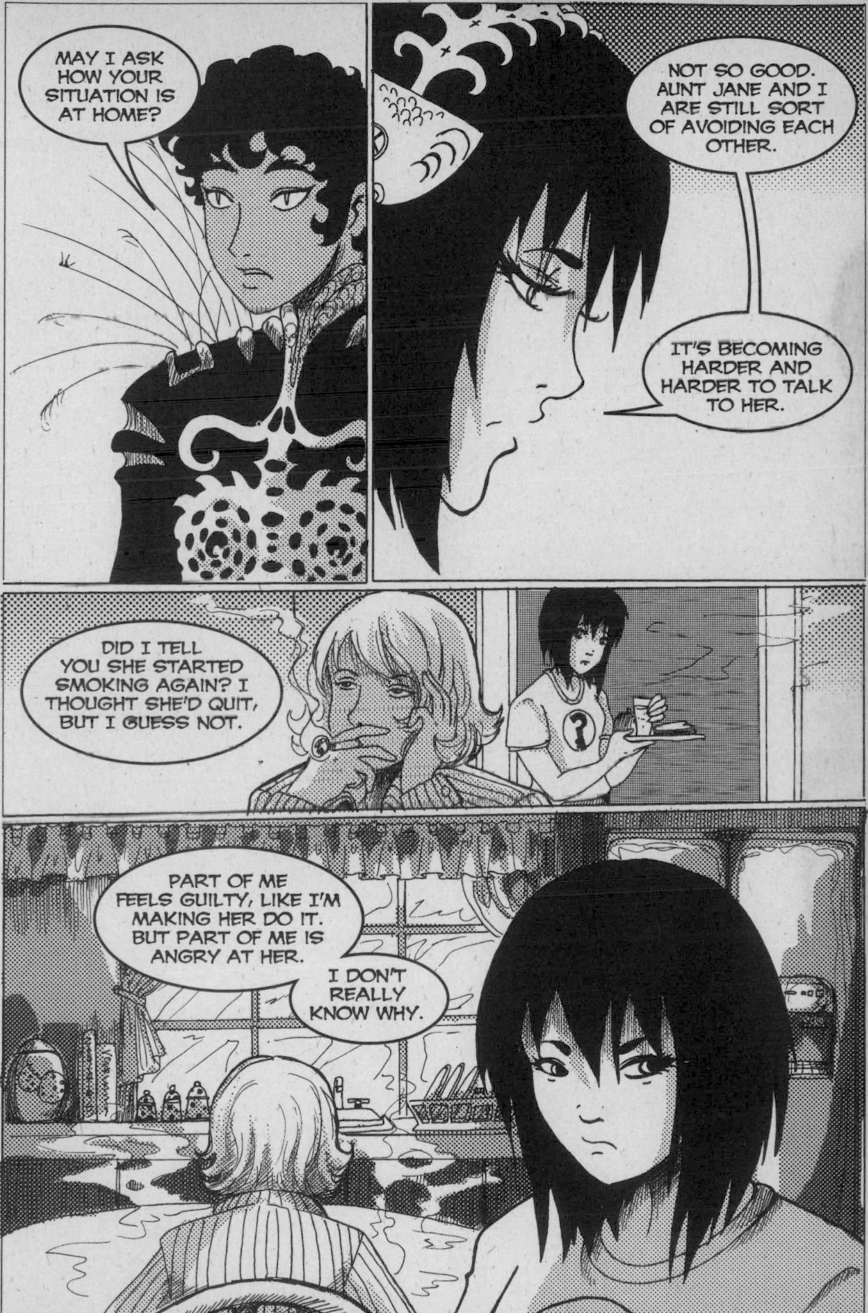
MAY I ASK HOW YOUR SITUATION IS AT HOME?
NOT SO GOOD. AUNT JANE AND I ARE STILL SORT OF AVOIDING EACH OTHER.
IT'S BECOMING HARDER AND HARDER TO TALK TO HER.
DID I TELL YOU SHE STARTED SMOKING AGAIN? I THOUGHT SHE'D QUIT, BUT I GUESS NOT.
PART OF ME FEELS GUILTY, LIKE I'M MAKING HER DO IT. BUT PART OF ME IS ANGRY AT HER.
I DON'T REALLY KNOW WHY.

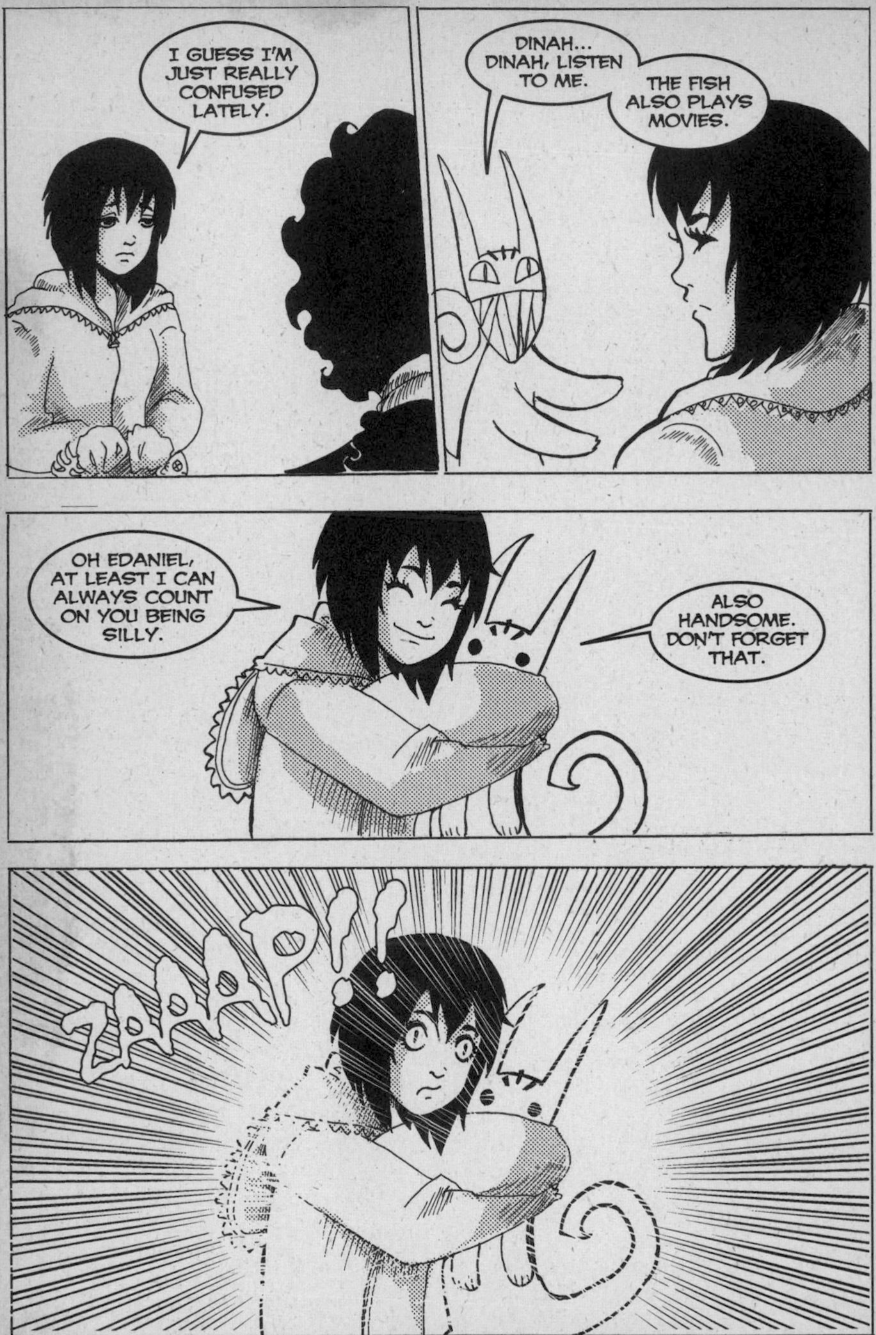
I GUESS I'M JUST REALLY CONFUSED LATELY.
DINAH... DINAH, LISTEN TO ME.
THE FISH ALSO PLAYS MOVIES.
OH EDANIEL, AT LEAST I CAN ALWAYS COUNT ON YOU BEING SILLY.
ALSO HANDSOME. DON'T FORGET THAT.
ZAAAP!!

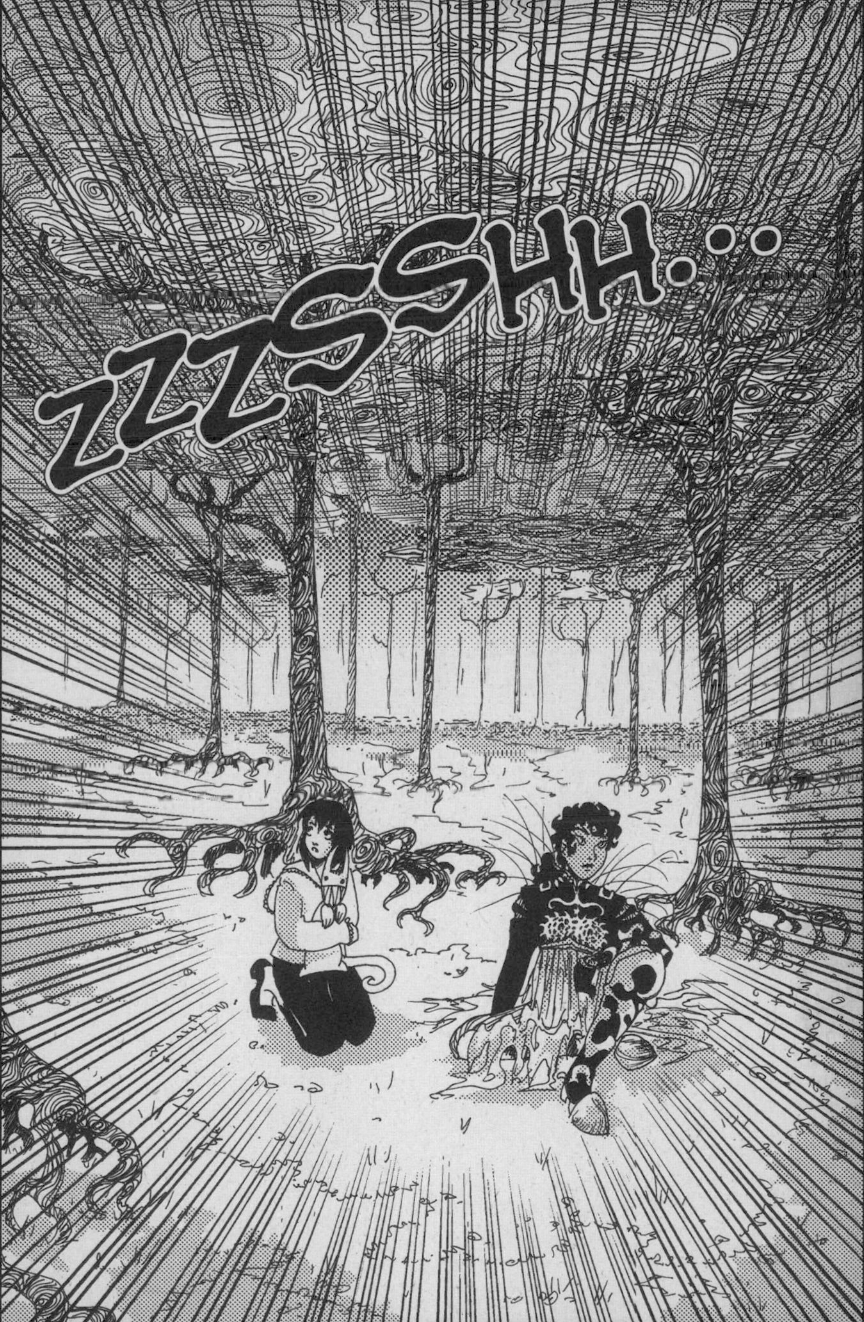
ZZZSHH...

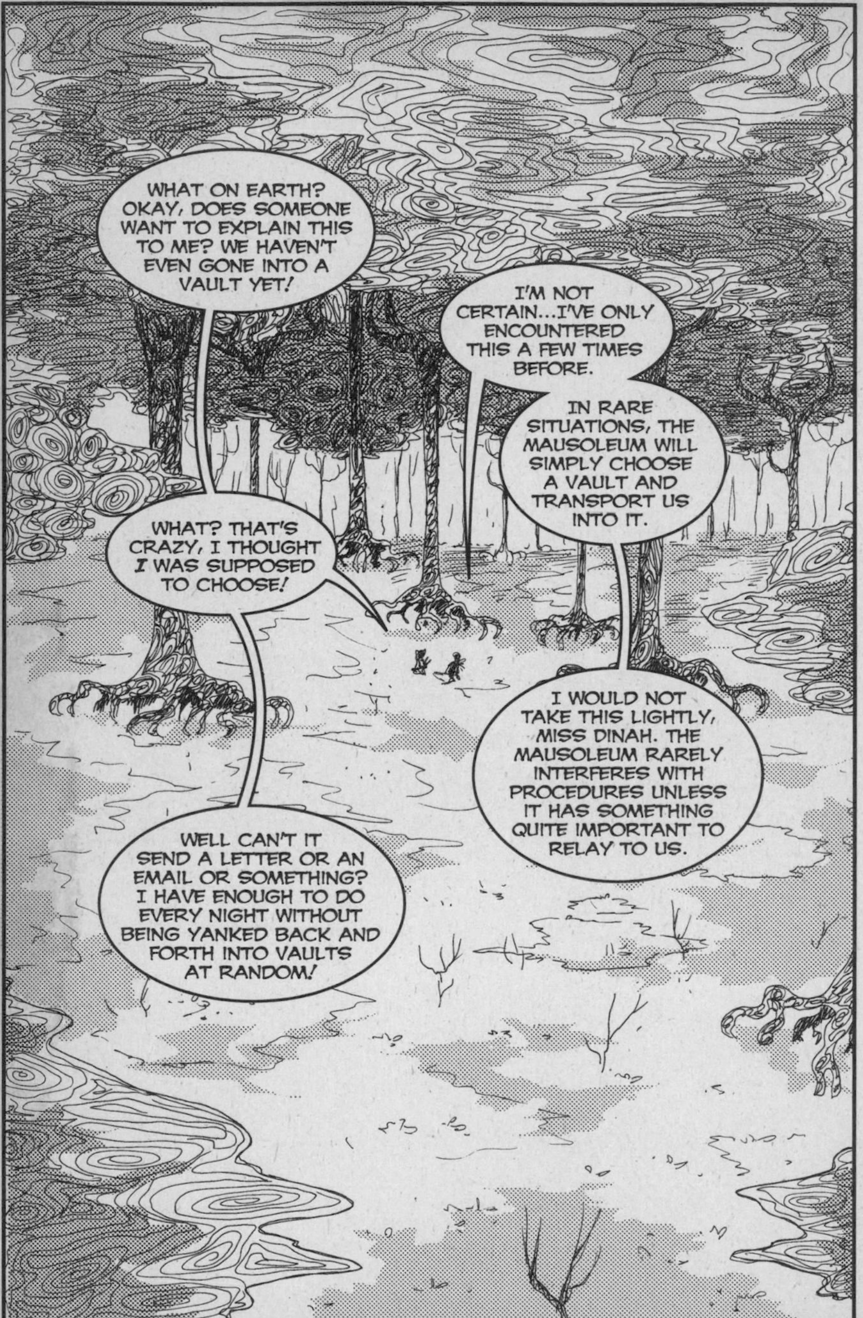
WHAT ON EARTH? OKAY, DOES SOMEONE WANT TO EXPLAIN THIS TO ME? WE HAVEN'T EVEN GONE INTO A VAULT YET!
I'M NOT CERTAIN...I'VE ONLY ENCOUNTERED THIS A FEW TIMES BEFORE.
IN RARE SITUATIONS, THE MAUSOLEUM WILL SIMPLY CHOOSE A VAULT AND TRANSPORT US INTO IT.
WHAT? THAT'S CRAZY, I THOUGHT *I* WAS SUPPOSED TO CHOOSE!
I WOULD NOT TAKE THIS LIGHTLY, MISS DINAH. THE MAUSOLEUM RARELY INTERFERES WITH PROCEDURES UNLESS IT HAS SOMETHING QUITE IMPORTANT TO RELAY TO US.
WELL CAN'T IT SEND A LETTER OR AN EMAIL OR SOMETHING? I HAVE ENOUGH TO DO EVERY NIGHT WITHOUT BEING YANKED BACK AND FORTH INTO VAULTS AT RANDOM!

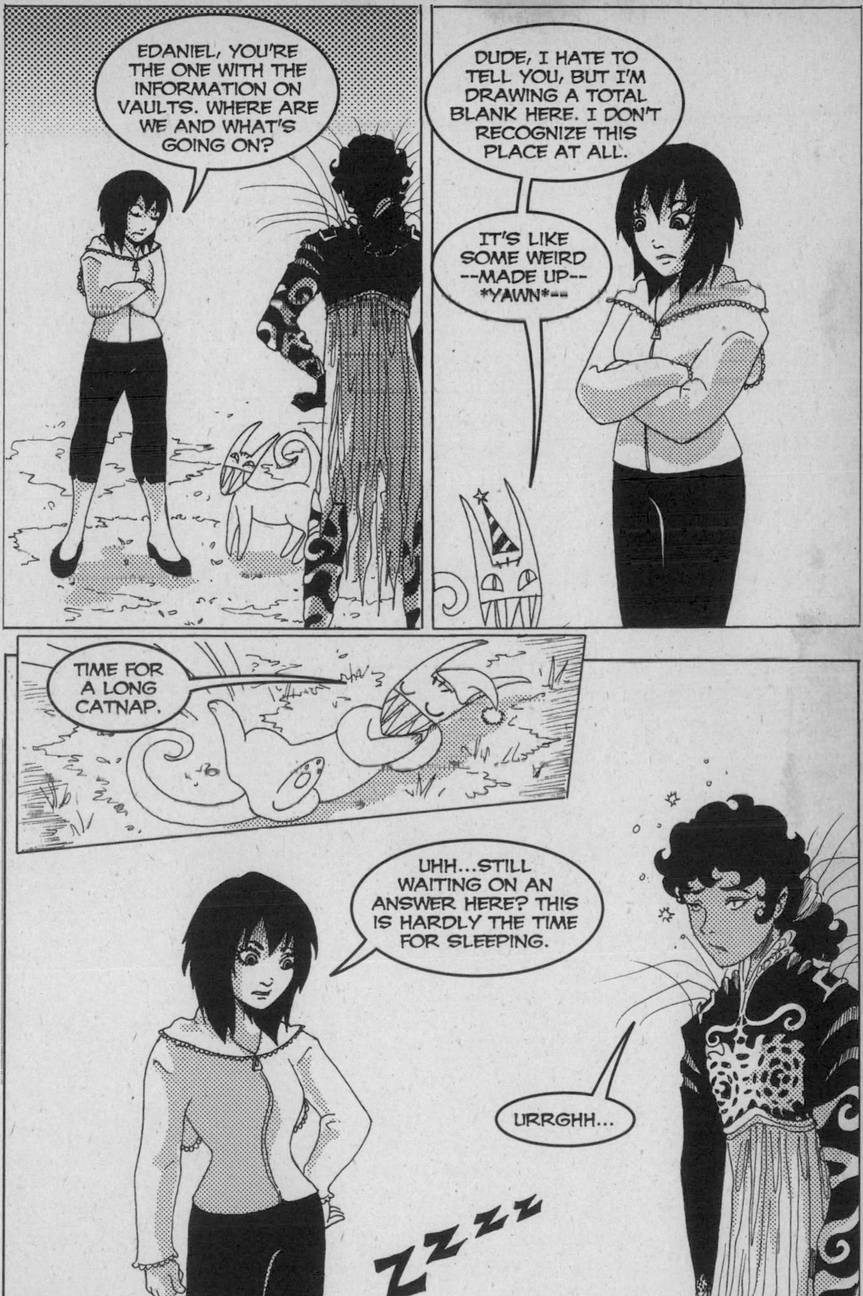
EDANIEL, YOU'RE THE ONE WITH THE INFORMATION ON VAULTS. WHERE ARE WE AND WHAT'S GOING ON?
DUDE, I HATE TO TELL YOU, BUT I'M DRAWING A TOTAL BLANK HERE. I DON'T RECOGNIZE THIS PLACE AT ALL.
IT'S LIKE SOME WEIRD --MADE UP-- *YAWN*--
TIME FOR A LONG CATNAP.
UHH...STILL WAITING ON AN ANSWER HERE? THIS IS HARDLY THE TIME FOR SLEEPING.
URRGHH...
...ZZZZZ

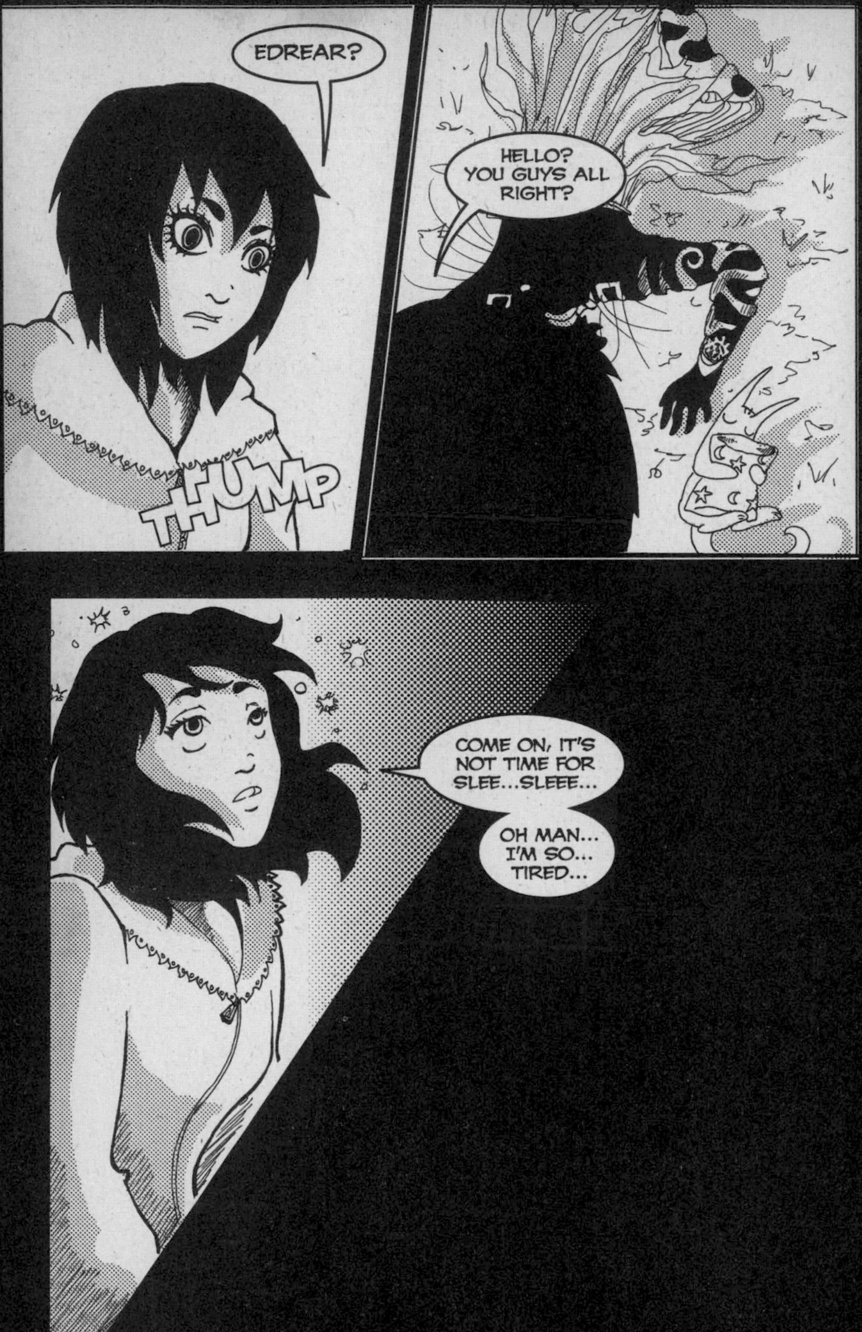
EDREAR?
THUMP
HELLO? YOU GUYS ALL RIGHT?
COME ON, IT'S NOT TIME FOR SLEE...SLEEE...
OH MAN... I'M SO... TIRED...

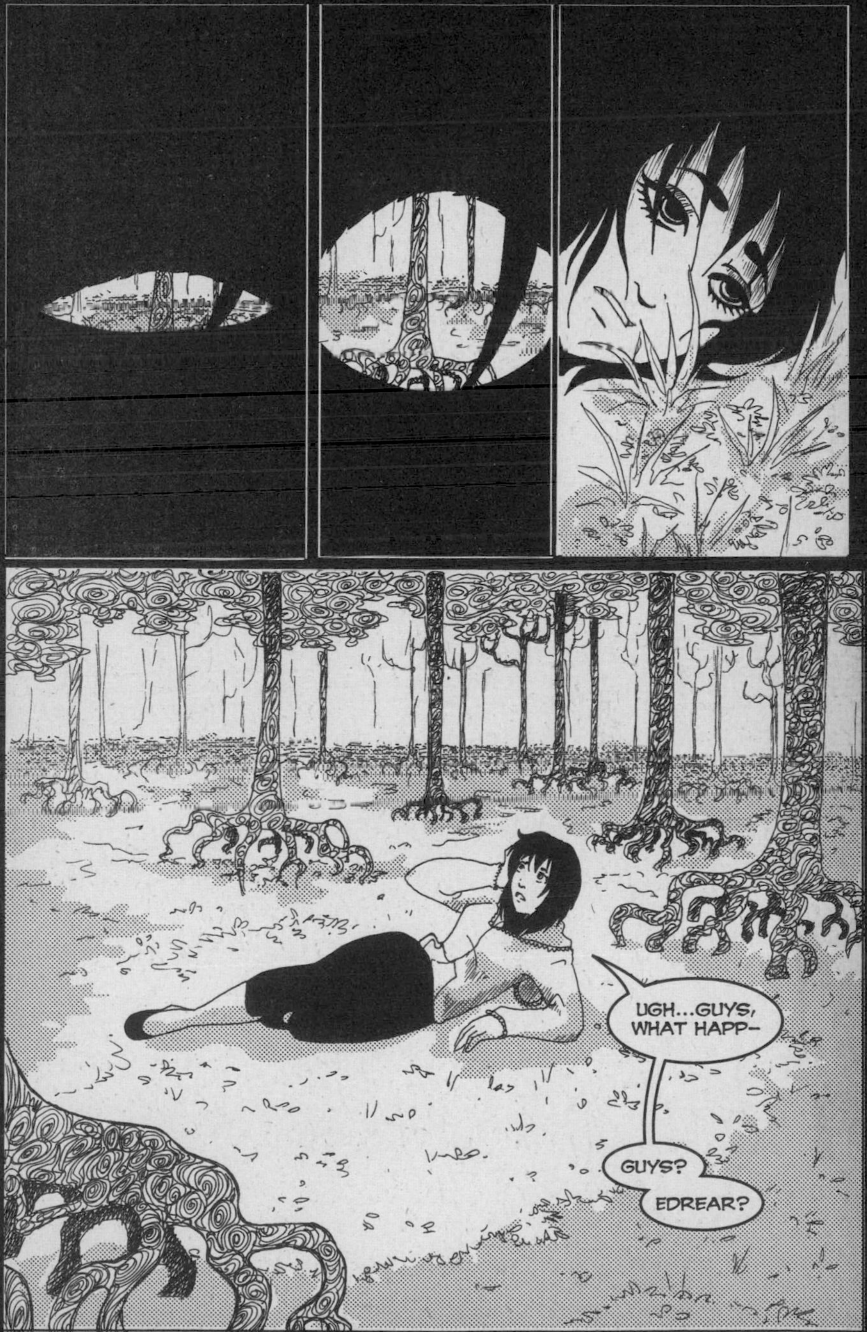
UGH...GUYS, WHAT HAPP-
GUYS?
EDREAR?

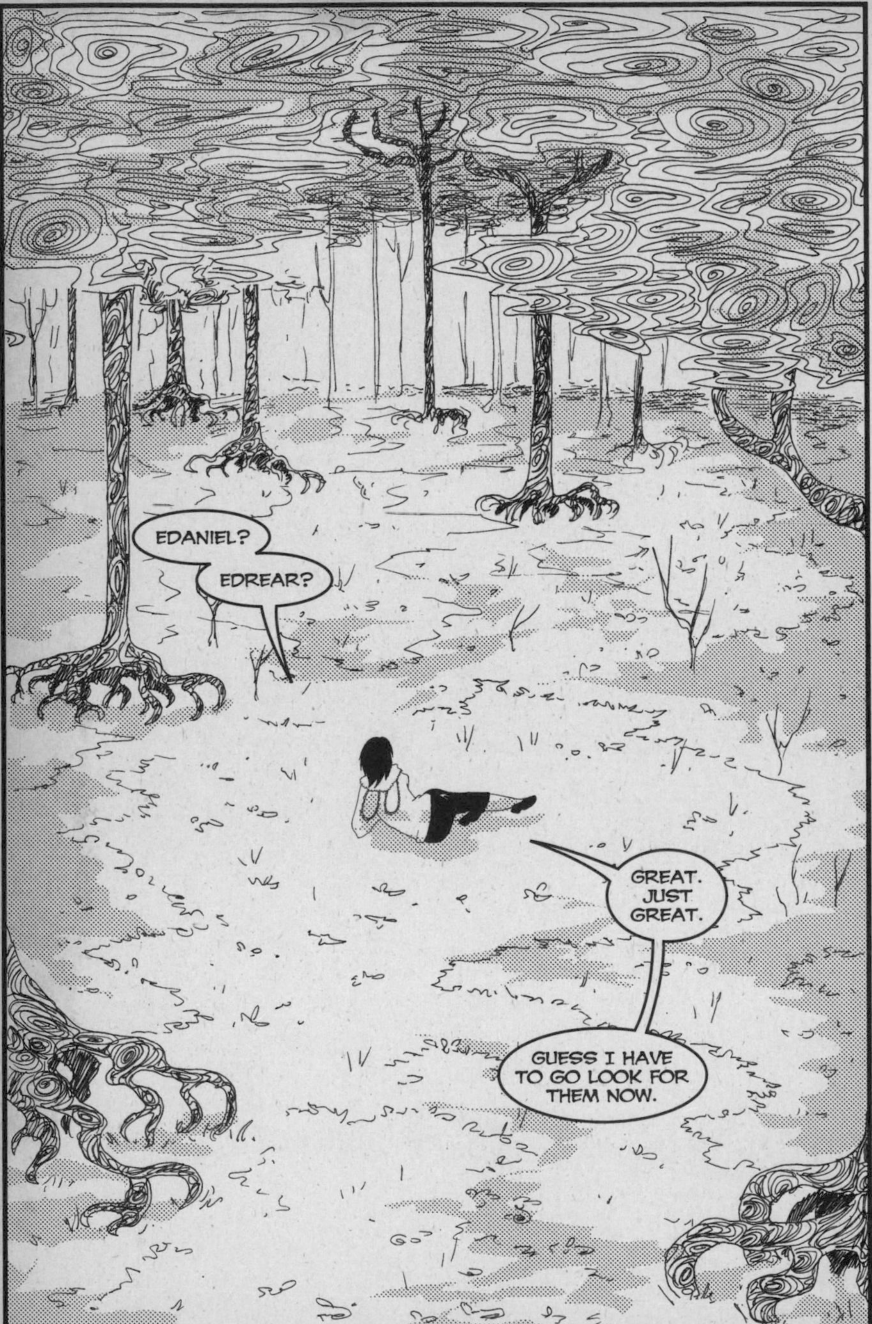
EDANIEL?
EDREAR?
GREAT. JUST GREAT.
GUESS I HAVE TO GO LOOK FOR THEM NOW.

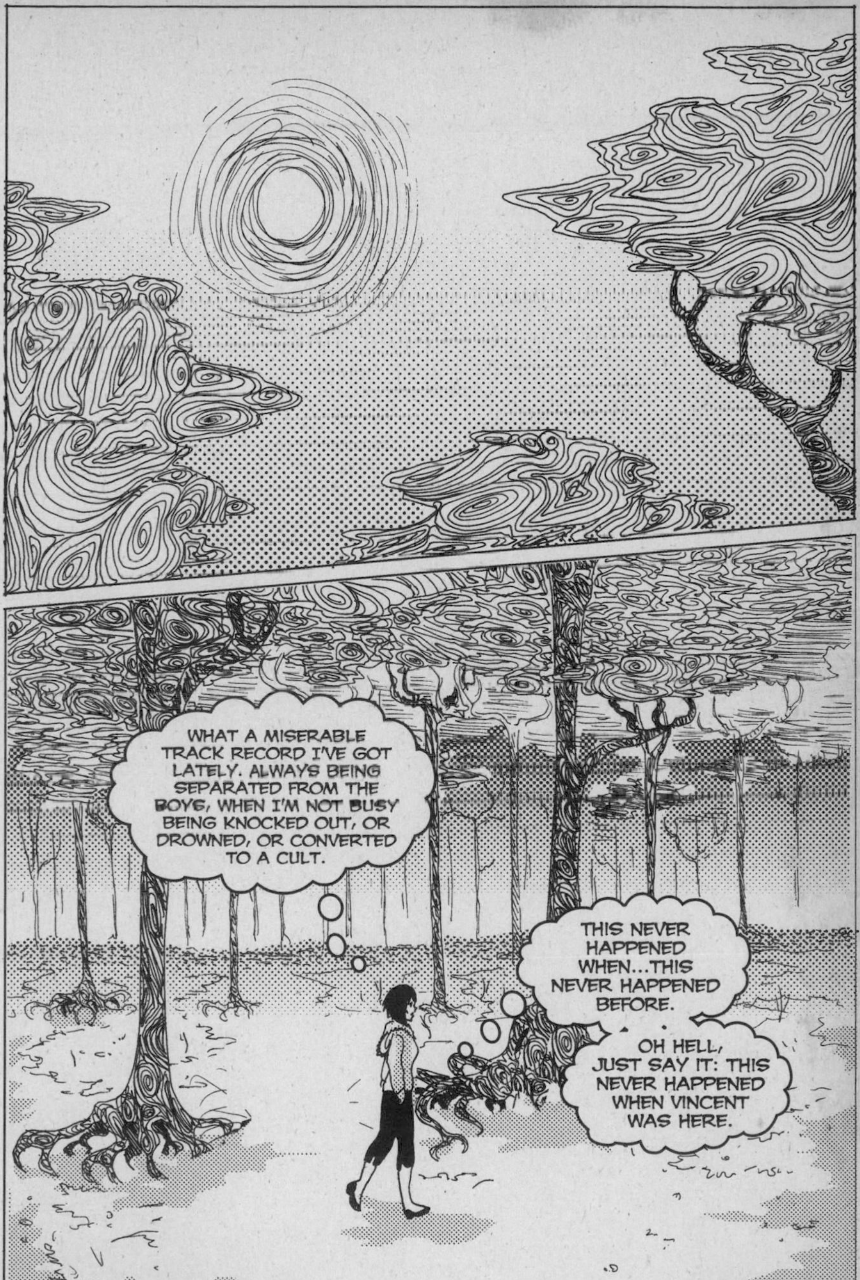
WHAT A MISERABLE TRACK RECORD I'VE GOT LATELY. ALWAYS BEING SEPARATED FROM THE BOYS, WHEN I'M NOT BUSY BEING KNOCKED OUT, OR DROWNED, OR CONVERTED TO A CULT.
THIS NEVER HAPPENED WHEN...THIS NEVER HAPPENED BEFORE.
OH HELL, JUST SAY IT: THIS NEVER HAPPENED WHEN VINCENT WAS HERE.

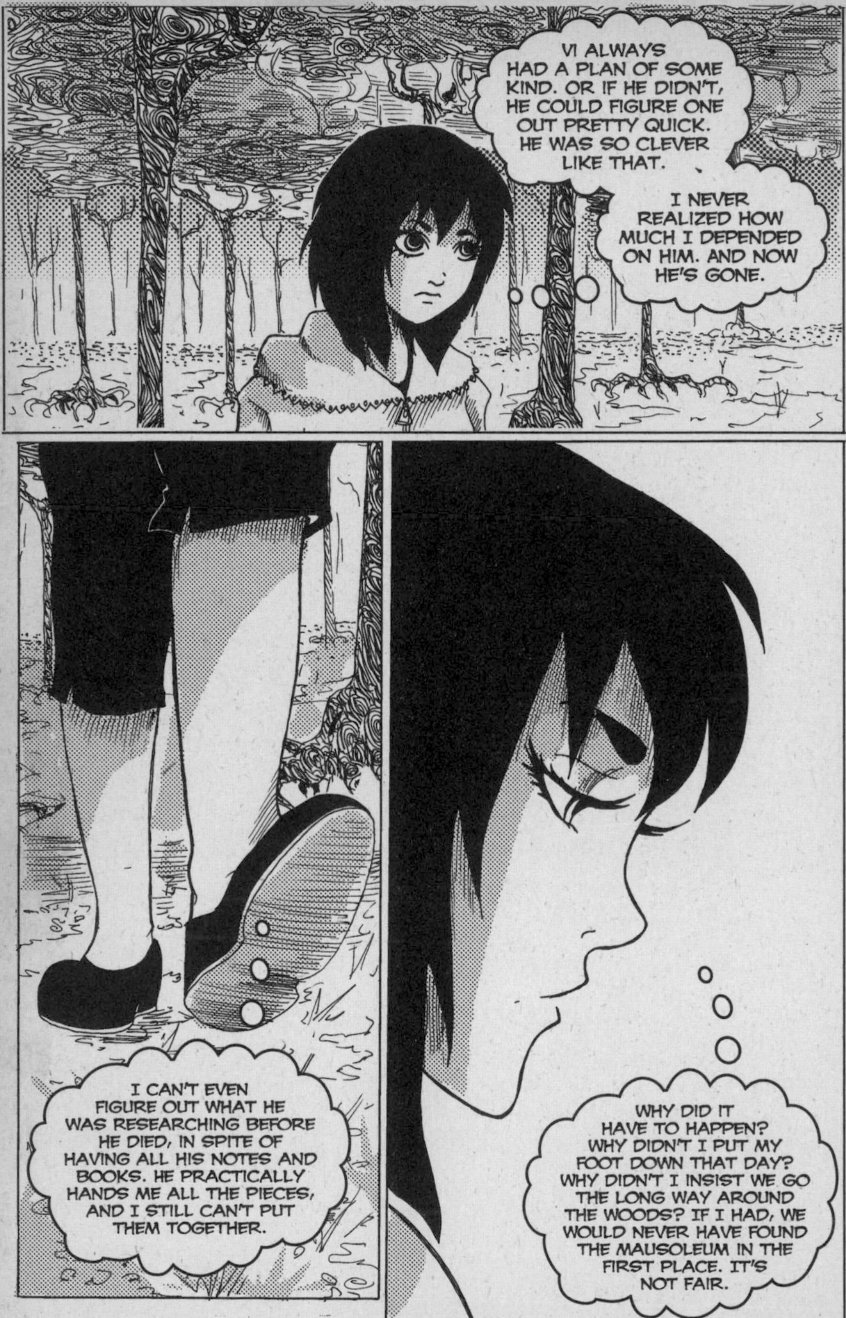
VI ALWAYS HAD A PLAN OF SOME KIND. OR IF HE DIDN'T, HE COULD FIGURE ONE OUT PRETTY QUICK. HE WAS SO CLEVER LIKE THAT.
I NEVER REALIZED HOW MUCH I DEPENDED ON HIM. AND NOW HE'S GONE.
I CAN'T EVEN FIGURE OUT WHAT HE WAS RESEARCHING BEFORE HE DIED, IN SPITE OF HAVING ALL HIS NOTES AND BOOKS. HE PRACTICALLY HANDS ME ALL THE PIECES, AND I STILL CAN'T PUT THEM TOGETHER.
WHY DID IT HAVE TO HAPPEN? WHY DIDN'T I PUT MY FOOT DOWN THAT DAY? WHY DIDN'T I INSIST WE GO THE LONG WAY AROUND THE WOODS? IF I HAD, WE WOULD NEVER HAVE FOUND THE MAUSOLEUM IN THE FIRST PLACE. IT'S NOT FAIR.

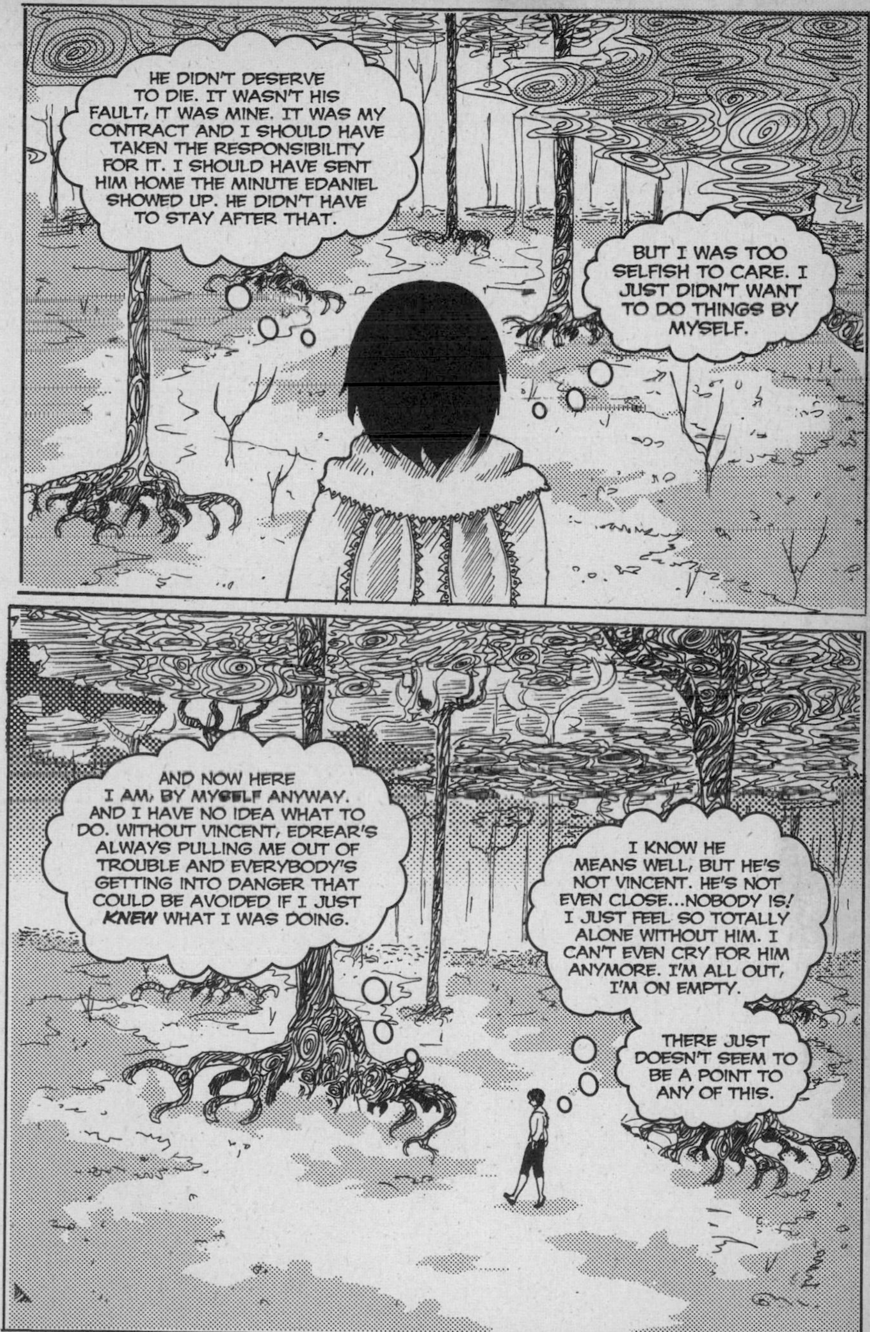
HE DIDN'T DESERVE TO DIE. IT WASN'T HIS FAULT, IT WAS MINE. IT WAS MY CONTRACT AND I SHOULD HAVE TAKEN THE RESPONSIBILITY FOR IT. I SHOULD HAVE SENT HIM HOME THE MINUTE EDANIEL SHOWED UP. HE DIDN'T HAVE TO STAY AFTER THAT.
BUT I WAS TOO SELFISH TO CARE. I JUST DIDN'T WANT TO DO THINGS BY MYSELF.
AND NOW HERE I AM, BY MYSELF ANYWAY. AND I HAVE NO IDEA WHAT TO DO. WITHOUT VINCENT, EDREAR'S ALWAYS PULLING ME OUT OF TROUBLE AND EVERYBODY'S GETTING INTO DANGER THAT COULD BE AVOIDED IF I JUST *KNEW* WHAT I WAS DOING.
I KNOW HE MEANS WELL, BUT HE'S NOT VINCENT. HE'S NOT EVEN CLOSE...NOBODY IS! I JUST FEEL SO TOTALLY ALONE WITHOUT HIM. I CAN'T EVEN CRY FOR HIM ANYMORE. I'M ALL OUT, I'M ON EMPTY.
THERE JUST DOESN'T SEEM TO BE A POINT TO ANY OF THIS.

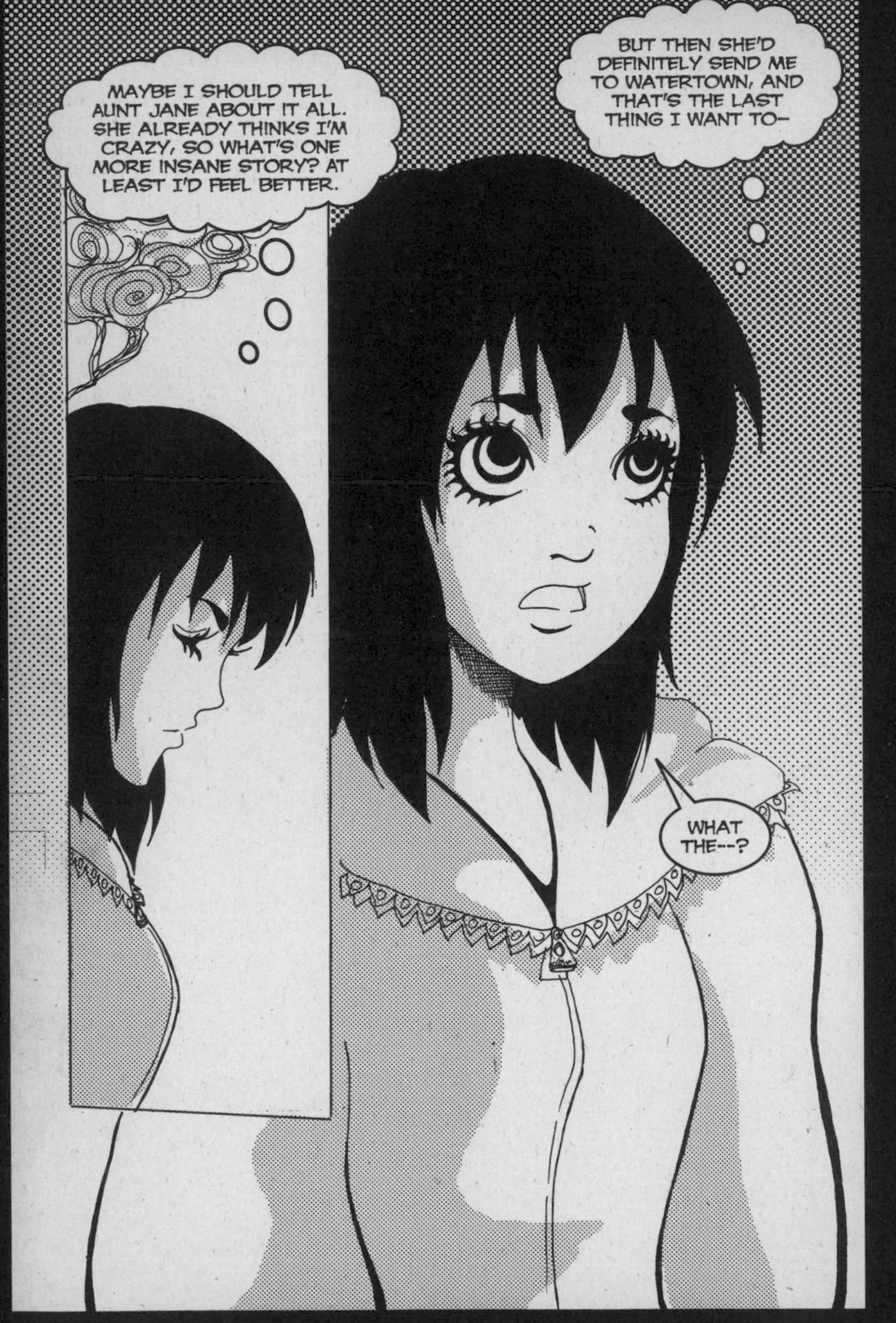
MAYBE I SHOULD TELL AUNT JANE ABOUT IT ALL. SHE ALREADY THINKS I'M CRAZY, SO WHAT'S ONE MORE INSANE STORY? AT LEAST I'D FEEL BETTER.
BUT THEN SHE'D DEFINITELY SEND ME TO WATERTOWN, AND THAT'S THE LAST THING I WANT TO-
WHAT THE--?

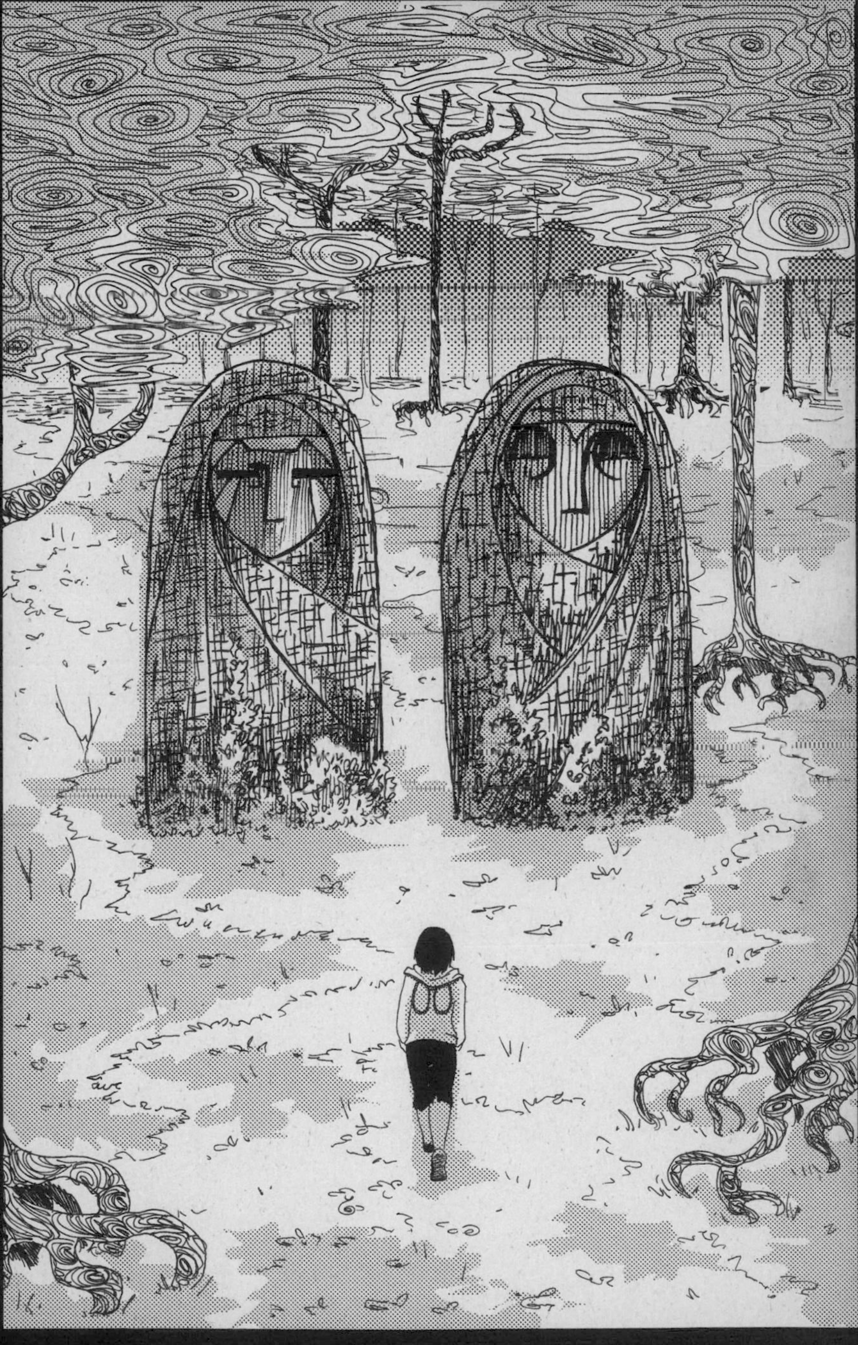

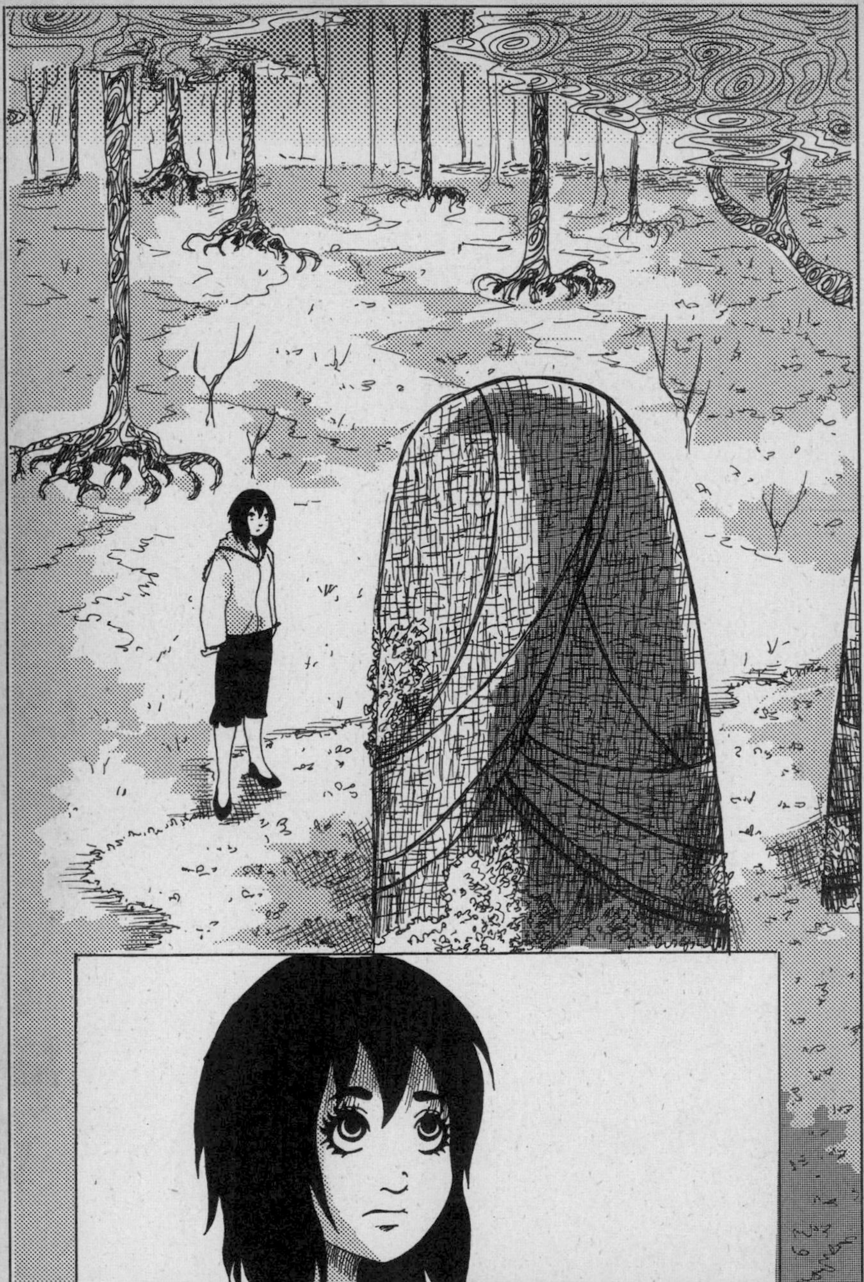

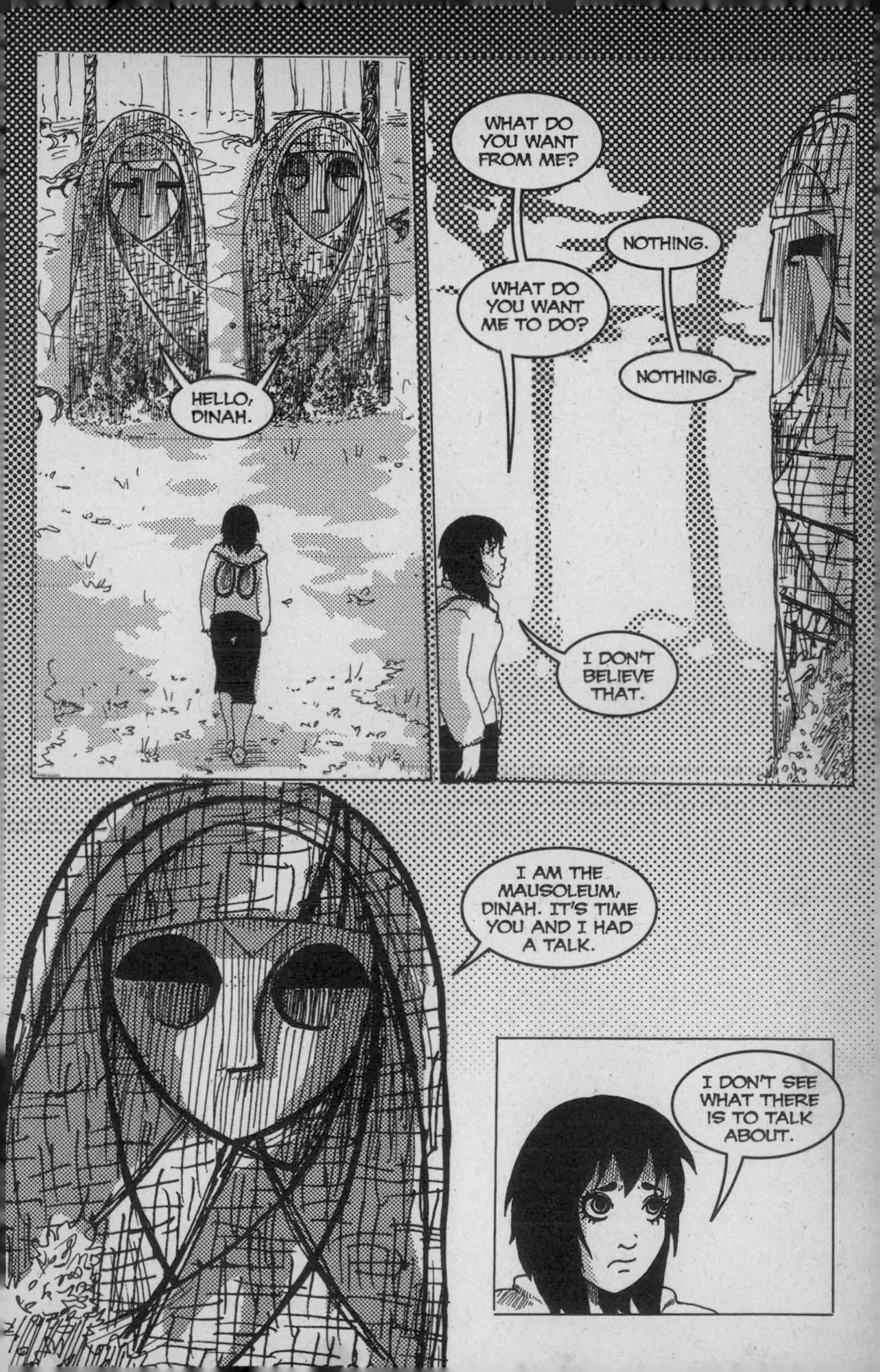
HELLO, DINAH.
WHAT DO YOU WANT FROM ME?
NOTHING.
WHAT DO YOU WANT ME TO DO?
NOTHING.
I DON'T BELIEVE THAT.
I AM THE MAUSOLEUM, DINAH. IT'S TIME YOU AND I HAD A TALK.
I DON'T SEE WHAT THERE IS TO TALK ABOUT.

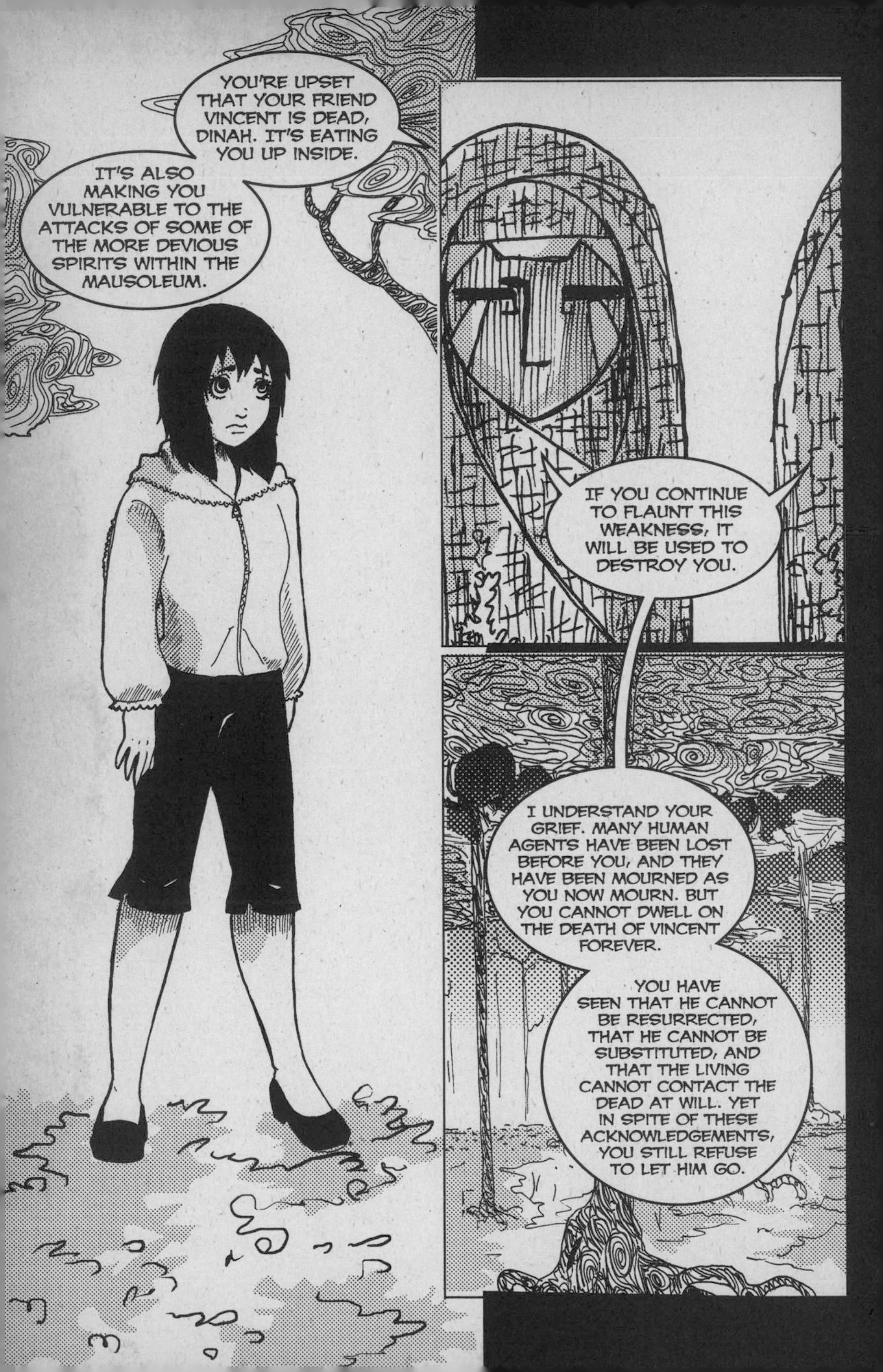
YOU'RE UPSET THAT YOUR FRIEND VINCENT IS DEAD, DINAH. IT'S EATING YOU UP INSIDE.
IT'S ALSO MAKING YOU VULNERABLE TO THE ATTACKS OF SOME OF THE MORE DEVIOUS SPIRITS WITHIN THE MAUSOLEUM.
IF YOU CONTINUE TO FLAUNT THIS WEAKNESS, IT WILL BE USED TO DESTROY YOU.
I UNDERSTAND YOUR GRIEF. MANY HUMAN AGENTS HAVE BEEN LOST BEFORE YOU, AND THEY HAVE BEEN MOURNED AS YOU NOW MOURN. BUT YOU CANNOT DWELL ON THE DEATH OF VINCENT FOREVER.
YOU HAVE SEEN THAT HE CANNOT BE RESURRECTED, THAT HE CANNOT BE SUBSTITUTED, AND THAT THE LIVING CANNOT CONTACT THE DEAD AT WILL. YET IN SPITE OF THESE ACKNOWLEDGEMENTS, YOU STILL REFUSE TO LET HIM GO.

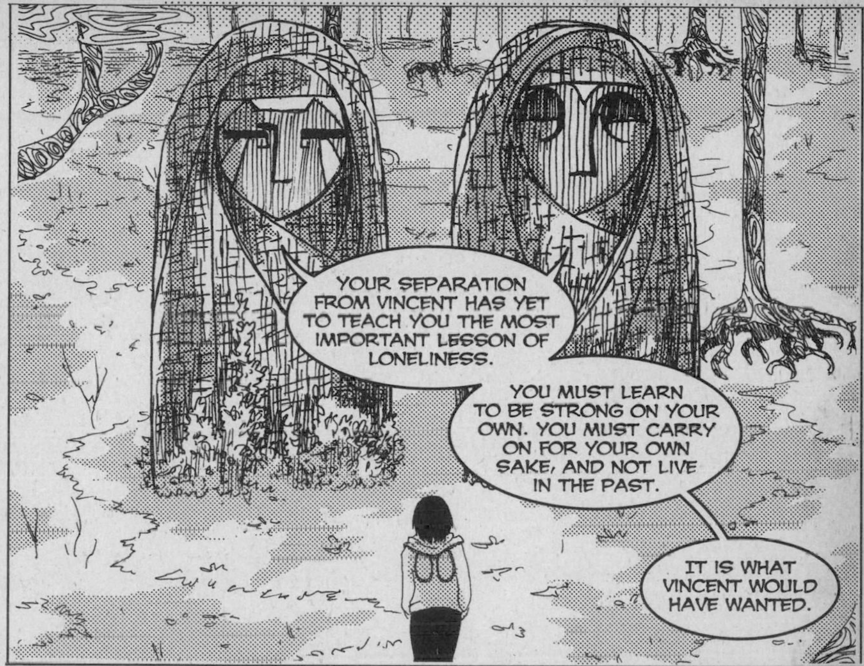
YOUR SEPARATION FROM VINCENT HAS YET TO TEACH YOU THE MOST IMPORTANT LESSON OF LONELINESS.
YOU MUST LEARN TO BE STRONG ON YOUR OWN. YOU MUST CARRY ON FOR YOUR OWN SAKE, AND NOT LIVE IN THE PAST.
IT IS WHAT VINCENT WOULD HAVE WANTED.

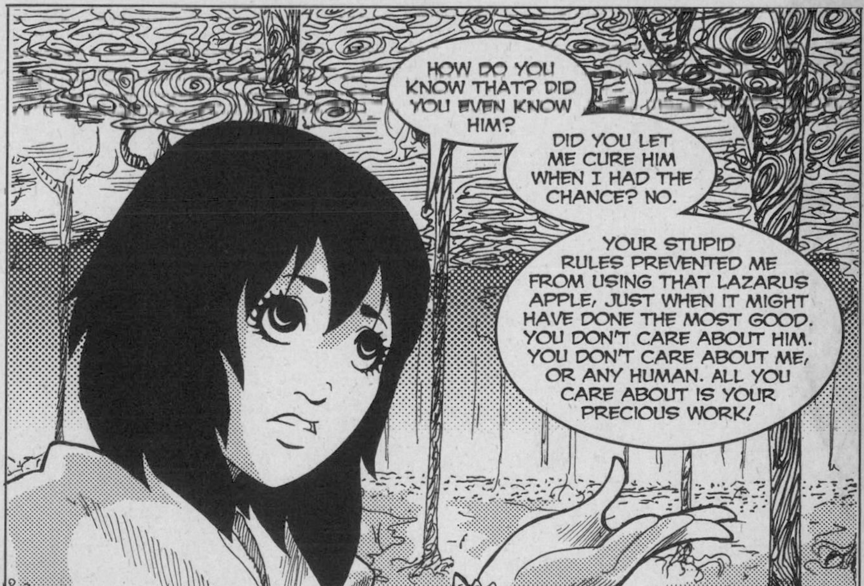
HOW DO YOU KNOW THAT? DID YOU EVEN KNOW HIM?
DID YOU LET ME CURE HIM WHEN I HAD THE CHANCE? NO.
YOUR STUPID RULES PREVENTED ME FROM USING THAT LAZARUS APPLE, JUST WHEN IT MIGHT HAVE DONE THE MOST GOOD. YOU DON'T CARE ABOUT HIM. YOU DON'T CARE ABOUT ME, OR ANY HUMAN. ALL YOU CARE ABOUT IS YOUR PRECIOUS WORK!

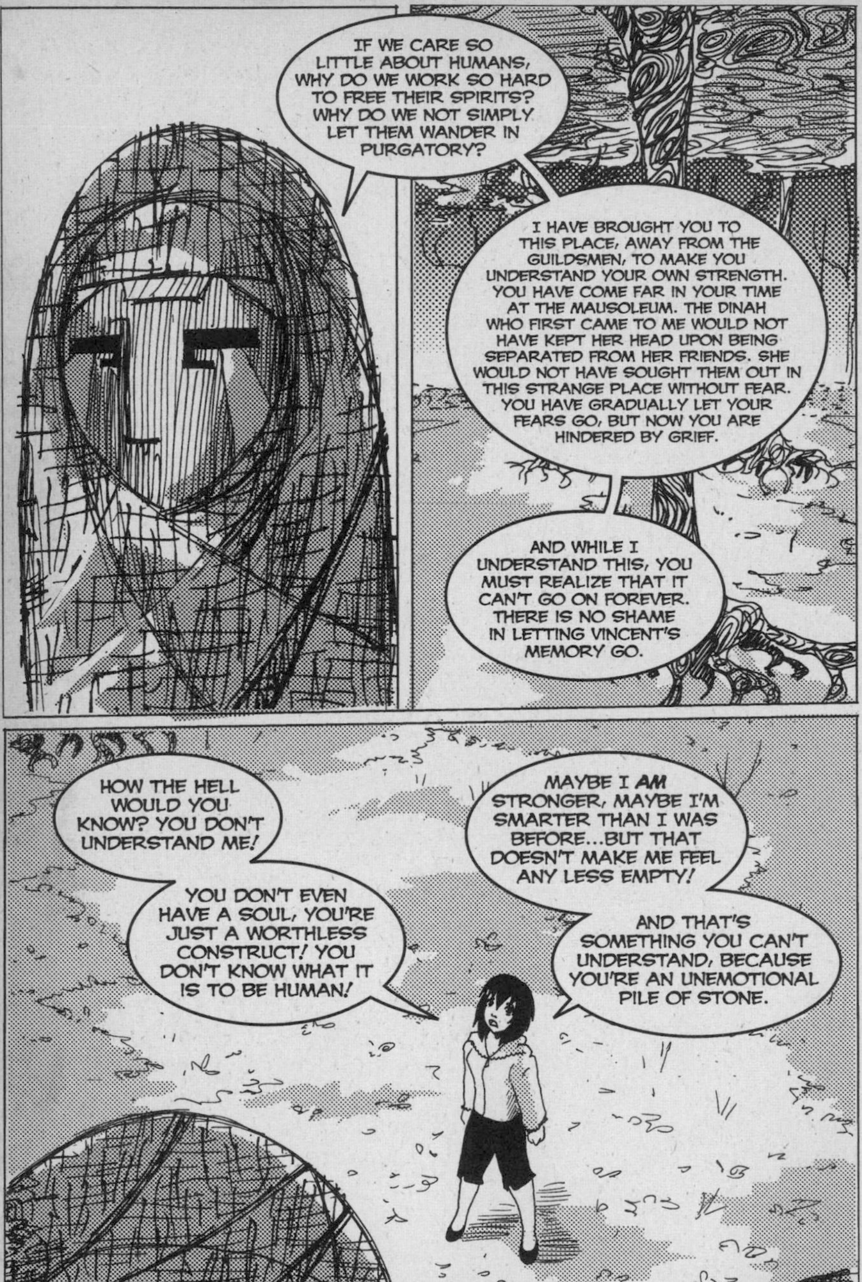
IF WE CARE SO LITTLE ABOUT HUMANS, WHY DO WE WORK SO HARD TO FREE THEIR SPIRITS? WHY DO WE NOT SIMPLY LET THEM WANDER IN PURGATORY?
I HAVE BROUGHT YOU TO THIS PLACE, AWAY FROM THE GUILDSMEN, TO MAKE YOU UNDERSTAND YOUR OWN STRENGTH. YOU HAVE COME FAR IN YOUR TIME AT THE MAUSOLEUM. THE DINAH WHO FIRST CAME TO ME WOULD NOT HAVE KEPT HER HEAD UPON BEING SEPARATED FROM HER FRIENDS. SHE WOULD NOT HAVE SOUGHT THEM OUT IN THIS STRANGE PLACE WITHOUT FEAR. YOU HAVE GRADUALLY LET YOUR FEARS GO, BUT NOW YOU ARE HINDERED BY GRIEF.
AND WHILE I UNDERSTAND THIS, YOU MUST REALIZE THAT IT CAN'T GO ON FOREVER. THERE IS NO SHAME IN LETTING VINCENT'S MEMORY GO.
HOW THE HELL WOULD YOU KNOW? YOU DON'T UNDERSTAND ME!
YOU DON'T EVEN HAVE A SOUL, YOU'RE JUST A WORTHLESS CONSTRUCT! YOU DON'T KNOW WHAT IT IS TO BE HUMAN!
MAYBE I *AM* STRONGER, MAYBE I'M SMARTER THAN I WAS BEFORE...BUT THAT DOESN'T MAKE ME FEEL ANY LESS EMPTY!
AND THAT'S SOMETHING YOU CAN'T UNDERSTAND, BECAUSE YOU'RE AN UNEMOTIONAL PILE OF STONE.

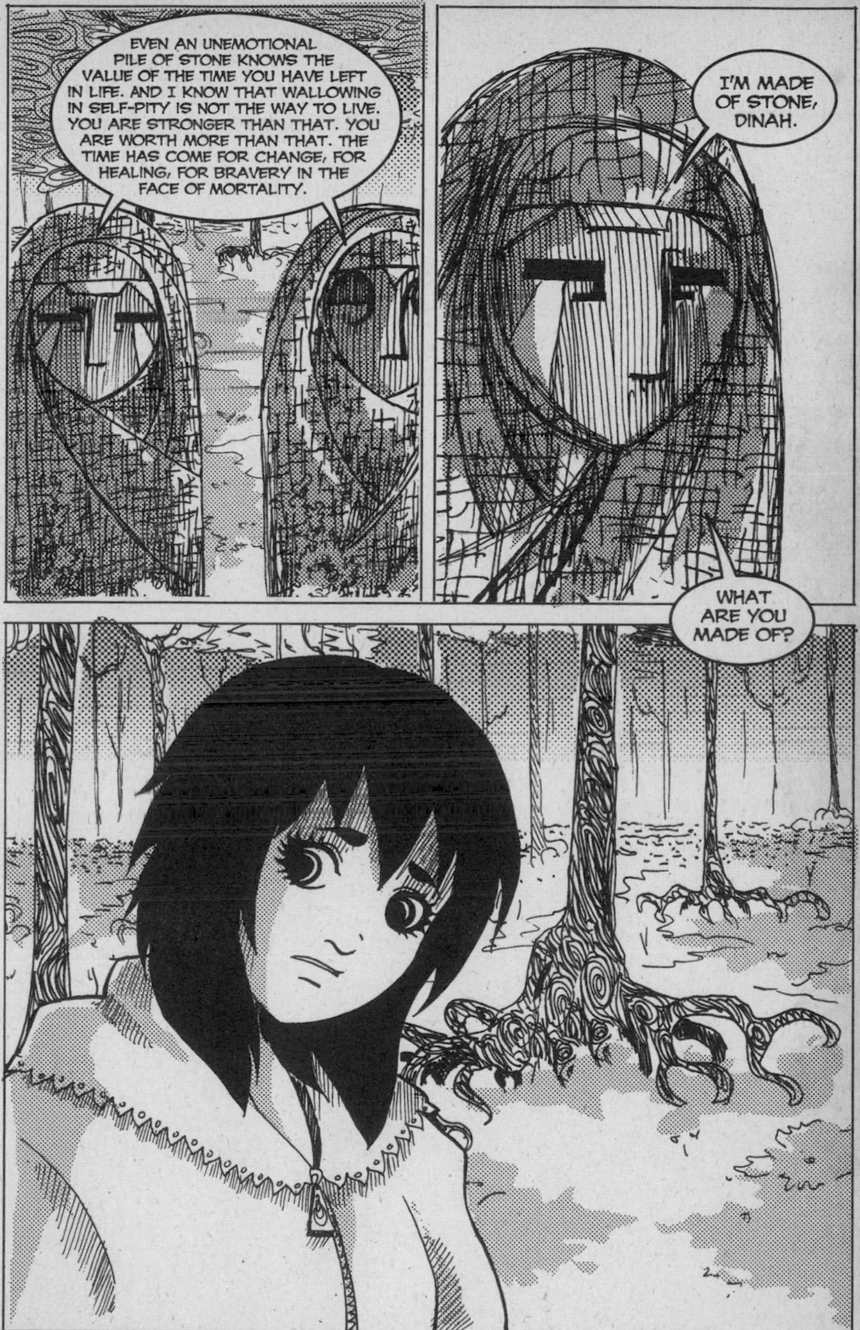
EVEN AN UNEMOTIONAL PILE OF STONE KNOWS THE VALUE OF THE TIME YOU HAVE LEFT IN LIFE. AND I KNOW THAT WALLOWING IN SELF-PITY IS NOT THE WAY TO LIVE. YOU ARE STRONGER THAN THAT. YOU ARE WORTH MORE THAN THAT. THE TIME HAS COME FOR CHANGE, FOR HEALING, FOR BRAVERY IN THE FACE OF MORTALITY.
I'M MADE OF STONE, DINAH.
WHAT ARE YOU MADE OF?

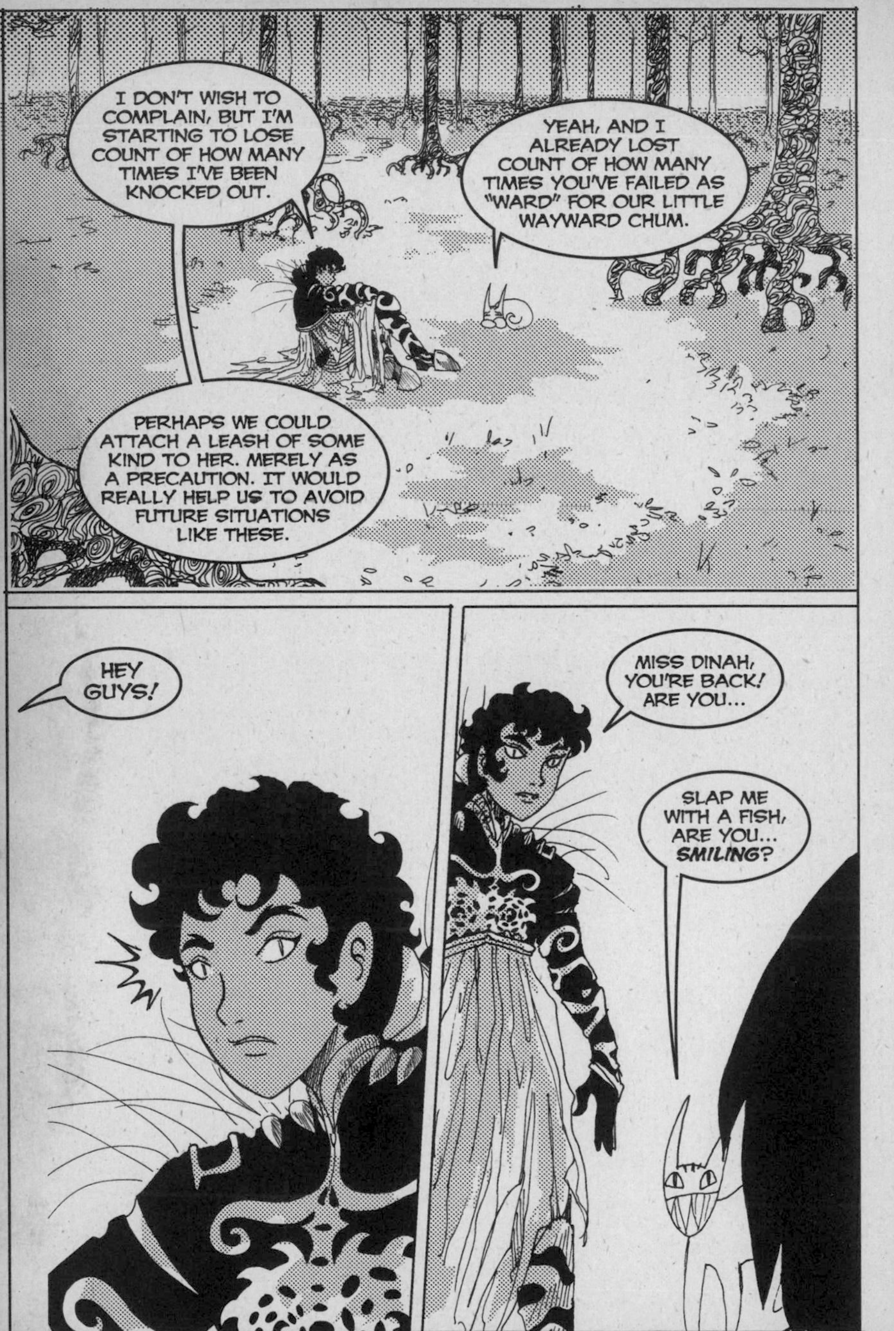
I DON'T WISH TO COMPLAIN, BUT I'M STARTING TO LOSE COUNT OF HOW MANY TIMES I'VE BEEN KNOCKED OUT.
YEAH, AND I ALREADY LOST COUNT OF HOW MANY TIMES YOU'VE FAILED AS "WARD" FOR OUR LITTLE WAYWARD CHUM.
PERHAPS WE COULD ATTACH A LEASH OF SOME KIND TO HER. MERELY AS A PRECAUTION. IT WOULD REALLY HELP US TO AVOID FUTURE SITUATIONS LIKE THESE.
HEY GUYS!
MISS DINAH, YOU'RE BACK! ARE YOU...
SLAP ME WITH A FISH, ARE YOU... *SMILING*?

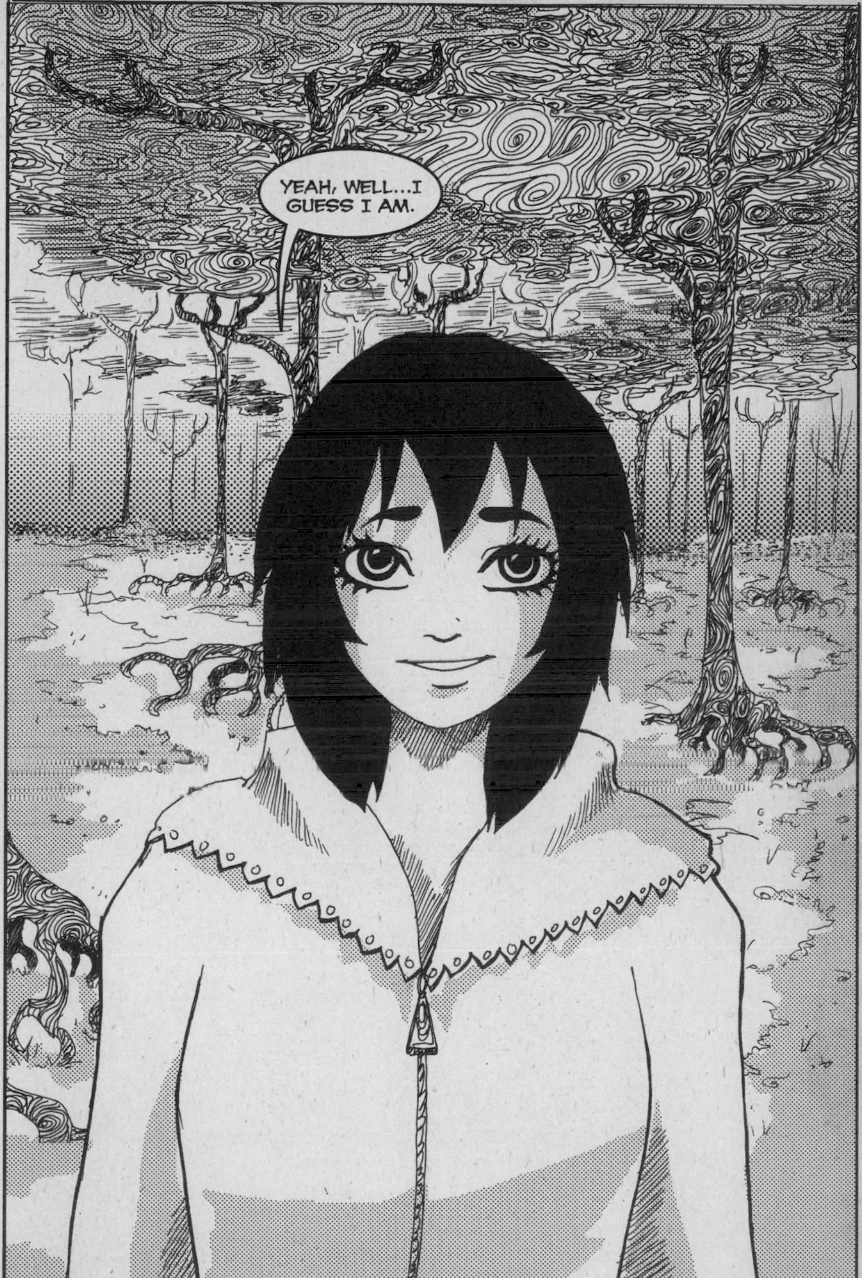
YEAH, WELL...I GUESS I AM.

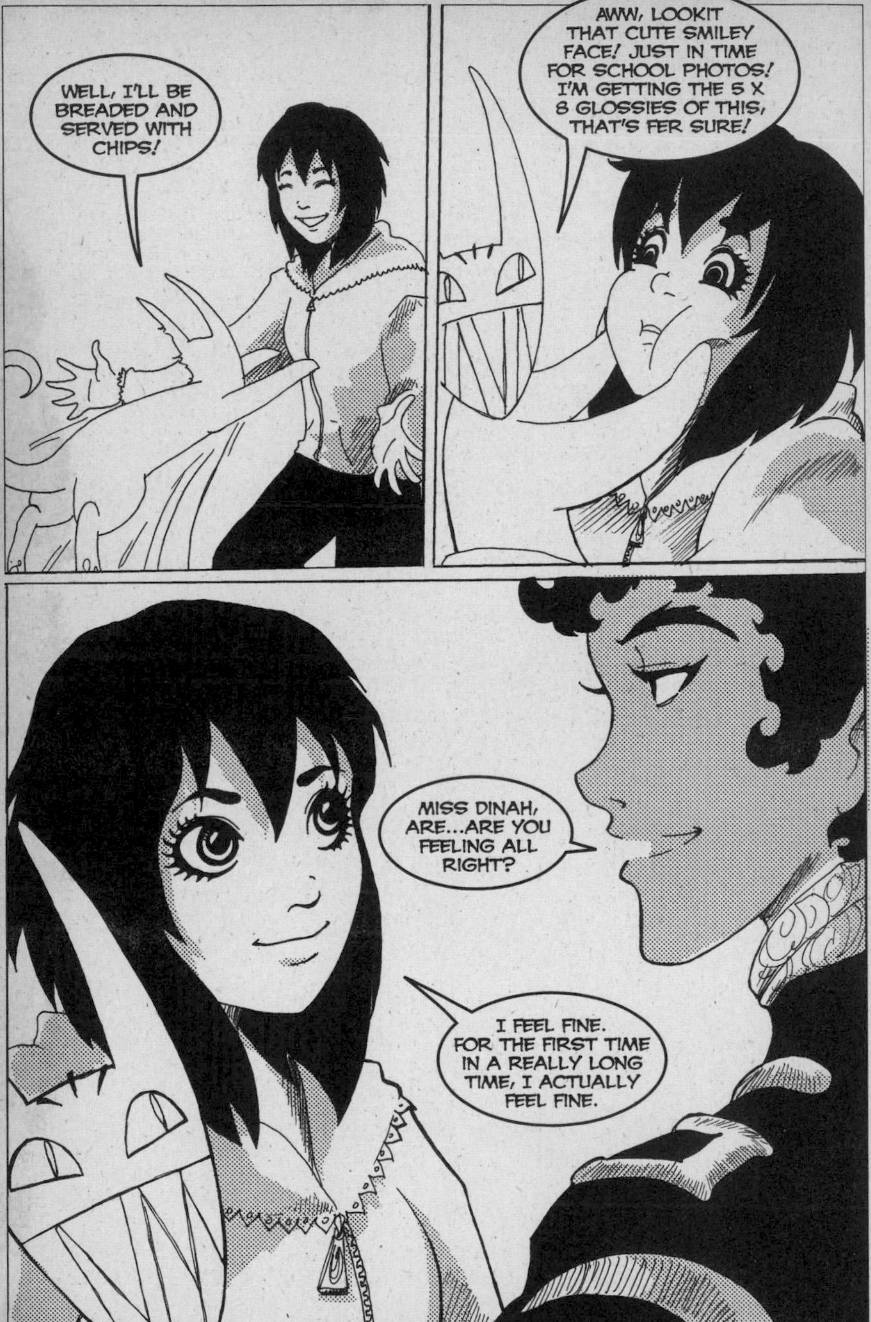
WELL, I'LL BE BREADED AND SERVED WITH CHIPS!
AWW, LOOKIT THAT CUTE SMILEY FACE! JUST IN TIME FOR SCHOOL PHOTOS! I'M GETTING THE 5 X 8 GLOSSIES OF THIS, THAT'S FER SURE!
MISS DINAH, ARE...ARE YOU FEELING ALL RIGHT?
I FEEL FINE. FOR THE FIRST TIME IN A REALLY LONG TIME, I ACTUALLY FEEL FINE.

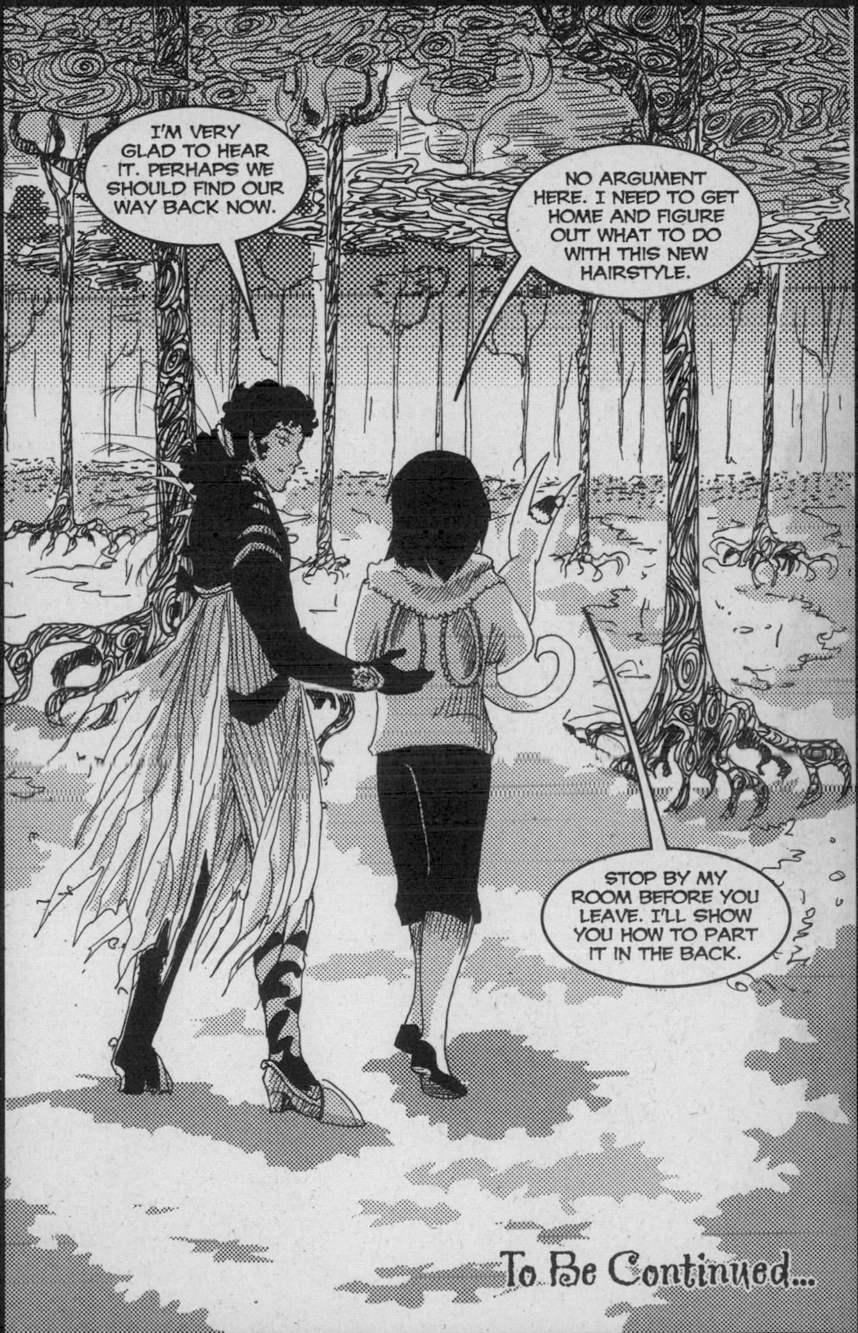

I'M VERY GLAD TO HEAR IT. PERHAPS WE SHOULD FIND OUR WAY BACK NOW.
NO ARGUMENT HERE. I NEED TO GET HOME AND FIGURE OUT WHAT TO DO WITH THIS NEW HAIRSTYLE.
STOP BY MY ROOM BEFORE YOU LEAVE. I'LL SHOW YOU HOW TO PART IT IN THE BACK.
To Be Continued...

In Volume six of Bizenghast:

Dinah may be back on track to taking care of her nightly tasks, but as the final vaults approach, these tasks are becoming increasingly difficult, and evermore deadly. Dinah's transformation from frightened and disturbed girl to courageous young woman is nearly complete, but more things haunt the Mausoleum than just unhappy spirits, and the horrifying story behind Vincent's secret research may finally be revealed...

Bizenghast

IN AUGUST OF 2007, I HAD A CONTEST TO DESIGN A
NEW OUTFIT FOR DINAH TO WEAR IN BOOK 5.
HERE ARE THE WINNERS!   *Stay tuned for more contests
in future volumes!*

OCTODRESS
BY ENLILY
HTTP://ENLILY.DEVIANTART.COM

THIS WAS SUCH A CUTE DESIGN!
I REALLY LIKE THE LITTLE
OCTOPI ALL OVER THE
DRESS...THEY'RE SO CUDDLY!

*Ooh, the combination of stripes,
cropped jacket and puffed sleaves
is killer! Great work!*

by_NatalietheGreat

http://nataliethegreat.
deviantart.com

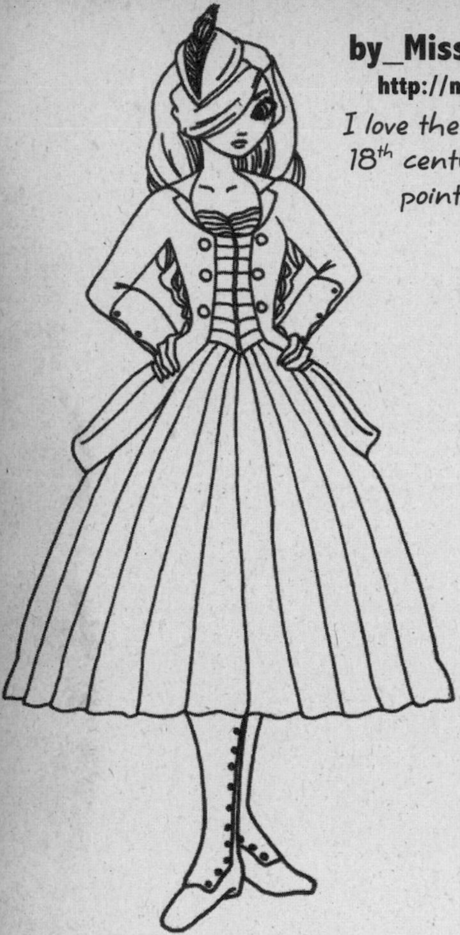

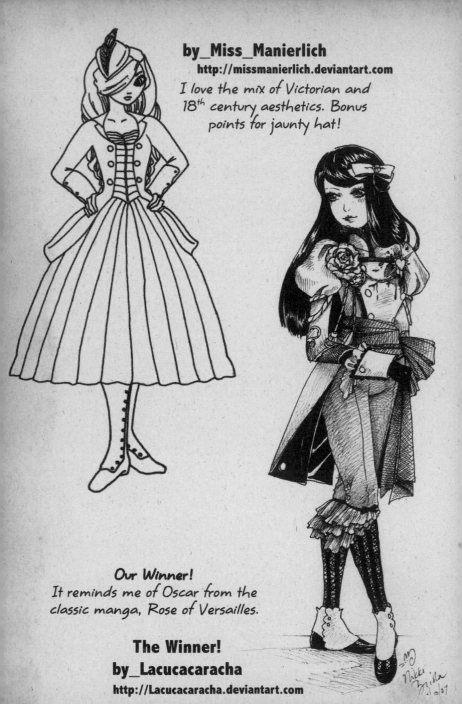

by_Miss_Manierlich

http://missmanierlich.deviantart.com

I love the mix of Victorian and 18th century aesthetics. Bonus points for jaunty hat!

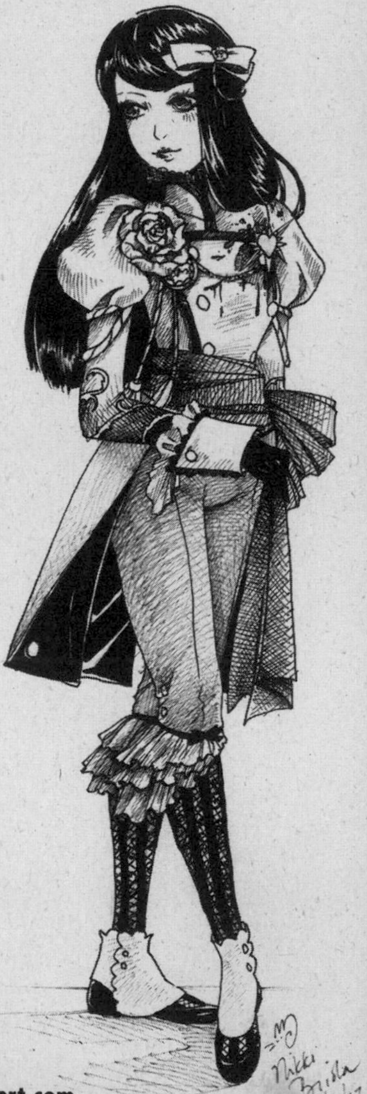

Our Winner!

It reminds me of Oscar from the classic manga, Rose of Versailles.

The Winner!

by_Lacucacaracha

http://Lacucacaracha.deviantart.com

COMING SOON . . .

BIZENGHAST: THE NOVEL

The first volume of this exciting new series
will arrive in stores in August 2008!

A  Prose Novel

TOKYOPOP Inc.
5900 Wilshire Boulevard, Suite 2000
Los Angeles, CA 90036
www.TOKYOPOP.com

STORY	Shawn Thorgersen
ILLUSTRATIONS	M. Alice LeGrow
INTERIOR DESIGN	John Lo
LAYOUT ARTIST	Michael Paolilli
SENIOR EDITOR	Jenna Winterberg
EDITOR	Michelle Prather
PRE-PRESS SUPERVISOR	Lucas Rivera
DIGITAL IMAGING MANAGER	Chris Buford
ART DIRECTOR	Al-Insan Lashley
CREATIVE DIRECTOR	Anne Marie Horne
MANAGING EDITOR	Vy Nguyen
EDITOR-IN-CHIEF	Rob Tokar
PUBLISHER	Mike Kiley
PRESIDENT AND COO	John Parker
CEO AND CHIEF CREATIVE OFFICER	Stu Levy

The Sickness

Dr. Morstan's stuff—Dinah couldn't remember the fancy name for it, though she knew the medication by its distinct taste of chalk dust—had been running its course through her ever since he'd arrived to treat her an hour or so earlier. Or maybe it was longer than that . . . the chalk stuff made time drip, drip along, as slow and strained as her heavy eyelids.

She lay in bed, her long curls splayed beneath her, dark rivers on the white shores of her aunt's linens. Outside her bedroom, the day had started: A cloudy morning had come to Bizenghast, the decrepit, all-but-forgotten mill town Dinah had called home since ... how long had it been now? The doctor's stuff made it hard to think. . . . Biting her lip until she left small red marks, she focused as much as the prescription would allow. How long, she thought . . . how long had she been here?

The answer materialized through the mists of her clouded mind: She'd been in Bizenghast since . . . yes, that was it: since the sudden bursting of a tire.

That's how the newspaper reporter had described it: "The sudden bursting of a tire."

Right. She took a breath. The medication must have been weakening. More breathing and more thinking, that was the trick. Dinah tried to remember that old newspaper clipping.

She'd read it only once—after all, she'd been riding in the back of the car when the accident happened, so she didn't need an article to tell her about an incident that had left her bumped and bruised . . . and her mother and father far worse. It had been—yes, now she recalled—seven years had passed since the accident. She had been eight years old, and up until then, it had never occurred to her that sometimes, parents die and leave their children all alone.

Weak as it was, that chalk stuff, that liquid Morpheus, beckoned her to sleep—but if she forced her blue eyes to remain open, and if she kept her thoughts whirring, she could escape its lulling whisper. Sometimes, though, her mind raced ahead of her, revealing memories she'd prefer to forget. Memories, for instance, of that night in Drury, when she'd heard the tire rupture, sharp like a pistol shot, the screeching—she'd felt her mother's hand fire back to safeguard Dinah as the sedan's wheels screeched and the headlights set the double-yellow lines of the highway alight until oncoming high beams washed the whole view into blinding white light, a light that seemed like heaven—until Dinah had awakened later, here on earth once more.

As her mind cleared, she could see the newspaper clipping again. At the age of twelve, she'd found it in a shoebox under her aunt's bed: a jagged-edged strip cut with a shaking hand and blunt scissors. Dinah remembered hating the reporter; in six words he'd summarized the moment when her life had cracked in two. But the part of the clipping that had hit her, smacked her, dropped her to her knees—was this:

"I just don't understand how it happened," said firefighter Neil Redmond. *"The busted tire we found was brand new with no defects or puncturing. It didn't even burst in a way you'd expect a tire would. It had a tiny puncture in it like a dart."*

How interesting! How curious! What's more, the reporter had added: "Police are investigating the scene for signs of foul play."

Dinah sat up. A lock of her hair fell in her face. Her gown had crept up during her rest, so she tugged it down over her knees. I'm awake, she thought to herself. Most times, she just poured the chalk stuff down the drain, but whenever Dr. Morstan was here, he watched her take it. Now, though, she was coherent; the memory of that night—the shock, rush, crash so fast you can't scream—had snapped her into a semblance of focus.

Foul play? No. Dinah knew there had been no foul play, and she'd known it all the seven years since moving from her parents' home in Pennsylvania to this Massachusetts graveyard town. It hadn't been foul play or fate that had caused the accident. Forget fate.

It had been random chance. Chaos, if you like. Dumb luck. A cruddy roll of the die.

She took a final breath, flipped off the bedcovers, and ran across her bedroom floor. It was a wide expanse; her bedroom had been a convalescent chamber back when the property was St. Lyman's School for Boys. After the accident, her aunt had received the deed and moved from Colorado; she'd renovated the place to provide a home for her and Dinah, whom she placed in the healing room, as it came with a bathroom and was safely stationed on the first floor. In other words, it was the perfect spot for her newly inherited, troubled child.

Dinah sat by the phone and dialed, twining the black cord in her pale fingers; these days, with Aunt Jane keeping her from attending school or leaving home for the most part due to her "illness," Dinah rarely saw the sun. Through the thin walls (Dinah suspected that some of the renovations had been done on the cheap), she could hear Dr. Morstan talking to Aunt Jane. Most of it sounded like mumbles, but she pieced together a few words—

words like "hospital" and "testing" and "for her safety." Now, she knew she'd beaten the medication. She was getting nervous again, which was partly what the stuff was supposed to prevent.

Likely, Aunt Jane hated having to assume responsibility for Dinah since the accident, and certainly believed there was something very wrong with her niece. Vincent, on the other hand . . .

Just when she thought she might get stuck talking to his voicemail, Vincent picked up. She listened to his breath; likely, he was outside somewhere, perhaps riding the outskirts of town on his bicycle. His breath, and then his voice, soothed her. She knew so few people here—heck, there were only sixty-four residents in the whole town, including herself, Aunt Jane, and Vincent. Vincent struck Dinah as the closest she'd ever come to meeting an adventurer; he was brave, he liked to explore the abandoned homes in town, and—the bottom line was—when he came around, the *other* inhabitants of the former St. Lyman's school, the ones only Dinah could see, left her alone.

"Hello?" he said. She imagined Vincent standing on a hill somewhere, his blond hair glistening with sweat from bicycling, but light and long enough to blow in the chill wind. Possibly, he had some interesting gadgets in his pockets, ripped from one of the local buildings. That's how he looked when she'd met him two years ago. He'd been dared to explore the weird old Lyman's school, and he'd arrived with an antenna knotted to his bicycle and some crown molding strapped to his back, as a knight might have strapped his sword. Vincent had startled her, but perhaps she'd startled him, too; he'd discovered her filling what likely resembled a miniature grave in the yard. She'd felt certain she'd scared the boy away, but two weeks later, Vincent had returned with a discovered copy of *Le Petit Prince,* salvaged from some of the town's other ruins. Dinah was thirteen at the time; she couldn't have guessed that this boy might become her dearest companion.

"Come over," Dinah answered. She paused, listening through the thin wall separating her bedroom from the foyer. Sometimes, Dr. Morstan stopped in simply to drop off meds, or for a quick exchange of paperwork along with a brief update—not this time. "I need you here. Dr. Morstan hasn't left yet."

On the other end, Vincent took a deep breath. His breathing slowed. "What do you want me to do? He and your aunt hate me."

"But they know!" she said, and then her voice fell to a whisper. There was no way she could allow Aunt Jane or Dr. Morstan to hear this next part: "They know about the ghosts!"

"Don't worry. I'll make him leave. I'll tell him what he wants to hear."

"Please hurry." She felt helpless—like a fair maiden on a faded movie poster, grasping the brave hero as he valiantly shields her from black-hearted villains. She hated the feeling almost as much as she hated the chalk stuff, but what could she do? She had no power. No authority. And anyway, what difference would it make if she *did* try something? Random chance could happen along and ruin things anyway. Forget that. So, she might as well leave it to Vincent, who was much better at taking care of things than she was.

"Hurry up," she said, "before he sends me away!"

She hung up the phone and listened. They were quiet on the other side of the wall. Had they overheard her conversation? She sidled to the wall that separated her bedroom from the main hall and cupped her hand to eavesdrop, trying to imagine what they were doing in such silence. In her mind's eye, she saw Dr. Morstan, a pale, bespectacled man in his late thirties, sporting a goatee. Likely, he felt it was fashionable, but Dinah often wondered whether he was just attempting to look like a legitimate psychiatrist—a young, hip, Freud, maybe. At Aunt Jane's request, he had been studying Dinah to ascertain the cause of her "fits," as he called them. Thus far, he'd discovered precious little—only that whatever had been troubling her through the years since her parents' passing and the move to her aunt's property often had left her screaming and bruised. He'd seen the fits himself, so any suspicion toward Aunt Jane had been quashed. He'd even tested her for the usual diagnosis, epilepsy, but that had come back negative. No, this was something else, and he hadn't figured it out yet, which is why Dr. Morstan had recently made his worst suggestion—that Dinah be removed to a hospital, where she could be better tested and treated.

When she'd heard that, she imagined towering white walls, wrinkled clothes reeking of bleach, and long, disinfected linoleum hallways spied through the reinforced glass square of solitary rooms. What an awful deal of the cards that would be, she thought. To be without parents was bad enough. To live in Bizenghast—which was, to her, the rotting cadaver of some colonist's dead vision—was to wilt alongside it. But to be alone, without even her aunt, or Vincent, her single friend, that would be the end for her. She'd never go to the hospital if she could help it, even if it somehow learning to cope with house full of ghosts.

If only Dr. Morstan could see what she saw. If only he could see the Walkers on the lawn, the shapes within the shadows here in her aunt's home . . . if he could see the governess, the matron ghost that would discipline Dinah, and realize that the creaks in the ancient floorboards were *not* the damned house settling, then he would know everything he needed to, and she wouldn't have to go to some hospital.

But the truth was that only Dinah saw these things. And in moments like these, staring at cracks in spackled walls, the eight-year-old inside her, who had been happy before the sudden bursting of a tire, wondered whether the new Dinah actually saw ghosts, or was simply mad as a hatter.

"Hurry, Vincent," she whispered.

***

The boy rode as quickly as he could, considering the chain on his bike sounded like it was going to rattle off and twirl around the rear wheel if he pedaled any faster over these dirt roads.

There, he saw it: The rusted, broken archway outside Dinah's home, informing any soul who came this way that this was St. Lyman's School for Boys. He'd always wanted to rip a chunk off that sign, partly as a souvenir, partly because a good hunk of iron presented so many possibilities. But this was Dinah's home, and even if her aunt didn't much like him, Vincent wasn't about to do wrong by Dinah.

He rode beneath the arch and past the brick walls, which were thick enough, he mused, to keep any of the old Lyman's boys from escaping, assuming the school still had a sturdy gate at the front (which it didn't). Vincent let his momentum take him the rest of the way, watching as the old school-turned-home grew large and looming, like a nightmare creature, in his vision. As was true of most of the buildings in town, Dinah's place needed work, and the boy wondered how long it would be before the ivy grew over the windows and covered the sharp rooftops.

Still, he loved his hometown of Bizenghast, and what some might label hopeless or strange, he called captivating, because you never knew how a thing might be if you fixed it up just right.

He could hear them talking about Dinah on the other side of the front door. Giving the bell-pull a good yank should hush up Aunt Jane, he figured, so he did just that. He grinned—she'd muttered something about killing him just as Dr. Morstan opened the door.

The doctor looked down his nose at Vincent the way some teachers did when they wanted to feel authoritative. Well, it wasn't going to work here. This doctor was a quack as far as Vincent was concerned, and even if he *did* know what he was doing, he was still hurting Dinah, and Vincent couldn't let that continue.

"Vincent," Dr. Morstan said, "what are you doing here?"

With as much innocence as he could muster, Vincent answered. "I came to see Dinah. Can I go inside?"

"Just a minute. Did Dinah . . ." At this, the doctor looked over his shoulder, glancing at Aunt Jane. "Has she had any fits lately?"

Fits? Vincent thought. Lying, he knew, was all about what you let stream through your head while speaking. To really, really, get out a good lie, it was important to actually *think* along the lines of what you spoke. So, Vincent thought, *This doctor IS off his rocker, asking such a ridiculous and bizarre question* (which wasn't hard for him to do). "Sir?" he answered, as if completely shocked by the question. He nearly believed himself.

"Fits, Vincent. Has she been well?"

For an instant, Vincent faltered. Deceiving him, his mind returned to a scene not two days past, when he'd nearly had to wrestle Dinah down from whatever phantom force had been troubling her. She'd grabbed the canopy of her bed and held on for dear life, screaming loud enough that Aunt Jane could have heard from anywhere in the large house, had she been home.

When he finally brought his mind back to the present, he realized he might not be able to craft a good lie again.

"Vincent?"

"Um, she's fine. She's been just fine." *Dammit*, he thought. *I don't even believe me.*

And neither, evidently, did Dr. Morstan. "Truthfully, Vincent. Are you quite sure of that?"

Again, his memories ruined a perfectly good deception. He struggled to move past an image of holding Dinah; she'd been cold to the touch, deathly white, eyes flared open as though to absorb a giant, terrible secret. And as much as he'd tried, he couldn't pull her hands down from her face until her . . . well, until her fit had passed.

Vincent looked to Aunt Jane. She was youngish and attractive (for a thirty-something-year old, anyway), with brown hair, lighter than Dinah's, fashioned in a short bob. Her curled ends made her appear youthful, but the way she furled her eyebrows and pressed her lips while talking about Dinah aged her. Sometimes, Vincent pitied her, although she preferred he not come around. After all, she wasn't a mother, hadn't planned on being one, but was nonetheless put in a hard spot. Tough break.

That's it, he thought. He shifted his focus to thinking of her—to using sympathy as a grounding point for a little lie that could help Dinah. So, was he quite sure that Dinah was just fine? *Focus,* he thought. "Sure as I'm standing here, sir," he said, and left the spot a trifle too quickly to fully drive home the point. No matter, though: He'd gotten past Dinah's guardians, and that was the real objective. They weren't his biggest fans, but nothing he could have said was going to change that, anyway.

He paused in the hallway, waiting to see if they would follow him. Dr. Morstan spoke first: "Well, fits or no," he said to Aunt Jane, "those cuts and bruises didn't make themselves."

Aunt Jane answered, incredulous. "Are you suggesting *they* did it?"

"Come now, Jane . . . we both know there's no such thing as ghosts."

With that, Vincent walked the short hall to Dinah's room. *So,* he thought, *they wondered about it, too.* While sneaking around inside abandoned homes these last few years, he'd had his share of scares: floors that bottomed out, rooftops that caved, and the occasional shadow that looked remarkably like an old owner staring at him as he looted the place. But truthfully, he'd never seen a ghost—not that he'd mind it if he did. Dinah said she saw them, and who was he to disagree? It didn't much trouble him, because in the end, he alone could help ease Dinah's troubles, and that was the thing that mattered to Vincent.

He opened her door, and saw her—she was a year younger than he was, and she always dressed, well, differently than the girls in school; it was always something elaborate with Dinah. But his favorite thing, upon seeing her for the first time each day, was her eyes—her blue eyes, wide and sad, waiting for him to give her a hand. And he would—any day she needed him, he'd be there.

★★★

TO BE CONTINUED . . .

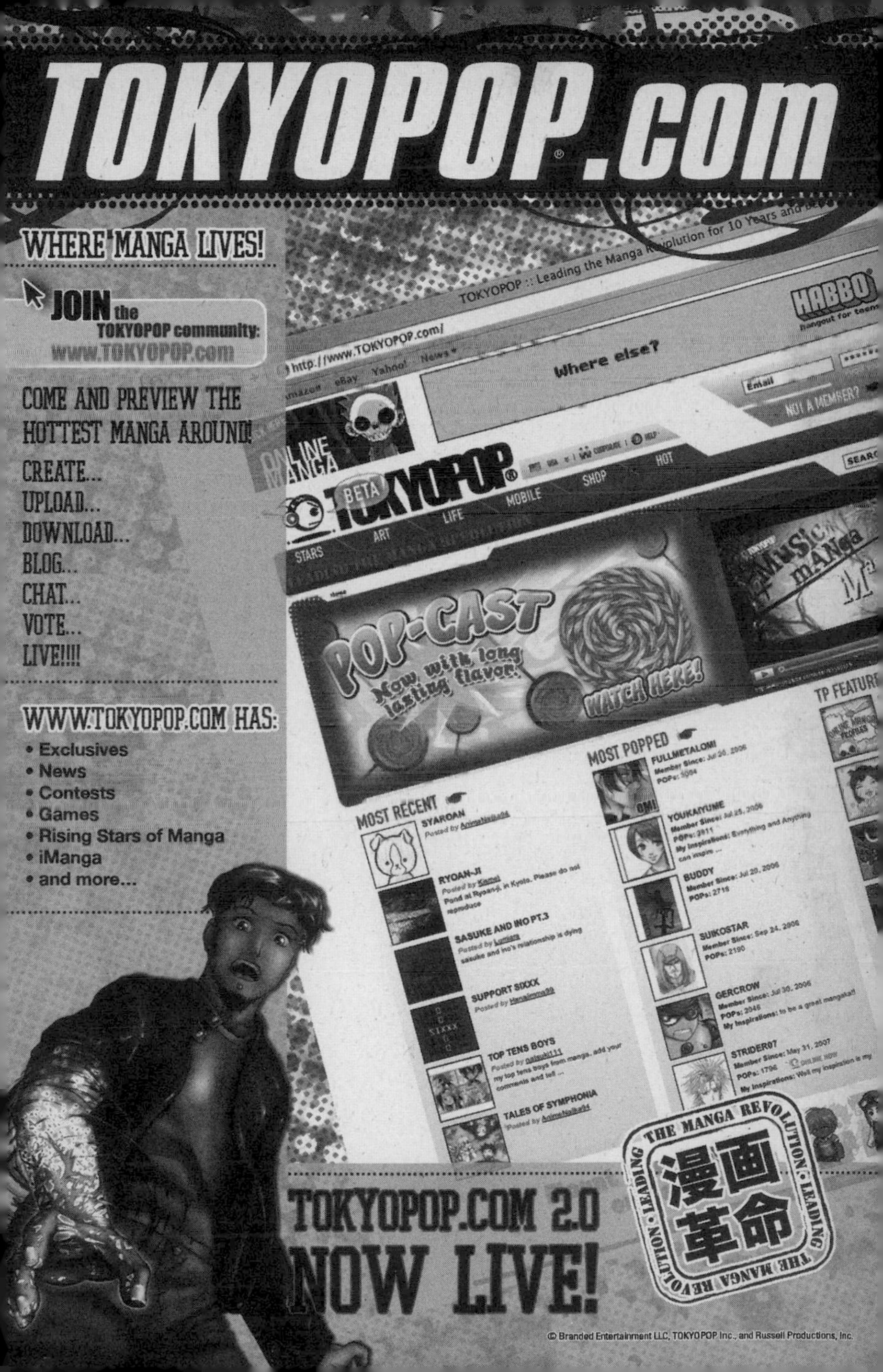
TOKYOPOP®.com
WHERE MANGA LIVES!
JOIN the TOKYOPOP community:
www.TOKYOPOP.com
COME AND PREVIEW THE HOTTEST MANGA AROUND!
CREATE...
UPLOAD...
DOWNLOAD...
BLOG...
CHAT...
VOTE...
LIVE!!!!
WWW.TOKYOPOP.COM HAS:
• Exclusives
• News
• Contests
• Games
• Rising Stars of Manga
• iManga
• and more...
TOKYOPOP.COM 2.0
NOW LIVE!
LEADING THE MANGA REVOLUTION
漫画革命
© Branded Entertainment LLC, TOKYOPOP Inc., and Russell Productions, Inc.

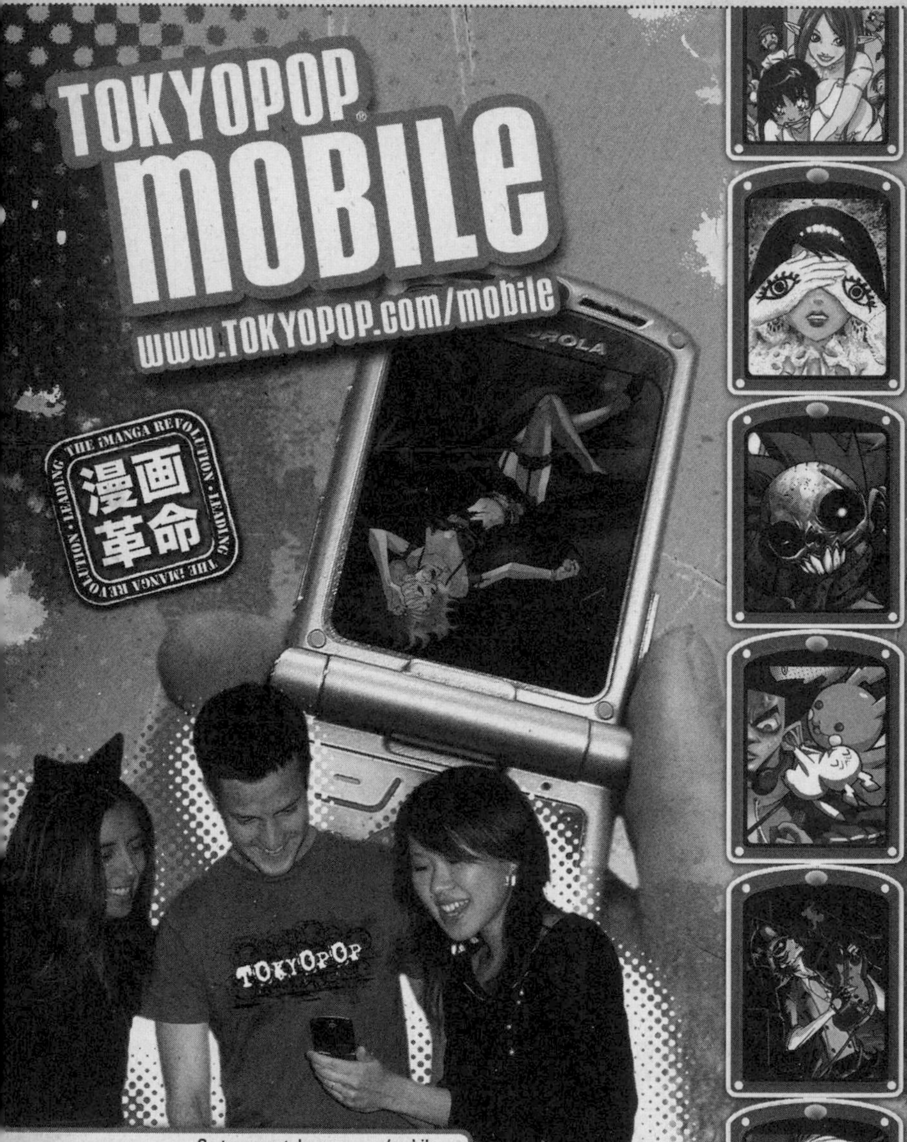
TOKYOPOP®
MOBILE
www.TOKYOPOP.com/mobile
THE iMANGA REVOLUTION • LEADING THE iMANGA REVOLUTION • LEADING
漫画
革命
TOKYOPOP
Go to www.tokyopop.com/mobile
for wallpapers, ringtones and more!
www.TOKYOPOP.com